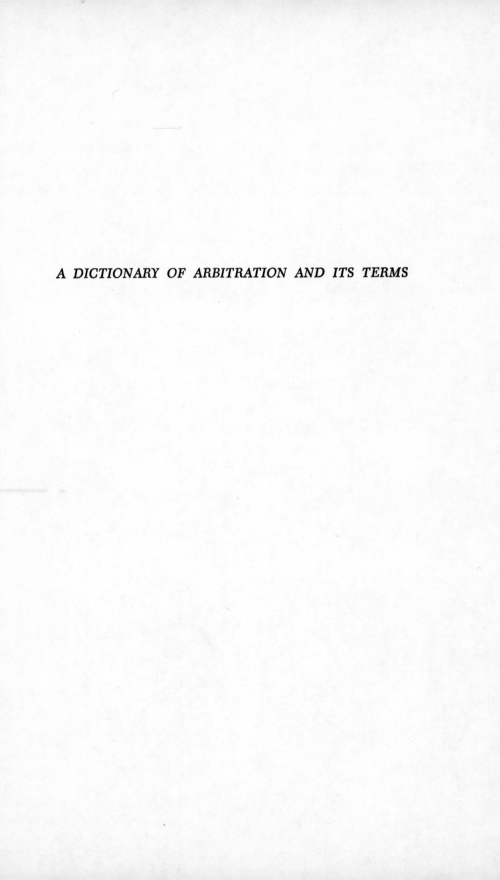

A DICTIONARY OF ARBITRATION AND ITS TERMS

A
Dictionary of Arbitration and its Terms

LABOR • COMMERCIAL • INTERNATIONAL

❋ ❋ ❋ ❋ ❋ ❋

A CONCISE ENCYCLOPEDIA OF
PEACEFUL DISPUTE SETTLEMENT

❋ ❋ ❋ ❋ ❋ ❋

Edited by
KATHARINE SEIDE

1970

PUBLISHED FOR THE EASTMAN LIBRARY OF THE
AMERICAN ARBITRATION ASSOCIATION

BY OCEANA PUBLICATIONS, INC.
DOBBS FERRY, NEW YORK

CONTENTS

CASES

PREFACE

This reference book was compiled and edited with the earnest hope and simple intention of providing the initial impulse toward a wider and better understanding of the subject of arbitration.

Grateful acknowledgement is made to the Bernheimer Fund of the Chamber of Commerce of the State of New York for a grant to aid in the completion and advancement of this work.

I owe many thanks to the officers of the American Arbitration Association, Donald B. Straus, President; Robert Coulson, Executive Vice President; John P. E. Brown, Edwin W. Dippold, Joseph S. Murphy, Morris Stone, Vice Presidents; Martin Domke, former Vice President; and Gerald Aksen, General Counsel, for their generous faith in my effort to extend the scope and usefulness of the arbitration library.

I would like to express my appreciation to Gerald Aksen especially for his unfailing patience and constant support.

I am very grateful to the members of the Library Committee of the Lucius R. Eastman Arbitration Library, Quigg Newton, Chairman, President of the Commonwealth Fund, Arthur A. Charpentier, Librarian of the Yale Law School; Lucius R. Eastman; and E. Nobles Lowe, General Counsel of the West Virginia Pulp and Paper Corporation, for sponsoring and encouraging this first edition of a dictionary of arbitration.

I am greatly indebted to Merton C. Bernstein, Professor of Law, Ohio State University College of Law; Thomas G. S. Christensen, Professor of Law and Executive Director, Institute of Labor Relations, New York University School of Law; and William M. Reisman, Research Associate of the Yale Law School, for their extremely helpful additions and corrections in serving as special consultants in the three major categories of dispute settlement.

I have received the most kind and courteous replies to my requests for information from David L. Cole in his capacity as Impartial Umpire of the AFL-CIO Internal Disputes Plan; J. P. A. François, Secretary-General of the Permanent Court of Arbitration; A. S. Fransen van de Putte of the Netherlands Arbitration Institute; D. G. Price, Secretary of the International Wool Textile Organisation; David Reid, Secretary of the Institute of Arbitrators; Jean Robert, Secretary General Counsel, International Union, United trage; Stephen I. Schlossberg, General Counsel, International Union, United Automobile & Agricultural Implement Workers of America-UAW; Richard F. Scott, Deputy Legal Adviser of the Organisation for Economic Co-operation and Development; and Emmett Thomas, Special Representative for Anthracite Affairs, United Mine Workers of America.

For their very willing assistance and cooperation, I wish especially to thank Mary Pelizza and Ellen Varady, and also with grateful appreciation Patricia Ann Colletti, Sally Cornwell, Marianne Gupta, Harry Herfurth, Susan Nadler, Jeri Socol and, as special typists, Patricia Bartolotta and Robert Cessna.

My special thanks also go to Helen E. Freedman and David G. Finkelstein, assistants to the General Counsel of the American Arbitration Association.

Others who did much preliminary and essential research and who deserve special mention are: Barry Bennett, Margaret Causey, Mark Denbeaux, Jeffrey Dubin, David Gould, and in particular Teresa McKellen.

Finally I would like to thank Michael Seide for his most vital and invaluable contribution in the writing of the definitions and the preparation of the text as writer-consultant through each and every phase of this project.

I would like to note also here that this Dictionary is a by-product of a Union Catalog of Arbitration which will be published at a later date and which is being funded by such foundations as The Beinecke Foundation, The Eastman (Lucius and Eva) Fund, Inc., The New York Foundation, The New York Times Foundation, The Pittsburgh Plate Glass Foundation, The Warburg (Mr. and Mrs. Paul Felix) Fund, the American Arbitration Association, and Anonymous Gifts.

Katharine Seide
Librarian
Lucius R. Eastman Arbitration Library
of the American Arbitration Association

INTRODUCTION

This publication is designed as a handbook of arbitration in a format which allows a reader to enter into an area of arbitration through a pertinent term or word, defined in straightforward, non-technical language. An effective guide, more in the form of an encyclopedia than a dictionary, it is, I think, also closely related to the digests with which we are all familiar. You will find in it not only the vacabulary of arbitration but also a liberal sprinkling of legal terms, statutes, cases and concepts with which an arbitrator or student may be concerned ("laches," "Adamson Act," "ex aequo et bono," "res judicata," and the like).

It is primarily intended as a handy, definitive working tool for the arbitrator, practioner, party, teacher or student interested in arbitration. One need not be a lawyer to use it.

This admirable project owes its existence to Katharine Seide, librarian of the American Arbitration Association. Mrs. Seide conceived this as part of a far larger project, the creation of a union list of arbitration materials held by leading libraries in this country.

Katharine is fortunate in being blessed with imaginative superiors who encouraged her work and provided initial financing. Donald B. Straus, President of the Association; Robert Coulson, Executive Vice President; and Gerald Aksen, the General Counsel, have all been active in implementing the concern of the Association's Library Committee under Quigg Newton, President of the Commonwealth Fund, that the Association act as a central clearing house for the dissemination of the knowledge of arbitration proceedings.

This reference book is the first manifestation of other projects. We all expect it to prove as useful in its sphere as the Association is unique and indispensable in the field of arbitration.

As for me, nothing is more satisfying to a law librarian than having the privilege of watching another librarian conceive and produce a good contribution to our work as her organization encourages and supports her on the way down the puzzling road of creation and compilation.

Arthur A. Charpentier
Yale Law School, 1969

EXPLANATORY NOTES

A careful reading of these explanatory notes will make it easier for the user of this dictionary to comprehend the information contained at each entry.

ORDER OF ENTRIES. The main entries follow each other alphabetically, in order, letter by letter, from *a* to *z*. For example, Labor Arbitration (Voluntary) comes after Labor Arbitration Reports; Nationality precedes National Joint Board.

CROSS REFERENCES. Each entry is further amplified by interlocking references found under the *See also* after the body of the explanatory matter following each definition. By remaining within the hierarchy of these references the user may accomplish preliminary research on individual subjects, such as, for example, Procedure, which is a broad subject, or Award, which is narrower in scope. The main categories of Commercial, International Commercial, International Public, and Labor Arbitration are each followed by the longest list of cross references. Referral to each of these individual references will lead into further and pertinent information.

ABBREVIATIONS

Adm.	administrative
Ann.	annotated
Ann. Rep.	annual report
Arb.	arbitration
Art.	article
Ass'n.	association
Bull.	bulletin
Cert.	certiorari
Cert. den.	certiorari denied
Civ.	civil
Co.	company
Com'l.	commercial
Comm.	committee
Comm'n.	commission
Conf.	conference
Corp.	corporation
Dept.	department
Doc.	document
Gen. Stat. Ann.	general statute annotated
Gov't.	government
Inc.	incorporated
Int'l.	international
Ltd.	limited
Mfg.	manufacturing
Nat'l.	national
Nav.	navigation
n.s.	new series
Proc.	proceedings
Pub.	public
Pub. L.	public law
Rev. ed.	revised edition
§	section
Sess.	session
Stat.	statute
Supp.	supplement
T.S.	treaty series
U.S.C.	United States code
v.	versus

ABBREVIATIONS OF PERIODICALS CITED

Albany L. Rev.	Albany Law Review
ALR	American Law Reports
Am. J. Int'l. L.	American Journal of International Law
Am. Jurist	American Jurist
Arb. J.	Arbitration Journal
Arb. J. of the Inst. of Arbitrators	Arbitration Journal of the Institute of Arbitrators
BC Ind. Com'l. L. Rev.	Boston College Industrial and Commercial Law Review
Brit. Y. B. Int'l. L.	British Yearbook of International Law
Buffalo L. Rev.	Buffalo Law Review
Bus. Law.	Business Lawyer
Colum. L. Rev.	Columbia Law Review
Cornell L. Q.	Cornell Law Quarterly (v. 53 no. 1 changed to Cornell Law Review)
Dick. L. Rev.	Dickinson Law Review
Duke L. J.	Duke Law Journal
Duquesne U. L. Rev.	Duquesne University Law Review
E. African L. J.	East African Law Journal
Fordham L. Rev.	Fordham Law Review
Geo. L. J.	Georgetown Law Journal
Geo. Wash. L. Rev.	George Washington Law Review
Georgia L. Rev.	Georgia Law Review
Harv. L. Rev.	Harvard Law Review
I.C.J. Y.B.	International Court of Justice Yearbook
Ind. and Labor Rels. Rev.	Industrial and Labor Relations Review
ICA Arb. Q.	Indian Council Arbitration Quarterly
Indian J. Int'l. L.	Indian Journal of International Law
Indian L. J.	Indian Law Journal
Int'l. & Comp. L. Q.	International and Comparative Law Quarterly
Int'l. Arb. J.	International Arbitration Journal
Int'l. L. Rep.	International Law Reports
Int'l. Lab. Rev.	International Labour Review
Int'l. Lawyer	International Lawyer
Int'l. Legal Materials	International Legal Materials
J. of Air L. & Commerce	Journal of Air Law and Commerce
J. Bus. L.	Journal of Business Law
J. Pub. L.	Journal of Public Law
Ky. L. J.	Kentucky Law Journal
Labor L. J.	Labor Law Journal
Law & Contemp. Prob.	Law and Contemporary Problems
Miami L. Q.	Miami Law Quarterly

Mich. L. Rev.	Michigan Law Review
Minn. L. Rev.	Minnesota Law Review
Mo. Lab. Rev.	Monthly Labor Review
Modern L. Rev.	Modern Law Review
Notre Dame Law.	Notre Dame Lawyer
NY L. J.	New York Law Journal
NY State Bar J.	New York State Bar Journal
NYU J. Int'l. L. & Politics	New York University Journal of International Law and Politics
NYU L. Rev.	New York University Law Review
Philippine Int'l. L. J.	Philippine International Law Journal
Q. Japan Com'l. Arb. Ass'n.	Quarterly of the Japan Commercial Arbitration Association
Rev. Jur. U.P.R.	Revista Juridica de la Universidad de Puerto Rico
Rutgers L. Rev.	Rutgers Law Review
Stan. L. Rev.	Stanford Law Review
Texas L. Rev.	Texas Law Review
U. Chicago L. Rev.	University of Chicago Law Review
U. Detroit L. J.	University of Detroit Law Journal
U. Missouri at K.C. L. Rev.	University of Missouri at Kansas City Law Review
U. of Pa. L. Rev.	University of Pennsylvania Law Review
U. Toronto Fac. of L. Rev.	University of Toronto Faculty of Law Review
UCLA L. Rev.	University of California at Los Angeles Law Review
Va. L. Rev.	Virginia Law Review
Vanderbilt L. Rev.	Vanderbilt Law Review
Washburn L. J.	Washburn Law Journal
Western Res. L. Rev.	Western Reserve Law Review
Wisconsin L. Rev.	Wisconsin Law Review
Yale L. J.	Yale Law Journal

ACRONYMS AND INITIALS

AAA	American Arbitration Association
ABA	American Bar Association
AFL	American Federation of Labor
AFL-CIO	American Federation of Labor and Congress of Industrial Organizations
ALAA	American Labor Arbitration Awards (Prentice-Hall, Inc.)
ARAMCO	Arabian American Oil Company
ARB	Labor Arbitration Awards (Commerce Clearing House)
BLS	Bureau of Labor Statistics
BNA	Bureau of National Affairs
BSEIU	Building Service Employees' International Union
CCH	Commerce Clearing House
CIM	Convention Internationale Concernant le Transport des Marchandises par Chemins de Fer (International Convention Concerning the Carriage of Goods by Rail)
CIO	Congress of Industrial Organizations
CIV	Convention Internationale Concernant le Transport des Vayageurs et des Bagages par Chemins de Fer (International Convention Concerning the Carriage of Passengers and Luggage by Rail)
COMSAT	Communications Satellite Corporation
CPLR	Civil Practice Law and Rules
ECAFE (U.N.)	Economic Commission for Asia and the Far East (United Nations)
ECE (U.N.)	Economic Commission for Europe (United Nations)
E.O.	Executive Order
FMCS	Federal Mediation and Conciliation Service
GAC	General Arbitration Council of the Textile Industry
GAOR (U.N.)	General Assembly Official Record (United Nations)
GERR	Government Employee Relations Report (Bureau of National Affairs)
IACAC	Inter-American Commercial Arbitration Commission
IBEW	International Brotherhood of Electrical Workers
IBRD	International Bank for Reconstruction and Development (World Bank)
ICA	Indian Council of Arbitration
ICAO	International Civil Aviation Organization
ICC	International Chamber of Commerce
ICJ	International Court of Justice
ICSID	International Centre for Settlement of Investment Disputes
ILC (U.N.)	International Law Commission (United Nations)
ILIR	Institute of Labor and Industrial Relations (University of Illinois)

ILO	International Labour Organization
INGO	International Non-Governmental Organization
INTELSAT	International Telecommunications Satellite Consortium
IUE	International Union of Electrical, Radio and Machine Workers
IWTO	International Wool Textile Organisation
JIL	Japan Institute of Labour
LA	Labor Arbitration Reports (Bureau of National Affairs)
LMRA	Labor Management Relations Act
L.N.T.S.	League of Nations Treaty Series
NAA	National Academy of Arbitrators
NAI	Netherlands Arbitration Institute
NLRA	National Labor Relations Act
NASA	National Aeronautics and Space Administration
NWLB	National War Labor Board
OAS	Organization of American States
OAU	Organization of African Unity
OCB	Office of Collective Bargaining (New York City)
OECD	Organisation for Economic Co-operation and Development
PERB	Public Employment Relations Board (New York State)
P-H	Prentice-Hall
PL Boards	Public Law Boards
TIAS	Treaties and other International Acts Series (United States State Department)
TVA	Tennessee Valley Authority
UAW	United Auto Workers
U.K.	United Kingdom
U.N.	United Nations
UNCITRAL	United Nations Commission on International Trade Law
UNIDROIT	International Institute for the Unification of Private Law
U.N.R.I.A.A.	United Nations Reports of International Arbitral Awards
U.N.T.S.	United Nations Treaty Series
USAA	United States Arbitration Act
U.S.C.A.	United States Code Annotated
US BLS	United States Bureau of Labor Statistics
US GPO	United States Government Printing Office

AAA

See: American Arbitration Association.

ABS-SHAWCROSS DRAFT CONVENTION ON INVESTMENTS ABROAD (1959)

A proposed treaty drafted to encourage the investment of capital in foreign countries by protecting the property of investors abroad through an international guarantee.

The Abs-Shawcross Draft Convention is an amalgam of two previous separate drafts, one drawn up under the chairmanship of Dr. Abs, and the other under that of Lord Shawcross. Arbitration was to be available as a means of settling disputes, though its use remained optional. The provisions for enforcing awards were extremely vague. Some attempt has been made to revitalize the draft through the Organisation for Economic Co-operation and Development. The basic aims of the Abs-Shawcross draft have also found partial expression in the Convention on the Settlement of Investment Disputes between States and Nationals of Other States, but with more sophisticated procedures and an effort to balance the interests of investors with those of the host States.

See also: Convention on the Settlement of Investment Disputes between States and Nationals of Other States; Draft Convention to Improve the Climate for Investment in Latin America by Facilitating the Settlement of Disputes; OECD Draft Convention on the Protection of Foreign Property.

Sources: [*Abs-Shawcross*] *Draft Convention on Investments Abroad,* 9 J. Pub. L. (1960); Organisation for Economic Co-operation and Development, *Draft Convention on the Protection of Foreign Property,* Oct. 12, 1967, (O.E.C.D. Publication No. 23081, Nov. 1967); E. Nwogugu, The Legal Problems of Foreign Investment in Developing Countries 147-148 (1965); Schwarzenberger, *The Arb. Pattern and the Protection of Property Abroad,* in Int'l. Arb. Liber Amicorum for Martin Domke 313 (P. Sanders ed. 1967).

ABU DHABI ARBITRATION (1951)
[*Petroleum Development (Trucial Coast) Ltd.* v. *Sheikh of Abu Dhabi*]

An international arbitration which determined whether or not an oil concession agreement of 1939 granted by the Sheikh of Abu Dhabi to a British corporation extended to the seabed and subsoil of the territorial waters of Abu Dhabi and to the continental shelf.

The Abu Dhabi Arbitration is interesting because of the method by which the Umpire, Lord Asquith of Bishopstone, arrived at the applicable law which he described as a "modern law of nature." The concession agreement had provided for the appointment of two arbitrators, and if these arbitrators could not agree, for an Umpire whose award was to be final. The arbitrators failed to come to a decision, and as a result, Lord Asquith was appointed Umpire. Each party had used a different version

1

of the concession contract translated from the original Arabic, and the Umpire had first to decide, by comparing the two versions, exactly what had been the true meaning of the governing agreement. As the contract was made in Abu Dhabi, and was to be performed wholly in that country, the logical applicable law would have been the law of Abu Dhabi. But no such law could be said to exist, since the Sheikh was an absolute feudal monarch, as Lord Asquith pointed out in his award, "administering a purely discretionary justice with the assistance of the Koran. . . . Clause 17 of the agreement . . . repels the notion that the municipal law of any country could be appropriate. The terms of that clause invite . . . the application of principles rooted in the good sense and common practice of the generality of civilised nations—a sort of 'modern law of nature.'"

See also: Applicable law. Int'l. pub. arb.; Concession contract; Economic development agreements; Enforcement of award (Int'l. pub. arb.); General principles of law recognized by civilized nations.

Sources: Petroleum Development Ltd. v. Sheikh of Abu Dhabi, 1951 I.L.R. (Arb. award September 1951); *In the Matter of an Arb. between Petroleum Development (Trucial Coast) Ltd. and the Sheikh of Abu Dhabi. Award of Lord Asquith of Bishopstone*, 1 INT'L. & COMP. L. Q. 247-261 (1952).

ACCESS TO THE ARBITRAL TRIBUNAL

The right of the disputing parties to have recourse to the facilities of an administrative agency for the arbitration of their dispute.

The facilities of most administrative agencies are open to the public only as parties. Some agencies reserve the right to refuse such access under certain specified circumstances. Certain commodity exchanges may require that at least one party to a dispute be a member of the exchange. Access rights are usually established by the rules of various national and international institutions and have been subjected to little public supervision. In international public arbitration, it is commonly understood that each party must be a State, but this may be a formal rather than a material requirement. In investment disputes, one party is usually a State, and the other party a national of another State. If an international convention controls the arbitration, access to the arbitral machinery is usually restricted to those nations which have ratified the convention.

See also: American Arb. Association; Convention on the Pacific Settlement of Int'l. Disputes of 1899 and 1907; Institutional arb.; Int'l. Centre for Settlement of Investment Disputes; Int'l. Chamber of Commerce; London Court of Arb.; Chamber of Commerce of the State of N. Y. Arb. Comm.; Permanent Court of Arb.

Sources: I.C.J. STAT. art. 34; Convention on the Recognition and Enforcement of Foreign Arbitral Awards, U.N. Doc. E/CONF.26/8/Rev. 1 (1958); Convention on the Settlement of Investment Disputes between States and Nationals of Other States, (submitted by I.B.R.D., March 18, 1965); U.N. ECE Handbook, U.N. Doc. TRADE/WP.1/ 15/Rev.1 (1958).

ADAMSON ACT [39 Stat. 721 (1916)] (September 5, 1916)

An act to establish an eight-hour day and avert a general strike in the railroad industry by legislating the terms of settlement in a single labor dispute.

Prior to the Adamson Act, the four railway brotherhoods of engineers, conductors, firemen, and trainmen had rejected arbitration which the railroads had requested. The Act complied with union demands for an eight-hour day, and provided for a presidential commission of three to observe the operation and the effects of such an eight-hour standard workday, and report its findings to President Woodrow Wilson and the Congress. The railroads waited to implement the Act until the United States Supreme Court held on its constitutionality. After a second threatened strike in March 1917, the dispute was finally settled with the appointment of a committee of mediation representing the Council of National Defense. Committee members were Secretary of the Interior Franklin K. Lane, Secretary of Labor William B. Wilson, Daniel Willard, President of the Baltimore and Ohio Railroad, and Samuel Gompers, President of the American Federation of Labor. The Agreement was signed on March 19, 1917, and the eight hour-day became a fact for the first time in the railroad industry.

See also: Arb. Act of 1888; Compulsory arb.; Erdman Act; Gov't. intervention; Newlands Act; Railroad Arb. Act; Railway Labor Act; Transportation Act of 1920.

Sources: Adamson Act, in U.S. GPO, COMPILATION OF LAWS RELATING TO MEDIATION, CONCILIATION AND ARB. 100-101 (1967); Berman, *The Threatened Railway Strike of 1916, the Adamson Act,* in LEGISLATIVE REFERENCE SERVICE OF THE LIBRARY OF CONGRESS FOR THE SENATE COMM. ON LABOR AND PUBLIC WELFARE, FEDERAL LEGISLATION TO END STRIKES 63-81 (1967).

ADHESION CONTRACT

A standard-form printed contract prepared by the more powerful party and submitted to the weaker on a take it or leave it basis.

The terms of such an adhesion contract are imposed by one party on the other, and are not reached as a result of any bargaining process. The arbitration clause is more vulnerable where it appears as "boiler plate" in standardized mass contracts. Arbitration statutes of Germany, Ethiopia, and Israel* provide that the arbitration agreement is not valid when one of the parties is in a superior position. The European Convention Providing a Uniform Law on Arbitration of January 20, 1966, also holds that "an arbitration agreement shall not be valid if it gives one of the parties . . . a privileged position with regard to the appointment of the arbitrator or arbitrators."

See also: Boiler plate.

Sources: Council of Europe, European Convention Providing a Uniform Law on Arb., Jan. 20, 1966, European Treaty Series 56, art. 3, Annex I; *M. DOMKE, THE LAW AND PRACTICE OF COMMERCIAL ARBITRATION 42-43 (1968); Goldberg, *A Supreme Court Justice Looks at Arbitration*, 20 ARB. J. (n.s.) 13-19 (1965); Kessler, *Contracts of Adhesion*, 43 COLUM. L. REV. 629 (1943).

AD HOC ARBITRATION

Non-institutional arbitration, either private or public, with all procedural matters indicated by the parties in their agreement to arbitrate or in their *compromis* or submission agreement.

The exact phrasing of the arbitration clause becomes very important in *ad hoc* arbitration with specific reference to such procedures as the appointment of arbitrators, the designation of the place of the arbitration, and the applicable law.

See also: Appointment of arbitrators; Arb. agreement; Institutional arb.; Procedure.

Sources: M. DOMKE, *supra* Adhesion contract at 36.

AD HOC ARBITRATOR

An arbitrator jointly selected by the parties to serve in a single arbitration only.

Such an *ad hoc* arbitrator or arbitration tribunal is common in commercial and international arbitration. In labor arbitration, where permanent arbitrators are also frequently used, many employers and unions want each case decided strictly on its merits on an individual basis, and feel that such decisions are more likely to be achieved if the arbitrator is chosen to serve in a single case only. Selection on an *ad hoc* basis also permits designation of specialists to arbitrate different types of cases. Even though an agreement establishes *ad hoc* arbitrators, the same individual or board may be used again if both union and management are satisfied with the original selection. Such a continuation enables the parties to secure some of the advantages of permanent arbitration, and at the same time retain their freedom to change or alternate arbitrators.

See also: Impartial chairman (Ad hoc); Impartial chairman system; Rotating panels; Umpire system.

Sources: U.S. B.L.S., BULL. No. 1425-6 MAJOR COLLECTIVE BARGAINING AGREEMENT, ARB. PROCEDURES, (1966).

ADJOURNMENT OF HEARINGS

The postponement of hearings in an arbitration.

The arbitrator has the power to postpone a hearing until another time upon the application of either party or when he himself decides to do so. Provisions establishing the authority of the arbitrator to grant adjournments may be found in most modern arbitration laws. Similar provisions may be included in the contract itself. The Uniform Arbitration Act and the California Arbitration Act declare that an award may be vacated if the arbitrators have refused to postpone a hearing when sufficient cause had been shown for adjournment. Other statutes including that of New York, merely state in broad terms without specific reference to adjournment that misconduct on the part of the arbitrator is a ground on which an award may be vacated.

See also: Hearing; Procedure; Uniform Arbitration Act; Vacating an award.

Sources: U.S. Arb. Act, 9 U.S.C. § 10(c) (1954); 9 Calif. Code of Civ. Proced. § 1286.2 (e); Uniform Arbitration Act, § 12 (9)(4); M. DOMKE, *supra* Adhesion contract at 249-251; 34 AAA LAWYERS' ARB. LETTERS 3-5 (1968).

ADJUSTMENT BOARD

A union-management board which frequently operates as the final stage of the grievance procedure.

An adjustment board may or may not be transformed into an arbitration board by the addition of a neutral member. An example of this type of board is the Adjustment Board of the San Francisco Hotel and Restaurant Industry which was instituted in 1941. Their Agreement at § 10 reads: "All complaints, disputes and grievances arising between the parties . . . and all questions of interpretation and application of this Agreement . . . including questions of arbitrability which cannot otherwise be adjusted, shall be submitted to an Adjustment Board. . . ." If the adjustment board is unable to agree, the case is then submitted to a five man board which shall include a chairman chosen by lot from a permanent panel of arbitrators. No chairman shall be chosen to serve in two consecutive arbitrations unless by mutual consent of the parties.

See also: Appeal systems; Bipartite board; Nat'l. Railroad Adjustment Board.

Sources: Railway Labor Act, 45 U.S.C. §§ 151-163, 181-188; V. KENNEDY, ARBITRATION IN THE SAN FRANCISCO HOTEL AND RESTAURANT INDUSTRIES 94-99 (1952); Hotel Employers Association of San Francisco and San Francisco Local Executive Board of the Hotel and Restaurant Employees and Bartenders International Union, AFL-CIO . . . Agreement . . . Effective July 1, 1966 at § 10.

ADMINISTRATIVE AGENCY (IMPARTIAL ARBITRAL INSTITUTION)

An institution, trade association, government agency, or international body which, among other services, may administer arbitration proceedings.

These arbitral services may be accessible to the general public. Or they sometimes may be restricted to the members of the institution. Such associations generally operate under their own rules and maintain panels of arbitrators. Agencies may appoint the arbitrator or a group of arbitrators either as provided in their rules or by the agreement of the parties. Or they may offer the parties lists from which to choose arbitrators. A number of associations maintain panels of arbitrators which are not selected by the parties, but are presented to them as a panel which acts as the arbitration board.

See also: Adm. appointment; Administrator; American Arb. Association; Appointing agency; Federal Mediation and Conciliation Service; Institutional arb.; Int'l. Centre for Settlement of Investment Disputes; Int'l. Chamber of Commerce; Trade association.

Sources: U.N. ECE, *supra* Access to the arbitral tribunal.

ADMINISTRATIVE APPOINTMENT

The appointment of the arbitrator by an administrative agency in a case under its administration when the parties themselves fail to agree on the selection of an arbitrator.

Most arbitration rules provide for the possibility of administrative appointments. The actual details of such a provision may vary from agency to agency. When parties have been sent lists and fail to agree on a mutual choice, the agency may reserve the right to make the appointment itself. Under certain circumstances, the parties may invite the agency to make the appointment without such a preliminary submission of lists. When a Tribunal in an international investment dispute has not been appointed within 90 days, Article 38 of the Convention on the Settlement of Investment Disputes permits the Chairman of the Administrative Council to appoint the arbitrator at the request of one party. after consulting as much as he can with both.

See also: Adm. agency; Appointment of arbitrators; Convention on the Settlement of Investment Disputes between States and Nationals of Other States.

Sources: Convention on the Settlement of Investment Disputes between States and Nationals of Other States, art. 38 (submitted by I.B.R.D., March 18, 1965); AAA COM'L. ARB. RULES AMENDED AND IN EFFECT JUNE 1, 1964 at § 12.

ADMINISTRATIVE EXPENSES

The costs of the arbitral proceedings charged by an administrative agency as established in its rules.

Such costs may include an administrative fee, hearing room fee, any charges for clerical services but not for transcripts of hearings, and may in some instances also include the fees and expenses of the arbitrators. Article 17 (a) of the London Court of Arbitration Rules provides that: "Every submission to arbitration shall be deemed to contain an undertaking by all parties . . . to pay the fees, costs and expenses of the arbitrator, arbitrators and umpire and the costs of the arbitration and award in such manner as may by the award be directed . . . ."

See also: Compensation of the arbitrator; Transcript of hearing.

Sources: M. DOMKE, *supra* Adhesion contract at 360; LONDON COURT OF ARB., RULES, 1964.

ADMINISTRATOR

An official of an administrative agency or the agency itself which is empowered to conduct and supervise an arbitration.

When an arbitration is initiated by the parties under the rules of a particular agency, that agency is known as the administrator. The administrator does not act as the arbitrator under normal circumstances.

See also: Adm. agency; Appointment of arbitrators; Trade association.

Sources: TRIBUNAL OF ARB. OF THE MANCHESTER CHAMBER OF COMMERCE, RULES AND FEES at art. 4.

ADVISORY ARBITRATION

An effort to resolve specific issues in a dispute by an arbitrator who renders an award which merely recommends possible solutions and is therefore not binding on the parties.

Advisory arbitration is used most frequently in public employee disputes. Government agencies have long been reluctant to surrender to an arbitrator what they feel are the discretions and responsibilities which are theirs by right of law. A committee appointed by the Mayor of New York City in 1946 recommended advisory arbitration of transit employee grievances. Under President John F. Kennedy's Executive Order 10988 of 1962, the federal government granted advisory arbitration to its employees. Use of such arbitration is limited to questions of majority status, bargaining unit determination, and grievances. The Secretary of Labor, who administers this type of arbitration, has drawn up forms and procedures which have not as yet been widely used.

See also: Executive Order 10988.

Sources: Employee-Management Cooperation in the Federal Service, E.O. No. 10988 § 6b, 27 F.R. 551, 3 C.F.R. 521, 523-4 (1959-1963 compilation 1962); AAA Voluntary Advisory Arb. Rules, 1962?; Dept. of Labor of the City of New York, Unresolved Disputes in Public Employment, Dec. 1955; U.S. Dept. of Labor, Rules for the Nomination of Arbitrators under § 11 of the Executive Order 10988, Aug. 14, 1964.

ADVISORY OPINION

An opinion which an arbitrator gives as his view on the employee-employer rights or on the rights of any parties to a contract.

An advisory opinion, unlike an award, is not binding.

See also: Tentative award.

Sources: M. DOMKE, *supra* Adhesion contract at 132.

AFFIDAVIT

A sworn statement or written declaration made upon oath before an authorized magistrate or officer.

An affidavit is one of the methods used to introduce evidence in an arbitration. Section 29 of Voluntary Labor Arbitration Rules of the American Arbitration Association declares: "The Arbitrator may receive and consider the evidence of witnesses by affidavit, but shall give it only such weight as he deems proper after consideration of any objections made to its admission." An affidavit may be rejected as evidence when its contents are controversial and the witness is not available for cross examination. Some state statutes explicitly permit the affidavit as evidence in an arbitral proceeding. They may also implicitly allow such use of an affidavit by declaring that the rules of evidence shall not be observed. Though used in arbitration, affidavits are generally excluded in court proceedings.

See also: Deposition.

Sources: 9 Calif. Code of Civ. Proced. § 1282.2(d); AAA COM'L. ARB. RULES, *supra* Adm. appointment at § 31; AAA VOLUNTARY LABOR ARB. RULES, AS AMENDED AND IN EFFECT FEB. 1, 1965 at § 29.

AFL AND CIO IMPARTIAL UMPIRE

See: No-Raiding Agreement; AFL-CIO Internal Disputes Plan.

AFL-CIO INTERNAL DISPUTES PLAN

A disputes plan established under Article XXI at the 1961 AFL-CIO Convention to succeed the No-Raiding Agreement.

The AFL-CIO Internal Disputes Plan, which became effective on January 1, 1962, was created to handle disputes through procedures which include an Impartial Umpire, as in the No-Raiding Agreement. All established collective bargaining relationships of union affiliates were to be respected. The AFL-CIO President was authorized to set up a panel of mediators drawn from within the labor movement to process complaints before they reached the Umpire. If mediation failed, the dispute was then submitted to an Impartial Umpire selected from a panel of Impartial Umpires composed of prominent and public figures.

The AFL-CIO Internal Disputes Plan deals with representational and work assignment disputes. The Umpire does not have the authority to make binding decisions as he did in the No-Raiding Agreement, but can only make recommendations which on appeal to a sub-committee of the AFL-CIO Executive Council may be confirmed or set aside by a majority vote of the Executive Council members. The Determinations of the Impartial Umpire are published biennially and continue the Decisions and Recommendations of the AFL-CIO Impartial Umpire published under the No-Raiding Agreement. David L. Cole who functioned as the sole Umpire under the No-Raiding Agreement is still acting as Umpire, but Howard W. Kleeb is also serving in this capacity.

See also: American Federation of Labor and Congress of Industrial Organizations; Jurisdictional disputes; No-Raiding Agreement (AFL & CIO); Representational disputes; Work assignment disputes.

Sources: AFL-CIO INTERNAL DISPUTES PLAN, DETERMINATIONS AND REPORTS (1962-63, 1964-65, 1966-67); Cole, *The AFL & CIO No-Raiding Agreement,* in 8 PROC. OF THE NAT'L. ACADEMY OF ARBITRATORS 149-154 (1955); Cole, *Interrelationships in the Settlement of Jurisdictional Disputes,* 10 LAB. L. J. 454-460 (1959).

AGREED AWARD

An award which appears to have been made by the arbitrator but has actually been arrived at by the parties concerned.

The agreed award is considered a violation of the arbitration process. Such an award is also known as a rigged award, informed award, or a fixed award. These are all alike in that someone who will be affected by the result of the award is ignorant of the fact that the award was agreed upon by the immediate parties to the contract, and was not made by the arbitrator himself, but with his knowledge and consent. The agreed award is perhaps most common in cases settling wage demands, a settlement which one or both parties feel unable to announce except through a third party, such as an arbitrator.

See also: Arbitrator; Award; Award upon settlement; Code of Ethics and Procedural Standards for Labor-Management Arb.; Consent award.

Sources: P. HAYS, LABOR ARB., A DISSENTING VIEW 62-65 (1966); Epstein, *The Agreed Case,* 20 ARB. J. (n.s.) 41-48 (1965); Fleming, *Some Problems of Due Process and Fair Procedures in Labor Arb.,* 13 STAN. L. REV. 248-250 (1961).

AGREEMENT TO ARBITRATE

See: Arb. agreement; Future disputes clause; Standard arbitration clause; Submission agreement.

AIR TRANSPORT AGREEMENTS

Treaties between two sovereign States for the purpose of sharing and exchanging aviation traffic rights.

Such treaties are called bilateral air transport agreements and are negotiated by governments on behalf of their national airlines. Many of these bilateral air transport agreements provide for arbitration of future disputes.

See also: Bermuda agreement; Convention on Int'l. Civil Aviation; Int'l. pub. arb.; Rate clauses; Warsaw Convention on Int'l. Air Transportation.

Sources: B. CHENG, THE LAW OF INT'L. AIR TRANSPORT (1962); Larsen, *Arb. in Bilateral Air Transport Agreements*, 2 ARKIV FOR LUFTRETT (1964).

ALAA

American Labor Arbitration Awards published by Prentice-Hall, Inc., Englewood Cliffs, N. J.

See also: American Labor Arbitration Awards.

ALABAMA ARBITRATION (GENEVA ARBITRATION)
(*United States v. Great Britain*) (1871-1872)

Arbitration of a dispute between Great Britain and the United States arising from the failure of Great Britain to maintain her neutrality during the American Civil War.

The United States alleged that Great Britain had violated her neutrality by allowing a number of vessels to be built in English shipyards for the use of the Confederate Navy, and sought to recover compensation for the damage caused by these Confederate cruisers. The British government denied its responsibility under international law. It was finally agreed by the Treaty of Washington of May 8, 1871, to submit the dispute to arbitration by a High Commission of five arbitrators. The arbitrators were to be selected, one each by the litigating governments, and three neutral arbitrators to be named one each by the King of Italy, the Emperor of Brazil, and the President of the Swiss Confederation. Charles Francis Adams was the United States arbitrator. The arbitration itself was to influence arbitral procedure for many years to come. The principle of the binding character of the arbitration award was stated by the British arbitrator, Sir Alexander Cockburn, as follows: ". . . While the award of the Tribunal appears to me to be open to . . . exception, I trust that it will be accepted by the British people . . . with the submission and respect which is due to the decision of a Tribunal by whose award it has freely consented to abide."*

See also: Applicable law. Int'l. pub. arb.; Binding character of award; Compliance with the award; Int'l. claims; Mixed claims comm'n.; Tripartite board.

Sources: 1 J. MOORE, HISTORY AND DIGEST OF INT'L. ARBITRATIONS TO WHICH THE U.S. HAS BEEN A PARTY 495-682 (1898); *The Alabama Claims, 4 Papers Relating to the Treaty of Washington of 1871, p. 544 (Foreign Relations of the United States, Vol. II, 1872) as cited in footnote 4, Schachter, *The Enforcement of Int'l. Judicial and Arbitral Decisions*, 54 AM. J. INT'L. L. 2 (1960).

ALTERNATIVE FINAL AWARD (BRITISH)

The practice in an arbitration of rendering two or more awards, as alternatives, under a single arbitration proceeding.

The alternative final award is resorted to under English law when the arbitrator proposes to request judicial advice on a point of law through the expedient of the special case.

See also: Special case (Great Britain).

Sources: F. RUSSELL, RUSSELL ON THE LAW OF ARB. (17th ed. 1963).

AMERICAN ARBITRATION ASSOCIATION
(140 West 51st Street, New York, N.Y. 10020)

A private, non-profit organization founded in 1926 to foster the study of arbitration, and to perfect the techniques of this voluntary method of dispute settlement under law, administering arbitration in accordance with the agreements of parties.

The American Arbitration Association is solely an administrative or impartial arbitration agency whose officials never act as arbitrators. It maintains panels from which arbitrators may be selected, and provides administrative personnel and procedures for cases being arbitrated under its rules. The five most important arbitration categories or tribunals are Commercial, Accident Claims, Labor, International, and Inter-American. The Association cooperates closely with members of the bar and various trade bodies, in many cases establishing special panels of arbitrators and separate rules to meet the particular needs of certain industries. It explores the possibility of using arbitration as a means of resolving disputes in such areas as landlord-tenant rent strikes, and other community grievances. The AAA also conducts programs at universities and law schools, bar associations, labor unions, trade associations, and civic organizations of all kinds, in order to bring about the widest possible understanding of the uses of arbitration. The American Arbitration Association maintains 21 regional offices.

See also: Access to the arbitral tribunal; Adm. agency; American Arbitration Association. Recommended arb. clause; Appointing agency; Arb. Journal; Arb. Law. A digest of court decisions; Arb. Magazine; Arb. News; Center for Dispute Settlement; Code of Ethics and Procedural Standards for Labor-Management Arb.; Construction Industry Arb. Rules; General Arb. Council of the Textile Industry. Arb. Rules; Institutional arb.; Inter-American Com'l. Arb. Comm'n.; Inter-association com'l. arb. agreement; Int'l. Arb. Journal; Motion Picture Industry Arb. System; Selection of arbitrators (AAA); Summary of Labor Arb. Awards (AAA); Uninsured motorist arb.

Sources: AAA, FACTS ABOUT THE AAA (1969); AAA, LABOR ARB. PROCEDURES AND TECHNIQUES (1968); F. ELKOURI and E. ELKOURI, HOW ARB. WORKS (Rev. ed. 1960).

AMERICAN ARBITRATION ASSOCIATION. NATIONAL PANEL OF ARBITRATORS

A list of some 26,000 men and women especially skilled in a particular trade, business, or profession who are available to serve as arbitrators throughout the United States.

The American Arbitration Association also carries listings of arbitrators in major cities throughout the world. Many of these persons were nominated to membership on the panel by leaders in their own trades and professions. Others were invited directly by the Association so that the panels could remain current as new fields of specialization appeared, and as the volume of cases increased. Labor arbitrators are carefully screened for impartiality before being appointed to the panel.

See also: Appointment of arbitrators; Selection of arbitrators (AAA).

Sources: AAA, MAY WE HAVE THE BENEFIT OF YOUR JUDGMENT (1968).

AMERICAN ARBITRATION ASSOCIATION. RECOMMENDED ARBITRATION CLAUSE

The following clause is recommended by the AAA for inclusion in commercial agreements where arbitration is desired: "Any controversy or claim arising out of or relating to this contract, or the breach thereof, shall be settled by arbitration in accordance with the Rules of the American Arbitration Association, and judgment upon the award rendered by the Arbitrator(s) may be entered in any Court having jurisdiction thereof."

Sources: AAA COM'L. ARB. RULES. *supra* Adm. appointment.

AMERICAN FEDERATION OF LABOR AND CONGRESS OF INDUSTRIAL ORGANIZATIONS (AFL-CIO)

A federation of trade unions in the United States and Canada, formed in December 1955 by the merger of the American Federation of Labor and the Congress of Industrial Organizations.

The American Federation of Labor was organized in 1886 from an earlier Federation of Organized Trade and Labor Unions in the United States of America and Canada which was founded in Pittsburgh in 1881. From the very beginning the Federation stressed the organization of skilled workers on a craft basis as opposed to an industrial one. Dissident members of the Committee for Industrial Organization, which had been formed late in 1935 to organize the mass production industries, were eventually expelled from the A. F. of L. This dissident group reorganized in 1938 as a permanent institution known as the Congress of Industrial Organizations. The Congress of Industrial Organizations merged in 1955 with the American Federation of Labor to form the AFL-CIO.

See also: AFL-CIO Internal Disputes Plan; No-Raiding Agreement (AFL and CIO).

Sources: COLUMBIA ENCYCLOPEDIA (3d ed. 1963).

AMERICAN LABOR ARBITRATION AWARDS

Arbitration awards published by Prentice-Hall, Inc., Englewood Cliffs, New Jersey, to be cited 13 ALAA ¶ 72,654.

This publication contains full texts of significant labor arbitration awards in more than thirteen volumes since 1946. Included are the arbitrators' opinions, covering every phase of contract negotiation and administration. Awards are indexed as to issues in dispute. Tables of cases are indexed by parties and arbitrators. The correct citation includes the volume, the abbreviation ALAA, and the paragraph number, as in 13 ALAA ¶ 72,654.

See also: Labor Arb. Awards (CCH); Labor Arb. Reports (BNA); Summary of Labor Arb. Awards (AAA); War Labor Reports (BNA).

AMERICAN MANUFACTURING COMPANY
[*United Steelworkers of America* v. *American Mfg. Co.*, 363 U.S. 564 (1960)]

The first of three United States Supreme Court cases known as the 1960 Trilogy, in which the Court held that the basic function of a federal court is to decide whether or not a dispute submitted to it is arbitrable under the contract regardless of the merit of the claim.

The *American Manufacturing Company* case was concerned with the return of an employee to his job in accordance with the seniority provision of the collective bargaining agreement, even though he had received workmen's compensation on the basis of a permanent partial disability. Upon being refused reinstatement, the employee filed a grievance. Suit was eventually brought to compel arbitration of this grievance. The company held that the dispute was not arbitrable. The United States Supreme Court in its decision held that: "The agreement is to submit all grievances to arbitration, not merely those the court will deem meritorious. The processing of even frivolous claims may have therapeutic values (of) which those who are not a part of the plant environment may be quite unaware. The union claimed in this case that the company had violated a specific provision of the contract. The company took the position that it had not violated that clause. There was, therefore, a dispute between the parties as to 'the meaning, interpretation and application' of the collective bargaining agreement. Arbitration should have been ordered. When the judiciary undertakes to determine the merits of a grievance under the guise of interpreting the grievance procedure of collective bargaining agreements, it usurps a function which under that regime is entrusted to the arbitration tribunal."

See also: Enterprise Wheel & Car Corp.; § 301 disputes; Substantive arbitrability; Trilogy; Warrior & Gulf Nav. Co.

Sources: United Steelworkers v. American Mfg. Co., 363 U.S. 564 (1960); Davey, *The Supreme Court and Arb.*, 36 NOTRE DAME LAWYER (1961); Feller & Freidin, *Discussion—Recent Supreme Court Decisions and the Arb. Process*, in 14 PROC. OF THE NAT'L. ACADEMY OF ARBITRATORS (1961); Kagel, *Recent Supreme Court Decisions*, in 14 PROC. OF THE NAT'L. ACADEMY OF ARBITRATORS 1-29 (1961); *Readings in Arb.*, 16 ARB. J. (n.s.) 34 (1961).

AMERICAN TREATY OF PACIFIC SETTLEMENT

See: Pact of Bogotá.

AMIABLE COMPOSITEUR

A French phrase for an arbitrator who has great freedom in formulating the terms of his award.

The concept of *amiable compositeur* is widely used in continental legal systems. It has been variously defined as conciliator, arbitrator *de facto*, or in the most extreme sense, an arbitrator under no obligation to observe the rule of law. An *amiable compositeur* is nevertheless subject to the rules of "natural justice" and must observe the fundamental rules governing judicial procedure and material law. He is distinguished from other arbitrators in that he is permitted to decide *ex aequo et bono*, although the literal meaning of the term, a "friendly" arbitrator, suggests that he is to conciliate both parties rather than secure absolute fairness at the expense of one. In France, Belgium, and Portugal, the parties waive the right of appeal if they authorize the arbitrator to act as an *amiable compositeur*. The term is not in use in the United States.

See also: Applicable substantive law. Int'l. com'l. arb.; Ex aequo et bono; Expert arbitrator.

Sources: Marx, *Amiable Compositeur*, 2 ARB. J. (n.s.) 211 (1947); Mezger, *La distinction entre l'arbitre dispensé d'observer la règle de la loi et l'arbitre statuant sans appel*, in INT'L. ARB. LIBER AMICORUM FOR MARTIN DOMKE 184 (P. Sanders ed. 1967).

ANNULMENT OF THE AWARD. INTERNATIONAL PUBLIC ARBITRATION

The nullifying of the legality of an arbitral award or a judgment.

Annulment of an award occurs only when there is some authoritative public or judicial confirmation of the ground for such an annulment. This confirmation might come from an international agency such as the International Court of Justice, although there is no statutory provision for such confirmation at the present time. Confirmation might also be based on international public opinion deriving from general principles of law common to all nations. Refusal by the losing party to comply with the award is not in itself equivalent to a lawful annulment. There are certain fundamental procedural rights upon which a State may rely in any international arbitration. The flagrant violation of such rights would lead to nullifying the award. It is commonly held in both the international and national communities that the validity of an award may be challenged by either party on several grounds. These may be that the tribunal has exceeded its powers, or that there was corruption on the part of a member of the tribunal, or a serious departure from a fundamental rule of procedure, including failure to state the reasons for the award. Conventions such as the Convention on the Settlement of Investment Disputes between States and Nationals of Other States may provide for challenging the award. Article 52 of the Convention has this provision: "Either party may request annulment of the award by an application in writing addressed to the Secretary General. . . ." If no other confirming agency had been designated by the parties, the Model Rules on Arbitral Procedure prepared by the International Law Commission, in Articles XXXV and XXXVI, offer specific conditions for testing the validity of the award, and provisions for annulling it through the International Court of Justice.

See also: Exces de pouvoir; Grounds of nullity; Int'l. Court of Justice Statute. Article 38; Int'l. pub. arb.; Misconduct of arbitrator; Model rules on arbitral procedure; Repudiation.

Sources: U.N. Int'l. Law Commission, Commentary on the Draft Convention on Arbitral Procedure, U.N. Doc. A/CN.4/92 (1955) at 105; A. BALASKO, CAUSES DE LA SENTENCE ARBITRALE EN DROIT INT'L. PUBLIC (1938), as cited in U.N. ILC, Commentary on the Draft Convention on Arbitral Procedure, U.N. Doc. A/CN.4/92 (1955) at 106; K. CARLSTON, THE PROCESS OF INT'L. ARBITRATION, 36-61, 222-233 (1946); E. NANTWI, THE ENFORCEMENT OF INT'L. JUDICIAL DECISIONS AND ARBITRAL AWARDS IN PUBLIC INT'L. LAW 148ff (1966).

ANSWERING STATEMENT

A reply in writing by the party who has not initiated the arbitration.

The answering statement denies in whole or in part that a dispute exists. The statement may also take the form of a counterclaim. If no answer is filed within the stated time, the assumption is that the claim is denied. Administrative agencies vary in their requirements concerning the answering statement. Under the Rules of the American Arbitration Association, failure to answer does not delay arbitration. The Rules of the International Chamber of Commerce state that the party not initiating the arbitration must reply within thirty days after receipt of the request for arbitration, and must also furnish in his reply a statement of the case, and any proposals or claims he may wish to make.

See also: Counterclaim; Demand for arb.; Procedure (Arbitration).

Sources: AAA Com'l. Arb. Rules, *supra* Adm. appointment at § 7; Int'l. Chamber of Commerce, Rules of Conciliation and Arb. in Force on 1st June 1955 at art. 9 & 10.

ANTHRACITE BOARD OF CONCILIATION

A board created by the Anthracite Coal Strike Commission in its Fourth Award of March 18, 1903, to be composed of three operators and three miners to hear and decide any grievance disputes in the industry.

An award made by a majority of such a Board of Conciliation was to be final and binding on all parties. If the Board was unable to decide any question, that question was to be submitted to an umpire. The umpire was to be appointed at the request of the Board of Conciliation by one of the judges of the United States Court of Appeals in Philadelphia. The decision of the umpire was to be final and binding. Grievance procedures have been perfected to simplify and strengthen the processing of grievances before the dispute is submitted to the Board of Conciliation. The Board of Conciliation is still in operation.

See also: Anthracite Coal Strike Commission; Umpire system.

Sources: Anthracite Board of Conciliation, Award of the Anthracite Coal Strike Commission 7-8 (July 1, 1953); T. Larkin, Fifty Years of Handling Labor Disputes 1-19 (1953).

ANTHRACITE COAL STRIKE COMMISSION

A Commission appointed by President Theodore Roosevelt after the United Mine Workers agreed in convention to go back to work on October 23, 1902, following a strike of twenty-three and a half weeks.

The Anthracite Coal Strike Commission established in its Fourth Award an Anthracite Board of Conciliation to handle all grievances which might develop as a result of these settlements.

See also: Anthracite Board of Conciliation; Grievance arb. (Rights arb.).

Sources: D. McDonald & E. Lynch, Coal and Unionism 58-61 (1939).

APPEAL

The process of seeking the reversal or amendment of a decision by a higher tribunal.

Though there is generally no right of appeal from an award in arbitration, there do exist methods by which an award may be challenged, so that the challenge itself would represent an appeal. Where arbitration statutes are in force, the challenge to an award may be made only on grounds specified in the statutes. Such a challenge will usually be based upon the partiality or bias of the arbitrator, or any misconduct that violates the basic rights of the parties to a fair hearing, or for some formal error, such as an incorrect computation. The most recent modern statutes permit a motion to an arbitrator to correct his own alleged error. The grounds for vacating or modifying an award at common law are essentially the same as those adopted in the statutes. Some arbitral procedures provide for an appeal to a higher arbitral tribunal, a procedure which is not common in the United States.

See also: Appeal boards of adm. agencies; Challenge of award; Confirming the award; Modifying the award; Statutory arb.; Vacating an award.

Sources: M. BERNSTEIN, PRIVATE DISPUTE SETTLEMENT (1968); M. DOMKE, *supra* Adhesion contract at 298-302.

APPEAL BOARDS OF ADMINISTRATIVE AGENCIES

A review procedure for challenging an award in arbitrations which are administered by various commodity exchanges and trade associations.

A review procedure has long been established in Great Britain and in most of the commodity exchanges and trade associations in Europe, although there seems to be no uniformity in such a practice. Such a procedure has been adopted by some associations in the United States. For example, under the rules of the Diamond Trade Center, the Fur Merchants' Association, or the American Spice Trade Association, an appeal board usually consists of other arbitrators who proceed to hear the case again. Some trade association arbitration rules provide for an appeal proceeding before the American Arbitration Association. Appeal systems exist in a number of international organizations. The Rules and Regulations of the International Centre for Settlement of Investment Disputes in Chapter VII, Rules 50, 51, and 52, provide for an application for the interpretation, revision or annulment of an award in international investment disputes.

See also: Appeal; Challenge of award; Institutional arb.; U.N. Handbook of Nat'l. and Int'l. Institutions Active in the Field of Int'l. Com'l. Arb.

Sources: AMERICAN SPICE TRADE ASSOCIATION, A GUIDE TO ARBITRATIONS 8 (1965); M. DOMKE, COM'L. ARB. 96-97 (1965); INT'L. CENTRE FOR SETTLEMENT OF INVESTMENT DISPUTES, ICSID REGULATIONS AND RULES IN EFFECT ON JANUARY 1, 1968; LIVERPOOL CORN TRADE ASSOCIATION, BYE-LAWS, ARB. APPEALS (1960); Benjamin, *A Comparative Study of Int'l. Institutional Arb.*, in 2 INT'L. COM'L. ARB. 389 (P. Sanders ed. 1960).

APPEAL SYSTEMS

The contractual use of joint boards of union and company members for the purpose of reviewing employee complaints and grievances.

An appeal system is a more formal procedure than the usual grievance machinery, and is in many cases the next to the last step in that
machinery. Boards of this nature are variously called Adjustment Boards,
Joint Boards, or Appeal Boards, and usually consist of two or more members appointed by the union and by the company. These boards follow
rules of procedure as established in the contract, which determine the
time, place, and frequency of meetings. If the members are unable to
agree on any matter submitted to them, the case automatically proceeds
to arbitration, except in the comparatively rare instances where the
Appeal Boards represent the final step.

See also: Adjustment board; Bipartite board; Council on Industrial Relations
for the Electrical Contracting Industry; Grievance procedure; Public
Review Board (United Auto Workers); Umpire system.

APPLICABLE LAW. INTERNATIONAL PUBLIC ARBITRATION

The law to be applied by the arbitrators as established by the disputing
parties in their *compromis* or arbitration agreement.

The parties in drawing up the *compromis* may determine within
certain limits the rules and principles which will serve as a basis for the
decision of the arbitrator. The *compromis* may thus provide that the
Tribunal shall decide according to the principles of international law,
or the substantive rules enumerated in Article 38 of the Statute of the
International Court of Justice, or the principles of law and equity, or
ex aequo et bono. The parties may also establish special rules of law,
though their freedom to determine the applicable law is not unlimited.
The parties are bound by accepted principles of justice and the general
framework or system of world law. If the *compromis* fails to define the
applicable law, it is implicitly understood that the arbitrator shall apply
international law as the basis of his award. Article 42 of the Convention
on the Settlement of Investment Disputes between States and Nationals
of Other States has this provision: "The Tribunal shall decide a dispute
in accordance with such rules of law as may be agreed by the parties.
In the absence of such agreement, the Tribunal shall apply the law of
the Contracting State party to the dispute (including its rules on the
conflict of laws) and such rules of international law as may be applicable." The Convention prohibits a finding of *non liquet*, but permits
the Tribunal to decide a dispute *ex aequo et bono* if the parties have so
agreed.

See also: Abu Dhabi Arb.; Alabama Arb.; Compromis; Ex aequo et bono;
General principles of law recognized by civilized nations; Int'l. Court
of Justice Statute. Article 38; Int'l. pub. arb.; Lena Goldfields Arb.;
Non liquet; Principles of law common to the parties; Trail Smelter
Arb.

Sources: 1 J. Moore, *supra* Alabama Arbitration at 549-550; I.C.J. STAT. art.

38; U.N. ILC, *supra* Annulment . . . at 34-44; K. CARLSTON, *supra* Annulment . . . ; Broches, *The Convention on the Settlement of Investment Disputes between States and Nationals of Other States,* in INT'L. ARB. LIBER AMICORUM FOR MARTIN DOMKE 12 (P. Sanders ed. 1967).

APPLICABLE PROCEDURAL LAW

The law which governs the arbitral proceedings.

The procedural law of the country or state in which the arbitration takes place will usually prevail. An example of such a law is the New York State Arbitration Law which establishes procedures for conducting the arbitration and enforcing the award, and guarantees the rights of the parties in the conduct of the arbitration. If the parties have not determined in their agreement where the arbitration is to take place, the question is commonly decided by the arbitrator. In arbitrations conducted under the rules of an agency, such as the International Chamber of Commerce, the place of the arbitration is determined by the Court of Arbitration, unless the parties themselves have agreed in advance on the place. Article 16 of the ICC Rules provides as follows: "The rules by which the arbitration proceedings shall be governed shall be these Rules and, in the event of no provision being made in these Rules, those of the law of procedure chosen by the parties or, failing such choice, those of the law of the country in which the arbitrator holds the proceedings."

See also: Applicable substantive law. Int'l. com'l. arb.; Int'l. com'l. arb.; Locale of arb.; Municipal law; Procedure; Special Case (Great Britain); U.N. ECAFE; U.N. ECE. Rules of Arb.

Sources: INDIAN COUNCIL OF ARB., INT'L. SEMINAR ON COM'L. ARB. (1968); ICC, *supra* Answering statement; Centre for Com'l. Arb., U.N. ECAFE, ECAFE Rules for Int'l. Com'l. Arb. and ECAFE Standards for Conciliation, 1966; Broches, *supra* Applicable law. Int'l. pub. arb. at 12; 2 INT'L. COM'L. ARB. 387 (P. Sanders ed. 1960); Wilner, *Determining the Law Governing Performance in Int'l. Com'l. Arb.* 19 RUTGERS L. REV. 646-691 (1965).

APPLICABLE SUBSTANTIVE LAW. INTERNATIONAL COMMERCIAL ARBITRATION

The law to be applied in defining and determining the merits or issues in a dispute.

If the parties in their contract have not decided on the applicable law, the place of arbitration may become an important factor in determining what law or laws the arbitrators should apply in solving the dispute. The terms of an international convention may be helpful in providing for the applicable substantive law. Article VII of the European Convention on International Commercial Arbitration declares in § 1:

"The parties shall be free to determine, by agreement, the law to be applied by the arbitrators to the substance of the dispute. Failing any indication by the parties as to the applicable law, the arbitrators shall apply the proper law under the rule of conflict that the arbitrators deem applicable. In both cases the arbitrators shall take account of the terms of the contract and trade usages." Article VII 4. (b) of the ECAFE Rules is similar in its rulings. The arbitrators under both procedures may act as *amiables compositeurs* if the parties authorize them to do so, and if it is authorized by the law applicable to the arbitration.

See also: Amiable compositeur; Applicable procedural law; Int'l. com'l. arb.; Locale of arb.; U.N. ECAFE.

Sources: European Convention on Int'l. Com'l. Arb., art. 7, §§ 1 & 2, U.N. Doc. E/ECE/423 & E/ECE/TRADE/48 (done at Geneva on 21 April 1961); Centre for Com'l. Arb., U.N. ECAFE, *supra* Applicable procedural law; Domke, *Int'l. Com'l. Arb. by the Centre for Com'l. Arb. of ECAFE*, in INDIAN COUNCIL OF ARB., INT'L. SEMINAR ON COM'L. ARB. (1968); Sanders, *Venue of Arbitration in Int'l. Com'l. Arb.*, in INDIAN COUNCIL OF ARB., INT'L. SEMINAR ON COM'L. ARB. (1968).

APPOINTING AGENCY

Another term for Administrative Agency, particularly as applied in this country to such institutions as the American Arbitration Association, the Federal Mediation and Conciliation Service, and the various State Mediation Boards in their respective roles as administrators of labor arbitration cases.

See also: Adm. agency; American Arb. Association; Federal Mediation and Conciliation Service; State Boards of Mediation.

APPOINTMENT OF ARBITRATORS

Arbitrators are chosen by the disputing parties in the manner established in their agreement to arbitrate.

Some agreements provide that each party appoints an arbitrator, and the third arbitrator is to be chosen by the two arbitrators. If the two arbitrators cannot agree, the third arbitrator may be appointed by the agency administering the arbitration. A common practice at present is to select a single arbitrator whose appointment may be governed by the rules of an impartial agency, or who can be designated in the agreement. Under modern arbitration statutes, if the method specified in the agreement does not result in an appointment, a court may make the appointment on the motion of one of the parties. If the parties are members of a commodity exchange or trade association, the association or exchange may automatically appoint an arbitrator, or in some cases act as the arbitrator itself, through a rotating arbitration board or a permanent arbitration committee. Methods for appointing arbitrators in international arbitrations are established in the *compromis* or agreement to arbitrate or in the governing treaty. In those cases where the parties fail to appoint an arbitrator within certain specified time limits as expressed in their agreement, the President of the International Court of Justice may be designated to select the arbitrator, or the arbitrator may be appointed by some head of state or important jurist. The typical tribunal of three arbitrators permits each of the parties to appoint one member of its own nationality. The *compromis* usually allows considerable latitude in the appointment of arbitrators.

See also: Adm. appointment; AAA. Nat'l. Panel of Arbitrators; Arb. agreement; Compromis; Impartial chairman system; Int'l. Court of Justice; Modern arb. statute; Number of arbitrators; Procedure; Rotating panels; Selection of arbitrators (AAA); Selection of arbitrators (FMCS); Sole arbitrator; Trade association; Umpire system; U.N. ECE. Rules of Arb.; Wal Wal Arb.

Sources: Model Rules on Arbitral Procedure, in Report of the ILC Covering the Work of Its Tenth Session 28 April-4 July 1958, 13 U.N. GAOR Supp. 9, U.N. Doc. A/3859 (1958); U.N. ILC, *supra* Annulment at 17-25; LIVERPOOL PROVISION TRADE ASSOCIATION, RULES EMBODYING THE TRADE CUSTOMS AND SYSTEM OF ARB. § 9, rule 70 (1958); J. SIMPSON & H. FOX, INT'L. ARB. LAW AND PRACTICE, 81ff (1959); U.N. SYSTEMATIC SURVEY OF TREATIES FOR THE PACIFIC SETTLEMENT OF INT'L. DISPUTES 1928-1948 at 89-107 (1948); François, *La liberté des parties de choisir les arbitres dans les conflits entre les Etats*, in INT'L. ARB. LIBER AMICORUM FOR MARTIN DOMKE 89 (P. Sanders ed. 1967).

APPRAISAL

A valuation of property by one or more especially qualified and impartial persons.

The appraiser makes his valuation according to his own skill, knowledge, and experience. Some courts have declared that an appraisal is not in itself an arbitration proceeding, since no controversy exists. Unless such a specific provision is made in the agreement, an appraisal provision is not regarded as an intention to take evidence, or to hear arguments in the presence of the parties. An appraisal in California is considered to be similar to an arbitration award. In New York State, CPLR § 7601 provides that a party may move to compel an appraisal, and that it shall be subject to the provisions of the law governing arbitration.

Sources: M. DOMKE, *supra* Adhesion contract at 6-7.

ARAMCO ARBITRATION (August 23, 1958)
(*State of Saudi Arabia* v. *Arabian American Oil Company*)

An arbitration concerned with the interpretation of a concession agreement made on May 29, 1933, between the Government of the State of

Saudi Arabia and the Standard Oil Company of California.

Although the initial concession was contracted with the Standard Oil Company of California, it was subsequently assigned to the California Arabian Standard Oil Company, which later changed its name to the Arabian American Oil Company, and was thereafter known as Aramco. The controversy concerned the right of Saudi Arabia to interfere with the transportation monopoly of Aramco granted by Saudi Arabia in the concession contract of 1933. The Government of Saudi Arabia had concluded a second agreement on January 20, 1954, with Mr. A. S. Onassis and his company, Saudi Arabian Maritime Tankers Co., Ltd., by which that company was given a thirty years "right of priority" for the transport of Saudi Arabian oil. The award made by a mixed arbitral tribunal held that Saudi Arabia had infringed its agreement with Aramco. Though the partisan arbitrator appointed by Saudi Arabia dissented, Saudi Arabia decided to comply with the award.

See also: Compliance with award; Concession contract; Economic development agreement.

Sources: Saudi Arabia v. Arabian American Oil Co. (Aramco), 27 I.L.R. 117-233 (Arb. Tribunal, Aug. 23, 1958).

ARB

Labor Arbitration Awards published by the Commerce Clearing House, 4025 West Peterson Ave., Chicago, Illinois 60646.

The correct citation includes the year, the abbreviation ARB, and the paragraph number, as 68-1 ARB ¶ 8254. The 1 in 68-1 refers to the volume for that year when there is more than one volume.

See also: Labor Arbitration Awards.

ARBITER

A term sometimes used in place of arbitrator.

An arbiter may serve as an umpire who makes the decision when arbitrators cannot agree. The term arbiter is now rarely used.

See also: Arbitrator.

Sources: WEBSTER'S INT'L. DICTIONARY, 2d ed.

ARBITRABILITY

The concept that an issue in dispute between parties is subject to arbitration as derived from their agreement to arbitrate, provided that certain specified steps have been exhausted prior to arbitration.

It is the arbitration clause or agreement which describes the specific nature and kinds of disputes subject to arbitration under the contract. Other factors determining arbitrability are whether or not the parties have a contract, and if it exists, whether it commits the parties to arbitrate this particular dispute, and whether all grievance procedures under the contract have been exhausted prior to arbitration. Who precisely determines questions of arbitrability depends on statutes in force, on rules of procedure which may apply or on court decisions, or on an international convention ratified by the parties. This means that the arbitrator or the courts may decide on arbitrability, or that its determination may be referred to an international organization. Arbitration will be ordered in labor arbitration subject to § 301 of the Taft-Hartley Act if a broad arbitration clause exists, or if a violation of the agreement is claimed, and the parties cannot be said "with positive assurance"* to have excluded the subject from arbitration.

See also: Enforcement of arb. agreements (Federal statutes); Jurisdiction; Procedural arbitrability; Stay of arb.; Substantive arbitrability; Trilogy; Warrior & Gulf Nav. Co.; Wiley v. Livingston.

Sources: *United Steelworkers v. Warrior & Gulf Nav. Co., 363 U.S. 574 (1960); Christensen, *The Developing Law of Arbitrability*, 11 SOUTHWESTERN LEGAL FOUNDATION, PROC. OF THE ANNUAL INSTITUTE ON LABOR LAW (1965); McDermott, *Arbitrability: The Courts Versus the Arbitrator*, 23 ARB. J. (n.s.) 18-37 (1968); Meltzer, *The Supreme Court, Arbitrability and Collective Bargaining*, 28 U. CHI. L. REV. 461-487 (1961); Smith & Jones, *The Impact of the Emerging Federal Law of Grievance Arb. on Judges, Arbitrators, and Parties*, 52 VA. L. REV. 831-912 (1966); Smith & Jones, *The Supreme Court and Labor Dispute Arb.*, 63 MICH. L. REV. 751-808 (1965).

ARBITRAL COURT (AFRICA)

A type of court found in the ancient tribal law of Africa.

The arbitral court in Africa was an informal means of settling disputes through negotiation with or without the use of an arbitrator. Usually such disputes were those within a family or an intra-family group most appropriately settled by the head of the family or its elders. Issues apart from quarrels included the adjustment of property rights in land or cattle, and the settlement of estates on the death of members of the family group. Arbitrations of this kind are universal in all African societies.

See also: Customary law.

Sources: A. ALLOTT, ESSAYS IN AFRICAN LAW 117ff. (1960).

ARBITRALE RECHTSPRAAK (Oppert 34, Rotterdam-1 and Teniersstraat 5, Amsterdam-7, The Netherlands)

A Dutch monthly journal on arbitration.

Arbitrale Rechtspraak began publication in 1919. The journal contains arbitral awards, with the arbitrators' opinions or reasons for making these awards, as required in Holland, as well as leading articles on arbitration law, and news about developments in the world of arbitration. The awards stem chiefly from the arbitration institutes of the organized branches of trade and industry.

Sources: Letter from A. S. Fransen van de Putte to the AAA, June 19, 1968; Sanders, *New Arbitration Institute in Holland*, 6 ARB. J. (n.s.) 40-41 (1951).

ARBITRAMENT (OBSOLETE)

An award or judgment which one or more persons make at the request of two parties to settle a dispute between them.

Sources: BLACK's LAW DICTIONARY (3d ed. 1933).

ARBITRAMENTUM AEQUUM TRIBUIT CUIQUE SUUM

A just arbitration renders to everyone his own.

Sources: BLACK's LAW DICTIONARY (3d ed. 1933).

ARBITRATION. A CONTRACTUAL CONCEPT

The concept that the arbitration clause in a contract binds the parties because in signing they have agreed to be so bound.

Any defects in this consent to arbitrate will void the process of arbitration, and will leave the dispute open to the more formal process of legal action.

ARBITRATION ACT OF 1888 (Pub. L. No. 304)

An act which established boards of arbitration for settling controversies between railroads and their employees.

The Arbitration Act of 1888 was the first federal law enacted in the United States to set up arbitration procedures in critical industries, in this case, the railroad industry. Though President Grover Cleveland, in a special message in April 1886, had recommended a permanent board for voluntary arbitration, the Arbitration Act of 1888 provided for neutral *ad hoc* arbitration boards to decide disputes whenever both parties so agreed. The Act empowered the President in any railroad labor dispute to appoint a board of investigation which was to make a public report with recommendations. The investigation provision was used only in the Pullman Strike of 1894. The voluntary arbitration provisions were never used. The Act proved ineffective and was replaced by the Erdman Act of 1898.

See also: Adamson Act; Erdman Act; Newlands Act; Railway Labor Act; Transportation Act of 1920.

Sources: Arbitration Act of 1888, in U.S. GPO, COMPILATION OF LAWS RELAT-
ING TO MEDIATION, CONCILIATION, AND ARB. 1-3 (1967); Railway
Labor Act, 45 U.S.C. §§ 151-163, 181-188; E. WITTE, HISTORICAL
SURVEY OF LABOR ARB. 8-9 (1952).

ARBITRATION AGENCY

See: Administrative agency; Appointing agency.

ARBITRATION AGREEMENT

That part of a contract or treaty which pledges the parties concerned to
use arbitration as a means of settling any present or future dispute.

Arbitration agreement is a term which is sometimes used inter-
changeably with arbitration clause. In actual practice, arbitration agreement is the more inclusive term, applying to the submission agreement
for existing disputes, and to the future disputes clause as well. If the
arbitration agreement is to be fully effective, it should define the questions to be arbitrated, determine the applicable law, and if possible, the
governing procedure. If the dispute is being arbitrated under the rules
of an administrative agency, such as the American Arbitration Association, a reference to these rules ensures their adoption in practice, and
establishes all the procedures necessary for arbitration. Modern statutes
in the United States generally require that agreements to arbitrate be
set down in writing. Where appropriate conventions govern, international
public disputes may be administered under the rules of an agency such
as the International Centre for Settlement of Investment Disputes. In
the absence of such a designated international agency, the parties may
specify in their treaties the detailed procedures to be followed in settling
disputes.

See also: Appointment of arbitrators; Arbitrator's authority; Compromis; Consent of the parties; Enforcement of arb. agreements (Common law);
Enforcement of arb. agreements (Federal statutes); Enforcement of
arb. agreements (State statutes); Enforcement of arb. agreements
(Int'l. com'l. arb.); Future disputes clause; Locale of arb.; Standard
arb. clause; Scope of arb. agreement; Submission agreement.

Sources: M. BERNSTEIN, *supra* Appeal at ch. III (1968); K. CARLSTON, *supra*
Annulment . . . at 65ff; J. SIMPSON & H. FOX, *supra* Appointment of
arbitrators at 42; W. STURGES, A TREATISE ON COM'L. ARBITRATIONS
AND AWARDS (1930); B. TOMSON, IT'S THE LAW (1960).

ARBITRATION AWARDS

See: American Labor Arb. Awards (P-H); Labor Arb. Awards (CCH); Labor
Arb. Reports (BNA); Summary of Labor Arb. Awards (AAA); War
Labor Reports (BNA).

ARBITRATION CLAUSE

See: Arb. agreement; Future disputes clause; Standard arb. clause.

ARBITRATION JOURNAL

A quarterly publication of the American Arbitration Association containing articles of a technical, theoretical, or legal nature on all phases of arbitration, and current bibliographies on the subject, as well as digests of court decisions on commercial, labor-management, and accident claims cases.

The Arbitration Journal includes articles by authorities on the subject in this country and abroad. Volumes 1-6 were published in collaboration with the Chamber of Commerce of the State of New York and the Inter-American Commercial Arbitration Commission. Publication was suspended during 1943-1945. It was resumed in 1946 with Volume 1 (new series).

See also: American Arb. Association.

ARBITRATION LAW. A DIGEST OF COURT DECISIONS

A quarterly digest of court decisions on the enforceability of arbitration agreements or awards published four times a year by the American Arbitration Association.

Arbitration Law has been published since 1952, and is indexed annually by case and subject.

See also: American Arb. Association.

ARBITRATION MAGAZINE

Published by the American Arbitration Association during the suspension of *The Arbitration Journal* in 1943 through 1945.

Volume 1 has the title *Arbitration in Action*.

See also: American Arb. Association.

ARBITRATION NEWS

A newsletter published ten times a year by the American Arbitration Association, and made available to its members, and to arbitrators on its National Panel.

Arbitration News contains brief comments on developments in all phases of arbitration of institutional as well as general interest.

See also: American Arb. Association.

ARBITRATION. THE JOURNAL OF THE INSTITUTE OF ARBITRATORS (16 Park Crescent, London, W.1, U.K.)

A quarterly published in London by the Institute of Arbitrators.

The title of the journal has varied. Volume I, new series, was called *The Arbitrator,* and began publication in October 1927, through Volume II, number 7, December 1928. With Volume II (n.s.) number 8 of February 1929, the name was changed to *The Journal of the Institute of Arbitrators Incorporated.* By 1952 the title had become *Arbitration, the Journal of the Institute of Arbitrators.* Articles are primarily concerned with commercial disputes, many of which are related to the construction industry.

See also: Institute of Arbitrators.

ARBITRATION (VOLUNTARY)

The referral of a dispute by the voluntary agreement of the parties to one or more impartial arbitrators for a final and binding decision.

An award in arbitration is made on the basis of evidence and argument presented by such parties who agree in advance to accept the decision of the arbitrator as final and binding. Arbitration between individual nations is contractual in source, and arises solely out of this voluntary agreement which may be in the form of a contract containing an arbitration agreement, or may be part of a treaty between two sovereign powers, or it may be the result of an adherence to the statute of an international tribunal or to a controlling international convention.

See also: Arsenal of weapons; Com'l. arb.; Compulsory arb.; Institutional arb.; Int'l. com'l. arb.; Int'l. pub. arb.; Labor arb. (Voluntary).

ARBITRATOR

An impartial person selected by the disputing parties to hear the evidence and deliver a final and binding decision as a determination of their dispute.

The labor arbitrator is usually selected because the parties have confidence in his knowledge of the common law of the shop, and because they have faith in his impartiality and in his personal judgment. The arbitrator is part of a system of self-government which the parties themselves have created.* Commercial arbitrators frequently are experts in a particular trade or profession. Parties are relatively free in the selection of individuals to serve as arbitrators, though the law establishes certain minimum standards of knowledge, impartiality, and moral character, standards which tend to equate the private arbitrator with the public judge. As long ago as 1731 the arbitrator was defined as follows: "The Arbitrators are private extraordinary Judges, chosen by the Parties to give Judgments between them, to end the Debate; they are called Arbitrators from the Word *Arbiter,* and the Arbitrary Power with which they are invested."**

See also: Ad hoc arbitrator; Agreed award; Appointment of arbitrators; Arbitrator's authority; Bias; Challenge of arbitrator; Code of Ethics and Procedural Standards for Labor-Management Arb.; Compensation of the arbitrator; Disqualification of arbitrator; Duty to disclose; Impartial chairman; Independent investigation by arbitrator; Indifferent gentlemen; Liability of arbitrator; Misconduct of arbitrator; Nationality of arbitrator; Neutral arbitrator; Oath of office; Permanent arbitrator; Presiding arbitrator; Removal of arbitrator; Schoeffen; Sole arbitrator; Testimony of arbitrator; Third arbitrator; Umpire; Waiver of right to object to arbitrator.

Sources: **THE COMPLEAT ARBITRATOR 72 (1731); R. FLEMING, THE LABOR ARBITRATION PROCESS 186-7 (1965); *Shulman, *Reason, Contract and Law in Labor Relations,* 68 HARV. L. REV. 999-1024 (1955).

ARBITRATOR REMUNERATION

The fee an arbitrator receives for his services.

See also: Compensation of the arbitrator.

ARBITRATOR'S AUTHORITY

The legal power or right of an arbitrator to hear and determine a dispute, an authority which is derived from law and from the will of the parties as expressed in their arbitration agreement or collective bargaining agreement.

The arbitrator determines the extent and limitations of his authority by examining the arbitration agreement. He also studies all other documents, such as the demand for arbitration in which the nature of the dispute is described, looks for the answering statement if there is one, or reviews the submission, and examines the rules of procedure as established by the parties or by the administrative agency. In international disputes, the authority of the arbitrator is derived from the *compromis,* or from a controlling convention. Justice Douglas in his opinion in *Steelworkers* v. *Enterprise Wheel & Car Corp.* defined the authority of the labor arbitrator as follows: "When an arbitrator is commissioned to interpret and apply the collective bargaining agreement, he is to bring his informed judgment to bear in order to reach a fair solution of a problem. . . . Nevertheless, an arbitrator is confined to interpretation and application of the collective bargaining agreement; he does not sit to dispense his own brand of industrial justice. He may of course look for guidance from many sources, yet his award is legitimate only so long as it draws its essence from the collective bargaining agreement. When the arbitrator's words manifest an infidelity to this obligation, courts have no choice but to refuse enforcement of the award."

See also: Arbitrability; Arb. agreement; Arbitrator; Collective bargaining agreement; Competence de la competence; Compromis; Exces de pouvoir; Jurisdiction; Party autonomy; Submission agreement.

Sources: United Steelworkers v. Enterprise Wheel & Car Corp., 363 U.S. 593 (1960); Chamberlain, *Job Security, Management Rights, and Arb.*, in 17 PROC. OF THE NAT'L. ACADEMY OF ARBITRATORS 224-251 (1964); Ouchi, *Problems of Competence of Int'l. Com'l. Arbitral Tribunals*, 3 PHILIPPINE INT'L. L. J. 16-32 (1964); Smith & Jones, *supra* Arbitrability.

ARBITRATOR'S DUTY TO DISCLOSE

See: Duty to disclose.

ARBITRATOR'S FEE

See: Compensation of the arbitrator.

ARBITRATORS, NUMBER OF

See: Number of arbitrators.

ARSENAL OF WEAPONS

A choice of dispute settlement procedures available to the President of the United States which he may use at his own discretion in handling threatened or actual strikes affecting the public interest.

Such settlement procedures may also be used by mayors or governors in public employee labor disputes. Included among these procedures are mediation, fact-finding with or without recommendations for settlement, cooling-off periods of various time limits enforceable by court injunction, plant seizure, retroactive pay orders, last-offer ballots, compulsory arbitration, sanctions or threat of sanctions, or final and binding arbitration. The advocates of the use of this arsenal of weapons cite the flexibility it provides in tailoring governmental intervention to particular collective bargaining situations. Some fear that its very availability will make intervention easy and thus frustrate bargaining. Others feel that the problem is primarily one of settling disputes, and not of stopping strikes.

See also: Arbitration (Voluntary); Compulsory arb.; Conciliation; Dispute settlement procedure; Fact-finding; Gov't. intervention; Impasse; Injunction; Mediation; Sanctions; Seizure of plant.

Sources: U.S. DEPT. OF LABOR, COLLECTIVE BARGAINING IN THE BASIC STEEL INDUSTRY 207-227 (1961).

ASSOCIAZIONE ITALIANA PER L'ARBITRATO (ITALIAN ARBITRATION ASSOCIATION) (Via Q. Sella, 69, Rome, Italy)

The Associazione Italiana per l'Arbitrato is based in Rome with facilities for administering arbitrations through its Court of Conciliation and Arbitration.

The Committee for the Articles, Regulations, Records and Arbitration of the Association appoints the Court which may not be composed of less than ten or more than twenty-five members who are chosen to serve for three years. Upon request of the parties, the Court submits to them a list of names of possible arbitrators, and conducts the arbitral proceedings according to its rules and regulations.

ATKINSON V. SINCLAIR REFINING CO.

[*Atkinson* v. *Sinclair Refining Co.*, 370 U.S. 238 (1962)]

A ruling by the United States Supreme Court which decided that the arbitration clause determined whether or not an employer's claim for damages against a union for an alleged violation of a no-strike pledge was subject to arbitration, and that the employer, therefore, could not bring any action for damages under § 301.

In *Atkinson* v. *Sinclair*, the arbitration clause excluded arbitration of any matter other than employee grievances, and did not provide for the submission of any grievances by the employer. As a result, it was not necessary to require a stay of the employer's damage suit pending arbitration.

See also: Breach of contract; Drake Bakeries, Inc.; No-strike clause; Second Trilogy; § 301 disputes; Sinclair Refining Co. v. Atkinson.

Sources: Atkinson v. Sinclair Refining Co., 370 U.S. 238 (1962); Smith & Jones, *supra* Arbitrability at 751-808.

ATOMIC ENERGY LABOR-MANAGEMENT RELATIONS PANEL
(1953-   ) (14th Street and Constitution Ave., N.W., Washington, D.C. 20004)

The Atomic Energy Labor-Management Relations Panel succeeded the Atomic Energy Labor Relations Panel, which President Harry Truman appointed in 1949, to recommend settlements in disputes in atomic energy plants in order to ensure the continuous operation of the atomic program without strikes or lockouts.

President Dwight D. Eisenhower in appointing the new Atomic Energy Labor-Management Relations Panel, on March 24, 1953, placed it under the Federal Mediation and Conciliation Service, which was authorized to certify a dispute to the Panel only after exhausting its own efforts at mediation. In 1957, the Panel was made an independent body, as its predecessor had been, which was available to assist parties in settling disputes only after the normal processes of collective bargaining, mediation, and conciliation had been fully used and exhausted. The ten member panel is selected by the President. Its recommendations are binding only on the Atomic Energy Commission. Since unions rarely fail to follow the recommended solution, work stoppages have been kept at a low level in these government owned but privately operated plants.

See also: Fact-finding; Federal Mediation and Conciliation Service; Mediation; Missile Sites Labor Comm'n.; President's Comm'n. on Labor Relations in the Atomic Energy Installations.

Sources: U.S. Atomic Energy Labor-Management Relations Panel, Report, Fiscal Years 1957-1964 (1964); Johnson, *Dispute-Settlement in Atomic Energy Plants,* 13 Ind. & Lab. Rel. Rev. 38-53 (1959); Straus, *Labor Disputes in Atomic Energy Commission Experience,* in 4 N.Y. University, Proc. of the Annual Conf. on Labor 233-259 (1951).

ATTACHMENT

A seizure of property or taking into custody of a person by virtue of a legal process for the purpose of acquiring jurisdiction over the person or property seized.

Attachments aid efficient arbitration by retaining the subject matter or assets with which the arbitration is concerned within the jurisdiction so as to ensure a meaningful award. Such a legal means of obtaining relief may be available as part of the arbitration process, though arbitration statutes do not provide for obtaining such relief. The United States Arbitration Act does provide for the libel and seizure of vessels in the arbitration of a maritime claim.

Sources: U.S. Arb. Act, 9 U.S.C. § 8 (1954); M. Domke, *supra* Adhesion contract at 266-267.

ATTORNEYS' FEES

The costs of an arbitration generally do not include attorneys' fees, and unless provision for their payment has been made in the contract of the parties, each party is responsible for the fee of the attorney who has acted as its counsel in the arbitration.

The New York State Civil Practice Law and Rules in § 7513 excludes attorneys' fees from any enforcement of the award unless the parties had so stipulated in their agreement. The California Code of Civil Procedure at § 1284.2, in allotting the costs of the arbitration, states: ". . . each party . . . shall pay his pro rata share of the expenses and fees . . . , not including counsel fees or witness fees or other expenses incurred by a party for his own benefit."

See also: Adm. expenses.

Sources: Calif. Code of Civ. Proced., § 1284.2; N.Y. CPLR § 7513; M. Domke, *supra* Adhesion contract at 355-356, 358-359.

AUTHORITY OF THE ARBITRATOR

See: Arbitrator's authority.

AUTOMOBILE INDUSTRY

See: Chrysler-UAW Impartial Chairman System; Ford-UAW Impartial Umpire System; General Motors Impartial Umpire System; Public Review Board (United lAuto Workers).

AWARD

The final and binding decision by an arbitrator in the full settlement of a dispute.

An award is given after taking testimony and hearing arguments from both parties, and must be in writing under modern arbitration statutes. An award may require specific performance as well as granting money damages. An arbitrator may also grant a party injunctive relief. Arbitrators in the United States and Great Britain need not state reasons for giving their award. In labor arbitration awards, reasons are generally given in the form of an opinion which accompanies the award, but is not a component part of it, unless otherwise specified by the arbitrator. In France and the Netherlands, an award given without reasons is invalid.

See also: Agreed award; Award by confession; Award upon settlement; Binding character of award; Challenge of an award; Confirming the award; Consent award; Enforcement of award; Enforcement of award (Labor); Enforcement of foreign arbitral awards; Injunctive relief; Modifying the award; Non liquet; Opinion; Specific performance; Unanimity of award; Unconfirmed award; Vacating an award.

Sources: AAA, A MANUAL FOR COM'L. ARBITRATORS (1959); AAA VOLUNTARY LABOR ARB. RULES, supra Affidavit; M. DOMKE, supra Adhesion contract at 263-294.

AWARD BY CONFESSION

An award by an arbitrator, or by the agency or person appointing the arbitrator, which is made at the request of the parties for money due or for money which will become due before an award is otherwise made.

An award by confession may be useful when the parties wish to have the award legally confirmed, though no controversy over liability is involved. All that is required to initiate such a procedure is a verified statement by each party containing an authorization to make the award, the amount of the award, or the method of arriving at the amount, and any fact relevant to the liability. An award by confession is treated in the same manner as an award which has been arrived at through the full arbitration procedure. Such a method relieves the parties of submitting their dispute to the full arbitration process in order to arrive at the amount of money due. An award by confession may be made at any time within three months after the verified statement.

See also: Award; Code of Ethics and Procedural Standards for Labor-Management Arb.; Consent award.

Sources: N.Y. CPLR § 7508; ASSOCIATION OF THE BAR OF THE CITY OF NEW YORK, AN OUTLINE OF PROCEDURE UNDER THE NEW YORK ARB. LAW 22-23 (1965).

AWARD UPON SETTLEMENT

An award which the arbitrator makes at the request of the parties on the terms of the settlement which the parties have arrived at themselves during the course of the arbitration.

See also: Agreed award; Award; Code of Ethics and Procedural Standards for Labor-Management Arb.; Compromise; Consent award.

Sources: AAA COM'L. ARB. RULES, *supra* Adm. appointment at § 43.

BACK PAY AWARDS

Unless deprived by the parties of the authority to do so, the arbitrator may award reinstatement with the amount of pay lost as remedy and compensation when discharge or wrongful layoff as a penalty seems too extreme.

Arbitrators may qualify such a penalty by reinstating without awarding back pay, or with a specified portion or full back pay allowed. They may also frequently require deduction for any compensation the employee has been receiving in the interim, as on a second job. Back pay may also be awarded in layoff in violation of seniority. The awards of some arbitrators provide for back pay with deduction for any unemployment compensation received. Some arbitrators feel that as the employee has already lost his available eligibility for future benefits in the same year, to make him return the benefits without restoring his eligibility might be considered an injustice. Contracts sometimes state that any unemployment benefits received must be taken into consideration in computing the amount of pay lost. The State of Connecticut has a statute which provides for such a procedure, requiring that the employer "shall be liable to pay the amount so deducted to the administrator who shall accept and credit the account of such person."

See also: Enterprise Wheel & Car Corp.; Reinstatement; Seniority.

Sources: Connecticut—Title 31, 257—General Statutes, as cited in 17 PROC. OF THE NAT'L. ACADEMY OF ARBITRATORS 185 at Note 23 (1964); Gorske, *Arb. Back-Pay Awards*, 10 LAB. L. J. 18-27 (1959); Gray, *Back Pay Awards and Unemployment Insurance*, 8 ARB. J. (n.s.) 114-116 (1953); Wolff, *The Power of the Arbitrator to Make Monetary Awards*, in 17 PROC. OF THE NAT'L. ACADEMY OF ARBITRATORS 176-193 (1964).

BANKRUPT

A person judicially declared insolvent.

Three questions frequently arise in a bankruptcy proceeding. The first is whether the bankruptcy of one party to an arbitration agreement automatically revokes the agreement. The second is whether the trustee in bankruptcy can be compelled to arbitrate. And the third is whether or not the trustee can compel arbitration.

Sources: 12 LAWYERS' LETTERS (1962), *supra* Adjournment of hearings at 1-2.

BENEFIT SENIORITY

See: Seniority

BERMUDA AGREEMENT (AIR SERVICES AGREEMENT)

An agreement reached in Bermuda in 1946 on air transport rights between the United States and the United Kingdom.

The Bermuda Agreement is important because it has become a primary and significant model for the bargaining of air traffic rights between nations throughout the world. It also makes detailed provisions for the arbitration of disputes.

See also: Air transport agreements; Convention on Int'l. Civil Aviation.

Sources: Agreement between the Gov't. of the U.S.A. and the Gov't. of the U.K. Relating to Air Services, February 11, 1946, T.I.A.S. 1507; B. CHENG, *supra* Air transport agreements; Larsen, *supra* Air transport agreements.

BIAS

Show of partiality.

Any special show of bias by the arbitrator towards one party may result in his being challenged by the other party. The United States Arbitration Act at § 10 provides that the court may vacate an award where "there was evident partiality or corruption in the arbitrators. . . ." Section 18 of the American Arbitration Association Commercial Arbitration Rules declares that an arbitrator is obligated to disclose "any circumstances likely to create a presumption of bias or which he believes might disqualify him as an impartial Arbitrator. . . ." Although the AAA Rules did not apply in its decision of November 18, 1968, in *Commonweath Coatings Corp.* v. *Continental Casualty Co. et al.*, the United States Supreme Court nevertheless held that: "This rule of arbitration . . . rest(s) on the premise that any tribunal permitted by law to try cases and controversies must not only be unbiased but must avoid even the appearance of bias. We cannot believe that it was the purpose of Congress to authorize litigants to submit their cases and controversies to arbitration boards that might reasonably be thought biased against one litigant and favorable to another."

See also: Arbitrator; Challenge of arbitrator; Disqualification of arbitrator;

Duty to disclose; Grounds of nullity; Misconduct of arbitrator; Removal of arbitrator; Vacating an award.

Sources: Commonwealth Coatings Corp. v. Continental Casualty Co. et al., 89 S. Ct. 337 (1968); Matter of Astoria Medical Group (HIP of New York) 11 N.Y. 2d 129, 227 N.Y.S. 2d 401 (1962) as cited in BERNSTEIN, *supra* Appeal at 152-156; 22 LAWYERS' LETTERS (1965), *supra* Adjournment of hearings at 1.

BILATERAL TREATY

See: Treaty.

BINDING CHARACTER OF AWARD

The established principle that an award in an arbitration is final and binding upon both parties.

An award which is within the scope of the arbitration agreement is as binding on the parties as was the agreement from which it grew, and in some instances, as binding as a judgment of a court. In states having no modern arbitration statutes, there may be some difficulty in enforcing an award made in another state. At the present time, many jurisdictions have statutory procedures whereby an award may be reduced to judgment. This judgment entered on the arbitral award is a judgment on the merits of the case, and can therefore be enforced in other states. In international law, the binding character of the award derives from the obligation of the basic contract: *pacta sunt servanda.*

See also: Alabama Arb.; Award; Confirming the award; Enforcement of award (Labor); Exequatur; Finality of award; Pacta sunt servanda; Res judicata.

Sources: K. CARLSTON, *supra* Annulment . . . ; J. SIMPSON & H. FOX, *supra* Appointment of arbitrators; 8 LAWYERS' LETTERS (1961), *supra* Adjournment of hearings at 2-4; Schachter, *supra* Alabama Arbitration at 8-9.

BIPARTITE BOARD

A board consisting of equal representatives from labor and management, which examines and acts on complaints as the last step in the grievance procedure prior to arbitration.

The bipartite board in some industries may be the final step in the grievance machinery. Such a board is also sometimes referred to as a joint board or an adjustment board.

See also: Adjustment board; Appeal systems; Conseil de prud'hommes; Council on Industrial Relations for the Electrical Contracting Industry; Nat'l. Railroad Adjustment Board.

BLS

See: Bureau of Labor Statistics.

BNA (BUREAU OF NATIONAL AFFAIRS)

See: Labor Arb. Reports; War Labor Reports.

BOARD OF ARBITRATION

A board, which may or may not be tripartite, established jointly by the parties, consisting of a chairman, sometimes referred to as a permanent chairman, and such other arbitrators as may be appointed with the approval of the parties, to assist the chairman in the hearing and deciding of arbitration cases.

A Board of Arbitration is one method of setting up a permanent umpire system which may be particularly useful in large corporations which maintain many plants. An example of such a board is the Board of Conciliation and Arbitration of the United States Steel Corporation and the United Steelworkers of America which was established in 1945 by mutual agreement of the parties and at that time was tripartite in organization. In 1951, the Board became the Board of Arbitration with the chairman reviewing his draft decisions with union and company representatives. Hearings by the Board are invoked after an unresolved grievance has passed through a four-step grievance procedure, or where both parties agree to by-pass one of the steps and proceed directly to arbitration, or where the officers of the parties submit a complaint to the Board in writing. The parties are obliged to stipulate as many agreed facts as possible, and to inform each other of their respective positions and principal items of evidence. Representatives of the parties meet with the Chairman in executive session to discuss his award. The Board also settles problems of compliance, and all its awards are final and binding. Decisions in such a system are valuable as precedents for the particular company and union involved.

See also: Discovery of documents; Impartial chairman system; Grievance arb. (Rights arb.); Precedent; Umpire system.

Sources: Board of Arb. of U.S. Steel Corp. & United Steelworkers, Rules of Procedure, Nov. 3, 1967 (Pittsburgh, Pa.); Killingsworth & Wallen, *Constraint and Variety in Arbitration Systems*, in 17 PROC. OF THE NAT'L. ACADEMY OF ARBITRATORS 69-71 (1964).

BOARD OF NINE MEN

A court of arbitration founded in 1647 by the Dutch burghers of New Amsterdam.

From this Board of Nine Men, three were chosen to serve together on each case. One was to be a merchant, another a farmer, and the third a burgher. The three who were to serve and make their binding decisions as arbitrators were to meet on Thursday, which was the usual Burgher Court Day.

Sources: COMM. ON ARB. OF THE N.Y. (STATE) CHAMBER OF COMMERCE, ANN. REP. 1 (1943); Jones, *Historical Development of Com'l. Arb. in the U.S.*, 12 MINNESOTA L. REV. 240-262 (1928).

BOARDS OF INQUIRY

See: Fact-finding; Emergency boards; Int'l. comm'n. of inquiry.

BOILER PLATE

A standard or stereotype clause which may appear in any contract, and which negotiators often accept verbatim instead of creating a freshly worded clause to insert in their own particular contract.

Clauses such as a management rights clause, or a clause against discrimination for union activity, tend to become stereotype, and are thus often referred to as boiler plate. A boiler plate in commercial contracts may be the arbitration clause itself when it appears in standardized mass contracts. Any fine print material appearing in such standardized mass contracts may be referred to as boiler plate.

See also: Adhesion contract.

Sources: Goldberg, *supra* Adhesion contract at 13-19.

BONA FIDE DISPUTE

See: Justiciable.

BOUNDARY DISPUTES

A controversy between nations over the territorial line which separates them.

A boundary dispute is closely related to a territorial dispute which is concerned with conflicting claims of sovereignty over a territory, rather than with the specific demarcation between two states. Boundary disputes constitute one of the three common types of disputes which are settled by means of international public arbitration. The other two are international claims, and investment disputes between a State and a foreign national. Under Jay's Treaty of 1794 between the United States and Great Britain, the northeastern boundary of the United States was a subject of arbitration. Recent boundary disputes have been the India-Pakistan dispute over the Rann of Kutch, the arbitration of the controversy between the Argentine Republic and the Republic of Chile,

November 24, 1966, and the United States-Mexico dispute over the Chamizal settled on December 13, 1968, after 53 years of negotiations.

See also: Chamizal Arb.; Convention on the Settlement of Investment Disputes between States and Nationals of Other States; Int'l. claims; Int'l. pub. arb.; Jay's Treaty; Northeastern Boundary Arb.; Territorial dispute.

Sources: *Hearings on Executive N, Convention with Mexico for Solution of the Problem of the Chamizal before the Senate Committee on Foreign Relations*, 88th Congress 1st Sess., (1963); GT. BRIT. FOREIGN OFFICE, AWARD OF HER MAJESTY QUEEN ELIZABETH II FOR THE ARB. OF A CONTROVERSY BETWEEN THE ARGENTINE REPUBLIC AND THE REPUBLIC OF CHILE (1966); 1 & 2 INT'L. ADJUDICATIONS ANCIENT AND MODERN, MODERN SERIES (J. Moore ed. 1929); Rao, *Indo-Pakistan Agreement on the Rann of Kutch*, 5 INDIAN J. INT'L. L. 176-185 (1965).

BREACH OF CONTRACT

To break or violate the terms of a contract.

It is the alleged breach of contract that many times causes one party to the contract to invoke the arbitration clause, or if there is no such clause, to request a submission of the dispute to arbitration. The asserted breach of an agreement containing an arbitration clause does not relieve the other party of his obligation to arbitrate claims otherwise subject to arbitration. The United States Supreme Court in its *Drake Bakeries* decision declared: "Arbitration provisions, which themselves have not been repudiated, are meant to survive breaches of contract, in many contexts, even total breach. . . ."

See also: Atkinson v. Sinclair Refining Co.; Drake Bakeries, Inc.; Fraudulent inducement of the contract; Irrevocability of the arb. agreement; No-strike clause; Sinclair Refining Co. v. Atkinson.

Sources: Drake Bakeries v. Local 50, American Bakery & Confectionery Workers, 370 U.S. 254 (1962).

BRIEF

A concise statement of fact and law in support of a party's case which is prepared by counsel or by the party itself, and which is then submitted to a court or an arbitrator.

See also: Post-hearing briefs.

BROAD ARBITRATION CLAUSE

See: Scope of the arb. agreement; Trilogy (1960).

BUREAU OF LABOR STATISTICS (BLS)
(14th Street and Constitution Ave., N.W., Washington, D.C. 20210)

The principal United States Government fact-finding agency in the field of labor economics.

The Bureau of Labor Statistics has no enforcement or administrative functions. It maintains regional offices in New York City, Boston, Atlanta, Chicago, San Francisco, and Kansas City, Missouri. It publishes a biennial *Directory of National and International Labor Unions*, and innumerable bulletins and statistical reports in the field of industrial relations, including valuable studies on arbitration procedures. The Bureau also collects and analyzes data on employment and manpower, productivity and technological developments, wages, industrial relations, work injuries, prices, and costs and standards of living. Its official publication is the *Monthly Labor Review*.

Sources: U.S. BLS, *supra* Ad hoc arbitrator; U.S. OFFICE OF THE FEDERAL REGISTER, U.S. GOVERNMENT ORGANIZATION MANUAL 347-351 (1968-69).

BUREAU OF NATIONAL AFFAIRS, INC. (BNA)

See: Labor Arbitration Reports; War Labor Reports.

BUSTAMANTE CODE (1928)
(Code of International Private Law Approved by the Sixth International Conference of American States)

A code adopted in Havana in 1928 which contains provisions on the recognition and enforcement of judicial and arbitral awards rendered in any of the signatory countries.

The Bustamante Code was signed by each of the Central American countries. Article 432 of the Code declares: "The procedure and effects regulated in the preceding articles shall be applied in the contracting States to awards made in any of them by arbitrators or friendly compositors, whenever the case to which they refer can be the subject of a compromise in accordance with the legislation of the country where the execution is requested." The requirements for enforcement of foreign arbitral awards under the Code are concerned with such procedural requirements as the competence of the Tribunal, the notification of the parties of the proceedings, compliance with public policy of the country where the award is to be enforced, and translation of the award when necessary by an official interpreter in the state of enforcement. Because of this Code and its enforcement provisions, the climate in Central America seemed propitious in 1969 for the creation of an effective international system of commercial arbitration.

See also: Inter-American Com'l. Arb. Comm'n.

Sources: V. VITA, COMPARATIVE STUDY OF AMERICAN LEGISLATION GOV-
ERNING COM'L. ARB. (1928); Norberg, *Inter-American Com'l. Arb.*, 1
LAWYER OF THE AMERICAS 25-41 (1969).

CALVO CLAUSE

A clause used in concession contracts between South American governments and foreign nationals in which these nationals promise not to
invoke the aid of their own government, but instead to abide by the
local law of the country in settling claims arising out of disputes under
their concession agreements.

The Calvo Clause was a doctrine first enunciated by Justice Carlos
Calvo of Argentina. There have been no International Court decisions
based on the Calvo Clause. The decision of the Mexican General Claims
Commission in the *North American Dredging Company of Texas Case*
(March 31, 1926), is generally held to be a reasonable and accurate
statement of the law. It reads in part as follows: "The Commission does
not feel impressed by arguments either in favor of or in opposition to
the Calvo clause, in so far as these arguments go to extremes. . . . The
problem is not solved by saying yes or no; the affirmative answer ex-
posing the rights of foreigners to undeniable dangers, the negative answer leaving to the nations involved no alternative except that of exclusion of foreigners from business. The present stage of international
law imposes upon every international tribunal the solemn duty of seeking for a proper and adequate balance between the sovereign right of
national jurisdiction, on the one hand, and the sovereign right of national
protection of citizens on the other. . . ."

See also: Concession contract; Exhaustion of local remedies; Int'l. claims.

Sources: North American Dredging Co. of Texas (U.S.A.) v. United Mexican
States, 4 U.N.R.I.A.A. 26-35 (1926); C. JENKS, THE PROSPECTS OF
INT'L. ADJUDICATION (1964); 8 M. WHITEMAN, DIGEST OF INT'L.
LAW 916 (1967).

CAREY V. WESTINGHOUSE

[*Carey* v. *Westinghouse Electric Corp.*, 375 U.S. 261 (1964)]

A decision of the United States Supreme Court which held that the
authority of the National Labor Relations Board over jurisdictional matters or unfair labor practices does not exclude arbitration as a means of
resolving work assignment or inter-union disputes.

This case was concerned with whether certain work assigned by
Westinghouse should be performed by members of one or the other
of two disputing unions. The Court enforced an order compelling
Westinghouse to arbitrate the matter with one of the unions under the
existing bargaining agreement. The Court held: "However the dispute
be considered—whether one involving work assignment or one concern-

ing representation—we see no barrier to use of the arbitration procedure. If it is a work assignment dispute, arbitration conveniently fills a gap and avoids the necessity of a strike to bring the matter to the Board. If it is a representation matter, resort to arbitration may have a pervasive, curative effect even though one union is not a party. . . . The superior authority of the Board may be invoked at anytime. Meanwhile the therapy of arbitration is brought to bear in a complicated and troubled area." The NLRB withheld jurisdiction until the outcome of the arbitration. The arbitrator in this case ruled that the employees should be split among the two units on the basis of job classifications, but the award was subsequently overruled by the NLRB as being unfair because one union was not a party to the arbitration. The NLRB ordered that a hearing be held to determine the proper certification of the workers.

See also: Concurrent jurisdiction; Joinder; Jurisdictional disputes; Representational disputes; § 10(k) proceedings; Trilateral arb.; Work assignment disputes.

Sources: Carey v. Westinghouse Electric Corp. 375 U.S. 261 (1964); *id.* 65-2 ARB. ¶ 8609; *id.* 1965 CCH NLRB ¶ 9796; Bernstein, *Jurisdictional Dispute Arb.*, 14 UCLA L. REV. 347-353 (1966); Bernstein, *Nudging and Shoving All Parties to a Jurisdictional Dispute into Arb.*, 78 HARV. L. REV. 784-797 (1965); Jones, *On Nudging and Shoving the Nat'l. Steel Arb. into a Dubious Procedure*, 79 HARV. L. REV. 327 (1965).

CASES. COURT DECISIONS

See: Arbitration Law. A Digest of Court Decisions; Cases. U.S. Court of Appeals (Labor); Cases. U.S. Supreme Court (Com'l.); Cases. U.S. Supreme Court (Labor).

CASES. INTERNATIONAL PUBLIC ARBITRATION

See: Abu Dhabi Arb.; Ambatielos Case (at Mixed claims commission); Aramco Arb.; Chamizal Arb.; Death of James Pugh Arb. (at Ex aequo et bono); Fur Seal Arb. (at Ex aequo et bono); Lake Ontario Claims Tribunal; Lena Goldfields Arb.; North American Dredging Co. of Texas Case (at Calvo Clause); Northeastern Boundary Arb.; Pious Fund Case; Trail Smelter Arb.; Victory Transport (at Tate Letter); Wal Wal Arb.

CASES (PUBLISHED LABOR ARBITRATION AWARDS AND OPINIONS)

See: American Labor Arb. Awards (P.H); Labor Arb. Awards (CCH); Labor Arb. Reports (BNA); Summary of Labor Arb. Awards (AAA).

CASES. UNITED STATES COURT OF APPEALS (LABOR)

See: Livingston v. John Wiley & Sons (at Procedural arbitrability).

CASES. UNITED STATES SUPREME COURT (COMMERCIAL)

See: Commonwealth Coatings Corp. v. Continental Casualty Co. (at Bias); Prima Paint Corp. . . .

CASES. UNITED STATES SUPREME COURT (LABOR)

See: American Manufacturing Co.; Atkinson v. Sinclair Refining Co.; Carey v. Westinghouse; Drake Bakeries, Inc.; Enterprise Wheel & Car Corp.; Fibreboard Paper Products Corp. v. NLRB; Lincoln Mills; Republic Steel v. Maddox; Sinclair Refining Co. v. Atkinson; Vaca v. Sipes; Warrior & Gulf Navigation Co.; Wiley & Sons v. Livingston.

CASSATION

Annulment

See also: Cour de cassation.

CCH (COMMERCE CLEARING HOUSE)

See: Labor Arbitration Awards.

CENTER FOR DISPUTE SETTLEMENT OF THE AMERICAN ARBITRATION ASSOCIATION
(1819 H Street, N.W., Washington, D.C. 20006)

A division of the American Arbitration Association established to employ proven dispute settlement techniques to solve community grievances such as landlord-tenant or parent-teacher disputes through the use of mutually acceptable neighborhood leaders.

See also: American Arb. Association.

Sources: AAA, THE CENTER FOR DISPUTE SETTLEMENT, 1969; AAA, Legal Rights and Housing Wrongs, 1968 (a study conducted under a grant from the O.E.O.); A. Zack, Dispute Settlement in the Ghetto, 1968; S. Zagoria, A Path to Campus Peace Aug. 23, 1968 (remarks at the Joint Convention of the Association of Labor Mediation Agencies and Nat'l. Association of State Labor Relations Agencies, St. Thomas, Virgin Islands); *Tenants' Grievances Pressed in Rabbinical Court*, 3 LAW IN ACTION 1-4 (1968); Zack, *Mediation, Arb. and the Poverty Program*, 2 LAW IN ACTION 1 (1968).

CENTRAL OFFICE FOR INTERNATIONAL RAILWAY TRANSPORT
(30 Gryphenhuebeliweg, 3006 Berne, Switzerland)

An office established in Berne by a group of nine European nations under the Convention on the Transport of Goods by Rail of October 14, 1890, which entered into force January 1, 1893.

The Central Office for International Railway Transport has continued to operate to this day. The Convention on the Transport of Goods by Rail has been superseded by the Convention on the Transport of Passengers and Luggage by Rail (CIV), and the Convention on the Transport of Goods by Rail (CIM), both signed on October 23, 1924, and entered into force on October 1, 1928. Both Conventions have been periodically revised. Under Article 57 of the 1890 Convention, the Central Office was to arbitrate disputes which might arise between railways when the parties concerned so demanded. The Director of the Central Office was to give the decision with the assistance of two judges-arbitrators to be designated by the Swiss Federal Council. The tribunal heard twenty-two such disputes between 1892 and 1942. According to procedures described in the Conventions which came into force on January 1, 1965, each Contracting State may nominate not more than two of its nationals who are specialists in international transport law for inclusion on the panel of arbitrators to be established and kept up to date by the Swiss Government. Though there have been no recent arbitrations, there are 29 Contracting States under the current conventions.

See also: Institutional arb.; Int'l. pub. arb.; Universal Postal Union.

Sources: Int'l. Convention Concerning the Carriage of Goods by Rail (CIM) (British Railways Board, Feb. 25, 1961); P. JESSUP, TRANSNATIONAL LAW (1958); YEARBOOK OF INT'L. ORGANIZATIONS (12th ed. -1968-1969); Hudson & Sohn, *Fifty Years of Arb. in the Union of Int'l. Transport by Rail*, 37 Am. J. Int'l. L. 597-610 (1943).

CHALLENGE OF ARBITRATOR

A right which a party may invoke in order to question the qualifications of an arbitrator with the aim of removing him from office.

This right of challenge may be provided for in an arbitration agreement or in the rules of an administrative agency administering the arbitration, or in a treaty. Many associations with facilities for arbitration have some procedure in their Rules for challenging an arbitrator by one party or both on the grounds that the arbitrator has disqualified himself. The Rules of the London Court of Arbitration at § 12 state: "If any arbitrator . . . becomes in the opinion of the Court unfitted to act . . . (the) Court may, on the application of any party, remove such arbitrator, . . . and appoint some other person . . . in his . . . place." The Rules of the International Centre for Settlement of Investment Disputes have related provisions after allowing the arbitrator due process for answering the charges. The Ford Motor Co. and the UAW in their collective agreement provide that "if at any time either party desires to terminate the service of the umpire, it shall give notice in writing to that effect, specifying the date of termination, and sending one copy to the umpire and one to the other party."

See also: Bias; Disqualification of arbitrator; Misconduct of arbitrator; Removal of arbitrator.

Sources: U.N. E.C.E, *supra* Access to the arbitral tribunal at 34-36; Ford Motor Co.-UAW Collective Bargaining Agreement, Oct. 25, 1967 at art. 7, § 22; AAA COM'L. ARB. RULES, *supra* Adm. appointment at § 19; ICSID, *supra* Appeal boards of adm. agencies at 84-85; LONDON COURT OF ARB., *supra* Adm. expenses at art. 12.

CHALLENGE OF AWARD

An attempt by the dissatisfied party to contest on specific statutory grounds the decision of the arbitrator.

An award may be challenged in several ways. The losing party may challenge the validity of the award by opposing any application to a court to have the award confirmed. The winning party may make such application any time within a year after delivery of the award. If time is an important factor, the losing party may proceed directly with a motion to have the award vacated. The application is usually made within 90 days after the award has been delivered, depending on the statute. Or the losing party may simply apply to have the award corrected or modified. The New York statute permits such application to be made directly in writing to the arbitrator within 20 days after delivery of the award for specific reasons such as a miscalculation of figures. Certain administrative agencies have review procedures for challenging awards within their own administrative framework. This is especially true in England in appeal boards of commodity exchanges and trade associations. Some trade associations in the United States have adopted a few similar appeal systems.

See also: Appeal; Appeal boards of adm. agencies; Award; Confirming the award; Modifying the award; Rehearing; Vacating an award.

Sources: U.S. Arb. Act, 9 U.S.C. § 10 & § 11 (1954); 9 Calif. Code of Civ. Proced. § 1284; N.Y. CPLR § 7509 & § 7511(c); M. DOMKE, *supra* Appeal boards of adm. agencies at 96; 19 LAWYERS' LETTERS (1964), *supra* Adjournment of hearings; 34 *id*. (1968).

CHAMBER OF COMMERCE

An association of businessmen to promote the commercial and industrial interests of a community, state, or nation.

Many such chambers of commerce were pioneers in promoting the use of arbitration.

See also: Chamber of Commerce of the State of N.Y.; Int'l. Chamber of Commerce; London Court of Arb.

CHAMBER OF COMMERCE OF THE STATE OF NEW YORK
(New York State Chamber of Commerce)

A chamber founded on April 5, 1768, and confirmed by the charter of King George III on March 13, 1770.

One of the functions outlined as a most important part of its activities at the earliest meetings of the New York State Chamber of Commerce in 1768 was the appointment of a committee on arbitration to settle disputes between merchants. The Chamber has administered the arbitration of commercial disputes from that early date to the present time. The Chamber of Commerce of the State of New York has been most influential in the development of commercial arbitration in New York State, especially in the support it gave to the drafting and passage of the New York Arbitration Law in 1920 and 1937, and the United States Arbitration Act of 1926.

See also: Chamber of Commerce of the State of N.Y. Arb. Comm.; Institutional arb.

Sources: N.Y. (STATE) CHAMBER OF COMMERCE, A BRIEF HISTORY OF COM'L. ARB. IN N.Y. (1927); N.Y. (STATE) Chamber of Commerce, Rules and Regulations Relating to Arb., Effective March 9, 1966.

CHAMBER OF COMMERCE OF THE STATE OF NEW YORK. ARBITRATION COMMITTEE

An arbitration committee first appointed by the Chamber of Commerce of the State of New York on May 3, 1768.

The State of New York passed certain laws concerning the New York Chamber of Commerce and its work for commercial arbitration. The first of these in 1874 created a Court of Arbitration, with the State bearing a portion of the operating expenses, and the Chamber offering its facilities and administrative personnel. The Court of Arbitration was very active through 1882, and with some changes in the law, less so until 1900. The Arbitration Committee of the Chamber of Commerce of the State of New York still exists. It acts as the administrator, maintaining a List of Official Arbitrators and providing rules and regulations for the conduct of such arbitrations, access to which is not limited to its own members. Arbitrations are still conducted under its own rules, though less frequently.

See also: Access to the arbitral tribunal; Institutional arb.; Sterling Iron Works Dispute.

Sources: N.Y. (STATE) CHAMBER OF COMMERCE ANN. REP. (1920); N.Y. (STATE) CHAMBER OF COMMERCE, *supra* Chamber of Commerce of the State of New York.

CHAMIZAL ARBITRATION (June 15, 1911)
(United States and Mexico)

A boundary dispute between the United States and Mexico arbitrated by the International Boundary Commission with the Canadian Commissioner added as the neutral member.

The difficulty arose because the original boundary marked by the Rio Grande River had been continually moving southward, thereby increasing the area of land north of the River, a portion of the 600 acres known as El Chamizal coming eventually within the city limits of El Paso, Texas. The award rendered on the 15th of June, 1911, in favor of Mexico, was protested by the United States because it divided the tract instead of deciding title to the entire area. The United States refused to comply with the award, or to resubmit a claim of nullity. Through further negotiations between the two countries, the Convention between the United States of America and the United Mexican States for the Solution of the Problem of the Chamizal was signed at Mexico City on August 29, 1963. After the 88th Congress passed the American-Mexican Chamizal Convention Act of 1964, a satisfactory settlement was negotiated to facilitate compliance with the Convention. The Presidents of Mexico and the United States saluted the final settlement at a ceremony on December 13, 1968, when the waters of the Rio Grande were diverted into a concrete-lined channel to form the boundary between the two countries.

See also: Boundary disputes; Enforcement of award (Int'l. pub. arb.).

Sources: The Chamizal Case, 11 U.N.R.I.A.A. 309-347 (1911); Cong. Rec. 15646 (daily ed. Sept. 9, 1963); American-Mexican Chamizal Convention Act of 1964, in ABA Section of Int'l. and Comparative Law, Proc. 1964, (1965); *Hearings on Executive N, supra* Boundary disputes; N. Y. Times, Dec. 14, 1968, at 18, col. 1.

CHARTER PARTY

A mercantile lease of a vessel.

The contract by which owners lease a vessel often contains an arbitration clause. Subcharters also are common and frequently provide for arbitration.

See also: Rule of court clause.

Sources: M. Domke, *supra* Appeal boards of adm. agencies at 49.

CHICAGO CONVENTION (1944)

See: Convention on Int'l. Civil Aviation.

CHRYSLER-UAW IMPARTIAL CHAIRMAN SYSTEM

The creation of an Impartial Chairman System by the Chrysler Company and the United Automobile Workers in 1943 under a directive from the War Labor Board.

The collective agreement between the company and union before 1943 had established joint appeal boards as part of the grievance procedure. Until 1962, the Impartial Chairman did not meet with the Appeal Board, but only received a written record of those cases the Board had not been able to settle. Later the chairman was given wider jurisdiction with the right to participate in all discussions and meetings of the Appeal Board. In the event that the Appeal Board was unable to settle the matter, it was to be determined by decision of the Impartial Chairman, and not by majority vote of the Board.

See also: Appeal systems; Ford-UAW Impartial Umpire System; General Motors-UAW Impartial Umpire System; Grievance arb. (Rights arb.); Precedent.

Sources: Chrysler-UAW Collective Bargaining Agreement, 1967; Killingsworth & Wallen, *supra* Board of arb. at 56; Wolff, *The Chrysler-UAW Umpire System,* in 11 PROC. OF THE NAT'L. ACADEMY OF ARBITRATORS (1958) at 111.

CIM

See: Central Office for Int'l. Railway Transport.

CITATIONS OF LABOR ARBITRATION AWARDS

See: American Labor Arb. Awards (P-H); Labor Arb. Awards (CCH); Labor Arb. Reports (BNA); Summary of Labor Arb. Awards (AAA).

CIV

See: Central Office for Int'l. Railway Transport.

CIVIL ARBITRATION

See: Commercial arbitration.

CIVIL AVIATION

See: Air Transport Agreements; Bermuda Agreement; Convention on Int'l. Civil Aviation; Int'l. Civil Aviation Organization; Rate clauses.

CIVIL SERVANT

See: Public employee.

CLAIMANT

The party who initiates the arbitration by giving notice to the respondent of his intention to arbitrate.

See also: Demand for arb.; Notice of intention to arbitrate; Respondent.

CLAUSE COMPROMISSOIRE

Arbitration clause in French practice.

See also: Arb. agreement; Compromis; Submission agreement.

Sources: U.N. ILC. A/CN.4/35 25 July 1952.

CLOSE CORPORATION

A business corporation controlled by a small and closely knit group of people.

The significant features of a close corporation are that its stock is owned by only a few individuals, frequently members of the same family, and that it is not sold on a national securities exchange. A close corporation is often nothing more than an incorporated partnership. It has been variously defined in different state statutes as a small business corporation with no more than ten shareholders, or a business incorporated for less than a million dollars, and having fewer than 500 shareholders, or a corporation with not more than 30 shareholders. Arbitration as a means of settling close corporation disputes is coming into greater use, especially in New York State.

Sources: Hornstein, Arb. in Incorporated Partnerships, 18 ARB. J. (n.s.) 229-234 (1963); Kessler, Arb. of Intra-Corporate Disputes under New York Laws, 19 ARB. J. (n.s.) 1-22, 85-97 (1964); 20 LAWYERS' LETTERS (1964), supra Adjournment of hearings; O'Neal, Developments in the Regulation of the Close Corporation, 50 CORNELL L. Q. 641-662 (1965).

CLOSING ARGUMENT

A final oral statement made by each party in an arbitration.

The arbitrator always allows the parties to make this closing argument or summation if they so desire, though he may impose time limitations. Closing arguments and post-hearing briefs serve much the same purpose. The parties may sometimes elect to do both, but more frequently they choose to use either one or the other as a means of emphasizing the arguments which they feel have proved their case.

See also: Post-hearing briefs; Procedure.

Sources: AAA MANUAL, supra Award; F. ELKOURI & E. ELKOURI, supra American Arb. Association at 158-159.

COAL INDUSTRY

See: Anthracite Board of Conciliation; Anthracite Coal Strike Commission; Umpire system.

CODE OF ETHICS AND PROCEDURAL STANDARDS FOR LABOR-MANAGEMENT ARBITRATION

A code drafted jointly by the American Arbitration Association and the National Academy of Arbitrators, and published in 1951 by the Bernheimer Arbitration Education Fund.

The Code of Ethics was also approved by the Federal Mediation and Conciliation Service. The drafters intended to devise a code of ethics primarily designed to meet those situations where the parties, having failed to resolve their differences through direct negotiations with or without the assistance of mediators have elected to submit their dispute to arbitration for a final and binding settlement.

See also: Agreed award; American Arb. Association; Arbitrator; Award by confession; Award upon settlement; Consent award; FMCS; Nat'l. Academy of Arbitrators; Privacy of arb.

Sources: CODE OF ETHICS & PROCEDURAL STANDARDS FOR LABOR-MANAGEMENT ARB. (1951).

CODE OF PRIVATE INTERNATIONAL LAW

See: Bustamante Code.

COLLATERAL ESTOPPEL

The doctrine that an issue which has already been legally determined can not be reopened or litigated again in a subsequent proceeding.

Collateral estoppel applies in arbitration cases as well as in civil suits. Even when a point not central to the case has been determined, that point is considered to be decided for any further cases which are concerned with the same matter and involving the same parties. Precedent does not apply to the arbitration of labor-management disputes. If a specific cause for grievance in labor arbitration has once been determined, it might so remain determined for the particular parties concerned.

See also: Precedent; Res judicata.

Sources: M. DOMKE, *supra* Adhesion contract at 338.

COLLECTIVE BARGAINING

A process of negotiation between union and management to effect changes in contracts concerning terms and conditions of employment.

Once negotiated and set down in writing, these working rules then become the collective bargaining agreement. New techniques are constantly being evolved to extend collective bargaining throughout the term of the contract, in an effort to sustain a continuous dialogue between representatives of management and labor in order to avoid last minute crisis bargaining. Negotiations between foreign investment firms and sovereign States very often take the form of collective bargaining, as do certain negotiations on treaties between nations. Some bilateral treaties include clauses which provide that treaty negotiations shall be reopened within a specified number of years. In collective bargaining agreements, concession contracts, or treaties, the final method of settling disputes concerning the interpretation or the application of their provisions is most frequently that of arbitration.

See also: Collective bargaining agreement; Labor arb. (Voluntary); Treaty.

Sources: S. SLICHTER ET AL., THE IMPACT OF COLLECTIVE BARGAINING ON MANAGEMENT 982 (1960); Cox & Dunlop, *The Duty to Bargain Collectively During the Term of an Existing Agreement*, 63 HARV. L. REV. 1097-1133 (1950).

COLLECTIVE BARGAINING AGREEMENT

A contract between a union and a company which contains the terms and conditions of employment for a stated period of time.

A collective bargaining agreement might be called a privately drawn code of laws or the common law of the plant. An arbitration clause is included in over 94% of such contracts. The application or interpretation of the terms of the contract is very often cause for dispute, and may be referred to an arbitrator for resolution, thus making him an integral part of this system of self-government created by the parties.

See also: Arbitrator's authority; Collective bargaining; Duty of fair representation; Exclusionary clause; Grievance arb.; Management rights; Recognition clause; Residual rights; Subcontracting.

Sources: Cox, *Reflections upon Labor Arb.*, 72 HARV. L. REV. 1498-1499 (1959); Shulman, *supra* Arbitrator.

COMITE FRANCAIS DE L'ARBITRAGE
(23, rue d'Anjou, Paris VIII°, France)

A society established in Paris in December 1953, with the purpose of acquainting the legal and business community with arbitration as a means of settling differences which might occur in domestic and international law.

The Comité Français promotes the growth of arbitration by means of public lectures on the subject. It sponsored the first international congress on arbitration in Paris in 1960, and closely cooperated with the second, which was held in Rotterdam in 1966. A third international congress on arbitration was convened in Venice in 1969. The Comité has prepared and is supporting the draft of a new French law concerning arbitration, which is being studied at the present time by various governmental bodies. The Comité publishes a quarterly review on arbitration, *Revue de l'Arbitrage*. Membership in the Comité Français de l'Arbitrage is limited to 200.

See also: Int'l. com'l. arb.; Revue de l'Arbitrage.

Sources: Memorandum by Jean Robert to the AAA, July 23, 1968.

COMMERCE CLEARING HOUSE (CCH)

See: Labor Arbitration Awards.

COMMERCIAL ARBITRATION

Arbitration used for the settlement of disputes in the general commercial or business world.

See also: Appointment of arbitrator; Arb. agreement; Arbitrator; Award; Bias; Cases. U.S. Supreme Court (Com'l.); Confirming the award; Discovery of documents; Future disputes clause; Initiating the arb. proceedings; Institutional arb.; Irrevocability of the arb. agreement; Modern arb. statute; Party autonomy; Procedure (Arb.); Trade association; Vacating an award; Waiver of arb. (Com'l.).

Sources: M. BERNSTEIN, *supra* Appeal; M. DOMKE, *supra* Adhesion contract; M. DOMKE, *supra* Appeal boards of adm. agencies.

COMMISSION OF INQUIRY

See: International Commission of Inquiry.

COMMON LAW

A body of written or unwritten rules and principles which derive their authority solely from customs or court decisions as distinguished from laws enacted by legislatures.

Common law as a term also applies to the Common Law of England which has become part of the law of all but one of the American States, as well as of certain nations associated with England. The force and authority of Common Law in the United States is dirived from that portion of the Common Law of England which had been adopted and was in force at the time of the American Revolution. The states in this country have continued the development of their own common law, though actual legislation has become increasingly important.

See also: Common law arb.

Sources: BLACK'S LAW DICTIONARY (3d ed. 1933); BOUVIER'S LAW DICTIONARY
(8th ed. 1914).

COMMON LAW ARBITRATION

The voluntary agreement of the parties to submit their dispute to the
decision of a mutually selected third person.

Such a submission agreement may be oral, and may be revoked at
any time before the rendering of the award. Common law arbitration
and all its procedures derive from court decisions rather than from any
statutes. These procedures include the agreement to arbitrate, the selection of arbitrators, the steps to be followed in the hearing, the award
itself, and its enforcement or annulment. Common law arbitration co-
exists with little or no modification with the various statutory systems.
Even if there is a state statute, federal law has priority in labor arbitration where § 301 of the Labor Management Relations Act applies.

See also: Enforcement of arb. agreements (Common law); Enforcement of arb.
agreements (State statutes); Irrevocability of the arb. agreement;
Lincoln Mills; § 301 disputes; Submission agreement; Vynior's Case.

Sources: F. ELKOURI & E. ELKOURI, *supra* American Arbitration Association;
Sturges & Reckson, *Common-Law and Statutory Arb.*, 46 MINN. L.
REV. 819-867 (1962).

COMMUNICATIONS SATELLITE CORPORATION (COMSAT)

A corporation created by the passage of the Communications Satellite
Act of August 31, 1962, as a joint enterprise of the United States Government and private business in order to establish with other nations a
commercial satellite system as part of an improved global communications
network.

The Communications Satellite Corporation is a private, profit-making,
government-sanctioned company. The President of the United States is
to supervise its relationship with foreign governments. In August 1964,
the Corporation became a party to the Special Agreement establishing
the International Telecommunications Satellite Consortium (INTEL-
SAT).

See also: INTELSAT; INTELSAT. Supplementary Agreement on Arb.

Sources: Communications Satellite Act of 1962, 76 Stat. 419-427, Pub. L. No.
87-624; Schrader, *The Communications Satellite Corp.*, 53 KY. L. J.
732-742 (1965).

COMPENSATION OF THE ARBITRATOR

The fee the arbitrator receives for his services.

Compensation for labor arbitrators in the United States is usually
on a *per diem* basis, with added allowance for study and travel. Parties

and arbitrators should come to some agreement in advance of the hearing on the compensation to be paid, or try to establish the basis on which such compensation will be determined. These arrangements should be made in the presence of both parties. Parties in disagreement about compensation should discuss the matter in the absence of the arbitrator. Administrative agencies frequently determine the question of compensation by notifying parties in advance of the *per diem* fees individual arbitrators charge, or they may establish the *per diem* fee in their rules. Commercial arbitrators in the United States may serve without fee, depending upon the rules of particular administrative agencies. Section 50 of the Commercial Arbitration Rules of the American Arbitration Association reads: "Members of the . . . Panel of Arbitrators serve without fee in commercial arbitrations. In prolonged or in special cases the parties may agree to the payment of a fee. . . ." In England, commercial arbitrators receive compensations. The arbitrator's fee in international public arbitration is frequently determined by the parties in the *compromis*. The interested States usually bear the expenses in equal parts, or provision is sometimes made that the expenses may be charged by the tribunal to the losing party. In some cases the matter is left to later agreement, or to be disposed of in the award.

See also: Arbitrator; Silk Association of America.

Sources: CODE OF ETHICS, *supra* Code of Ethics and Procedural Standards for Labor-Management Arb. at 10; W. GILL, EVIDENCE AND PROCEDURE IN ARB. (1965).

COMPETENCE DE LA COMPETENCE

The power of a court or arbitrator to determine his own jurisdiction.

See also: Arbitrator's authority; Jurisdiction.

Sources: K. CARLSTON, *supra* Annulment . . . at 74, 75; A. SHIHATA, THE POWER OF THE INT'L. COURT TO DETERMINE ITS OWN JURISDICTION (1965).

COMPETITIVE STATUS SENIORITY

See: Seniority.

COMPLIANCE WITH THE AWARD

The voluntary acceptance of the decision of an arbitrator by the losing party, including his consent to comply with the final and binding terms of the award.

The vast majority of arbitration awards are voluntarily accepted by the disputing parties, because it is unlikely that they would have submitted their dispute to arbitration if they had not been willing to risk an unfavorable decision. This has been true in labor arbitration as it is true in commercial and international public arbitration. The legal doctrine that an arbitration award is binding on the parties and must be carried out in good faith is almost universally accepted.

See also: Alabama Arb.; Aramco Arb.; Binding character of award; Int'l. pub. arb.; Repudiation.

Sources: HAMBRO, L'EXECUTION DES SENTENCES INTERNATIONALES (1936); STUYT, SURVEY OF INT'L. ARB. 1794-1938 (1939); Schachter, *supra* Alabama Arbitration at 1-24.

COMPROMIS

The *compromis* is the arbitration agreement between sovereign States which empowers them to arbitrate an existing dispute.

By means of a *compromis,* the procedures to be followed are determined such as the time allowed for appointing arbitrators, the form, order, and time in which the pleadings before the Tribunal may be made, and also the amount of the initial sum which each party must deposit in advance to defray expenses. The *compromis* may also define the manner of appointing arbitrators, and ascribe any special powers which may eventually belong to the Tribunal, as well as the particular language to be used, and all other determining conditions on which the parties are agreed. A clear definition of the question to be arbitrated should be given wherever possible. Though the *compromis* is a document used only in existing disputes, its subject matter is very similar to the arbitration agreement for settling future disputes, an agreement which is an integral part of many bilateral treaties. Unless a *compromis* states otherwise, it is either an express or an implied condition that the arbitrator shall apply international law as the basis of his decision. In commercial disputes in France, if the bare arbitration clause is to be applied, that is, the *clause compromissoire,* a submission or *compromis* must be made before the arbitration can proceed.

See also: Applicable law. Int'l. pub. arb.; Appointment of arbitrators; Arb. agreement; Arbitrator's authority; Clause compromissoire; Consent of the parties; Int'l. pub. arb.; Obligatory compromis; Pious Fund Case; Submission agreement; Treaty; Wal Wal Arb.

Sources: Convention on the Pacific Settlement of Int'l. Disputes (The Hague, July 28, 1899, revised Oct. 18, 1907); K. CARLSTON, *supra* Annulment . . . ; J. SIMPSON & H. FOX, *supra* Appointment of arbitrators at 42; Wilner, *supra* Applicable procedural law at 665.

COMPROMISE

The settlement of a dispute in arbitration when the parties involved reach their own agreement.

The parties may ask the arbitrator to render an award based upon their own agreement to compromise. *A Manual for Commercial Arbitra-*

tors published by the American Arbitration Association defines the procedures of such a compromise as follows: "During an arbitration parties or their attorneys may see an opportunity for compromise they may have overlooked before. They may ask for an adjournment for the sake of further negotiation or withdraw the matter from arbitration. They may even ask the arbitrator to incorporate a settlement in his award, thereby giving the agreement strong recognition in law. This is permissible and may be regarded as a collateral advantage of arbitration, *as long as the compromise results from the action of the parties themselves, without the participation of the arbitrator.*"

See also: Award upon settlement; Consent award.

Sources: AAA Manual, *supra* Award at 19.

COMPULSORY ARBITRATION

A system whereby the parties to a dispute are forced by the government to forego their right to strike and are compelled to accept the resolution of their dispute through arbitration by a third party.

Compulsory arbitration compels the parties to submit their dispute for a final and binding decision, under a state statute or federal order, by an arbitrator who is normally appointed by the government. There have been other types of compulsory arbitration, such as those intended to cope with congested court calendars by the arbitration of small claims. This has been used most extensively in the Pennsylvania system established in 1952.

See also: Adamson Act; Arbitration (Voluntary); Arsenal of weapons; Compulsory arb. (Australia); Conseil de prud'hommes; Emergency boards; Gov't. intervention; Labor arb. (Voluntary); Labor court; Nat'l. Railroad Adjustment Board; Nat'l. War Labor Board; Pennsylvania compulsory arb. of small claims; Railroad Arb. Act.; Sanctions; War Labor Disputes Act.

Sources: H. ROBERTS, COMPULSORY ARB.: PANACEA OR MILLSTONE? (1965); Jones, *Compulsion and the Consensual in Labor Arb.*, 51 VA. L. REV. 369-395 (1965); Sturges, *Compulsory Arb.—What Is It?*, 30 FORDHAM L. REV. 1-16 (1961).

COMPULSORY ARBITRATION. AUSTRALIA

A public method in Australia of settling major labor disputes over the terms of a contract on both state and federal levels.

This system of compulsory arbitration is administered by the Conciliation and Arbitration Commission, and by the Commonwealth Industrial Court. There are five distinct jurisdictions: the Commonwealth, and the four states of New South Wales, Queensland, South Australia, Western Australia. Though there is a procedure for settling grievances, as well as contract terms, the major dispute settlement machinery is concerned with what in the United States would be the terms of a new contract. Most grievances are settled at the plant level and never reach arbitration. All arbitrators are public officials and are never selected by the parties concerned. Though strikes are generally forbidden, they still do occur. The great majority of disputes determined by the Commonwealth Industrial Court are concerned with such strike cases.

See also: Compulsory arb.; Conseil de prud'hommes; Labor court; Nat'l. Railroad Adjustment Board; National War Labor Board.

Sources: AUSTRALIA COURT OF CONCILIATION AND ARB., COMMONWEALTH ARB. REPORTS (1905 to date); P. BRISSENDEN, THE SETTLEMENT OF LABOR DISPUTES ON RIGHTS IN AUSTRALIA (1966); Laffer, *The Working of Australian Compulsory Arb.*, in THE CHALLENGE OF INDUSTRIAL RELATIONS IN THE PACIFIC-ASIAN COUNTRIES (H. Roberts & P. Brissenden eds. 1965).

COMPULSORY ARBITRATION. PUBLIC EMPLOYEES

The compulsory resolution of public employee disputes which have erupted into strikes, or which threaten to become strikes, by a board of impartial labor relations experts appointed with or without the consent of the parties.

Such compulsory arbitration is complicated by the fact that arbitrators, when their decision is stated to be final and binding, would be acting without the traditional checks and balances fundamental to the development of the law in the United States. A decision by the arbitrators in favor of wage demands of one particular group of employees might require budgetary action by the legislature, an action which the lawmakers might not be willing or able to make. The New York State Committee on Public Employee Relations in its report of March 31, 1966, proposed in preference to arbitration boards the use of fact-finding boards which would submit their reports to the legislature and the chief executive officer prior to the budget-submission date of the government agency involved in the particular negotiation. Since the legislature or the local legislative body concerned represents all of the people and has the power to tax, a final solution might more easily be reached. Even so, recent laws in Pennsylvania and Rhode Island may point to the use of compulsory arbitration for policemen and firemen in cases of impasse.

See also: Compulsory arb.; Labor court; National Railroad Adjustment Board; N.Y. State PERB.; OCB; Public employee; Taylor Law.

Sources: Pa. Stat. Ann. Title 43, §§ 217.1 to 217.10; R.I. Gen. Laws, Title 28, Chs. 9.1, 9.2, §§ 28--9.1-1 to 28-9.2-14; N.Y. (State) Governor's Committee on Pub. Employee Relations, Interim Report, June 17, 1968, at 13-16; GOV'T. EMPLOYEE REL. REP. F-1, G-1, H-1 (No. 267, 1968); *id, Recommendations for Changes in N.Y. State Law*, GOV'T. EMPLOYEE REL. REP. G-1 (No. 283, 1969).

COMSAT

See: Communications Satellite Corporation.

CONCESSION CONTRACT

A contract between a State and a private foreign investor.

A concession contract is the term employed to describe contracts for the investment of private foreign capital in developing the resources of another country. These investments may be for the development of natural resources such as coal, lumber, ore, or oil, or for the construction and management of gas and electrical utilities. The private corporation usually receives compensation in the form of profits. A characteristic feature of such an agreement is the elaborately detailed legal machinery included to govern the performance of the concession. Concession contracts usually contain an arbitration clause as a means of settling future disputes. The word concession is often said to imply a basic inequality in the negotiation of such contracts, and as such may conceal the essential bilateral character of the transaction. Many prefer to use the term Economic Development Agreement rather than concession contract.

See also: Abu Dhabi Arb.; Aramco Arb.; Calvo Clause; Convention on the Settlement of Investment Disputes between States and Nationals of Other States; Economic development agreements; Enforcement of award (Int'l. pub. arb.); Int'l. pub. arb.; Int'l. Centre for Settlement of Investment Disputes; Lena Goldfields Arb.; OECD Draft Convention on the Protection of Foreign Property.

Sources: H. CATTAN, THE LAW OF OIL CONCESSIONS IN THE MIDDLE EAST AND NORTH AFRICA 200 (1967); G. DELAUME, LEGAL ASPECTS OF INT'L. LENDING AND ECONOMIC DEVELOPMENT FINANCING (1967); S. SIKSEK, THE LEGAL FRAMEWORK FOR OIL CONCESSIONS IN THE ARAB WORLD (1960).

CONCILIATION

A dispute settlement procedure which uses a neutral third party to clarify the issues in a dispute so that the parties concerned may themselves arrive at a mutually acceptable agreement.

In labor management relations, little distinction seems to be made between mediation and conciliation, mediation at present being the preferred term. The Taft-Hartley Act provides for the conciliation of labor disputes through the Federal Mediation and Conciliation Service in industries affecting commerce. Many international treaties contain procedures for the use of conciliation with the consent of the parties prior to arbitration. The Permanent Court of Arbitration permits the use of conciliation as well as arbitration. Chapter III of the Convention on the Settlement of Investment Disputes establishes procedures to be used when conciliation is selected by the parties as a means of settling their dispute. Conciliation has long been the method most often used for settling controversies in Japan. Although the Japanese Civil Code provides for arbitration, it is seldom used, conciliation having been the preferred procedure in Japanese villages as far back as the early 17th Century. In recent times, conciliation laws in Japan have become broader and more various, and include such transactions as house and land lease, and disputes in the mining industry, as well as in domestic and personal affairs.

See also: Arsenal of weapons; Emergency boards; Federal Mediation and Conciliation Service; Good offices; Int'l. comm'n. of inquiry; Labor arb. (Voluntary); Mediation; Nat'l. Mediation Board; State boards of mediation.

Sources: Convention on the Settlement of Investment Disputes between States and Nationals of Other States (submitted by I.B.R.D., March 18, 1965); D. HENDERSON, CONCILIATION AND JAPANESE LAW (1965); Sanders, Types of Labor Disputes and Approaches to Their Settlement, 12 LAW & CONTEMP. PROB. 215 (1947).

CONCURRENT JURISDICTION (ARBITRATION)

A jurisdiction which is or may be shared by the courts, the National Labor Relations Board, and the arbitrator.

When such concurrent jurisdiction exists, each of the above has the power to decide a dispute based on identical or closely related issues in the same case. Such concurrence is established when the collective bargaining agreement and the National Labor Relations Act protect the same rights, as when under the collective agreement, if a worker is discharged, his grievance is subject to arbitration. If, however, he is discharged for union activities, such undue discrimination is an unfair labor practice within the Board's jurisdiction as established by the National Labor Relations Act. The question then becomes which of these has final jurisdiction. To cope with a possible conflict, the National Labor Relations Board has tried to establish a working set of principles in its so-called Spielberg doctrine, where an award has already been rendered. Where no award has been made, the Board will withhold its jurisdiction in favor of arbitration if certain conditions clearly establish the need for arbitration.

See also: Carey v. Westinghouse; Nat'l. Labor Relations Board; Preemption; Spielberg doctrine; Unfair labor practice; Wagner Act; Work assignment disputes.

Sources: NLRB ANN. REPS.; 20 PROC. OF THE NAT'L. ACADEMY OF ARBITRATORS (1968); McCulloch, Arb. and/or the NLRB, 18 ARB. J. (n.s.) 3-16 (1963); Waks, The "Dual Jurisdiction" Problem in Labor Arb., 23 ARB. J. (n.s.) 201-227 (1968).

CONDON-WADLIN ACT (NEW YORK STATE)
(§ 108, Civil Service Law)

A New York State law prohibiting public employees from striking.

The Condon-Wadlin Act provided drastic penalties for individual workers who went out on strike. The act was passed in 1947 after a strike by teachers in Buffalo. The severity of the penalties was reduced in 1963, and reinforced in 1965. After the difficulties arising out of the New York City Transit Workers strike in 1966, the Condon-Wadlin Act was replaced in September 1967 by the Taylor Law.

See also: Taylor Law.

Sources: Pauletti & Wolk, *The Condon-Wadlin Act*, 40 N.Y. STATE B. J. 86-93 (1968).

CONFIRMING THE AWARD

The process of having an award confirmed by a court so that it can be enforced as a court judgment.

To complete this process, the winning party on notice to the defeated party makes a motion before the court to have the award confirmed. If all legal requirements have been met in the award, and there has been no successful motion to vacate, the court will enter judgment on it. The New York State statute has this to say on the subject: "The Court shall confirm an award upon application of a party made within one year after its delivery to him, unless the award is vacated or modified upon a ground specified in § 7511." When the losing party willingly complies with the award, it therefore becomes neither practical nor necessary to have the award confirmed.

See also: Appeal; Award; Binding character of award; Challenge of award; Entry-of-judgment clause; Judgment; Judgment-roll; Vacating an award.

Sources: N.Y. CPLR § 7510; Ass'n. OF THE BAR OF THE CITY OF N.Y., *supra* Award by confession; 32 LAWYERS' LETTERS (1967), *supra* Adjournment of hearings.

CONGRESS ON INDUSTRIAL CONCILIATION AND ARBITRATION

One of the first congresses on labor arbitration sponsored by the Civic Federation of Chicago, and held in Chicago in November 1894.

The Civic Federation of Chicago had been prominent in its attempts to settle the Pullman Strike of 1894. Its Provisional Board of Conciliation, which was appointed with the hope of settling the strike, proved to be ineffective, but out of these efforts plans were developed for the convening of this Congress, of which Jane Addams was secretary. The Congress was attended by prominent leaders in industry, labor, and government. A later and second congress was held in 1901.

See also: National Civic Federation.

Sources: E. WITTE, *supra* Arb. Act of 1888.

CONSEIL DE PRUD'HOMMES (COUNCIL OF MEN OF EXPERIENCE AND INTEGRITY)

A conciliation board as well as a labor court elected from employee and employer representatives for the purpose of settling labor disputes in France.

    This system of handling grievances, which has been employed in France since the era of Napoleon I, is said to be the oldest labor court in the world. These conciliation boards and labor courts are established by law and are competent to hear disputes arising out of the individual contract of employment. There is no arbitrator or any other neutral representative on the board. Deadlocks are referred for final resolution to judges of the local regular courts.

See also: Labor court; Bipartite board; Compulsory arb.; Compulsory arb. Australia; Nat'l. Railroad Adjustment Board.

Sources: W. McPHERSON & F. MEYERS, THE FRENCH LABOR COURTS (1966).

CONSENT AWARD

An award which was arrived at by the parties themselves, and which the arbitrator consents to make.

    A consent award may have been made prior to the hearing, or during the hearing itself, or prior to the rendering of the award. The award as submitted to the arbitrator should be a statement signed by both parties specifying the terms of the settlement, and the allocation of expenses incurred in the arbitration. The statement should also declare that the arbitrator is authorized to render a consent award. It should indicate at which stage of the proceedings the settlement occurred, in the unlikely event that the consent award should later be contested in court. In the Code of Ethics and Procedural Standards for Labor-Management Arbitration, the arbitrator is advised that he may upon the request of the parties and at his own discretion give the terms of their voluntary settlement the status of an award, the parties having given a full and satisfactory explanation of the reasons behind their settlement.

See also: Agreed award; Award by confession; Award upon settlement; Code of Ethics and Procedural Standards for Labor-Management Arb.; Compromise.

Sources: CODE OF ETHICS, *supra* Code of Ethics and Procedural Standards for Labor-Management Arb.; M. DOMKE, *supra* Adhesion contract at 277-278.

CONSENT DECREE

A decree entered with the consent of the disputing parties and adopted as such by the court.

A consent decree represents the ultimate disposition of a suit, and the accurate and specific representation of the rights of the parties as contained in their own agreement. It was under a consent decree that the Motion Picture Industry Arbitration System came into existence.

See also: Motion Picture Industry Arb. System.

Sources: BOUVIER's LAW DICTIONARY (8th ed. 1914); WEBSTER's INT'L. DICTIONARY (3rd ed. 1966).

CONSENT OF THE PARTIES

Consent rests in the agreement of the parties to arbitrate.

Disputing parties may often waive certain limitations as outlined in their agreement, and by so doing may expand the scope of that agreement. The parties consent to grant jurisdiction to the arbitrator in their arbitration agreement. In international public arbitration, the consent between sovereign States rests in an arbitration treaty or *compromis,* or in an arbitration agreement included in a treaty. Such consent must be mutual, as must be any alteration in the agreement. The parties may often abandon, waive, or ignore the award, and thus render it ineffectual, subject to statutes in force or general international law. Consent of the parties may also refer to the continuing mutual consent which is required during the hearing to implement such procedural matters as a request by the arbitrator for permission to inspect a plant or consult with experts.

See also: Arb. agreement; Compromis; Delegation of arbitrator's authority; Future disputes clause; Independent investigation by arbitrator; Int'l. pub. arb.; Model rules on arbitral procedure; Party autonomy; Permanent Court of Arb. Rules of Arb. and Conciliation for Settlement of Int'l. Disputes between Two Parties of Which Only One Is a State; Submission agreement; U.N. ECE. Rules of Arb.

Sources: K. CARLSTON, *supra* Annulment at 63-64.

CONSOLIDATION OF CASES

Two or more arbitration cases which are heard as one.

Consolidation of arbitration proceedings may be granted by a court for substantially the same reasons as for the consolidation of any legal action, that is, when the issues are the same, and there is at least one party common to all of the arbitrations.

See also: Joinder; Multiple grievances; Procedure.

Sources: FINKELSTEIN, *Consolidation of Arb.* . . . , 162 N.Y.L.J., Oct. 14 & 15, 1969.

CONSTRUCTION INDUSTRY ARBITRATION RULES (March 8, 1966)

Rules which were drafted by a joint committee from organizations in the construction industry, and which were to be administered by the American Arbitration Association.

Prior to 1966, construction industry arbitration cases, under the existing American Institute of Architects Conditions, were either arbitrated informally by the parties, or were administered by the American Arbitration Association under its Commercial Arbitration Rules. A joint committee of architects and engineers which began a study of the use of arbitration in the industry, was augmented in 1965 by the addition of representatives from the principal associations in the construction industry. After further study, the Construction Industry Arbitration Rules were adopted. The National Construction Industry Arbitration Committee was established with representatives from the various industry and professional associations. Regional advisory committees work with the American Arbitration Association to enlarge the panels of arbitrators, and to serve in an advisory capacity on administrative problems.

See also: American Arb. Association; Standard arb. clause.

Sources: AAA, CONSTRUCTION CONTRACT DISPUTES (1968); AAA CONSTRUCTION INDUSTRY ARB. RULES, EFFECTIVE DATE MARCH 8, 1966; Aksen, *Resolving Construction Contract Disputes through Arb.* 23 ARB. J. (n.s.) 141-161 (1968).

CONTAINER CONTRACT

A contract which contains an arbitration clause.

The importance of the container contract for arbitration is that under certain conditions, the arbitration provision is regarded as separable from the contract in which it appears.

See also: Fraudulent inducement of the contract; Irrevocability of the arb. agreement; Prima Paint Corp.; Separability doctrine; U.S. Arb. Act.

Sources: Bernstein, *The Impact of the Uniform Com'l. Code upon Arb.*, 42 NYU L. REV. 8-33 (1967); Collins, *Arb. and the Uniform Com'l. Code*, 41 NYU L. REV. 736-756 (1966).

CONTRACT ARBITRATORS

See: Rotating panels.

CONVENTION

A pact or written agreement which establishes a legal relation between the cosigning sovereign States.

A convention may be simply defined as a written instrument. States may, however, incur legal obligations other than through written agreements. Conventions usually refer to international agreements between more than two signatory nations (multilateral). Treaties refer to agreements between two nations (bilateral). Custom permits use of the term multilateral treaty rather than convention. International organizations, such as the United Nations or the World Bank, may themselves have the authority to conclude international agreements with States.

See also: Convention on Int'l. Civil Aviation; Convention on the Execution of Foreign Arbitral Awards; Convention on the Pacific Settlement of Int'l. Disputes; Convention on the Recognition and Enforcement of Foreign Arbitral Awards; Convention on the Settlement of Investment Disputes between States and Nationals of Other States; European Convention on Int'l. Com'l. Arb.; Int'l. customary law; Int'l. law; Permanent Court of Arb. Rules of Arb. and Conciliation for Settlement of Int'l. Disputes between Two Parties of Which Only One Is a State; Protocol on Arb. Clauses; Treaty.

Sources: U.N. ILC Draft Laws of Treaties, art. 2(1)(a).

CONVENTION ON INTERNATIONAL CIVIL AVIATION (CHICAGO CONVENTION)

An agreement drafted at the International Civil Aviation Conference in Chicago in 1944, providing for the adoption of international standards of air transportation, and the creation of the International Civil Aviation Organization.

Chapter XVIII of the Chicago Convention provided for two types of dispute settlement procedures for disputes between contracting States relating to the interpretation and application of the convention. One was by executive decisions of the ICAO Council, and the other by the choice of an appeal from these decisions to an *ad hoc* arbitral tribunal, or to the then Permanent Court of International Justice. The ICAO system is particularly interesting in that it established sanctions for the enforcement of awards. Article 87 empowers nations to prohibit the use of their air space to airlines which have not complied with the terms of an award. Arbitration clauses are found in almost all air transport bilateral treaties. Most recent agreements refer disputes to a tripartite *ad hoc* tribunal. Though the disputes are between private air carriers, the arbitrations are conducted by their governments under the bilateral air transport agreements. None of these agreements had been invoked until the 1963 air traffic rights dispute between the United States and France. Arbitration of the bilateral agreement with Italy, initiated by the United States in 1965, is the second such action.

See also: Air transport agreements; Bermuda Agreement; Int'l. Civil Aviation Organization; Int'l. pub. arb.; Rate clauses; Sanctions.

Sources: Convention on Int'l. Civil Aviation, Dec. 7, 1944, 61 Stat. 1180, T.I.A.S. 1591; B. CHENG, *supra* Air transport agreements; Domke, *Int'l. Civil Aviation Sets New Pattern*, 1 INT'L. ARB. J. 20-29 (1945); Hingorani, *Dispute Settlement in Int'l. Civil Aviation*, 14 ARB. J. (n.s.)

14-25 (1959); Larsen, *supra* Air transport agreements at 145-164; Larsen, *The U.S.-Italy Air Transport Arb.*, 61 AM. J. INT'L. L. 496-520 (1967); Larsen, *Arb. of the U.S.-France Air Traffic Rights Dispute,* 1965 J. AIR L. & COMMERCE 231-247.

CONVENTION ON THE EXECUTION OF FOREIGN ARBITRAL AWARDS (1927) (GENEVA CONVENTION)

A convention which provided for the enforcement of awards rendered according to an arbitration agreement covered by the Protocol on Arbitration Clauses of 1923, and adopted by the Assembly of the League of Nations on September 26, 1927.

Each Contracting State is required under the terms of the convention to recognize awards rendered in another contracting State as binding and enforceable under certain stated conditions. The award must have been made in accordance with a valid arbitration agreement on the subject matter capable of settlement by arbitration under the law of the country in which enforcement is being sought. The arbitral tribunal must have been appointed according to the wishes of the parties. The award must comply with the legal requirements governing the arbitration, and becomes final in the country in which it was rendered, if no proceeding for vacating the award is pending, or if enforcement of the award is not contrary to public policy of the country in which it is to be enforced. Recognition and enforcement of the award may be rejected by the court if certain procedural irregularities are proved to have existed. The United States is not a party to this convention.

See also: Convention; Enforcement of foreign arbitral awards; Protocol on Arb. Clauses.

Sources: Convention on the Execution of Foreign Arbitral Awards, (signed at Geneva, Sept. 26, 1927, in force July 25, 1929); Comm. on Com'l. Arb. of the Ministry of Commerce, Government of India, *Report,* in TRADE/CA/NEWS 3 ECAFE CENTRE FOR COM'L. ARB. NEWS BULL. 24 (1965); Hoare, *Preface to Int'l. Arb. A Review of World Wide Com'l. Dispute Settlement,* 35 ARB. JOURNAL OF THE INSTITUTE OF ARBITRATORS 30-65 (1969).

CONVENTION ON THE PACIFIC SETTLEMENT OF INTERNATIONAL DISPUTES OF 1899 AND 1907

A convention adopted at the Peace Conference at The Hague on October 29, 1899, and revised at a second conference in 1907, for the purpose of codifying the law and practice relating to arbitration, and providing for the establishment of the Permanent Court of Arbitration.

Article 37 of the revised Convention of 1907 declared that "International arbitration has for its object the settlement of disputes between States by judges of their own choice and on the basis of respect for law." Sixty-three States have become parties to the Convention. Under certain conditions, the Registry of the Permanent Court of Arbitration will lend its facilities for arbitrations between two parties of which only one is a nation and the other an important private company or person.

See also: Access to the arbitral tribunal; Convention; Int'l. pub. arb; Permanent court of arb.

Sources: Convention on the Pacific Settlement of Int'l. Disputes (Oct. 18, 1907) 36 Stat. 2199, TS 536, 1 Bevans 566; M. HUDSON, INT'L. TRIBUNALS PAST AND FUTURE (1944); PERMANENT COURT OF ARB., RULES OF ARB. AND CONCILIATION FOR SETTLEMENT OF INT'L. DISPUTES BETWEEN TWO PARTIES OF WHICH ONLY ONE IS A STATE (1962).

CONVENTION ON THE RECOGNITION AND ENFORCEMENT OF FOREIGN ARBITRAL AWARDS (UN CONVENTION) (NEW YORK CONVENTION)

A multilateral treaty drafted at a United Nations Conference on international commercial arbitration.

The United Nations Conference was convened in New York City on May 20 and ended on June 10, 1958. The subject of international commercial arbitration had been under study by an *Ad Hoc* Committee since 1954. The Convention on the Recognition and Enforcement of Foreign Arbitral Awards entered into force on June 7, 1959. As of April 9, 1969, thirty-three countries had become parties to it. Under the terms of the Convention, each Contracting State undertakes to recognize arbitral awards as binding, and to enforce them in accordance with the rules of procedure of the territory where the award is to be recognized. Arbitrations may be conducted according to existing rules, or special rules drafted for a specific arbitration, or under the law of the country in which the arbitration takes place. A party seeking enforcement of the award need only produce the award, or a certified copy of it, including the agreement to arbitrate, in the country where such enforcement is being sought.

See also: Convention; Enforcement of arb. agreements (Int'l. com'l. arb.); Enforcement of foreign arbitral awards; European Convention on Int'l. Com'l. Arb.; Foreign arbitral award; Int'l. com'l. arb.; U.N. Conf. on Int'l. Com'l. Arb.

Sources: Convention on the Recognition and Enforcement of Foreign Arbitral Awards, U.N. Doc. E/CONF.26/8/Rev. 1 (1958); CONVENTION ON THE RECOGNITION AND ENFORCEMENT OF FOREIGN ARBITRAL AWARDS, MESSAGE FROM THE PRESIDENT TRANSMITTING THE CONVENTION, SENATE EXEC. E., 90th Cong., 2d Sess. (1968); U.S. Dep't. of State, Official Report of the U.S. Delegation to the U.N. Conf. on Int'l. Com'l. Arb., May 20-June 10, 1958; G. HAIGHT, CONVENTION ON THE RECOGNITION AND ENFORCEMENT OF FOREIGN ARBITRAL AWARDS: SUMMARY ANALYSIS OF RECORD OF U.N. CONF., MAY/JUNE 1958 (1958); Cohn, *The Fifth Report of the Private Int'l. Law Comm.*, 25 MODERN L. REV. (1962); Domke, *The U.N. Conf. on*

Int'l. Com'l. Arb., 53 AM. J. INT'L. L. 416 (1959); Minoli, *L'Italie et la Convention de New York,* in INT'L. ARB. LIBER AMICORUM FOR MARTIN DOMKE (P. Sanders ed. 1967).

CONVENTION ON THE SETTLEMENT OF INVESTMENT DISPUTES BETWEEN STATES AND NATIONALS OF OTHER STATES

A convention drafted by the International Bank for Reconstruction and Development which provides facilities on a voluntary basis for the settlement through conciliation and arbitration of investment disputes between member States and nationals of other member States.

A National is defined as being either a private person or a corporation. The Convention on the Settlement of Investment Disputes is one of several proposals designed to stimulate and protect the flow of private international capital into developing countries. It differs from three previous draft conventions in that it offers to member States and foreign investors a permanent forum for the settlement of their disputes according to specific rules of procedure. The International Centre for Settlement of Investment Disputes has been established with offices at the Bank's principle office in Washington, D.C., but with its own autonomous Secretariat for the administration of dispute settlement procedures. The Convention entered into force on October 14, 1966, after it had been ratified by twenty member States.

See also: Concession contract; Economic development agreements; Exhaustion of local remedies; Int'l. Centre for Settlement of Investment Disputes; Investment disputes.

Sources: Convention on the Settlement of Investment Disputes between States and Nationals of Other States, 17 UST 1270, TIAS 6090, 575 UNTS 159; Broches, *supra* Applicable law. Int'l. pub. arb.; Delaume, *Convention on the Settlement of Investment Disputes between States and Nationals of Other States,* 1 INT'L. LAWYER 64-80 (1966); Farley, *Commentary: The Convention on the Settlement of Investment Disputes between States and Nationals of Other States,* 5 DUQUESNE U. L. REV. 19-30 (1966); Sirefman, *The World Bank Plan for Investment Dispute Arbitration,* 20 ARB. J. (n.s.) 168-178 (1965).

CONVENTION ON THE TRANSPORT OF GOODS BY RAIL

See: Central Office for Int'l. Railway Transport.

CONVENTION ON THE TRANSPORT OF PASSENGERS AND LUGGAGE BY RAIL

See: Central Office for Int'l. Railway Transport.

COSTS OF ARBITRATION

See: Administrative expenses.

COUNCIL OF EUROPE
(Avenue de l'Europe, Strasbourg, France)

A consultative body founded by ten Western European nations on May 5, 1949, to achieve a greater unity between its members and facilitate their economic and social progress.

The Council of Europe was the first European political institution to have an international Parliament. It is governed by a Committee of Ministers made up of the Foreign Ministers of the member countries, and a Consultative Assembly, consisting of representatives appointed by the various national Parliaments. The Council has been particularly helpful in its comments on various draft proposals containing arbitration procedures, such as its Opinion 39 of 1963 on the OECD Draft Convention on the Protection of Foreign Property. The Council itself has submitted a European Convention Providing a Uniform Law on Arbitration opened for signature on January 20, 1966, and a European Convention for the Peaceful Settlement of Disputes (1957). There were 17 member nations as of 1970.

See also: European Convention for the Peaceful Settlement of Disputes; European Convention Providing a Uniform Law on Arb.; Organisation for Economic Co-operation and Development; OECD Draft Convention on the Protection of Foreign Property.

Sources: Council of Europe, Agreement Relating to Application of the European Convention on Int'l. Com'l. Arb., European T.S. 42; COUNCIL OF EUROPE, CATALOGUE OF PUBLICATIONS 3 (1967); Consultative Assembly of the Council of Europe, *Opinion on O.E.C.D. Draft Convention on the Protection of Foreign Property, Opinion No. 39* (1963), 3 INT'L. LEGAL MATERIALS 133-150 (1964).

COUNCIL OF EUROPE. OPINION NO. 39

See: Organisation for Economic Co-operation and Development. Draft Convention on the Protection of Foreign Property.

COUNCIL ON INDUSTRIAL RELATIONS FOR THE ELECTRICAL CONTRACTING INDUSTRY

A twelve member judicial body established by the International Brotherhood of Electrical Workers and the National Electrical Contractors Association at their respective conventions in 1921 and 1922 to serve as the supreme court of the electrical contracting industry.

The Council is composed of six representatives of the National Electrical Contractors Association and six members of the IBEW. They meet quarterly and hear the cases brought before them. These consist of matters in dispute or interpretations of existing agreements. Both sides are heard and whatever decision is reached must be unanimous. As there is no third party or neutral member, the Council on Industrial

Relations is not an arbitral tribunal. This Council still continues to function.

See also: Bipartite board.

Sources: COUNCIL ON INDUSTRIAL RELATIONS FOR THE ELECTRICAL CONTRACT-
       ING INDUSTRY, [FACTS CONCERNING THE COUNCIL] (8th ed. 1964).

COUNTERCLAIM

An opposing claim made by the respondent in his answering statement to the claim raised by the initiating party in his demand for arbitration.

See also: Answering statement; Respondent.

Sources: M. DOMKE, *supra* Adhesion contract.

COUR DE CASSATION

The supreme court of appeals in any country, such as the highest court of France, the judiciary committee of the House of Lords, or the United States Supreme Court.

Sources: A. WALTON, INTRODUCTION TO FRENCH LAW (2d ed. 1963).

CRUCE, EMERIC

A French theorist of the early 17th century, who advocated a genuine plan for international arbitration in his book *Le Nouveau Cynée.*

"Why should I," he wrote, "a Frenchman, wish harm to an English-man, a Spaniard, or a Hindoo? I cannot do it, when I consider that they are men like me, that I am subject like them to error and to sin, and that all nations are united by a natural, and consequently indissoluble bond." Eméric Crucé proposed that a permanent assembly of ambassadors representing all the nations of the world should sit in Venice. All disputes between states were to be settled by the whole assembly, and if anyone rebelled against the decision of so notable a body, he would thereby incur the disdain and disapproval of all the other princes, who would then proceed to bring him to reason and justice.

Sources: THE NEW CYNEAS OF EMÉRIC CRUCÉ 83-85 (T. Balch ed. 1909), as
       cited in Fraser, *A Sketch of the History of Int'l. Arb.*, 11 CORNELL L.
       Q. 181 (1926).

CUSTOMARY LAW

A traditional source of law which remains unwritten, and which has been established by long usage through the collaboration and consent of our ancestors.

The three traditional sources of law are customary law, statutory law, and judge-made law. Customary law in commercial arbitration is particularly significant in that it is frequently the reason for the use of arbitration instead of litigation, since arbitrators, unlike judges, are familiar with the various trades and customs involved. Past practice as it has developed in labor-management relations might be considered a customary law of a particular plant or factory. Customary law was often administered by English merchant courts in medieval times. In folk societies, customary law usually denotes the unwritten law governing the various public aspects of that culture. In contemporary society customary law is simply law which does not derive from official sources of decision making.

See also: Arbitral court (Africa); Expert arbitrator; General principles of law recognized by civilized nations; Institutional arb.; Int'l. customary law; Law merchant; Panchayat; Past practice.

Sources: ALLEN, LAW IN THE MAKING (7th ed. 1964); A. ALLOT, *supra* Arbitral court.

DEATH OF THE ARBITRATOR

If an arbitrator dies after being appointed, his successor may be designated by the party or parties involved, or by the court, or by the administrative agency which chose him originally.

The arbitration rules of most administrative agencies provide for the replacement of an arbitrator. When an arbitration agreement declares that the award shall be made by a majority of a board of arbitrators, and if one of the arbitrators dies before the hearings have ended, and before the arbitrators have had a chance to consult with each other, the other members of the board cannot continue the hearings or render an award. Such has been the almost unanimous opinion in the applicable court decisions. The Commercial Arbitration Rules of the American Arbitration Association at § 19 read: "If any Arbitrator should . . . die . . . the AAA may . . . declare the office vacant. Vacancies shall be filled in accordance with the applicable provisions of these Rules and the matter shall be reheard unless the parties shall agree otherwise." The Regulations and Rules of the International Centre for Settlement of Investment Disputes state that vacancies on the Tribunal shall be filled in the same way in which the original appointment had been made. Its Rule 12 (Resumption of Proceedings after Filling a Vacancy) declares that: "As soon as a vacancy on the Tribunal has been filled, the proceeding shall continue from the point it had reached at the time the vacancy occurred. The newly appointed arbitrator may, however, require that the oral procedure be recommenced, if this had already been started."

Sources: Model Rules, *supra* Appointment of arbitrators at art. 5; AAA COM'L. ARB. RULES, *supra* Adm. appointment at § 19; ICC, *supra* Answering statement at art. 7 (5); ICSID, *supra* Appeal boards of adm. agencies at 86-87; 5 AMERICAN JURISPRUDENCE 591-592 (2d ed. 1962); 5 LAWYERS' LETTERS (1961), *supra* Arjournment of hearings at 3-5.

DEATH OR INCOMPETENCY OF A PARTY

The disability or death of any of the parties directly involved in an arbitration proceeding.

Where there is no arbitration statute and the common law controls, the death of a party revokes the arbitration agreement, unless the parties had explicitly stipulated in their submission that the agreement to arbitrate will survive such a death. Under most modern arbitration statutes, the arbitration proceeding does not necessarily end upon the death of either one of the parties. The New York Civil Practice Law and Rules § 7512 provides: "Where a party dies after making a written agreement to submit a controversy to arbitration, the proceedings may be begun or continued upon the application of . . . his executor or administrator. . . . Upon the death or incompetency of a party, the court may extend the time within which an application to confirm, vacate or modify the award or to stay arbitration must be made. Where a party has died since an award was delivered, the proceedings thereupon are the same as where a party dies after a verdict."

Sources: N.Y. CPLR § 7512; M. DOMKE, *supra* Adhesion contract at 74; M. DOMKE, *supra* Appeal boards of adm. agencies at 51; 24 LAWYERS' LETTERS (1965), *supra* Adjournment of hearings.

DECLARATORY JUDGMENT

See: Advisory opinion.

DEFAULT

The failure of a party to appear and participate in an arbitration proceeding.

In the event of such a failure, arbitrators may hear testimony and render awards as if both parties had actually participated. Under the commercial and voluntary labor arbitration rules of the American Arbitration Association, an award may not be automatically entered upon the default alone. The arbitrator conducts a hearing and gives an award to the party present only if that party proves its claim. Similar practice holds in international law. Whether a disputant joins or abstains from the proceedings, an international tribunal may not award in favor of the initiating party unless that party has proved his case to the satisfaction of the arbitration court.

See also: Evasion of arb.; Ex parte arb.; Lena Goldfields Arb.; Montevideo Treaty; Participation in arb.

Sources: N.Y. CPLR § 7506(c); I.C.J. STAT. art. 53; Model Rules, *supra* Appointment of arbitrators at art. XXV; M. DOMKE, *supra* Adhesion contract at 343; F. ELKOURI & E. ELKOURI, *supra* American Arb. Association at 146; ICC, *supra* Answering statement at art. 19(2); Broches, *supra* Applicable law. Int'l. pub. arb. at 12; 1 LAWYERS'

LETTERS (1960), *supra* Adjournment of hearings at 1-2; 8 *id.* (1961) at 2-4.

DELEGATION OF THE ARBITRATOR'S AUTHORITY

The authority of the arbitrator to decide on issues of fact and law cannot be delegated, no matter what outside assistance or consultation is judged to be necessary.

The arbitrator should obtain the consent of the parties when he deems it necessary to consult outside experts to verify certain facts. Such consultation is not a delegation of the arbitrator's authority, since the ultimate decision still rests with him. To protect arbitrators from a charge of delegating authority, most agencies establish procedures in their rules for the use of outside experts, or for any inspections to be made by the arbitrators. Article 20 of the International Chamber of Commerce Rules provides that the arbitrator ". . . may also appoint one or more technical or legally qualified experts and request them to report on technical or legal issues, provided that their terms of reference are laid down in advance." Rule 36 of the International Centre for Settlement of Investment Disputes Regulations and Rules states: "If the Tribunal considers it necessary to visit any place connected with the dispute or to conduct an inquiry there, it shall make an order to this effect. The order shall define the scope of the visit or the subject of the inquiry, the time limit, the procedure to be followed and other particulars. The parties may participate in any visit or inquiry. Minutes shall be kept in accordance with Rule 37, *mutatis mutandis.*"

See also: Independent investigation by arbitrator; Int'l. Centre for Settlement of Investment Disputes; Procedure; Special case.

Sources: M. DOMKE, *supra* Adhesion contract at 247-248; M. DOMKE, *supra* Appeal boards of adm. agencies at 82; ICSID, *supra* Appeal boards of adm. agencies at 102-103; ICC, *supra* Answering statement at art. 20.

DELIVERY OF AWARD

The transmission of the award to the parties in an arbitration.

Delivery usually consists of mailing the award to the parties at their last known address by the arbitrator or by a representative of the administrative agency. The New York State arbitration statute provides that the arbitrator shall deliver a copy of the award to each party in the manner provided in the agreement. If there is no such provision in the agreement, the award may be delivered personally, or be sent by registered or certified mail, so that a return receipt may be obtained, or in any manner prescribed by law. At common law, once the award is delivered, the arbitrator becomes *functus officio.*

See also: Execution of award; Functus officio; Personal service; Procedure.

Sources: N.Y. CPLR § 7507; AAA Com'l. Arb. Rules, *supra* Adm. appointment; M. Domke, *supra* Adhesion contract at 286; ICC, *supra* *Answering* statement at art. 28.

DEMAND FOR ARBITRATION

The initial notice by one party to the other of an intention to arbitrate their dispute under the arbitration clause in their contract.

The demand for arbitration should contain in writing a statement of the nature of the controversy. In addition to this specific description of the dispute, the demand should also contain the names of the parties, a copy of the arbitration clause, and a statement of the remedy or relief being sought. The governing arbitration statute should be consulted in order to ensure that all legal requirements have been met. If the arbitration is being administered under the rules of an administrative agency, the demand usually consists of a form supplied by that agency. A copy of the demand is sent to the opposing party, and another is filed with the administrative agency.

See also: Notice of hearing; Notice of intention to arbitrate.

Sources: N.Y. CPLR § 7503(c); AAA Com'l. Arb. Rules, *supra* Adm. appointment at § 7; M. Domke, *supra* Adhesion contract at 136-137.

DEPOSITION

The taking of testimony under oath on petition of or on behalf of an absent party to be used as evidence in an arbitration.

A few state arbitration statutes provide for the use of depositions. The Florida Arbitration Code § 682.08(2) states as follows: "On application of a party to the arbitration and for use as evidence, the arbitrators, or the umpire in the course of his jurisdiction, may permit a deposition to be taken, in the manner and upon the terms designated by them or him of a witness who cannot be subpoenaed or is unable to attend the hearing."

See also: Affidavit; Discovery of documents; Examination before trial.

Sources: Connecticut Arb. Act, 52 Gen. Stats. Ann. ch. 909; N.Y. CPLR § 3102(c); Ohio Rev. Code Ann., ch. 2711, § 2711.07; Pennsylvania Arb. Act, 5 Purdon's Pa. Stats. Ann. ch. 4, § 167; 31 Lawyers' Letters (1967), *supra* Adjournment of hearings.

DETERMINATION OF A DISPUTE

The settling and ending of a dispute by a judicial or arbitral decision.

See also: Binding character of award.

DISCLOSURE BY ARBITRATOR

See: Duty to disclose.

DISCOVERY OF DOCUMENTS

A legal procedure invoked before a trial to inform both parties of the facts in a dispute in order to narrow the issues and save time and expense.

Such statements of disclosure may be made under oath before an officer of the court. Discovery may reveal such facts as the identity of persons who are to appear as witnesses, and the substance of their contemplated testimony. It makes available certain documents and other relevant evidence which would expose the relative strengths and weaknesses in the positions of the disputing parties. Exposure such as this often results in pretrial settlements. Discovery of documents as a procedure has not been used often in arbitration, since arbitration is itself an informal and simplified procedure. But there are situations in arbitration where disclosure of certain specific information is required if the arbitrator is to have the facts he may need for a satisfactory decision. This is true in both commercial and labor arbitration. Some states have provided legal solutions to the problem of discovery. The Connecticut, Florida, Ohio, and Pennsylvania Arbitration Acts provide that depositions may be taken to be used as evidence in arbitration, either on request of the arbitrator, or by one or both of the parties. The New York State CPLR § 3102(c) has this provision: "Before an action is commenced, disclosure to aid . . . in arbitration . . . may be obtained, but only by court order. The court may appoint a referee to take testimony. . . ."

See also: Board of arb.; Deposition; Examination before trial; Legalisms; Prehearing conf.; Procedure; Provisional remedies.

Sources: Connecticut Arb. Act, 52 Gen. Stats. Ann., ch. 909; Florida Arb. Code, § 682.08; N.Y. CPLR § 3102(c); Ohio Rev. Code Ann., ch. 2711, § 2711.07; Pennsylvania Arb. Act, 5 Purdon's Pa. Stats. Ann. ch. 4, § 167; W. GILL, *supra* Compensation of the arbitrator; Jones, *Blind Man's Buff and the Now-Problems of Apocrypha, Inc. and Local 711*, 116 U. PA. L. REV. 571-610 (1968); Jones, *Evidentiary Concepts in Labor Arb.*, 13 UCLA L. REV. 1241-1297 (1966).

DISPUTE

See: Labor dispute.

DISPUTE SETTLEMENT PROCEDURE

All the possible means available to parties or governments for the peaceful settlement of a controversy.

See also: Arb. (Voluntary); Arsenal of weapons; Compulsory arb.; Conciliation; Fact-finding; Good offices; Gov't. intervention; Injunction; Mediation; Sanctions; Seizure.

DISQUALIFICATION OF ARBITRATOR

An arbitrator may be disqualified on grounds of some form of misconduct such as the failure to show strict impartiality.

Bias on the part of the arbitrator is one of the most frequent reasons for challenging the validity of the award. The fact that the arbitrator did not disclose the possibility of a bias, such as a personal relationship with the lawyer or law firm representing one or the other of the parties might constitute sufficient grounds for nullifying the award. Once such biased relationships have been disclosed, parties do frequently choose to disregard them. Other and obvious grounds for disqualification of the arbitrator would include the same tenets of unethical behavior which would disqualify a judge. If a party has known of relationships the arbitrator has had with a party and fails to make objection, he has waived the right to object on this ground once the award has been rendered.

See also: Arbitrator; Bias; Challenge of arbitrator; Duty to disclose; Removal of arbitrator; Vacating an award; Waiver of the right to object to arbitrator.

Sources: M. DOMKE, *supra* Adhesion contract at 202-214.

DISTRESSED GRIEVANCE PROCEDURES

An accumulation of minor grievance cases which have reached the final step of arbitration because they have not been resolved at any of the steps in the grievance procedure.

Arbitration thus becomes a substitute for the grievance procedure rather than a means of strengthening it. Arbitrators themselves sometimes find ways of helping with short-cut procedures. Especially when the arbitrator is permanent, he may play a useful role in helping a union and company restore the effectiveness of the grievance procedure and reduce the case load.

See also: Grievance procedure.

Sources: Ross, *The Arb. of Discharge Cases*, in 10 PROC. OF THE NAT'L. ACADEMY OF ARBITRATORS at 21 (1957); Ross, *Distressed Grievance Procedures and Their Rehabilitation*, in 16 PROC. OF THE NAT'L. ACADEMY OF ARBITRATORS at 104-145 (1963).

DOCTRINE OF OUSTER (BRITISH)

The principle that parties to an arbitration cannot in their agreement exclude the jurisdiction of the ordinary court in questions of law.

The doctrine of ouster, out of which grew the jurisdiction of the English courts over the fact and substance of arbitration, is today founded on statute. Two practical considerations influenced the establishment of this doctrine, first that it would be best to keep the law uniform, and second, that the strict impartiality of arbitration would be protected if it were kept open to judicial review. Under modern arbitration statutes in the United States, judicial review of an award is concerned only with whether an agreement to arbitrate exists, and if it does exist, with the fact that the parties had agreed to arbitrate this particular dispute. In United States practice, the court does not consider either the sufficiency of evidence, or the merits of the award.

See also: Judicial review in arb.; Special case.

Sources: Ass'n. of the Bar of the City of N.Y., *supra* Award by confession at 5, 6, 13; Schmitthoff, *The Supervisory Jurisdiction of the English Courts*, in Int'l. Arb. Liber Amicorum for Martin Domke 294-296 (P. Sanders ed. 1967).

DRAFT CONVENTION ON ARBITRAL PROCEDURES

See: International Law Commission.

DRAFT CONVENTION ON INTERNATIONAL COMMERCIAL ARBITRATION (1967)

A convention drafted by the Inter-American Juridical Committee to serve as a complement to the Draft Uniform Law on International Commercial Arbitration of 1956 and to include the four or five fundamental standards governing the commercial arbitration system of the Americas.

These standards include the validity of the arbitration agreement and the principle that arbitration awards shall have the force of a final judgment, and may be enforced "in the same manner as a judgment of a court, national or foreign, according to the respective procedural laws." Article 3 of the convention establishes the applicable law and rules of procedure.

See also: Draft conventions and uniform laws; Second Conf. on Inter-American Com'l. Arb.

Sources: Draft Convention on Int'l. Com'l. Arb. (Rio de Janeiro, Oct. 5, 1967); Inter-American Juridical Comm., Report on the Draft Convention on Int'l. Com'l. Arb., OEA/Ser. I/VI. 1, Feb. 19, 1968 (Rio de Janeiro, Oct. 5, 1967).

DRAFT CONVENTION ON THE PROTECTION OF FOREIGN PROPERTY

See: Organisation for Economic Co-operation and Development. Draft Convention on the Protection of Foreign Property.

DRAFT CONVENTION TO IMPROVE THE CLIMATE FOR INVESTMENT IN LATIN AMERICA BY FACILITATING THE SETTLEMENT OF DISPUTES

A draft convention adopted in Rio de Janeiro, at the Second Special Meeting of November 1-5, 1965, on Legal and Institutional Aspects of Foreign Private Investments of the Inter-American Institute of International Legal Studies.

The purpose of this Convention is to encourage investment in Latin American countries by recognizing the inviolability of contracts, and by protecting the investors who are parties to an agreement from the confiscation of their property. The Convention provides that when a dispute occurs, parties may dispense with the necessity of exhausting local remedies and proceed immediately to *ad hoc* arbitration. The Tribunal is to be composed of three members, one selected by each party, and the third by the other two members. The decision of the Tribunal is to be by majority vote and is not subject to appeal.

See also: Abs-Shawcross Draft Convention on Investments Abroad; Convention on the Settlement of Investment Disputes between States and Nationals of Other States; Exhaustion of local remedies; OECD Draft Convention on the Protection of Foreign Property.

Sources: Draft Convention to Improve the Climate for Investment in Latin America by Facilitating the Settlement of Disputes (Inter-American Institute of Int'l. Legal Studies, Second Special Meeting on Legal and Institutional Aspects of Foreign Private Investment, Rio de Janeiro, Nov. 1-5, 1965).

DRAFT CONVENTIONS AND UNIFORM LAWS

See: Draft Convention on Int'l. Com'l. Arb.; Draft Convention to Improve the Climate for Investments in Latin America . . . ; Draft Uniform Law on Inter-American Com'l. Arb.; European Convention for the Peaceful Settlement of Disputes (Council of Europe); European Convention Providing a Uniform Law on Arb. (Council of Europe); Int'l. Institute for the Unification of Private Law; OECD Draft Convention on the Protection of Foreign Property.

DRAFT UNIFORM LAW ON INTER-AMERICAN COMMERCIAL ARBITRATION (INTER-AMERICAN COUNCIL OF JURISTS)

A draft uniform law approved by Resolution VIII of the Third Meeting of the Inter-American Council of Jurists held in Mexico City in 1956.

The Montevideo Conference of 1933 had recommended the adoption of standard rules of arbitration. The Inter-American Council of Jurists, meeting in 1950 in Rio de Janeiro, authorized the Inter-American Juridical Committee to draft a Uniform Law. As approved in 1956, this law established the validity of the arbitration clause, provided for the appointment of arbitrators, and recognized the procedural rules of the

Inter-American Commercial Arbitration Commission. The Uniform Law was one of many such efforts in Europe and in North and South America to make uniform under one procedure the widest variety of arbitration statutes.

See also: European Convention Providing a Uniform Law on Arb.; IACAC; Law merchant; Montevideo Conf.; Organization of American States; Uniform Arb. Act.

Sources: INTER-AMERICAN COM'L. ARB. COMMISSION, *supra* IACAC; INTER-AMERICAN COUNCIL OF JURISTS, REPORT OF THE EXECUTIVE SECRE-TARY, THIRD MEETING, MEXICO CITY, Jan. 17-Feb. 4, 1956 (1956); INTER-AMERICAN JURIDICAL COMMITTEE, REPORTS, DRAFTS AND OTHER DOCUMENTS APPROVED DURING ITS 1967 SESSION, Doc. OEA/ Ser. I/VI.1, CIJ-91; DOMKE, *infra* Institutional arb.

DRAKE BAKERIES, INC.
[*Drake Bakeries, Inc.* v. *Local 50, American Bakery and Confectionery Workers International*, AFL-CIO, 370 U.S. 254 (1962)]

A decision of the United States Supreme Court which ruled that if an arbitration clause requires both parties to arbitrate, a company is obliged to arbitrate rather than sue the union for breach of a no-strike clause.

The ruling of the Supreme Court was that: "If the union did strike in violation of the contract, the company is entitled to its damages; by staying this action, pending arbitration, we have no intention of depriving it of those damages. We simply remit the company to the forum it agreed to use for processing its strike damage claims. . . ."

See also: Atkinson v. Sinclair Refining Co.; Breach of contract; No-strike clause; Second trilogy; § 301 disputes; Sinclair Refining Co. v. Atkinson.

Sources: Drake Bakeries v. Local 50, American Bakery & Confectionery Work-ers, 370 U.S. 254 (1962); Smith & Jones, *supra* Arbitrability.

DUAL EMPLOYMENT
See: Moonlighting.

DUAL JURISDICTION
See: Concurrent jurisdiction.

DUE PROCESS (ARBITRATION)

A fair procedure practice in an arbitration which protects the rights of individuals other than the original parties in a dispute, as well as safe-guarding the rights of the parties themselves.

Adequate representation may also be required for an individual who may not even be party to the collective bargaining agreement, or to the arbitration in process under that agreement, but who may never-theless be affected by its eventual outcome. This is particularly true in cases involving questions of discharge or seniority. Seniority cases may refer to people who are not directly involved, and are therefore not present at the arbitration hearing.

See also: Individual rights; Intervention.

Sources: Fleming, *Some Problems of Due Process and Fair Procedures in Labor Arb.*, 13 STAN. L. REV. 235 (1961); Stockman, *Discussion—Due Process of Arb.*, in 11 PROC. OF THE NAT'L. ACADEMY OF ARBITRA-TORS 37-46 (1958); Wirtz, *Due Process of Arb.*, *id.* at 1-36.

DUTY OF FAIR REPRESENTATION

The moral and legal obligation of a union to protect the fundamental rights of all its members.

Duty of fair representation is derived from federal labor statutes which confer these rights and responsibilities on a union. Some unions acknowledge in their constitutions this obligation to protect the rights of all their members. Many union constitutions also provide remedies for members who are dissatisfied with the union's handling of their grievances. Such a duty to represent its members in a fair manner does not obligate a union to carry every individual grievance to the final step of arbitration.

See also: Individual rights; Public Review Board; Recognition clause; Vaca v. Sipes.

Sources: Vaca v. Sipes, 386 U.S. 171 (1967); Summers, *Labor Arb.: A Private Process with a Public Function*, 34 REV. JUR. U.P.R. 477-496 (1965).

DUTY TO DISCLOSE

The obligation of an arbitrator to reveal any fact or circumstance which might impair his ability to render a fair and just award.

Such duty to disclose exists from the moment the arbitrator is ap-pointed, and remains his constant and continuing obligation. If anything develops which might cast doubt on the impartiality of an arbitrator, but which was not known at the outset of the hearing, the arbitrator should reveal it at once to the parties, or to the agency administering the arbitration. Section 18, American Arbitration Association Commercial Arbitration Rules, states that the ". . . neutral Arbitrator shall disclose any circumstances likely to create a presumption of bias or which he believes might disqualify him as an impartial Arbitrator. . . ." This would include relationships, past or current, of his employer or firm with either of the parties or with their counsel, not only of a financial or pro-fessional nature, but social as well. Failure to disclose may be ground for vacating an award.

See also: Arbitrator; Bias; Disqualification of the arbitrator; Misconduct of arbitrator; Removal of arbitrator; Vacating an award; Waiver of right to object to the arbitrator.

Sources: Model Rules, *supra* Appointment of arbitrators at art. VI; AAA COM'L. ARB. RULES, *supra* Adm. appointment at § 18; J. SIMPSON & H. FOX, *supra* Appointment of arbitrators at 89; 17 LAWYERS' LETTERS (1964), *supra* Adjournment of hearings at 1.

ECAFE CENTRE FOR COMMERCIAL ARBITRATION

See: United Nations Economic Commission for Asia and the Far East (ECAFE) Rules.

ECAFE RULES ON COMMERCIAL ARBITRATION

See: United Nations Economic Commission for Asia and the Far East (ECAFE).

ECONOMIC DEVELOPMENT AGREEMENTS

Contracts between a sovereign State and a corporation of another country.

An economic development agreement is primarily concerned with the development of natural resources, such as oil reserves. In such a contractual relationship one party offers raw materials and the other party the means for developing them. Arbitration clauses included in these agreements detail the rules under which arbitration would be administered in case of a dispute.

See also: Abu Dhabi Arb.; Aramco Arb.; Concession contract; Convention on the Settlement of Investment Disputes between States and Nationals of Other States; Enforcement of award (Int'l. pub. arb.); Int'l. Centre for Settlement of Investment Disputes; Lena Goldfields Arb.; OECD Draft Convention on the Protection of Foreign Property.

Sources: H. CATTAN, *supra* Concession contract; G. DELAUME, *supra* Concession contract.

ELECTRICAL INDUSTRY

See: Council on Industrial Relations for the Electrical Contracting Industry.

EMERGENCY BOARDS

Boards created under special statutes to investigate a single case in which a strike or a threat of a strike involves the public interest.

There are two federal statutes which have made provision for such emergency boards. The Railway Labor Act § 10 calls for the creation of Emergency Boards when the regular machinery set up under the law has been unable to settle disputes that threaten a substantial interruption of interstate commerce. The Taft-Hartley Act at § 206 requires the President to establish such a board in national emergency disputes that may imperil the nation's health and safety. Under the Railway Labor Act, the boards have the power to investigate the facts, report the circumstances of the dispute, and make recommendations aimed at a settlement. These recommendations are advisory rather than binding. Under the Taft-Hartley Act, the report shall include a statement of the facts, but shall not contain any recommendations for their solution.

See also: Compulsory arb.; Conciliation; Fact-finding; Gov't. intervention; Mediation; Nat'l. Mediation Board; Railroad Arb. Act; Railway Labor Act; Taft-Hartley Act.

Sources: Labor Management Relations Act, 29 U.S.C. §§ 141-197; Railway Labor Act, 45 U.S.C. §§ 151-163, 181-188.

EMPLOYEE-MANAGEMENT COOPERATION IN THE FEDERAL SERVICE

See: Executive Order 10988; Executive Order 11491 (at EO 10988).

ENFORCEMENT OF ARBITRATION AGREEMENTS (COMMON LAW)

No effective means exist under common law to enforce an arbitration agreement or to make it binding.

In the absence of an arbitration statute, the agreement to arbitrate may be revoked by either one of the parties at any time before the award has been made. After the arbitrator has rendered an award, the parties to the agreement are bound by the award at common law, and the award can be made enforceable, and suit cannot be brought again on the same subject matter. This is true for arbitration agreements under union contracts, and for agreements to arbitrate commercial disputes in the absence of an arbitration statute or controlling federal law. Recent court decisions have provided for specific means for the enforcement of common law agreements to arbitrate. The most influential of these decisions is that of the United States Supreme Court in *Textile Workers Union* v. *Lincoln Mills*. In this decision, the Supreme Court chose to qualify the common law nature of the collective agreement by finding legislative support in § 301 of the Taft-Hartley Act.

See also: Arb. agreement; Common law arb.; Enforcement of arb. agreements (State statutes); Irrevocability of the arb. agreement; Lincoln Mills; Oral arb. agreement; § 301 disputes; Submission agreement; Vynior's Case.

Sources: Sturges & Reckson, *supra* Common law arb. at 819-867.

ENFORCEMENT OF ARBITRATION AGREEMENTS (FEDERAL STATUTES)

The power granted to the Federal Courts under the United States Arbitration Act to compel parties to honor their agreement to arbitrate commercial disputes under contracts involving interstate commerce or maritime transactions.

Included in the United States Arbitration Act was an exemption for "contracts of employment," which has been interpreted by some courts as meaning that this Act does not apply to union contracts. With the enactment of the Taft-Hartley Act of 1947, the federal courts were given the power to enforce union contracts under § 301. The United States Supreme Court decision in the *Lincoln Mills* case held that this authority included the power to compel compliance with an arbitration clause in such a contract. Under both statutes, as in all modern arbitration acts, the agreement to arbitrate excludes court suit on issues covered by the agreement. The awards that result are subject to very limited court review.

See also: Arbitrability; Arb. agreement; Lincoln Mills; Prima Paint . . . ;
§ 301 disputes; Stay of suit; U.S. Arb. Act.

Sources: U.S. Arb. Act, 9 U.S.C. § 1-14 (1954).

ENFORCEMENT OF ARBITRATION AGREEMENTS (INTERNATIONAL COMMERCIAL ARBITRATION)

The process by which arbitration agreements in international commercial arbitration can be enforced by the power of the courts in those States where applicable treaties and conventions have been ratified.

The Convention on the Recognition and Enforcement of Foreign Arbitral Awards (the U.N. Convention) and the European Convention on International Commercial Arbitration (the Geneva Convention of 1961) define the arbitration agreement and provide for its enforcement. Article II of the United Nations Convention declares that the Contracting States shall recognize the validity of the arbitration agreement, which must be in writing, and be on a subject capable of being settled by arbitration. A court of a Contracting State shall upon the request of one of the parties compel arbitration when a suit has been brought on a subject within the scope of the agreement, "unless . . . the said agreement is null and void, inoperative or incapable of being performed." The European Convention applies to arbitration agreements concluded with the purpose of settling international trade disputes between persons who reside in different Contracting States. The arbitration agreement may take any form authorized by law, such as an arbitration clause in a contract, or an agreement contained in an exchange of letters, telegrams, or in a communication by teleprinter. The European Convention provides at § 3, Article VI for stay of suit in favor of arbitration.

See also: Arb. agreement; Convention on the Recognition and Enforcement of Foreign Arbitral Awards; Enforcement of foreign arbitral awards; European Convention on Int'l. Com'l. Arb.; Future disputes clause; Inter-association com'l. arb. agreements; Int'l. com'l. arb.; Protocol on Arb. Clauses; Stay of suit; U.N. Economic Comm'n. for Europe; U.S. Treaties of Friendship, Commerce and Navigation.

Sources: Convention on the Recognition and Enforcement of Foreign Arbitral Awards, U.N. Doc. E/CONF.26/8/Rev. 1 (1958); European Convention on Int'l. Com'l. Arb., art. 6, U.N. Doc. E/ECE/423 & E/ECE/TRADE/48 (done at Geneva on 21 April 1961); M. DOMKE, *supra* Adhesion contract; 28 LAWYERS' LETTERS (1966), *supra* Adjournment of hearings at 1-2.

ENFORCEMENT OF ARBITRATION AGREEMENTS (STATE STATUTES)

Agreements to arbitrate can be enforced and made binding under those arbitration statutes which contain provisions for such enforcement.

There are 47 state arbitration statutes in the United States concerned with commercial agreements to arbitrate. The extent to which these agreements are enforceable differs widely. In overruling the common law, many statutes distinguish between agreements to submit pending disputes to arbitration, and agreements to arbitrate unknown future disputes. Almost all states may enforce submission agreements of existing disputes, subject to certain exclusions and conditions. It is permissible in most states to include future dispute clauses in a contract. Provision for their enforcement is not universal. Modern statutes uniformly provide for such enforcement. A modern statute such as the New York State CPLR § 7501 states as follows: "A written agreement to submit any controversy thereafter arising or any existing controversy to arbitration is enforceable without regard to the justiciable character of the controversy and confers jurisdiction on the courts of the state to enforce it and to enter judgment on an award. . . ." The court may compel arbitration when a party applies for such an order. If the application is granted, it may also include a stay of a pending suit on issues in the case which are subject to arbitration.

See also: Arb. agreement; Common law arb.; Enforcement of arb. agreements (Common law); Enforcement of arb. agreements (Int'l. com'l. arb.); Evasion of arb.; Future disputes clause; Injunction; Irrevocability of the arb. agreement; Modern arb. statute; Motion to compel arb.; Rule of court clause; Stay of suit; Submission agreement.

Sources: M. DOMKE, *supra* Adhesion contract at 164-171; Aksen, *supra* Construction Industry Arb. Rules at 141-161.

ENFORCEMENT OF AWARD

See: Appeal; Award; Challenge of an award; Confirming the award; Enforcement of award (Int'l. pub. arb.); Enforcement of award (Labor); Enforcement of foreign arbitral awards; Modifying the award; Vacating an award.

ENFORCEMENT OF AWARD (INTERNATIONAL PUBLIC ARBITRATION)

Formal enforcement procedures in cases of non-compliance with an award are provided for in those arbitrations which take place under such international conventions as the Convention on the Settlement of Investment Disputes between States and Nationals of Other States or the Convention on International Civil Aviation.

The one convention provides for annulment, and the other offers sanctioning mechanisms to be used as a means of enforcement, initiated by the winning party in case of non-compliance with a valid award. The enforcement of non-institutional or *ad hoc* international arbitrations generally depends upon the efforts of the winning party. There is a variety of self-help measures which may be taken though not all have received universal acceptance by the international community. The State seeking enforcement may have recourse to traditional diplomatic negotiation which may be reinforced by economic pressures as in the *Lena Goldfields Arbitration*, where the British Government brought pressure on the Soviet Union by linking discussions of a trade agreement with payment of the *Lena* award. Occasionally property belonging to the debtor State may be attached.

See also: Abu Dhabi Arb.; Chamizal Arb.; Convention on the Settlement of Investment Disputes between States and Nationals of Other States; Execution; Int'l. Civil Aviation Organization; Lena Goldfields Arb.; Northeastern Boundary Arb.; Pact of Bogotá; Pious Fund Case.

Sources: K. CARLSTON, *supra* Annulment . . . ; E. NANTWI, *supra* Annulment . . . ; Reisman, *The Enforcement of Int'l. Judgments*, 63 AM. J. INT'L. L. 1-27 (1969); Schachter, *supra* Alabama Arb. at 1-24.

ENFORCEMENT OF AWARD (LABOR)

Section 301 of the Taft-Hartley Act authorizes federal courts to rule on suits involving violations of union contracts, and grants the courts the power to enforce awards made under the arbitration clause in union contracts affecting interstate commerce.

In a practical sense, judicial enforcement of awards is rarely invoked, since awards are seldom challenged. Awards are respected in the majority of labor cases because it was the intention of the parties originally to be so bound by the award. A court is not free to substitute its interpretation of the merits of the case when it is asked to enforce an award, unless the submission to arbitration limits the arbitrator's authority in this respect.

See also: Arbitrator's authority; Award; Enterprise Wheel & Car Corp.; Judicial review in arb.; Lincoln Mills; § 301 disputes; Trilogy.

Sources: United Steelworkers v. American Mfg. Co., 363 U.S. 564 (1960); United Steelworkers v. Enterprise Wheel, 363 U.S. 593 (1960).

ENFORCEMENT OF COLLECTIVE BARGAINING AGREEMENT

See: Lincoln Mills; § 301 disputes.

ENFORCEMENT OF FOREIGN ARBITRAL AWARDS

An award made in one State which is to be enforced in another must rely on the courts of that State to aid in its enforcement if the countries concerned have not ratified a convention or treaty providing for such enforcement.

A number of international conventions, such as the Geneva Convention, the Geneva Protocol on Arbitration Clauses, the European Convention on International Commercial Arbitration, and most important, the United Nations Convention on the Recognition and Enforcement of Foreign Arbitral Awards, seek to standardize enforcement in the courts of the Contracting States. In countries where the United Nations Convention has been ratified, the enforcement of an award in an international commercial arbitration is virtually assured, if the necessary procedures have been followed. Article III of the U.N. Convention provides as follows: "Each Contracting State shall recognize arbitral awards as binding and enforce them in accordance with the rules of procedure of the territory where the award is relied upon. . . ." The party seeking enforcement of the award need only produce the award or a certified copy of it, as well as the agreement to arbitrate, in the appropriate court in the country where enforcement is being sought. Procedures for challenging the award are set forth in Article V § 1 of the Convention. Grounds for such a challenge may include the absence of a valid arbitration agreement, the failure to give the losing party a fair opportunity to present his case, the rendering of an award outside the terms of the agreement, any improper arbitral procedure such as the appointment of the arbitrators, or the inconclusive nature of the final award.

See also: Award; Convention on the Execution of Foreign Arbitral Awards; Convention on the Recognition and Enforcement of Foreign Arbitral Awards; Enforcement of arb. agreements (Int'l. com'l. arb.); European Convention on Int'l. Com'l. Arb.; Exequatur; Foreign arbitral award; Int'l. com'l. arb.; Montevideo Treaty; Protocol on Arb. Clauses; U.N. Conf. on Int'l. Com'l. Arb.; U.S. Treaties of Friendship, Commerce and Navigation.

Sources: Domke, *supra* Convention on the Recognition and Enforcement of Foreign Arbitral Awards at 414.

ENTERPRISE WHEEL & CAR CORP.

[*United Steelworkers of America* v. *Enterprise Wheel & Car Corp.*, 363 U.S. 593 (1960)]

The third in a series of three United States Supreme Court landmark decisions known as the 1960 Trilogy in which the Court refused to review the merits of the award.

The Supreme Court limited itself to determining whether or not the arbitrator exceeded his jurisdiction in making his award. The award involved workers who were discharged in violation of the collective bargaining agreement during the term of the contract. The contract had expired and the employer's operations continued without its renewal. The arbitrator rejected the contention that expiration of the contract barred reinstatement. He then ordered reinstatement with back pay, minus pay for a 10-day suspension, and such sums as the employees might have received from other employment. The company attacked the award on the grounds that the arbitrator exceeded his authority. The majority decision of the Court was that ". . . the question of interpretation of the collective bargaining agreement is a question for the arbitrator. It is the arbitrator's construction which was bargained for; and so far as the arbitrator's decision concerns construction of the contract, the courts have no business overruling him because their interpretation of the contract is different from his." The Court ordered modification so that the amounts due to the employees could be determined by arbitration, but refused to rule on the reinstatement and accrual of back pay beyond the expiration date of the agreement, holding that ". . . mere ambiguity in the opinion . . . is not a reason for refusing to enforce the award. Arbitrators have no obligation to the court to give their reasons for an award. To require opinions free of ambiguity may lead arbitrators to play it safe by writing no supporting opinions. . . ."

See also: American Manufacturing Co.; Arbitrator's authority; Back pay awards; Enforcement of award (Labor); Exces de pouvoir; Opinion; Reinstatement; Testimony of arbitrator; Trilogy; Warrior & Gulf Nav. Co.

Sources: United Steelworkers v. Enterprise Wheel & Car Corp., 363 U.S. 593 (1960); Aaron, *Arb. in the Federal Courts*, 9 UCLA L. REV. 361 (1962); Smith & Jones, *supra* Arbitrability.

ENTRY INTO FORCE

The date and the method by which a treaty shall become enforceable.

A treaty enters into force in such a manner and upon such a date as may be provided in the treaty itself, or as the negotiating States may agree. Failing any such provision or agreement, a treaty enters into force as soon as consent to be bound by the treaty has been established for all the States concerned. Most treaties provide for ratification and entry into force. The following provision is more or less standard: "This treaty shall enter into force as soon as the instruments of ratification have been exchanged. It shall remain in force for five years from the date of its entry into force, and it shall thereafter remain in force for successive periods of five years, unless denounced by either Contracting Party by notice given in writing to the other at least six months before the expiration of any five-year period."

See also: Treaty.

Sources: Treaty for Conciliation, Judicial Settlement and Arb. between the United Kingdom of Great Britain and Northern Ireland and the Swiss Confederation, Gt. Brit. T.S. No. 42 (1967); Fitzmaurice, *(First) Report on the Law of Treaties*, [1956] 2 Y.B. INT'L. L. COMM'N. 104-129, U.N. Doc. A/CN.4/101 (1956).

ENTRY-OF-JUDGMENT CLAUSE

A provision in an arbitration agreement which states that the award may be entered in any court having jurisdiction in order to ensure its enforcement.

Standard arbitration clauses recommended by agencies administering commercial arbitration provide that ". . . judgment upon the award rendered by the Arbitrator(s) may be entered in any Court having jurisdiction thereof." A judgment entered on an arbitration award has the same force and effect as a judgment entered in a court action. Judgment cannot be entered unless the award complies with statutory arbitration requirements, nor will judgment be entered in those states where the common law rules, unless the award is in accord with the precepts of common law.

See also: Confirming the award; Judgment; Judgment-roll; Rule of court clause; Standard arb. clause.

Sources: AAA COM'L ARB. RULES, *supra* Adm. appointment at 2; 5 AM. JUR., *supra* Death of the arbitrator at 637-638; ASS'N. OF THE BAR OF THE CITY OF N. Y., *supra* Award by confession; M. DOMKE, *supra* Adhesion contract at 48.

EQUITY (IN ARBITRATION) (EQUAL OR APPLYING TO ALL)

The state of equality and fairness in dealing, within the precincts of the law.

In international law, equity is generally used in the sense of tempering the application of strict rules of law in order to avoid injustice or hardship in a particular case, so that law itself includes equity. The arbitrator needs no special mandate to apply equity as used in this sense, as it is part of his general obligation to apply law. Equity may also be used in contradistinction to law, as in the determination of the issue *ex aequo et bono*. In such a case, equity represents conformity not to law, but to a different value system. An arbitrator in international public or private cases usually applies equity in this sense, or *ex aequo et bono*, only by special authorization to do so from the parties concerned.

See also: Ex aequo et bono; General principles of law recognized by civilized nations; Jay's Treaty; Trail Smelter Arb.

Sources: M. HUDSON, *supra* Convention on the Pacific Settlement of Int'l. Disputes; C. JENKS, *supra* Calvo Clause; Mezger, *supra* Amiable compositeur at 184; Sohn, *Arb. of Int'l. Disputes Ex Aequo et Bono*, in INT'L. ARB. LIBER AMICORUM FOR MARTIN DOMKE 330 (P. Sanders ed. 1967).

ERASMUS, DESIDERIUS [1466(?)-1536]

Dutch scholar who advocated and spoke out for arbitration and world peace.

In his *Adagia*, under the caption "dulce bellum inexpertis," he said, "The world has so many grave and learned bishops, so many venerable abbots, so many grey-haired grandees wise by long experience, so many councils, so many senates instituted not in vain by our ancestors. Why should not the childish quarrels of princes be settled through the arbitration of these learned men?"

Sources: D. ERASMUS, ADAGIA, Chil. IV, Centur, I, Prov. I, as cited in Fraser, *supra* Crucé, Eméric at 180.

ERDMAN ACT (Pub. L. No. 115, 1898)

A federal act which established arbitration procedures for the railroad industry, replacing the earlier arbitration Act of 1888.

The Erdman Act provided that the Chairman of the Interstate Commerce Commission and the Commissioner of Labor would mediate and conciliate in case of a controversy. If their efforts failed, the dispute could be submitted to a board of arbitration consisting of three persons, one to be chosen by the employer, one by the union, and the third to be chosen by both. In its early years, this law was weakened by the power of the carriers, but as the railroad unions grew stronger sixty-one disputes were subsequently settled in the period from 1906 to 1913. Twenty-eight of these were resolved by mediation, four by arbitration, eight by a combination of mediation and arbitration, and twenty-one by outside agreement. The Erdman Act was replaced in 1913 by the Newlands Act.

See also: Adamson Act; Arb. Act of 1888; Nat'l. Mediation Board; Nat'l. Railroad Adjustment Board; Newlands Act; Railroad Arb. Act; Railway Labor Act; Transportation Act.

Sources: G. EGGERT, RAILROAD LABOR DISPUTES (1967); COMPILATION OF LAWS RELATING TO . . . ARBITRATION . . . BETWEEN EMPLOYERS AND EMPLOYEES 4-8 (Washington, GPO, 1967).

ESPOUSAL

The support of a case by a State on behalf of one of its nationals in his claim against a foreign country.

The Government of the United States may or may not decide to espouse the claim of one of its citizens. Such discretion is vested in the President, and exercised on his behalf by the Secretary of State. The President may waive or settle a claim against a foreign State without the consent of the national involved. Before espousing a claim, governments usually require that their citizens first exhaust all local remedies.

See also: Exhaustion of local remedies; Int'l. claims; Int'l. pub. arb.; Joint claims comm'n.; Lake Ontario Claims Tribunal; Lump sum settlement; Mixed arbitral tribunal; Mixed claims comm'n; Pious Fund Case; Trail Smelter Arb.

Sources: 8 M. WHITEMAN, *supra* Calvo Clause at 769-807 (1967).

EUROPEAN CONVENTION FOR THE PEACEFUL SETTLEMENT OF DISPUTES (COUNCIL OF EUROPE) (April 29, 1957)

A draft convention for the settlement of international controversies prepared on the recommendation of the Consultative Assembly of the Council of Europe of 1950.

The European Convention for the Peaceful Settlement of Disputes provides for three types of resolution: judicial, conciliatory, and arbitral. The provisions for arbitration are described in Chapter III of the Convention. The Arbitral Tribunal shall consist of five members, the parties each nominating one. The other three arbitrators are to be chosen by agreement from among the nationals of third States, and are to be of different nationalities, and not resident in the territory of either of the parties. Article 26 provides that if the parties in a special agreement have made no other rules, the Tribunal shall decide *ex aequo et bono*, with due regard given to the general principles of international law and the contractual obligations binding on the parties. Failure to comply with a judgment of the International Court of Justice or an Arbitral Tribunal may be appealed to the Committee of Ministers of the Council of Europe, which may then, by a two-thirds majority of the representatives, make recommendations to ensure compliance.

See also: Convention; Council of Europe; Enforcement of award (Int'l. pub. arb.); Int'l. pub. arb.

Sources: European Convention for the Peaceful Settlement of Disputes, (Council of Europe, European T. S. 23).

EUROPEAN CONVENTION ON INTERNATIONAL COMMERCIAL ARBITRATION (GENEVA CONVENTION, 1961)

A convention drawn up by the United Nations Economic Commission for Europe which is designed to develop a uniform arbitration procedure to be used in international trade disputes between persons who live in different Contracting States in Eastern and Western Europe.

The European Convention on International Commercial Arbitration was approved at a special meeting of twenty-two nations in Geneva, April 10-21, 1961. Unlike the New York Convention which limited itself to the problems of the recognition and enforcement of awards, the European Convention considers procedural matters, particularly those which the parties might omit to specify clearly in the agreement. These are such procedural matters as the place of the arbitration, the methods of appointing arbitrators, and the applicable law. Special emphasis is placed on problems of East-West trade. The basic intention of the Convention is to allow the parties to govern as much of the arbitration procedure as possible, with certain built-in guarantees against possible delays. Provisions may be found in Article IV, and in the Annex to the Convention, for a special committee to ensure impartial decisions between the interests of the East and West where the parties cannot agree on established procedures. The Convention entered into force January 7, 1964. Fourteen nations had ratified the Convention as of April 9, 1969.

See also: Applicable procedural law; Applicable substantive law. Int'l. com'l. arb.; Convention; Convention on the Recognition and Enforcement of Foreign Arbitral Awards; Enforcement of arb. agreements (Int'l. com'l. arb.); Enforcement of foreign arbitral awards; Int'l. com'l. arb.; Party autonomy; U.N. Economic Comm'n. for Europe; U.N. ECE. Rules of Arb.

Sources: European Convention on Int'l. Com'l. Arb., U.N. Doc. E/ECE/423 & E/ECE/TRADE/48 (done at Geneva on 21 April 1961); Benjamin, *The European Convention on Int'l. Com'l. Arb.*, 37 Brit. Y. B. Int'l. L., 1961 (1962); Cohn, *The Rules of Arb. of the U.N. ECE*, 16 Int'l. & Comp. L. Q. 946-981 (1967); 3 Int'l. Com'l. Arb., *supra* Applicable procedural law at 262-321.

EUROPEAN CONVENTION PROVIDING A UNIFORM LAW ON ARBITRATION (COUNCIL OF EUROPE) (1966)

A convention to establish a uniform code on arbitration by eliminating whatever differences may exist in the laws of 18 separate member nations of the Council of Europe.

A Committee of Experts on Arbitration was appointed by the Council of Europe. The Committee subsequently adopted the Draft Uniform Law on Arbitration prepared by the Rome Institute in 1954 as the preliminary basis of its work. The final draft of the Convention was completed by this Committee of Experts in March 1964. The Convention obligates the contracting parties to incorporate the Uniform Law into their national legislation, subject to certain reservations. It is concerned only with voluntary arbitration between private parties, and applies only to cases concerned with commercial or private law disputes. The Uniform Law on Arbitration deals mainly with the form of the arbitration agreement, the choice of arbitrators, and the arbitration proceedings as well as with the enforcement of the award. The Convention was opened for signature on January 20, 1966.

See also: Council of Europe; Draft Uniform Law on Inter-American Com'l. Arb.; Int'l. com'l. arb.; Int'l. Institute for the Unification of Private Law; Law merchant; Uniform Arb. Act.

Sources: European Convention Providing a Uniform Law on Arbitration (Council of Europe, European T.S. 56, Jan. 20, 1966); INT'L. INSTITUTE FOR THE UNIFICATION OF PRIVATE LAW, DRAFT OF A UNIFORM LAW ON ARB. IN RESPECT OF INT'L. RELATIONS OF PRIVATE LAW AND EXPLANATORY REPORT, U.P.L. 1954–DRAFT III(3); Jenard, *Draft European Convention Providing a Uniform Law on Arbitration,* 3 INT'L. COM'L. ARB. 370-399 (P. Sanders ed. 1965).

EVASION OF ARBITRATION

Delaying tactics used to avoid arbitration by a party to a contract or to a treaty containing an arbitration clause.

The rules of many impartial arbitration agencies are expressly designed to cope with such evasions. Modern arbitration statutes also provide against undue or unnecessary delay. In commenting on Rules 8 and 11, (*Incapacity or Resignation of Arbitrators and Filling Vacancies on the Tribunal*), in its Regulations and Rules, the International Centre for Settlement of Investment Disputes declares as follows: "While no person can be prevented from resigning as arbitrator, the Convention in Article 56(3) (and this Rule in paragraph (2)) requires that if such an arbitrator was appointed by one of the parties the Tribunal must decide whether it 'consents' to the resignation. If the Tribunal fails to do so, the consequence is not that the arbitrator must continue to serve, but rather that his replacement will be appointed by the Chairman of the Administrative Council and not by the party that had made the original appointment (Rule 11(2)(a)). The intention of this provision is to lessen the possibility of a party inducing an arbitrator appointed by it to resign, so as either to enable his replacement by a more tractable person or merely to delay the proceeding."

See also: Convention on the Settlement of Investment Disputes between States and Nationals of Other States; Default; Enforcement of arb. agreements (State statutes); Ex parte arb.; Model rules on arbitral procedure; Stay of suit; U.N. ECE. Rules of Arb.

Sources: N.Y. CPLR § 7503; ICSID, *supra* Appeal boards of adm. agencies at 84.

EVIDENCE

See: Parol evidence rule; Rules of evidence.

EX AEQUO ET BONO (ACCORDING TO WHAT IS JUST AND GOOD)

A power explicitly conferred on arbitrators by the parties in their arbitration agreement or *compromis,* permitting the arbitrator to go outside the bounds of law in order to reach a decision based primarily on concepts of fair dealing and good faith.

Parties in international disputes, public or private, must expressly state in the arbitration agreement that the arbitrator is authorized to decide *ex aequo et bono.* International legal authorities differ as to the definition of the term *ex aequo et bono.* Though generally used to describe a decision based on equity rather than on literal law, it is a decision still guided by general principles and standards accepted by a majority of nations. A few international cases were so determined in the 19th and early 20th Centuries. An example of such a case was *The Death of James Pugh Arbitration* of July 6, 1933, between Great Britain and Panama, in which the arbitrator was required by the *compromis* to decide *ex aequo et bono* as to whether the Panamanian police had used excessive force in the arrest of the seaman James Pugh, who was said to have been intoxicated. The arbitrator was to try to decide in all fairness whether: "(A)s a result of such excess did the death of said James Pugh occur? In the event that such excess did exist, . . . is there certainty that the acts of the agents . . . were malicious . . . and should the Panamanian Government . . . pay . . . an indemnity for such death?" The arbitrator determined that the death had not been due to malicious acts on the part of the Panamanian police, and that the government therefore was not to pay an indemnity. *Ex aequo et bono* may have legislative rather than judicial implications. In the *Fur Seal Arbitration* between Great Britain and the United States, the Tribunal was to determine *ex aequo et bono,* or according to "natural law" as the Treaty described it, on the legal responsibility of both parties for the conservation of animals in their wild state, a determination which had never been made before. *Ex aequo et bono* does not govern commercial arbitration in the United States, although arbitrators sometimes resolve disputes on the basis of absolute equity rather than strictly according to law. In Italian law an arbitrator not confined to the rule of law is known as a "free arbitrator," or "arbitrato libero."

See also: Amiable compositeur; Applicable law. Int'l. pub. arb.; Applicable substantive law. Int'l. com'l. arb.; Equity; Expert arbitrator; General principles of law recognized by civilized nations; Int'l. Court of Justice Statute. Art. 38.

Sources: Fur Seal lArb., in 1 J. MOORE, INT'L. ARBITRATIONS 922-929 (1898); In the Matter of the Death of James Pugh, 3 U.N.R.I.A.A. 1441-1453 (1933); *The North Atlantic Coast Fisheries Case,* in THE HAGUE COURT REPORTS 174-176 (J. Scott ed. 1916); C. JENKS, *supra* Calvo Clause at 316ff; J. SIMPSON & H. FOX, *supra* Appointment of arbitrators; W. WENGER, ZUM OBLIGATIONENRECHTLICHEN SCHIEDSVERFAHREN IM SCHWEIZERISCHEN RECHT (1968); Scheuner, *Decisions ex aequo et bono by Int'l. . . . and Arbitral Tribunals,* in INT'L. ARB.

LIBER AMICORUM FOR MARTIN DOMKE 275-288 (P. Sanders ed. 1967); Sohn, *supra* Equity at 330.

EXAMINATION BEFORE TRIAL

The examination of witnesses under the supervision of a court before the actual arbitration begins.

Most courts consider this procedure to be incompatible with the nature of the arbitration proceeding. Other judicial bodies would make such examination available if it is provided for by the parties in their agreement.

See also: Deposition; Discovery of documents; Prehearing conference; Provisional remedies.

Sources: AAA COM'L. ARB. RULES, *supra* Adm. appointment at § 46; 1 LAWYERS' LETTERS (1960), *supra* Adjournment of hearings at 2-3.

EXCES DE POUVOIR (EXCESS OF POWER)

The validity of an award may be challenged when the arbitrators exceed the jurisdiction conferred on them by the arbitration agreement or *compromis*.

In international public arbitration, the question of excess of power or jurisdiction is a question of treaty interpretation. The award must be carefully compared with the relevant provisions of the *compromis* which is the submission the two powers have made of their dispute, and which is therefore the governing document in the arbitration. A charge that the tribunal has departed from the terms of the submission, or that it has exceeded its jurisdiction, should be clear and substantial. Article XXXV of the Model Rules on Arbitral Procedure drafted by the International Law Commission cites the following grounds for challenging the validity of an award: "That the tribunal has exceeded its powers; that there was corruption on the part of a member of the tribunal; that there has been a failure to state the reasons for the award or a serious departure from a fundamental rule of procedure. . . ."

See also: Annulment . . . ; Arbitrator's authority; Enterprise Wheel & Car Corp.; Grounds of nullity; Model rules on arbitral procedure; Northeastern boundary arb.; Vacating an award.

Sources: Model Rules, *supra* Appointment of arbitrators at art. 35; U.N. ILC, *supra* Annulment . . . at 108.

EXCLUSIONARY CLAUSE

A clause in the collective bargaining agreement which specifies that certain subjects, such as subcontracting, be excluded from the arbitration process.

Examples of such exclusion may also be found in a management rights clause, as well as in a general arbitration clause.

See also: Collective bargaining agreement; Management rights; Residual rights.

Sources: Smith & Jones, *The Supreme Court, supra* Arbitrability.

EXECUTION

A synonym for the term enforcement as used in international public arbitration.

See also: Enforcement of award (Int'l. pub. arb.).

EXECUTION OF AWARD

The signing and delivery of the award by the arbitrators with whatever formalities required by law.

Execution of award is the method by which the arbitrator or arbitrators make known their decision in an arbitration. Statutes differ in their requirements on an arbitrator's signature. Under some jurisdictions, the signature must be attested to by witnesses according to prescribed rules or statutes. The New York CPLR 7507 requires the signature on the award of "the arbitrator making it." The United States Arbitration Act does not contain provision on this point. In international arbitration, execution is frequently used as a synonym for enforcement.

See also: Delivery of award; Procedure; Signature on award.

Sources: M. Domke, *supra* Adhesion contract at 285-286.

EXECUTIVE ORDER 10988. EMPLOYEE-MANAGEMENT COOPERATION IN THE FEDERAL SERVICE (January 17, 1962)

An order by President John F. Kennedy which established a program of employee-management cooperation in the United States federal civil service with a clear-cut policy on the right of employees to organize.

Executive Order 10988 covers all federal employees, except those in the investigative, intelligence, or security divisions. Employees are granted the right to join or not to join any labor organization. Management's rights are extensive and include a prohibition against employees' striking. The Order also leaves room for the possibility of advisory rather than binding arbitration. Executive Order 10988 was replaced by Executive Order 11491 of October 29, 1969, "Labor-Management Relations in the Federal Service." EO 11491 became effective January 1, 1970. The new document is expected to strengthen the federal labor relations system by equating it with practices in the private sector.

See also: Advisory arb.; Mediation; President's Task Force on Employee-Management Relations in the Federal Service; Public employee.

Sources: Employee-Management Cooperation in the Federal Service, E.O. No.

10988, § 6b, 27 F.R. 551, 3 C.F.R. 521, 523-4 (1959-1963 compilation 1962); W. VOSLOO, COLLECTIVE BARGAINING IN THE U.S. FEDERAL CIVIL SERVICE (1966); Abner, *FMCS Increasing Mediation Efforts in Public Sector Disputes*, GERR A-1 (No. 265, 1968).

EXEQUATUR

A Latin phrase, *let it be executed.*

Exequatur is an order used in certain European countries for enforcing and validating arbitration awards. Without this stamp by the judicial authority, the award would not be legally in effect.

See also: Binding character of award; Enforcement of foreign arbitral awards.

Sources: Schachter, *supra* Alabama Claims Arb.

EXHAUSTION OF LOCAL REMEDIES

A rule of international law that a corporation or a person residing in a foreign country must first exhaust all legal means unto the court of last resort in that country where he temporarily resides before seeking the assistance of his own government.

Exhaustion of local remedies is covered by the municipal law of the host country. Most alien complaints are settled on this level. The parties to a dispute may agree in their contract that they need not exhaust local remedies before arbitrating. Article 26 of the Convention on the Settlement of Investment Disputes between States and Nationals of Other States declares: "Consent of the parties to arbitration under this Convention shall, unless otherwise stated, be deemed consent to such arbitration to the exclusion of any other remedy. A Contracting State may require the exhaustion of local administrative or judicial remedies as a condition of its consent to arbitration under this Convention." Article 19 of the 1961 Harvard Draft Convention on International Responsibility* provides that local remedies shall be considered as exhausted if the claimant has used all administrative, arbitral, or judicial remedies which were made available to him in the State against which he is making the claim.

See also: Calvo Clause; Convention on the Settlement of Investment Disputes between States and Nationals of Other States; Draft Convention to Improve the Climate for Investment in Latin America by Facilitating the Settlement of Disputes; Int'l. claims; Mixed arbitral tribunals; Mixed claims comm'n.

Sources: The Ambatielos Claim, 12 U.N.R.I.A.A. 87-153 (1956); Convention on the Settlement of Investment Disputes between States and Nationals of Other States (submitted by I.B.R.D., March 18, 1965); J. SIMPSON & H. FOX, *supra* Appointment of arbitrators; *M. WHITEMAN, *supra* Calvo Clause at 777-778; Schwebel & Wetter, *Arb. and the Exhaustion of Local Remedies*, 60 AM. J. INT'L. L. 484 (1966).

EX PARTE ARBITRATION (ON ONE SIDE ONLY)

An arbitration in which a party does not participate because he is unwilling to submit to arbitration.

Most administrative agency rules allow for *ex parte* proceedings. Various state arbitration statues, and § 4 of the United States Arbitration Act, provide that when one party fails to participate in an arbitration, the other party may petition the court to order arbitration to proceed. Use of such a procedure is not required under agency rules, if some act of the resisting party, such as agreeing on the selection of an arbitrator, is not essential to complete the arbitral machinery. The American Arbitration Association Commercial Arbitration Rules at § 29 may be considered a fairly standard procedure. This section reads as follows: "Unless the law provides to the contrary, the arbitration may proceed in the absence of any party, who, after due notice, fails to be present or fails to obtain an adjournment. An award shall not be made solely on the default of a party. The Arbitrator shall require the party who is present to submit such evidence as he may require for the making of an award."

See also: Default; Evasion of arb.; Participation in arb.

Sources: N. Y. CPLR § 7503(a); AAA Com'l. Arb. Rules, *supra* Adm. appointment at § 29; AAA Voluntary Lab. Arb. Rules, *supra* Affidavit at § 27; Bradford Chamber of Commerce, Arb. Rules § 5 (Rev. ed. 1962); 1 Lawyers' Letters (1960), *supra* Adjournment of hearings at 1-2; 8 *id*. (1961) at 2-4.

EXPERT ARBITRATOR

An arbitrator selected by the parties because he has a special and professional knowledge of the subject under dispute.

Trade associations and other administrative agencies maintain panels of arbitrators who are experts in specific trades and industries.

See also: Amiable compositeur; Ex aequo et bono; Institutional arb.

EXPERT WITNESS

A person with special skill or experience in a trade, or professional knowledge of a specific subject.

See also: Delegation of arbitrator's authority.

FACT-FINDING

An investigation of a dispute by a public or private body which examines the issues and facts in a case, and as a result, may or may not recommend settlement procedures.

Fact-finding panels usually consist of three or five impartial members. Such boards may be appointed by state or local officials, or by the United

Nations, or by the President of the United States when the parties have reached an impasse in negotiations. Private industries such as the steel, longshore, and meat packing industries have established tripartite study committees to find facts and improve collective bargaining. In the federal government, there are two types of fact-finding boards provided by law. The first, under the Railway Labor Act, has the authority specifically to make recommendations. The second, under the Taft-Hartley Act, has no such power. Provisions for fact-finding were established under the New York State Taylor Law. Under this statute, fact-finding is "a formal proceeding which is conducted by an appointed fact-finder or panel of not more than three fact-finders, that sit in the joint presence of both parties and to whom facts are presented to support each party's position. These facts are weighed by the fact-finder(s) with a view to issuing subsequent recommendations."* Strikes and lock-outs are usually forbidden when such fact-finding boards are in session, and the status quo is maintained for a specified time after the report has been made. The strength of fact-finding as a dispute settlement procedure lies in the publicity given to the facts at issue, and the consequent appeal to public opinion.

See also: Arsenal of weapons; Atomic Energy Labor-Management Relations Panel; Emergency boards; Good offices; Impasse; Int'l. comm'n. of inquiry; Mediation; Nat'l. Defense Mediation Board; Nat'l. Mediation Board; Office of Collective Bargaining; Public Employment Relations Board; Railway Labor Act; Taft-Hartley Act; Taylor Law.

Sources: *N.Y. (State) Public Employment Relations Board, Guide for Fact-Finders, October 23, 1968; Cole, *Discussion—Neutral Consultants in Collective Bargaining*, in 15 PROC. OF THE NAT'L. ACADEMY OF ARBITRATORS 97 (1962); Hildebrand, *The Use of Neutrals in Collective Bargaining*, in 14 PROC. OF THE NAT'L. ACADEMY OF ARBITRATORS 141-147 (1961); McKelvey, *Fact finding in public employment disputes*. 22 IND. AND LAB. REL. REV. 528-543 (1969).

FEDERAL ARBITRATION ACT

See: United States Arbitration Act.

FEDERAL MEDIATION AND CONCILIATION SERVICE (FMCS)

A service established as an independent agency of the Federal Government under Title II of the Labor Management Relations Act, 1947, to mediate and conciliate labor disputes in any industry affecting commerce other than those occurring in the railroad and air transportation industries.

The United States Conciliation Service had operated since 1913 as a function of the Office of the Secretary of Labor. One of the major responsibilities imposed on the Service by the Labor Management Relations Act of 1947 was the prevention of labor-management disputes. In an effort to follow this concept of prevention, the Service has sought to provide labor and management assistance in the form of preventative mediation on a year round voluntary basis. The Service also makes available full and adequate governmental facilities for conciliation, mediation, and voluntary arbitration. These functions are in accordance with its own published arbitration regulations, or with those procedures specified in the labor agreements of the parties. The Director of FMCS is appointed by the President with the advice and consent of the Senate.

See also: Adm. agency; Appointing agency; Atomic Energy Labor-Management Relations Panel; Code of ethics and procedural standards for labor-management arb.; Conciliation; Mediation; Missile Sites Labor Comm'n.; Nat'l. Labor-Management Panel; Preventive mediation; Selection of arbitrators (FMCS); Taft-Hartley Act.

Sources: Labor Management Relations Act, 29 U.S.C.A. §§ 141-197; 1 FMCS ANN. REP. (1948); 21 id. (1968).

FEES

See: Attorney's fees; Compensation of the arbitrator.

FIBREBOARD PAPER PRODUCTS CORP.
[Fibreboard Paper Products Corp. v. NLRB, 379, U.S. 203 (1964)]

The leading United States Supreme Court decision on subcontracting.

The Fibreboard Paper Products Corp. contracted out its maintenance work without prior notice or consultation with the union. The result was the replacement of the maintenance staff by employees of a subcontractor. The National Labor Relations Board ruled that failure to bargain the subcontracting issue with the union was an unfair labor practice, and directed the employer to reinstate the displaced workers. The decision was upheld by the United States Supreme Court without clearly indicating the full range of its application. The Court declared that the company merely replaced existing bargaining unit employees with those of an independent contractor to do the same work in order to cut the high cost of maintenance work. It held therefore that the employer's freedom to manage his business is not significantly disturbed by requiring him to give the union an opportunity to bargain on the subcontracting issue, when there is a likelihood that employees in the bargaining unit will be laid off. Disputed subcontracting rights, which are included in the collective bargaining agreement, may be subject to the jurisdiction of the arbitrator.

See also: Management rights; Subcontracting; Recognition clause.

Sources: Fibreboard Paper Products Corp. v. NLRB, 379 U.S. 203 (1964); F. YOUNG, THE CONTRACTING OUT OF WORK 23-24 (1964); Dunau, Subcontracting and Unilateral Employer Action, in 18 N.Y. UNIVERSITY, PROC. OF THE ANNUAL CONF. ON LABOR 219-234 (1966).

FINALITY OF AWARD

The principle that an award is final and binding upon the parties concerned, subject to being vacated on statutory or common law grounds.

Finality is a clear and essential requirement for an arbitral award. All issues raised or counterclaims made by either party must be disposed of in the award. Any failure to resolve such issues may endanger the validity of an award. To ensure the absolute finality of the award, it should contain a separate finding on each item, if at all possible.

See also: Binding character of award; Counterclaim; Full settlement clause.

Sources: 3 LAWYERS' LETTERS (1960), *supra* Adjournment of hearings.

FMCS

See: Federal Mediation and Conciliation Service.

FORCED COMPROMIS

See: Obligatory compromis.

FORD–UAW IMPARTIAL UMPIRE SYSTEM

A permanent umpire procedure established in 1943 by the Ford Motor Company and the United Automobile Workers.

The collective bargaining agreement between the parties established joint review boards from which appeals could be made to the Impartial Umpire. There have been three umpires since 1943. Harry Shulman held that office from 1943 to 1955. He often made use of mediation, and by his informal approach helped the parties resolve a very difficult labor-management relationship. Harry Platt was Impartial Umpire from 1955 to 1967, and during his tenure the office became more truly that of a permanent umpire. James J. Healy was appointed Umpire in January 1968. The decisions are published as *Decisions of the Umpire*, A-1, 1943–.

See also: Chrysler-UAW Impartial Chairman System; General Motors-UAW Impartial Umpire System; Grievance arb. (Rights arb.); Impartial chairman; Precedent; Umpire.

Sources: Ford Motor Co., *supra* Challenge of arbitrator at art. 7; Killingsworth & Wallen, *supra* Board of arb. at 67-68.

FOREIGN ARBITRAL AWARD

An arbitration award which is made in one country and enforced in another.

At the present time there is no universally accepted definition of a foreign arbitral award. Various legal systems depend on such differing criteria as the territorial principle, the nationality of the parties involved, or the nationality of the procedural law used in the arbitration.

See also: Convention on the Recognition and Enforcement of Foreign Arbitral Awards; Enforcement of foreign arbitral awards; U.N. Conf. on Int'l. Com'l. Arb.

Sources: U. S. Dept. of State, *supra* Convention on the Recognition and Enforcement of Foreign Arbitral Awards; P. FOUCHARD, L'ARBITRAGE COM'L. INT'L. (1965); G. HAIGHT, *supra* Convention on the Recognition and Enforcement of Foreign Arbitral Awards; Cohn, *supra* Convention on the Recognition and Enforcement of Foreign Arbitral Awards.

FOREIGN CLAIMS SETTLEMENT COMMISSION OF THE UNITED STATES

An independent agency created in 1954 with jurisdiction to determine claims of United States nationals against foreign governments.

Though the Foreign Claims Settlement Commission is not an arbitration court, it is nevertheless related to the whole aspect of international claims disputes. Its three members are appointed by the President of the United States to serve for 3-year terms. Available funds for settling claims are derived from settlements of international claims, or from the liquidation of foreign assets in the United States.

See also: Int'l. claims; Lake Ontario Claims Tribunal—U.S. and Canada; Lump-sum settlement.

Sources: R. LILLICH, INT'L. CLAIMS: THEIR ADJUDICATION BY NATIONAL COMMISSIONS (1962); U.S. OFFICE OF THE FEDERAL REGISTER, *supra* Bureau of Labor Statistics at 470.

FRAUDULENT INDUCEMENT OF THE CONTRACT

A ground for nullifying the agreement in a case where one party has tried to defraud the other by withholding or falsifying certain facts which were true prior to the drafting and signing of the contract.

The issue of fraud is for the arbitrator to decide, if and when the arbitration clause is broad enough to cover it, and if the separability doctrine applies. If the arbitration clause itself is alleged to have been fraudulently induced, then that becomes an issue which must first be determined by a court.

See also: Breach of contract; Container contract; Prima Paint Corp. . . . ; Scope of the arb. agreement; Separability doctrine.

Sources: Robert Lawrence Co., v. Devonshire Fabrics, Inc., 271 F. 2d 402 (2d Cir. 1959) [cert granted 362 U.S. 909, appeal dismissed per stipulation, 364 U.S. 801 (1960)]; Mosely v. Electronic & Missile Facilities, Inc., 374 U.S. 167 (1963); Prima Paint Corp. v. Flood & Conklin Mfg. Co., 388 U.S. 395, (1967); M. DOMKE, *supra* Adhesion contract at 57-60; 5 LAWYERS' LETTERS (1961), *supra* Adjournment of hearings; 25 *id.* (1966).

FREE ARBITRATOR (ARBITRATO LIBERO)

See: Ex aequo et bono.

FULL SETTLEMENT CLAUSE

A statement in the award to the effect that this "is in full settlement of all claims submitted to arbitration by either party against the other."

The inclusion of the full settlement clause does not mean that the award cannot be challenged. A party may challenge the award by showing that the arbitrator did not actually consider all the claims and counterclaims. The full settlement clause clearly presumes that the arbitrator did fulfill all of his functions and duties. To make certain that the finality of the award cannot be challenged, the award should contain whenever possible a separate finding on each claim or counterclaim.

See also: Counterclaim; Finality of award.

Sources: 3 LAWYERS' LETTERS (1960), *supra* Adjournment of hearings.

FUNCTUS OFFICIO

A task performed.

Any officer who has fulfilled the duties and functions of his office, or whose term of office has expired, becomes *functus officio,* that is, he no longer has official status or authority. The doctrine of *functus officio* as applied to arbitration has meant the termination of an *ad hoc* arbitrator's authority after rendering and delivering his award. Under New York State Civil Practice Law and Rules, after an award has been rendered and delivered, a party may ask the arbitrator to correct it, and the arbitrator is empowered to make corrections if he believes they are warranted. Several statutes provide for resubmission to the original arbitrator if an award has been vacated, but allow the courts discretion on whether to send the case back to the old, or to new arbitrators.

See also: Delivery of award; Interim award; Modifying the award; Rehearing; Reopening of hearings.

Sources: N.Y. CPLR §§ 7509, 7511(c); 15 LAWYERS' LETTERS (1963), *supra* Adjournment of hearings.

FUTURE DISPUTES CLAUSE

A clause in a contract which provides for the arbitration of any dispute which may occur during the life of the contract.

An agreement to submit to arbitration any future dispute occurring under the contract usually includes all questions which might arise during the life of the contract. If specific reference is not made to the rules of an administrative agency, the wording of the clause becomes a matter of importance since the parties must include procedures to be followed in any eventual arbitration to ensure an effective and efficient award. Modern arbitration statutes, including the United States Arbitration Act and § 301 of the Taft-Hartley Act, make such a future disputes clause specifically enforceable by court order, and prohibit court suit of any claim related to the arbitration agreement. Under some of the older statutes, as well as at common law, future disputes clauses are not enforceable when a party refuses to abide by the agreement.

See also: Arb. agreement; Consent of the parties; Enforcement of arb. agreements (Int'l. com'l. arb.); Enforcement of arb. agreements (State statutes); Institutional arb.; Int'l. Chamber of Commerce. Arb. clause; London Court of Arbitration. Arb. clause; Modern arb. statute; Standard arb. clause; Submission agreement.

Sources: U. S. Arb. Act, 9 U.S.C. § 2 (1954); Labor Management Relations Act, 29 U.S.C.A. §§ 141-197; N.Y. CPLR § 7501; M. DOMKE, supra Adhesion contract at 30-45.

GARMENT INDUSTRY

See: Impartial chairman; Impartial chairman system; Protocol of peace.

GENERAL ARBITRATION COUNCIL OF THE TEXTILE INDUSTRY ARBITRATION RULES

A separate division of the American Arbitration Association, operating under its own rules in administering arbitration disputes in the textile industry.

The General Arbitration Council appoints and maintains an official list of available arbitrators which includes, but is not limited to members of the various divisions of the textile industry represented in the Council.

See also: American Arb. Association; Silk Association of America.

Sources: AAA GENERAL ARB. COUNCIL OF THE TEXTILE INDUSTRY ARB. RULES AS AMENDED AND IN EFFECT Feb. 1, 1968.

GENERAL MOTORS-UAW IMPARTIAL UMPIRE SYSTEM

The office of the Impartial Umpire was established in the General Motors-United Auto Workers collective bargaining agreement of June 24, 1940.

The collective bargaining agreement provided that the permanent arbitrator, to be known as the Umpire, was to be given limited authority, with jurisdiction only over those cases carefully defined in the contract, and relating particularly to disciplinary action, seniority, and job classification. Four uniform steps for all plants were established in the grievance procedure. These four steps were in order: presentation of a grievance to a foreman, a submission of it to the shop committee, an appeal to the corporation and the international union, and finally an appeal to the Impartial Umpire, providing the case is one in which the Umpire has authority to act. The contract limits the functions of the Impartial Umpire. He is appointed to serve for one year, but may remain in office longer if he continues to be acceptable to both parties. The contract states that all cases are to be presented to the Umpire in the form a written brief prepared by each party. He has the option of holding a public hearing, and in practice most cases are presented at a hearing.

See also: Chrysler-UAW Impartial Chairman System; Ford-UAW Impartial Umpire System; Grievance arb.; Impartial chairman; Precedent; Umpire; Umpire system.

Sources: General Motors Corp.-UAW Collective Bargaining Agreement, Effective Jan. 1, 1968; Alexander, *Impartial Umpireships*, in 12 PROC. OF THE NAT'L. ACADEMY OF ARBITRATORS 108-160 (1959); Killingsworth & Wallen, *supra* Board of arb. at 62-65.

GENERAL PRINCIPLES OF LAW RECOGNIZED BY CIVILIZED NATIONS

A primary source of international law other than treaties and customary law.

These general principles as a source of international law have been particularly important in the development of international arbitration. Arbitrators have had frequent recourse to these principles as a basis for their decisions. Such examples can be found in most of the major arbitrations of the last one hundred and fifty years. It has become customary for international oil concession agreements to refer to the general principles of law as one of the applicable laws governing the agreement. Article 38(1)(c) of the Statute of the International Court of Justice provides that the Court shall apply, together with international conventions and custom, "the general principles of law recognized by civilized nations."

See also: Abu Dhabi Arb.; Applicable law. Int'l. pub. arb.; Customary law; Equity; Ex aequo et bono; Int'l. customary law; Int'l. law; Int'l. pub. arb.; Lena Goldfields Arb.; Pacta sunt servanda; Principles of law common to the parties.

Sources: I. C. J. STAT. art. 38(1)(c); B. CHENG, GENERAL PRINCIPLES OF LAW (1953); C. JENKS, THE COMMON LAW OF MANKIND (1958); C. JENKS, *supra* Calvo Clause at 266ff.

GENEVA CONVENTION

See: Convention on the Execution of Foreign Arbitral Awards.

GENEVA CONVENTION OF 1961

See: European Convention on International Commercial Arbitration.

GENEVA PROTOCOL

See: Protocol on Arbitration Clauses.

GOOD OFFICES

A dispute settlement procedure in which a respected third party or a neutral State acting on request or at its own discretion seeks through diplomatic means to persuade the disputing parties to meet and resume direct negotiation.

Good offices is not synonymous with mediation. It is essentially a technique which is confined to the initiation by a disinterested third party of direct negotiations without any further participation by this same third party. The term has been in diplomatic and judicial use for some time, Chief Justice John Marshall of the United States Supreme Court having used the term as far back as 1812. According to the definition of good offices in the Pact of Bogotá, the task of the third party is to bring the parties together, so that they may arrive at a solution themselves.

See also: Conciliation; Fact-finding; Int'l. Comm'n. of Inquiry; Mediation.

Sources: Sucharitkul, *Good Offices as a Peaceful Means of Settling Regional Differences*, in INT'L. ARB. LIBER AMICORUM FOR MARTIN DOMKE 338-339 (P. Sanders ed. 1967).

GOVERNMENT INTERVENTION

The intervention of the President of the United States in a national emergency dispute in an effort to influence its settlement.

The policy of the United States, as stated by the Congress in the Wagner Act and in subsequent legislation, is that the parties must first resort to collective bargaining as a means of settling their dispute. The pressure of public opinion may often induce the President of the United States to intervene in national emergency disputes.

See also: Adamson Act; Arsenal of weapons; Compulsory arb.; Emergency boards; Nat'l. Mediation Board; Railroad Arb. Act; Sanctions; Seizure of plant; Taft-Hartley Act; War Labor Disputes Act.

Sources: U.S. DEPT. OF LABOR, *supra* Arsenal of weapons at 207ff.

GOVERNOR'S TASK FORCE

See: Taylor Committee Report.

GRIEVANCE

A complaint made by an employee, or his union representative, against his employer in the belief that he has been wronged in some area or aspect of his employment.

The grievance may result from some harmful or disciplinary action against the employee by his employer. Any complaint of an employee relating to his job, pay, working conditions, or the way he is treated is generally considered to be a grievance. A grievance may also be a complaint which an employer has against a union or union officials.

See also: Grievance arb.; Grievance arb. clause; Grievance procedure; Grievance procedure—Level of steps.

Sources: U.S. Bureau of Labor Statistics, Bull. No. 1425-1, Major Collective Bargaining Agreements, Grievance Procedures (1964).

GRIEVANCE ARBITRATION CLAUSE

A provision in a contract between a union and a company which makes arbitration the last step in a grievance procedure.

See also: Grievance; Grievance arb.; Grievance procedure; Grievance procedure—Level of steps.

Sources: U.S. BLS, supra lAd hoc arbitrator; U.S. BLS, supra Grievance.

GRIEVANCE ARBITRATION (RIGHTS ARBITRATION)

The final and binding decision of an arbitrator or arbitrators in disputes involving the infringement of employee-employer rights.

Infringements of such rights are known as grievances, and may range from discipline and discharge, to minor violations of the contract, such as coffee breaks or wash-up time. The arbitrator acts as a quasi-judge, and determines the meaning of the contract which the parties have established as the law of their relationship, and clarifies and interprets its terms. He may also decide if the grievance in question is covered by the contract and if the penalties are just. Jurisdiction of the arbitrator is frequently limited to those disputes which involve the interpretation or application of the contract. However, the grievance procedure prior to arbitration may allow consideration of a wider range of disputes. Arbitration in almost all contracts is the last step in the grievance procedure.

See also: Anthracite Coal Strike Comm'n.; Arbitrator's authority; Board of arb.; Chrysler-UAW Impartial Chairman System; Collective bargaining agreement; Ford-UAW Impartial Umpire System; General Motors-UAW Impartial Umpire System; Grievance; Grievance arb. clause; Grievance procedure; Grievance procedure—Level of steps; Impartial chairman system; Interest arb.; Labor arb. (Voluntary); Nat'l. Railroad Adjustment Board; Umpire system.

Sources: U.S. BLS, supra Ad hoc arbitrator, U.S. BLS, supra Grievance.

GRIEVANCE MEDIATION

The mediation by a third party in a dispute before arbitration is invoked.

This is a step sometimes provided in the grievance procedure in an effort to settle the dispute before it reaches arbitration.

See also: Grievance procedure; Mediation.

GRIEVANCE PROCEDURE

The steps established in a contract for the effective handling of complaints made by employees or employers against each other.

The essence of a grievance procedure is to provide a means by which an employee can express a complaint without endangering his job. The procedure should be orderly from the initial presentation of the grievance through varying levels of appeal, with the primary intent of settling the dispute before it reaches the final step of arbitration. The grievance procedures thus permit both management and labor to carry on a form of continuing collective bargaining to solve mutual problems. There is still debate as to whether the grievance procedure, up to and including arbitration, is actually part of the collective bargaining process, or whether it is essentially the administration or adjudication of particular established rights.

See also: Grievance; Grievance arb.; Grievance mediation; Grievant; Office of Collective Bargaining; Open-end grievance procedure; Procedural arbitrability; Republic Steel v. Maddox; Warrior and Gulf Nav. Co.; Wiley v. Livingston.

Sources: F. ELKOURI & E. ELKOURI, *supra* American Arb. Association; U.S. BLS, *supra* Grievance; Kuhn, *The Grievance Process*, in FRONTIERS OF COLLECTIVE BARGAINING (J. Dunlop & N. Chamberlain eds. 1967).

GRIEVANCE PROCEDURE—LEVEL OF STEPS

Grievance machinery usually consists of a series of procedural steps to be taken within specified time limits.

These procedural steps may vary from contract to contract. A grievance may be taken by the aggrieved employee to the foreman, and if no settlement is reached, it may be appealed through successive steps in the management hierarchy. The grievant may be represented by various union officials. Smaller companies tend to have shorter grievance procedures, consisting of three or more steps, usually concluding with arbitration. In larger companies, or in the case of multi-plant contracts, there may be grievance committees with union-management representatives, followed by joint boards, which are in turn followed by permanent umpire systems.

See also: Appeal systems; Grievance arb.; Grievance procedure; Grieve; Joint board; Procedural arbitrability; Wiley v. Livingston.

Sources: U.S. BLS, *supra* Grievance.

GRIEVANT

An employee who registers a complaint against his employer.

Grievant is a term used for the most part only in a union-company relationship where specific machinery has been established for the hearing of such complaints.

See also: Grievance procedure.

GRIEVE (TO GRIEVE)

The invoking of the grievance machinery to correct a wrong which a union member believes he has suffered.

See also: Grievance procedure.

GROTIUS, HUGO (1583-1645)

Dutch scholar who is known as the "father of international law."

In Books 2 and 3 of *De Jure Belli et Pacis,* his famous work, Grotius proved the antiquity, and demonstrated the reasonableness, of international arbitration as a dispute settlement method. "For if," he wrote, "in order to avoid trials by judges who were not of the true religion, both Jews and Christians appointed arbitrators of their own, and it was recommended by St. Paul, how much more ought it to be employed to avoid war, which is far more injurious? . . . And for this reason as well as for others, it would be profitable, nay rather in a certain manner it would be necessary, that there be certain assemblages of the Christian powers, where controversies might be settled by disinterested parties: and that steps even be taken for compelling the disputants to accept peace in accordance with just laws."

Sources: H. GROTIUS, DE JURE BELLI ET PACIS, Lib. II, c. 23, § 8 (2d ed. 1631), as cited in Fraser, *supra* Crucé, Eméric at 182.

GROUNDS OF NULLITY

The basis on which the validity of an arbitration award may be challenged.

Article XXXV of Model Rules on Arbitral Procedure adopted by the International Law Commission defines these grounds as follows: "That the tribunal has exceeded its powers; that there was corruption on the part of a member of the tribunal; that there has been a failure to state the reasons for the award or a serious departure from a fundamental rule of procedure; that the undertaking to arbitrate or the *compromis* is a nullity."

See also: Annulment . . . ; Arbitrator's authority; Bias; Exces de pouvoir; Misconduct of arbitrator; Model Rules on Arbitral Procedure; Repudiation.

Sources: *U.N. ILC, supra* Annulment . . . ; A. BALASKO, *supra* Annulment . . . ; K. CARLSTON, *supra* Annulment . . . .

GUT DAM CLAIMS. UNITED STATES AND CANADA

See: Lake Ontario Claims Tribunal–United States and Canada.

HAGUE. INTERNATIONAL COURT OF JUSTICE

See: International Court of Justice.

HAGUE. PERMANENT COURT OF ARBITRATION

See: Permanent Court of Arbitration.

HAGUE. PERMANENT COURT OF INTERNATIONAL JUSTICE

See: Permanent Court of International Justice.

HANDBOOK OF NATIONAL AND INTERNATIONAL INSTITUTIONS ACTIVE IN THE FIELD OF INTERNATIONAL COMMERCIAL ARBITRATION

See: United Nations Handbook of National and International Institutions Active in the Field of International Commercial Arbitration.

HEARING

The oral presentation of a case in an arbitration.

The basic requirements for a valid hearing at common law and under the arbitration statutes are that the arbitrators be present, that the persons whose rights are affected be given notice of the proceedings, and that the parties are entitled to be heard, to present evidence, and to cross examine witnesses appearing at the hearing. Article 41 of the Rules of the London Court of Arbitration states that: "The arbitration shall be held in private and no person shall be entitled to be present except the parties, their representatives or agents, the witnesses, and the officers of the Court."

See also: Adjournment of hearings; Individual rights; Notice of hearing; Oath of office; Posthearing briefs; Prehearing conference; Privacy of arb.; Procedure; Rules of evidence; Transcript of hearing.

Sources: Uniform Arb. Act; 5 AM. JUR., *supra* Death of the arbitrator at 600; LONDON COURT OF ARB., *supra* Adm. expenses at art. 41.

IACAC

See: Inter-American Commercial Arbitration Commission.

IBRD

See: International Bank for Reconstruction and Development.

ICA ARBITRATION QUARTERLY

See: Indian Council of Arbitration. ICA Arbitration Quarterly.

ICAO

See: International Civil Aviation Organization (ICAO).

ICC

See: International Chamber of Commerce (ICC).

IMPARTIAL CHAIRMAN

A permanent arbitrator who is the only impartial member of an arbitration board established jointly by a union and a company.

An impartial chairman may not necessarily be the chairman of any official board or committee. The decision of the impartial chairman is the final and binding step in the grievance procedure, subject always to the authority granted him by the collective bargaining agreement. Under some agreements, he may arbitrate some or all of the terms of a new contract. He may also take into account the long-term interests of the parties in deciding disciplinary cases. An impartial chairman system was established early in the 20th Century in the men's clothing industry. The duties of the impartial chairman of that period were much broader than those of a later date. Various forms of mediation as well as arbitration were used.

See also: Chrysler-UAW Impartial Chairman System; Ford-UAW Impartial Umpire System; General Motors-UAW Impartial Umpire System; Impartial chairman system; Neutral arbitrator; No-Raiding Agreement (AFL & CIO); Permanent arbitrator; Presiding arbitrator; Protocol of peace; Tripartite board; Umpire.

Sources: Aaron, *Some Procedural Problems in Arb., Symposium on Arb.*, 10 VAND. L. REV. 733-748 (1957); Killingsworth & Wallen, *supra* Board of arb.

IMPARTIAL CHAIRMAN (AD HOC)

A title sometimes used to designate the neutral member of an arbitration board chosen by the mutual consent of the parties to serve in a single case only.

The other members of such an *ad hoc* arbitral tribunal are known as party or partisan arbitrators, each having been chosen by one of the parties. The award is usually rendered by the neutral arbitrator with the concurrence or dissent of the party-appointed arbitrators merely noted. The party-appointed arbitrators may write a separate opinion, though this is seldom done in practice. The use of the title, Impartial Chairman, is not to be confused with the permanent arbitration procedure established in labor arbitration through the Impartial Chairman Systems in the early part of the century.

See also: Ad hoc arbitrator; Arbitrator; Impartial chairman system; Presiding arbitrator; Tripartite board.

IMPARTIAL CHAIRMAN SYSTEM

A historical method for settling disputes in which an impartial chairman selected by a union and an employer would be free to mediate as well as to arbitrate all disputes that occur during the life of a particular contract.

The Impartial Chairman System was one of two successful permanent arbitration procedures to be used in the United States. The Impartial Chairman System came into existence with the appointment of an impartial chairman in Chicago in 1911, by Hart, Schaffner and Marx and the Amalgamated Clothing Workers. Their collective bargaining agreement was brief and was stated in general terms. The scope of arbitration had much latitude, allowing any problem that might arise between management and labor to be submitted to the impartial chairman. The settlements were originally most often mediated. The first impartial chairmen also participated actively in the contract negotiations of the parties. An earlier permanent arbitration procedure was the Umpire System, which began with the award in 1903 made by the Anthracite Coal Strike Commission.

See also: Ad hoc arbitrator; Appointment of arbitrators; Board of arb.; Grievance arb.; Impartial chairman (ad hoc); Interest arb.; Labor arb. (Voluntary); Mediation; Umpire system.

Sources: Killingsworth & Wallen, *supra* Board of arb. at 56-59.

IMPASSE

A deadlock in negotiations.

An impasse in labor relations is reached when collected bargaining has been brought to a standstill, and unresolved issues are still on the bargaining table. A deadlock may be resolved by pressure from strikes, lockouts, or arbitration, depending on the terms of the contract. Mediation or fact-finding panels are often used, particularly in public employee disputes in an attempt to resolve such an impasse.

See also: Arsenal of weapons; Collective bargaining; Fact-finding; Mediation;

Office of Collective Bargaining; Taylor Law.

INDEPENDENT INVESTIGATION BY ARBITRATOR

An investigation of the case which the arbitrator makes without the knowledge or consent of the parties concerned, and which therefore may be declared improper by the courts.

Such an investigation should be made only if the arbitrator receives the permission of the parties. This permission may be obtained by an explicit provision in the agreement itself, or it may be provided during the course of the arbitration. No matter how important arbitrators may feel further tests to be, if any critical examination is made without the knowledge or consent of the parties, the validity of the award might thereby be endangered. However, an arbitrator may sometimes make an independent investigation when it will not seriously affect his final decision, and it is concerned with a minor and obvious detail about which a court is accustomed to take judicial notice.

See also: Arbitrator; Consent of the parties; Delegation of the arbitrator's authority; Judicial notice; Misconduct of arbitrator; Procedure.

Sources: 6 LAWYERS' LETTERS (1961), *supra* Adjournment of hearings at 1.

INDIAN COUNCIL OF ARBITRATION
(Federation House, New Delhi-1, India)

A non-profit organization established in April 1965 by the Government of India.

The main purposes of the Indian Council of Arbitration are to promote and administer the use of commercial arbitration or conciliation as a means of settling international trade disputes. Its membership includes representatives of the Government and of those organizations in India which provide for international commercial arbitration, including the major chambers of commerce. As part of its educational function the Council publishes the *ICA Arbitration Quarterly*, as well as surveys, reports, and various seminar proceedings.

See also: ICA Arb. Quarterly.

Sources: Indian Council or Arb., What It Is and How It Helps, Feb. 1967, at 4-6; 1 INDIAN COUNCIL OF ARB. NEWSLETTER 1-2 (No. 3, 1966); 1 *id.* 1 (No. 4, 1966).

INDIAN COUNCIL OF ARBITRATION. ICA ARBITRATION QUAR-
TERLY. (Journal of the Indian Council of Arbitration)
(Federation House, New Delhi-1, India)

An arbitration quarterly which began publication in India with Volume

II in April 1967, and which informs those interested in foreign trade of important developments in the field of commercial arbitration.

Volume I was printed as a mimeographed *Newsletter*. The *Quarterly* appears in January, April, July, and October of each year. It contains case notes, and notices of seminars and conferences on international commercial arbitration.

See also: Indian Council of Arb.

Sources: *Introduction,* 2 INDIAN COUNCIL ARB. Q. (No. 1, 1967).

INDIFFERENT GENTLEMEN

A phrase occasionally used to describe arbitrators, as early as Tudor England, indifferent meaning gentlemen of strict impartiality understood to be living in the county where the dispute occurred, who would therefore be acquainted with the parties, and able to judge the credibility of the witnesses, and thus ensure the settlement of the dispute without strife or disruption of the peace.

Many of the submissions at that time in England use such phrases as to achieve a "frendly and quyet end."* Occasionally the description of the arbitrators was some "indyferent citizen of London,"* or "gentlemen in the country."*

See also: Arbitrator; Board of nine men; Schoeffen.

Sources: *J. DAWSON, A HISTORY OF LAY JUDGES 168-169 (1960); Jones, *Power and Prudence in the Arb. of Labor Disputes,* 11 UCLA L. REV. 675-790 (1964).

INDIVIDUAL RIGHTS

Those rights which individual employees still retain despite the designation of a union as their exclusive bargaining agent.

An employee may sue his union if he believes it has failed to represent him fairly, but that same employee has no absolute right to have any personal grievance taken to arbitration. Although the union is the representative of all the employees, union interests rest with the majority, and the union must be free to decide what might be very minor grievances. The majority of reported cases in which union members have sought legal protection of their rights were concerned with disciplinary discharges. The Supreme Court of Canada vacated an award in a case in which the employee was not permitted to attend the arbitration and where the union opposed his claim. The Court found that the employee had been denied "natural justice." Employees in Sweden are permitted to bring suit in the Labor Court to protect their individual rights.

See also: Due process; Duty of fair representation; Intervention; Public Review Board (United Auto Workers); Republic Steel v. Maddox; Vaca v. Sipes.

Sources: Hoogendoorn and Greening Metal Products & Greening Equipment

Co. et al. (1968) 65 D.L.R. (2d) 641 (S.C.C.) as cited in Rossman, *Labour Arbitration and Natural Justice*, 26 U. TORONTO FAC. OF L. REV. 1-15 (1968); R. FLEMING, *supra* Arbitrator; Aaron, *Labor Relations Law*, in AMERICAN ASSEMBLY, CHALLENGES TO COLLECTIVE BARGAINING 120-121 (1967); Summers, *supra* Duty of fair representation at 482.

INITIATING THE ARBITRATION PROCEEDINGS

See: Compromis; Demand for arbitration; Notice of intention to arbitrate; Submission agreement.

INJUNCTION

A court order restraining a person or a group of persons from performing an act which the court believes would result in serious injury to the property or other rights of another person or group.

An injunction may also be an order requiring specific actions. Any violation of an injunction is punishable as contempt of court. Injunctions may be used to order a union not to strike, and were effectively so used prior to the passage of the Norris-LaGuardia Act in 1932, which severely limited the powers of federal courts to issue injunctions. A number of states have adopted similar statutes. Injunctions may also be used in national emergency disputes under the Taft-Hartley Act, postponing a strike for a period of up to eighty days. Some labor arbitrators have issued the equivalent of injunctions against slowdowns and strikes. Arbitrators in commercial transactions have been known to order specific performance of a negative obligation which is usually in the form of some type of injunction. Courts may enjoin suits in violation of an agreement to arbitrate under modern arbitration statutes. In New York State, courts may under certain circumstances stay arbitration proceedings. The United States Supreme Court in its decision on *Sinclair Refining Co.* v. *Atkinson* ruled that an employer should not be allowed to enjoy the benefits of the injunction along with the right which Congress had given him in § 301 to sue for breach of a collective bargaining agreement. At the present time, injunctions are most frequently used to halt strikes by public employees.

See also: Arsenal of weapons; Enforcement of the arb. agreements (State statutes); Injunctive relief; Norris-LaGuardia Act; Provisional remedies; Sinclair Refining Co. v. Atkinson; Specific performance; Stay of suit; Taft-Hartley Act.

Sources: N.Y. CPLR § 7503(a)(b); Sinclair Refining Co. v. Atkinson [370 U.S. 195 (1962)]; M. BERNSTEIN, *supra* Appeal at 593, 637, 640; Fleming, *Arbitrators and the Remedy Power*, 48 VA. L. REV. 1199 (1962); 4 LAWYERS' LETTERS (1960), *supra* Adjournment of hearings at 1; Stein, *Remedies in Labor Arb.*, in 13 PROC. OF THE NAT'L. ACADEMY OF ARBITRATORS 47 (1960).

INJUNCTIVE RELIEF

A remedy which an arbitrator may grant in his award, prohibiting a person from continuing a course of action which is considered to be a violation of the contract.

Though injunctive relief is seldom used, some collective agreements may empower an arbitrator to hold an expedited hearing of any claim that the no-strike or no-lockout clause has been violated, and if the claim is found to be valid, he may issue an order enjoining the violation.

See also: Award; Injunction; No-strike clause.

Sources: AAA MANUAL, *supra* Award at 22; Aaron, *The Strike and the Injunction*, *in* 18 N. Y. UNIVERSITY, PROC. OF THE ANNUAL CONFERENCE OF LABOR 93-116 (1966).

INSTITUTE OF ARBITRATORS
(16 Park Crescent, London, W. 1, United Kingdom)

An organization established in 1915 and incorporated in 1925 to supply the business community with commercial arbitrators who are acquainted with the legal aspects of arbitration and skilled in various technical branches of commerce and industry.

The Institute of Arbitrators seeks to advance the interests of arbitration, and to promote its use through simplified rules of procedure for the appointment of arbitrators. The Institute maintains a panel of competent arbitrators for ordinary or highly specialized arbitrations. Although the widest range of professions is represented in the membership of the Institute, there is an especially large number of members connected with architecture and allied professions. The Institute publishes the quarterly *Arbitration, The Journal of the Institute of Arbitrators,* (q.v.) and maintains a library on arbitration as well as standing committees on arbitration law and on education. The Institute sponsors annual lecture series on various aspects of arbitration, and conducts training sessions for arbitrators. Courses at universities are also developed in a concerted effort to interest students in arbitration.

See also: Arb. The Journal of the Institute of Arbitrators.

Sources: Addison, *President's Inaugural Address*, 34 ARB. J. INST. OF ARBITRATORS 234-237 (1968).

INSTITUTIONAL ARBITRATION

Arbitration conducted under the rules of a permanent and impartial agency, either national or international, such as the American Arbitration Association or the International Chamber of Commerce.

Institutional arbitration is administered by many business organizations, chambers of commerce, commodity exchanges, trade associations, and inter-governmental agencies throughout the world. Access to the arbitration tribunal may or may not be restricted to the members of the institution, depending on its rules. Such agencies provide facilities for arbitration, including arbitrators or lists from which the parties may select arbitrators, as well as administrative personnel, and rules of procedure. These services help to ensure that the arbitration will be conducted under strict procedural rules. Any explicit reference in an arbitration clause to the rules of a specific administrative agency is one preferred method of incorporating those rules as part of the agreement.

See also: Access to the arbitral tribunal; Adm. agency; American Arb. Association; Appeal boards of adm. agencies; Associazione Italiana . . . ; Central Office for Int'l. Railway Transport; Com'l. arb.; Customary law; Expert arbitrator; Future disputes clause; Inter-association com'l. arb. agreements; Int'l. Centre for Settlement of Investment Disputes; Int'l. Chamber of Commerce; Int'l. com'l. arb.; Int'l. pub. arb.; Int'l. Wool Textile Organisation; Japan Com'l. Arb. . . . ; London Court of Arb.; Netherlands Arb. Institute; N. Y. State Chamber of Commerce. Arb. Comm.; Standard arb. clause; Statutory arb.; Trade association; Umpire; U.N. Economic Comm'n. for Asia and the Far East; U.N. Handbook of Nat'l. and Int'l. Institutions Active in the Field of Int'l. Com'l. Arb.; Universal Postal Union.

Sources: Domke, *Int'l. Arb. of Com'l. Disputes,* in PROC. OF THE 1960 INSTITUTE ON PRIVATE INVESTMENTS ABROAD (1960).

INTELSAT (August 20, 1964)

The official acronym for the International Telecommunications Satellite Consortium which was established under the impetus of the United Nations General Assembly Resolution No. 1721 in order to make available to all countries a single global communications satellite system.

Two international agreements were set up to create the Consortium. The first is called the Agreement Establishing Interim Arrangements for a Global Commercial Communications Satellite System, to which only governments were parties. The second agreement is known as the Special Agreement. Parties to this Special Agreement are representatives of governments, or of public or private telecommunications corporations designated by governments. The Special Agreement is concerned with financial and technical matters and sets forth the basic principles and objectives. COMSAT is a signatory of this agreement, and as the largest single investor with 61% of the capital required during interim arrangements, is also manager of the Consortium. Arbitration procedures were developed in a Supplementary Agreement on Arbitration. The Agreement of 1964 provided for a review within five years of these interim procedures. The Conference on Definitive Arrangements for the International Telecommunications Satellite Consortium convened at Washington on February 24, 1969, with the 65 member countries represented.

See also: Communications Satellite Corp.; INTELSAT. Supplementary Agreement on Arb.

Sources: Communications Satellite System, agreement establishing interim arrangements for a global com'l. communications satellite system, Aug. 20, 1964, TIAS 5646; J. Washburn, INTELSAT: Resort to Arb. after Nov. 21, 1966, under the Supplementary Agreement on Arb., Sept. 18, 1967; *Ambassador Marks Holds Press Briefing on the INTELSAT Conference*, 60 DEPT. STATE BULL. 224-230 (1969); *INTELSAT Conference Opens at Washington*, *id.* 231-234; Washburn, *Arb. Procedures for INTELSAT's Legal Disputes*, 23 ARB. J. (n.s.) 97-102 (1968).

INTELSAT. SUPPLEMENTARY AGREEMENT ON ARBITRATION

The third in a series of international agreements concerned with the creation of the International Telecommunications Satellite Consortium.

The Supplementary Agreement was drafted in London, October 1964-March 1965, by legal experts from eleven countries, and entered into force on November 21, 1966. It provides machinery for settling legal disputes which may arise from the agreements establishing INTELSAT. The Supplementary Agreement provides for arbitration procedures, and for the appointment of the Tribunal, which will consist of three members, one designated by each party, and the third selected by these two from a Panel of seven experts who are to be nominated every two years by the signers of this Agreement.

See also: Communications Satellite Corp.; INTELSAT; Int'l. pub. arb.

Sources: Int'l. Telecommunications Satellite Consortium, Supplementary Agreement on Arb., entered into force Nov. 21, 1966, Jan. 1967 reprint of TIAS 5646 at 77; Washburn, *supra* INTELSAT at 97-102.

INTER-AMERICAN COMMERCIAL ARBITRATION COMMISSION
(IACAC) (Director General, Av. Franklin Roosevelt 115 grupo 405, Rio de Janeiro, Brazil. General Counsel, Federal Bar Building West, Room 310, Washington, D.C. 20006, U.S.A.)

An administrative body of delegates from National Sections created by Resolution XLI of the Seventh International Conference of American States in December 1933 to establish an Inter-American system for the non-governmental arbitration of commercial disputes.

The American Arbitration Association and the Council on Inter-American Relations were jointly to undertake the organization of this Commission. Its practical operation was conducted by National Committees appointed in each of the 21 Republics. Rules of procedure were drafted, and panels of arbitrators were appointed from nominations made by members of these Committees. The IACAC is presently being reorganized. Three meetings in 1967 initiated steps toward revising the Charter. A Second Conference on Inter-American Commercial Arbitration was held in Mexico City, November 7-9, 1968, with further plans for revitalizing the arbitration system of the Americas.

See also: American Arb. Association; Int'l. com'l. arb.; Montevideo Conf.; Second Conf. on Inter-American Com'l. Arb.; Draft Uniform Law on Inter-American Com'l. Arb.

Sources: INTER-AMERICAN COM'L. ARB. COMM'N., INTER-AMERICAN COM'L. ARB., A REPORT (1968); *id.*, RULES OF PROCEDURE AS AMENDED AND IN EFFECT April 1, 1969; D. Straus, Remarks . . . at the Conf. of Inter-American Com'l. Arb., Buenos Aires, April 3-4, 1967; Domke, *Inter-American Com'l. Arb.*, 4 MIAMI L. Q. (1950).

INTER-AMERICAN CONFERENCE. NINTH

See: Pact of Bogotá.

INTER-AMERICAN COUNCIL OF JURISTS

See: Draft Convention on Int'l. Com'l. Arb.; Draft Uniform Law on Inter-American Com'l. Arb.; Organization of American States.

INTER-AMERICAN INSTITUTE FOR LEGAL STUDIES CONVENTION TO IMPROVE THE CLIMATE FOR INVESTMENT IN LATIN AMERICA

See: Draft Convention to Improve the Climate for Investment in Latin America by Facilitating the Settlement of Investment Disputes.

INTER-ASSOCIATION COMMERCIAL ARBITRATION AGREEMENTS

A clause in the rules of impartial arbitral agencies throughout the world which makes available the reciprocal use of their arbitration facilities in the countries covered by the agreement.

The American Arbitration Association has many such joint agreements. Under these arrangements, arbitration to be held in Japan, for example, shall be conducted under the rules of the Japan Commercial Arbitration Association, while arbitrations to be held in the United States shall be conducted in accordance with the rules of the American Arbitration Association. Methods for determining the place of the arbitration and the appointment of arbitrators are explicitly stated in the agreement between the two associations. The various associations cooperate in advancing international commercial arbitration.

See also: American Arb. Association; Enforcement of arb. agreements (Int'l. com'l. arb.); Institutional arb.; Int'l. com'l. arb.; Japan Com'l. Arb. Association; Netherlands Arb. Institute; Trade association.

Sources: Japan-American Trade Arb. Agreement, Sept. 16, 1952 (agreement between the AAA and the Japan Com'l. Arb. Association); Rao, *supra* Boundary disputes.

INTEREST

The sum of money accrued and due with the passage of time on the amount that is awarded in an arbitration.

The arbitrator is empowered to include interest allowances as part of an award, unless the parties provide otherwise. He may also determine the date from which the interest shall run, as from the date of the breach of the contract or from the date of the award. Arbitrators often ignore the interest due in making an award. In some jurisdictions the courts may have the discretion to add interest from the exact date of the award. If a court were to add interest from a date prior to the award, it would infringe on the authority of the arbitrator.

Sources: 18 LAWYERS' LETTERS (1964), *supra* Adjournment of hearings.

INTEREST ARBITRATION

The arbitration of the terms of a new contract.

When contract negotiations reach an impasse and cannot be resolved by normal collective bargaining, the issues in dispute are sometimes submitted to an arbitrator. Most strikes occur because of the inability of the parties to negotiate new contract terms. The San Francisco hotel industry, as well as transit, printing, and public utilities, often have collective bargaining agreements with provisions for arbitrating new contract terms. Contracts providing for impartial chairmen sometimes include the arbitration of contract terms. Even after a strike, the parties may resort to arbitration, as in the New York City sanitation dispute of 1968. Most unions and private employers are reluctant to accept arbitration as a means of settling disputes on terms of a new contract.

See also: Compulsory arb. Public employees; Grievance arb.; Impartial chairman system; Labor arb. (Voluntary); Nat'l. Mediation Board.

Sources: Cushman, *Voluntary Arb. of New Contract Terms*, 16 LAB. L. J. 765 (1965); Katz, *Arb.—Favored Child of Pre-emption*, in 17 N.Y. UNIVERSITY, PROC. OF THE ANNUAL CONF. ON LABOR 32-36 (1964); Miller, *Arb. of New Contract Wage Disputes*, 20 IND. & LAB. REL. REV. 250 (1967).

INTERIM AWARD

A partial or temporary award rendered on only part of the whole dispute.

Most arbitration statutes in the United States require that arbitration awards must be final, and must determine all of the issues submitted. Partial or interim awards in this sense would therefore have no legal sanction, especially under the rule that once an arbitrator renders an award, he is *functus officio*. Such a rule might not be observed in a case where the parties either expressed or implied consent for an interim award. Interim awards are permitted under British practice.

See also: Functus officio; Tentative award.

Sources: Arb. Act of 1950, 14 Geo. 6, ch. 27, § 14; Fleming, *Interim Relief and Provisional Remedies in Arbitration*, in 17 N.Y. UNIVERSITY, PROC. OF THE ANNUAL CONF. ON LABOR 49-63 (1964).

INTERNATIONAL ARBITRATION

See: International public arbitration.

INTERNATIONAL ARBITRATION JOURNAL

A journal of which four issues were published during 1945 by the American Arbitration Association.

The *International Arbitration Journal* was dedicated in its first number to the task of advancing arbitration as a science of the pacific settlement of international controversy. The *Journal* was discontinued in 1946 when publication of *The Arbitration Journal* was resumed.

See also: American Arbitration Association.

INTERNATIONAL BANK FOR RECONSTRUCTION AND DEVELOPMENT (IBRD) (WORLD BANK) (1818 H Street, N.W., Washington, D.C. 20433)

An inter-governmental financial institution and specialized agency of the United Nations which assists in the reconstruction and development of its member countries by facilitating the investment of capital for productive purposes.

The International Bank for Reconstruction and Development was established on December 27, 1945, when the Articles of Agreement were signed by 28 nations. Operations of the Bank were begun on June 25, 1946. The Bank has been influential in furthering the use of arbitration in investment disputes through the Convention on the Settlement of Investment Disputes between States and Nationals of Other States. Another important development has been that loan agreements sponsored by the Bank contain arbitration clauses.

See also: Convention on the Settlement of Investment Disputes between States and Nationals of Other States; Int'l. Centre for Settlement of Investment Disputes.

Sources: Convention on the Settlement of Investment Disputes between States and Nationals of Other States (submitted by I.B.R.D., March 18, 1965); G. DELAUME, *supra* Concession contract at 172.

INTERNATIONAL CENTRE FOR SETTLEMENT OF INVESTMENT DISPUTES (ICSID)
(1818 H Street, N.W., Washington, D.C. 20433)

An international organization created in 1966 by the Convention on the Settlement of Investment Disputes between States and Nationals of Other States.

The Convention was formulated by the Executive Directors of the International Bank for Reconstruction and Development with the assistance of international legal experts, and entered into force on October 14, 1966. At the same time the ICSID also came into existence as the newest and only non-financial member of the World Bank group of organizations. The governing body of the Centre is its Administrative Council which is composed of one representative of each Contracting State. The primary function of the International Centre for Settlement of Investment Disputes is to provide facilities for the resolution of any future disputes, and assistance in settling those disputes that have already occurred. Panels of Conciliators and Arbitrators are maintained, most of whom are nominated by the Contracting States. The jurisdiction of the Centre is based on the consent given by both parties to such a means of settling an investment dispute. One of these parties must be the Government of a Contracting State, or a constituent subdivision or agency designated by such a Government, and the other must be a national of another Contracting State.

See also: Access to the arbitral tribunal; Adm. agency; Concession contract; Convention on the Settlement of Investment Disputes between States and Nationals of Other States; Delegation of arbitrator's authority; Economic development agreements; Evasion of arb.; Institutional arb.; Int'l. Bank for Reconstruction and Development; Int'l. pub. arb.

Sources: ICSID, *supra* Appeal boards of adm. agencies; INT'L. CENTRE FOR SETTLEMENT OF INVESTMENT DISPUTES, DOCUMENTS CONCERNING THE ORIGIN AND THE FORMULATION OF THE CONVENTION ON THE SETTLEMENT OF INVESTMENT DISPUTES, Vol. 2, Doc. 1-146 (1968); INT'L. CENTRE FOR SETTLEMENT OF INVESTMENT DISPUTES, MODEL CLAUSES RECORDING CONSENT TO THE JURISDICTION OF THE CENTRE (1968); Int'l. Centre for Settlement of Investment Disputes, What It Is, What It Does, and How It Works, Sept. 1, 1967.

INTERNATIONAL CHAMBER OF COMMERCE (ICC)
[38, Cours Albert—1er, Paris (VIIIe), France]

A chamber founded in Paris in 1919, following a decision taken at the International Trade Conference of 1919 in Atlantic City to establish a permanent organization of world business.

The Court of Arbitration attached to the International Chamber in Paris is the only arbitral center in Europe specializing in international legal affairs. Through the inclusion of an arbitration clause of the ICC in an agreement, the Rules of Conciliation and Arbitration to which the clause refers are also incorporated in the contract. The Court deals not only with purely commercial matters, but also with transactions arising out of international trade and investment in the broadest sense of these terms. The National Committees nominate suitably qualified persons for appointment as arbitrators to the Court. ICC arbitration does not attempt to duplicate national arbitration systems, or the highly specialized arbitration facilities developed within certain trade associations. Its facilities are meant to be used primarily for a form of arbitration which is neutral and international.

See also: Access to the arbitral tribunal; Chamber of commerce; Institutional arb.; Int'l. Chamber of Commerce. Arb. clause; Int'l. com'l. arb.; Int'l. non-governmental organization.

Sources: INT'L. CHAMBER OF COMMERCE, BIENNIAL REPORT (1965/1967); ICC, *supra* Answering statement.

INTERNATIONAL CHAMBER OF COMMERCE. ARBITRATION CLAUSE

The clause reads as follows: "All disputes arising in connection with the present contract shall be finally settled under the Rules of Conciliation and Arbitration of the International Chamber of Commerce by one or more arbitrators appointed in accordance with the Rules."

See also: Future disputes clause; Institutional arb.; Int'l. Chamber of Commerce; Standard arb. clause.

Sources: ICC, *supra* Answering statement.

INTERNATIONAL CIVIL AVIATION ORGANIZATION (ICAO)
(International Aviation Building, Montreal 3, Quebec, Canada)

An association of nations to encourage the growth and development of international air transport and to ensure that the rights of member States are fully respected.

The International Civil Aviation Organization was created by the Convention on Internationl Civil Aviation signed at Chicago on December 7, 1944, and was established formally as a permanent organization in April 1947. The Convention on International Civil Aviation was ratified by the President of the United States on August 6, 1946. The Convention provided for the arbitration of disputes. The International Civil Aviation Organization is a specialized agency of the United Nations. Its activities are concerned with such various fields of civil aviation as the encouragement of uniformity in methods of improving air navigation, the preparation of conventions on private international air law, and the maintenance of up-to-date statistics in air transport matters and recommendations to facilitate the movement of air passengers and freight across international boundaries. The ICAO has 116 member States.

See also: Convention on Int'l. Civil Aviation.

Sources: B. CHENG, *supra* Air transport agreements; U.S. OFFICE OF THE FEDERAL REGISTER, *supra* Bureau of Labor Statistics at 611; YEARBOOK OF INT'L. ORGANIZATIONS, *supra* Central Office for Int'l. Railway Transport at 639; Domke, *supra* Convention on Int'l. Civil Aviation.

INTERNATIONAL CLAIMS

A claim which a citizen of one country makes against another State under the auspices of his own government for loss or injury sustained.

An international claim is sometimes called the diplomatic protection of citizens abroad. A United States citizen with a claim against a foreign country seeks the assistance of the State Department. Governments usually refuse to espouse the claim of a citizen until all local remedies provided under the laws of the host country have been exhausted. There are three procedures which are commonly used for the settlement of international claims: diplomatic channels, lump sum settlements, or an agreement submitting all claims to an international arbitral commission. Any or all of these methods may be employed. This relatively modern practice of a State representing private claims against a foreign government began with Jay's Treaty between the United States and Great Britain in 1794.

See also: Alabama Arb.; Calvo Clause; Espousal; Exhaustion of local remedies; Foreign Claims Settlement Comm'n. of the U.S.; Int'l. pub. arb.; Joint claims comm'n.; Lake Ontario Claims Tribunal—U.S. and Canada; Lump sum settlement; Mixed arbitral tribunal; Mixed claims comm'n.; Pious Fund Case; Trail Smelter Arb.

Sources: M. HUDSON, *supra* Convention on the Pacific Settlement of Int'l. Disputes; R. LILLICH, *supra* Foreign Claims Settlement Comm'n. of the U.S.; M. WHITEMAN, *supra* Calvo Clause at ch. 24; Griffin, *Int'l. Claims of Nationals of Both the Claimant and Respondent States*, 1 INT'L. LAWYER 400-423 (1967); Lillich, *Int'l. Claims*, in INT'L. ARB. LIBER AMICORUM FOR MARTIN DOMKE 143-156 (P. Sanders ed. 1967).

INTERNATIONAL COMMERCIAL ARBITRATION

Arbitration of disputes in international trade or business transactions between parties residing in different countries.

See also: Amiable compositeur; Applicable procedural law; Applicable substantive law; Convention on the Execution of Foreign Arbitral Awards; Convention on the Recognition and Enforcement of Foreign Arbitral Awards; Enforcement of arb. agreements (Int'l. com'l. arb.);

Enforcement of foreign arbitral awards; European Convention on Int'l. Com'l. Arb.; European Convention Providing a Uniform Law on Arb.; Ex aequo et bono; Institutional arb.; Inter-association com'l. arb. agreements; Inter-American Com'l. Arb. Comm'n.; Int'l. Chamber of Commerce; Int'l. Institute for the Unification of Private Law; Int'l. Wool Textile Arb. Agreement; Law merchant; London Court of Arb.; Procedure; Protocol on Arb. Clauses; Uniform laws; U.N. Comm'n. on Int'l. Trade Law; U.N. ECAFE; U.N. ECE. Rules of Arb.; U.N. Handbook on Nat'l. and Int'l. Institutions Active in the Field of Int'l. Com'l. Arb.; U.N. Resolution of the U.N. Conf. on Int'l. Com'l. Arb.

Sources: U.N. Comm'n. on Int'l. Trade Law, Int'l. Com'l. Arb., Report of the Secretary-General, U.N. Doc. A/CN.9/21 (1969); INT'L. ARB., *supra* Doctrine of ouster; INT'L. COM'L. ARB., *supra* Applicable procedural law; Domke, *supra* Applicable substantive law; Domke, *supra* Institutional arb. at 131-184; Hoare, *supra* Convention on the Execution of Foreign Arbitral Awards at 30-64; Wilner, *supra* Applicable procedural law.

INTERNATIONAL COMMISSION OF INQUIRY

A fact-finding board set up to conduct an impartial investigation of an international dispute when the States concerned are unwilling to submit their dispute to arbitration.

The use of international commissions of inquiry was one of the methods for dispute settlement provided in the Convention on the Pacific Settlement of International Disputes of 1899. Commissions of this kind are an alternate means of settling disputes afforded by the Permanent Court of Arbitration.

See also: Fact-finding; Int'l. pub. arb.; Permanent Court of Arb.

INTERNATIONAL CONFERENCE OF INTER-AMERICAN STATES. SEVENTH

See: Montevideo Conference.

INTERNATIONAL CONVENTION CONCERNING THE CARRIAGE OF GOODS BY RAIL (CIM)

See: Central Office for Int'l. Railway Transport.

INTERNATIONAL CONVENTION CONCERNING THE CARRIAGE OF PASSENGERS AND LUGGAGE BY RAIL (CIV)

See: Central Office for Int'l. Railway Transport.

INTERNATIONAL COURT OF JUSTICE (ICJ)
(Palais de la Paix, The Hague, The Netherlands)

A court of justice established as the principal judicial organ of the United Nations under its Charter of 1945, with jurisdiction over all cases which the member States submit to it, and all other legal matters specifically provided for in the Charter or in treaties and conventions in force.

The President of the International Court of Justice is frequently authorized in arbitration agreements or treaties to appoint an arbitrator when the parties themselves fail to agree to do so. The Court has also had some influence on submission of disputes to arbitration, as in its judgment of May 19, 1953, in which it held that the United Kingdom was under obligation to submit to arbitration its differences with Greece on the validity of the Ambatielos claim. The Court may also deliver advisory opinions on request from member nations. Article 38 of the International Court of Justice Statute is often referred to as a source for the applicable law to be used in international public arbitrations.

See also: Appointment of arbitrators; Int'l. Court of Justice Statute. Article 38.

Sources: The Ambatielos Claim, 12 U.N.R.I.A.A. 87-153 (1956); I.C.J. STAT., U.N. CHARTER; I.C.J. Y.B. (1946-47); S. ROSENNE, LAW AND PRACTICE OF THE INT'L. COURT (1965).

INTERNATIONAL COURT OF JUSTICE STATUTE. ARTICLE 38

The provisions of this Article may be referred to in a *compromis* in a dispute between States as the applicable law to be used by the Arbitration Court in reaching its decision.

The provisions read as follows:

1. The Court, whose function is to decide in accordance with international law such disputes as are submitted to it, shall apply:
   a. international conventions, whether general or particular, establishing rules expressly recognized by the contesting states;
   b. international custom, as evidence of a general practice accepted as law;
   c. the general principles of law recognized by civilized nations;
   d. subject to the provisions of Article 59, judicial decisions and the teachings of the most highly qualified publicists of the various nations, as subsidiary means for the determination of rules of law.

2. This provision shall not prejudice the power of the Court to decide a case *ex aequo et bono*, if the parties agree thereto.

See also: Applicable law. Int'l. pub. arb.; Ex aequo et bono; Int'l. Court of Justice.

Sources: I.C.J. STAT. CHARTER OF THE U.N. Dep't. of State Publication 2353.

INTERNATIONAL CUSTOMARY LAW

A body of law which acquired its authority through custom and practice rather than through treaties or conventions.

The three traditional sources of international law are: treaties, custom, and general principles of law recognized by civilized nations. The distinctive characteristic of custom as opposed to treaties and general principles is that custom does not require the express consent of States to render it into law. In making their decisions, international judges and arbitrators may assure that States accept certain practices as customary law by referring to actual practice, together with the psychological acceptance of it as law through previous judicial opinions.

See also: Conventions; Customary law; General principles of law recognized by civilized nations; Int'l. law.

Sources: STUDIES IN WORLD PUBLIC ORDER (M. McDougal ed. 1960).

INTERNATIONAL INSTITUTE FOR THE UNIFICATION OF PRIVATE LAW (UNIDROIT) (ROME INSTITUTE)
(28, Via Panisperna, Rome, Italy)

An organization of 43 member countries formed to study methods for harmonizing and co-ordinating private law and to prepare uniform laws and conventions between States or groups of States.

The International Institute for the Unification of Private Law was originally established on April 20, 1926, by the agreement between the Italian Government and the Council of the League of Nations, and reconstituted by a multilateral agreement of April 21, 1940. Its working members are lawyers appointed by their own countries. Among its many draft conventions is a Draft of a proposed Uniform Law on Arbitration, which in early versions had far-reaching provisions as to the enforcement of awards, ruling that when an award has been declared enforceable by the courts of one of the countries where this Uniform Law is in force, it may be enforced in any of the other countries. This Convention on Uniform Law became the basis for the European Convention Providing a Uniform Law on Arbitration, which was drafted by the Council of Europe, and opened for signature by its member States on January 20, 1966.

See also: European Convention Providing a Uniform Law on Arb.; Int'l. com'l. arb.

Sources: 1 INT'L. COM'L. ARB., *supra* Applicable procedural law at 31; INT'L. INST. FOR THE UNIFICATION OF PRIVATE LAW, *supra* European Convention Providing a Uniform Law on Arb.; INT'L. INST. FOR THE UNIFICATION OF PRIVATE LAW Y.B. (1966); YEARBOOK OF INT'L. ORGANIZATIONS, *supra* Central Office for Int'l. Railway Transport.

INTERNATIONAL LABOUR ORGANISATION (ILO)
(Ch 1211, Geneva 22, Switzerland)

A specialized agency of the United Nations which was originally established in 1919 under the Covenant of the League of Nations.

Among other types of technical aid, the ILO provides assistance in framing laws at the request of governments. It publishes the *International Labour Review* and the *Legislative Series*, which give the texts of labor statutes in member countries throughout the world. The United States joined this autonomous inter-governmental agency in 1934, and is at present one of 121 member countries which finance its operation. The ILO is tripartite in organization with representation on its executive council of governments, labor, and management.

Sources: ILO; U.S. OFFICE OF THE FEDERAL REGISTER, *supra* BLS at 613.

INTERNATIONAL LAW COMMISSION

A commission established as a subsidiary organ by the United Nations General Assembly to encourage the progressive development and codification of international law.

The International Law Commission was elected at the third regular session of the General Assembly from a list of candidates nominated as authorities in international law by their own governments. At present the Commission is a permanent, part time body of twenty-five members elected by the General Assembly for a term of five years. No two members of the Commission can be nationals of the same State. Members serve as individuals rather than as government representatives. Annual sessions take place in Geneva and last on an average of ten weeks. At its first session in 1949, the Commission selected arbitral procedure as one of the topics on which international law might be codified. A draft Convention on Arbitral Procedure was adopted in 1952, and subsequently revised and submitted to the General Assembly. In its final form of Model Rules on Arbitral Procedure, the Commission's work on arbitration remains one of the most significant contributions made in decades in this area of international law.

See also: Int'l. pub. arb.; Model Rules on Arbitral Procedure.

Sources: Model Rules, *supra* Appointment of arbitrators; U.N. ILC, *supra* Annulment . . . ;H. BRIGGS, THE INT'L. LAW COMMISSION (1965); Carlston, *Int'l. Arb. Procedure*, 9 ARB. J. (n.s.) 83-88 (1954).

INTERNATIONAL LAW (IN ARBITRATION)

A body of rules derived from custom, treaty, or general principles of law recognized by civilized nations, and including arbitral and judicial opinions aimed at governing the relations between States.

Arbitrations are held to be governed by the rules established by the parties in their agreement to arbitrate. In international public arbitrations, this agreement to arbitrate may be a treaty or *compromis*. When this agreement is ambiguous or if it does not provide specific procedures, or when the law selected to govern the contract is not applicable, recourse is sometimes made to what is known as general principles of law recognized by civilized nations. Some agreements to arbitrate refer specifically to this body of general principles as the applicable substantive law.

See also: Abu Dhabi Arb.; Applicable law. Int'l. pub. arb.; Compromis; Convention; General principles of law recognized by civilized nations; Int'l. customary law; Lena Goldfields Arb.; Party autonomy; Treaty.

INTERNATIONAL NON-GOVERNMENTAL ORGANIZATION (INGO)

An organization primarily concerned with international interests and activities, and composed of individuals rather than nations.

International non-governmental organizations are often made up of private institutions with expert knowledge based on specialized experience in a single field. The importance of such organizations was officially recognized for the first time in Article 71 of the United Nations Charter, which specifically provides for consultation with non-governmental organizations, and specifies: "The Economic and Social Council may make suitable arrangements for consultation with non-governmental organizations which are concerned with matters within its competence. . . ." Nongovernmental organizations such as the International Chamber of Commerce, the Institute of International Law, and the International Law Association, are among a few of these international non-governmental organizations which have had a particular interest and influence in the development of arbitration.

See also: Int'l. Chamber of Commerce; U.N. Conf. on Int'l. Com'l. Arb.

Sources: U.N. CHARTER, art. 71; L. WHITE, INT'L. NON-GOVERNMENTAL ORGANIZATIONS (1968).

INTERNATIONAL PRIVATE ARBITRATION

See: International commercial arbitration.

INTERNATIONAL PUBLIC ARBITRATION

The settlement of disputes between States by judges of their own choice on the basis of respect for law.

International public arbitration is a procedure for the settlement of disputes between States as the result of an undertaking voluntarily accepted. The procedure may apply to existing disputes, or to disputes arising in the future. The modern history of international arbitration is traditionally said to have begun with Jay's Treaty of 1794, under which

Great Britain and the United States submitted certain important boundary disputes to arbitration by mixed commissions.

See also: Air transport agreements; Annulment . . . ; Applicable law. Int'l. pub. arb.; Boundary disputes; Cases. Int'l. pub. arb.; Central Office for Int'l. Railway Transport; Compliance with the award; Compromis; Concession contract; Consent of the parties; Convention; Draft conventions and uniform laws; Enforcement of award (Int'l. pub. arb.); Espousal; Ex aequo et bono; Exhaustion of local remedies; General principles of law recognized by civilized nations; Institutional arb.; INTELSAT. Supplementary Agreement on Arb.; Int'l. Centre for Settlement of Investment Disputes; Int'l. claims; Int'l. Law Commission; Investment disputes; Mixed arbitral tribunal; Mixed claims comm'n.; Model Rules on Arbitral Procedure; Permanent Court of Arb.; Procedure; Repudiation; Universal Postal Union.

Sources: Convention on the Pacific Settlement of Int'l. Disputes (The Hague, July 28, 1899, revised Oct. 18, 1907); K. CARLSTON, *supra* Annulment . . . ; J. SIMPSON & H. FOX, *supra* Appointment of arbitrators; U.N. ILC, *supra* Annulment. . . .

INTERNATIONAL TELECOMMUNICATIONS SATELLITE CONSORTIUM

See: INTELSAT.

INTERNATIONAL WOOL TEXTILE ARBITRATION AGREEMENT

An agreement for voluntary arbitration of disputes in the wool textile trade between organizations of different nations.

The International Wool Textile Arbitration Agreement was first signed on September 26, 1924, by representatives of the Bradford Chamber of Commerce in England and the Chambers of Commerce of Roubaix and Tourcoing in France. In 1925, the Agreement was also signed on behalf of the wool textile industry in Belgium, and later by the German industry in Berlin, and subsequently by the Italian industry on October 27, 1926. The basis of the Agreement is that commercial disputes are best settled by arbitration, conducted by an arbitration tribunal in the country of the seller. Later, when the membership of the IWTO had become extended to all five continents, it was agreed that the principle of arbitration in the country of the seller was not sacred and that where there are long-standing arbitration arrangements in trading in wool and wool textiles between countries, the arbitration of disputes can take place in the accustomed manner. Article II of the Agreement states in part: ". . . Where no arbitration clause is formally recommended by the National Committee so as to conform with National Law, the following clause should be included in all contracts: — 'Any dispute . . . arising out of this contract shall be settled by arbitration in accordance with the IWTO Arbitration Agreement and the competent body to conduct the arbitration shall be . . .' Here is to be inserted the name of the National Committee affiliated to the IWTO or the Chamber of Commerce or other competent organisation of the country of the seller . . ." with the exception that "(w)here there are long-standing arbitration arrangements in application to trade in wool and wool textiles between countries, the arbitration of disputes can take place in the accustomed manner. . . ." The text of the International Wool Textile Arbitration Agreement is periodically revised, the latest revision being that adopted at the 34th International Wool Conference in London in 1965.

See also: Int'l. com'l. arb.; Int'l. Wool Textile Organisation.

Sources: Int'l. Wool Textile Organisation, Int'l. Wool Textile Arb. Agreement, 1965 (adopted at the 34th Int'l. Wool Conf., London); INT'L. YEARBOOK ON CIVIL AND COM'L. ARB. 286 (A. Nussbaum ed. 1928); Comité Central Belge de la Laine, Arb. Regulations, June 1956; Letter from D. G. Price, Secretary, IWTO, to the AAA, March 12, 1969.

INTERNATIONAL WOOL TEXTILE ORGANISATION (IWTO)
(Commerce House, Cheapside, Bradford, United Kingdom)

An association of member organizations subscribing to the International Wool Textile Arbitration Agreement in order to maintain it, and in addition, to promote mutual interests in international economic affairs related to the wool textile industry.

The International Wool Textile Organisation was founded in 1929 at Bradford, England, following the arbitration agreement of 1924 between the Bradford Chamber of Commerce and the Chambers of Commerce of Roubaix and Tourcoing in France. Subsequently the agreement was signed by wool textile organizations in Belgium, Germany, Italy, and other countries. At the present time, there are organizations in 26 countries, including the United States, which subscribe to the International Wool Textile Arbitration Agreement.

See also: Institutional arb.; Int'l. Wool Textile Arb. Agreement; Textile arb.

Sources: Int'l. Wool Textile Organisation, Int'l. Wool Textile Arb. Agreement, 1965 (adopted at the 34th Int'l. Wool Conf., London).

INTER-UNION DISPUTES

See: Jurisdictional disputes; Representational disputes.

INTERVENTION

The act by which a third party requests to be acknowledged as a party in a suit or in an arbitration pending between two other parties.

In some interventions, as in seniority cases, three employees may be concerned, although only one employee is actually represented in the arbitration. The right of one or both of the other employees to intervene has usually been denied by arbitrators on the ground that the arbitration is between the union and the company and therefore subject to their control. An arbitrator must often determine whether the intervener's interests are adequately represented by the existing parties. Arbitrators have usually been reluctant to grant intervention over the objection of the parties. The Council of Europe allowed for intervention in Article 33-1 of its Draft European Convention for the Peaceful Settlement of Disputes which states: "In . . . arbitral procedure, if a third State should consider that its legitimate interests are involved, it may submit to the . . . Arbitral Tribunal a request to intervene as a third party."

See also: Due process; European Convention for the Peaceful Settlement of Disputes; Individual rights; Seniority.

Sources: European Convention for the Peaceful Settlement of Disputes, (Council of Europe, European T.S. 23); Fleming, *supra* Agreed award at 70-78; Shapiro, *Some Thoughts on Intervention before Courts, Agencies, and Arbitrators*, 81 HARV. L. REV. 721-772 (1968); Summers, *Individual Rights in Collective Agreements and Arb.*, 37 NYU L. REV. 362 (1962).

INTERVENTION (2)

See: Government intervention.

INVESTMENT DISPUTES

See: Abs-Shawcross Draft Convention on Investments Abroad; Abu Dhabi Arb.; Aramco Arb.; Concession contract; Convention on the Settlement of Investment Disputes; Draft Convention to Improve the Climate for Investment in Latin America by Facilitating the Settlement of Investment Disputes; Lena Goldfields Arb.; OECD Draft Convention on the Protection of Foreign Property.

IRREVOCABILITY OF THE ARBITRATION AGREEMENT

Once an arbitration agreement has been properly executed or incorporated in a contract, that agreement to arbitrate cannot be evaded under modern arbitration statutes, unless the entire contract itself is revoked.

An arbitration agreement under common law may be revoked at the discretion of either party until an award has been rendered. Section 2 of the United States Arbitration Act reads: "A written provision in . . . a contract . . . to settle by arbitration a controversy thereafter arising out of such contract . . . , or the refusal to perform the whole or any part thereof, or an agreement in writing to submit to arbitration an existing controversy arising out of such a contract, . . . shall be valid, irrevocable, and enforceable, save upon such grounds as exist at law or in equity for the revocation of any contract." Similar provisions are to be found in many modern state statutes.

See also: Breach of contract; Common law arb.; Container contract; Enforce-
    ment of arb. agreements (Common law); Enforcement of arb.
    agreements (State statutes); Modern arb. statute; Separability doc-
    trine; Submission agreement.

Sources: U.S. Arb. Act, 9 U.S.C. § 2 (1954); N.Y. CPLR § 7501.

JAPAN COMMERCIAL ARBITRATION ASSOCIATION
(14, 3-chome, Marunouchi, Chiyoda-ku, Tokyo, Japan)

An association established in 1950 to promote Japanese foreign trade
by encouraging the settlement of business disputes through the use of
conciliation and arbitration.

The Japan Commercial Arbitration Association has branch offices in
Nagoya, Osaka, Kobe, and Yokohama. It maintains an international panel
of arbitrators, and has facilities for consultation as well as for conciliation
and arbitration. It also seeks close cooperation with foreign arbitration
associations, and the conclusion of arbitration agreements with them as a
step in promoting trade. Each year the Japan Commercial Arbitration
Association sponsors a number of conferences and seminars for local trade
groups and government officials. Its publications include the *Quarterly
of the Japan Commercial Arbitration Association* in English, and the
monthly *Foreign Trade Claims and Arbitration* in Japanese. The Japan
Commercial Arbitration Association and the American Arbitration Association concluded in 1952 the Agreement . . . to Facilitate the Use
of Commercial Arbitration in Trade between Japan and the United
States. . . .

See also: Institutional arb.; Inter-association com'l. arb. agreements.

Sources: JAPAN COM'L. ARB. ASSOCIATION. Rules Revised June 14, 1963; Japan
    Com'l. Arb. Association, *Articles, Revised June 14, 1963*, TRADE/
    CA/NEWS 6 ECAFE CENTRE FOR COM'L. ARB. NEWS BULL. 7
    (1967); 3 *id.* 13 (1965); Q. JAPAN COM'L. ARB. ASS'N. 5 (No. 15,
    1964).

JAY'S TREATY (1794)

A treaty between England and the United States which provided that
various questions and disputes arising out of the American Revolutionary
War of 1776 be referred to arbitration.

This Treaty of Friendship, Commerce and Navigation gave great
impetus to the institution of arbitration. Jay's Treaty marks the beginning
of the modern period of arbitration.

See also: Boundary disputes; Equity.

Sources: Treaty of amity, commerce and navigation with U.K., Nov. 19, 1794,
    8 Stat. 116, TS 105; S. BEMIS, JAY'S TREATY (Rev. 1962).

JOINDER

A procedure whereby multiple grievances affecting many employees of the same company can be combined and arbitrated as a single case.

When joinder is used, the arbitrator's award will then bind all involved, and will therefore foreclose needless multiplicity and expense of proceedings. Joinder may also refer to the joining of two separate unions in a trilateral arbitration over a work assignment dispute, though only one of these unions has an arbitration agreement with the employer.

See also: Carey v. Westinghouse; Consolidation; Distressed grievance procedure; Multiple grievances; Trilateral disputes; Work assignment disputes.

JOINT BOARD

See: Adjustment board; Bipartite board; Grievance procedure—Level of steps; Nat'l. Joint Board for the Settlement of Jurisdictional Disputes in the Building and Construction Industry.

JOINT CLAIMS COMMISSION

A non-arbitral tribunal for the settlement of international claims.

International claims are those claims which a citizen of one country makes against the government of another for some infringement of his rights. Members of a joint claims commission are appointed by the disputing States. The States usually appoint their own nationals, thus maintaining a controlling influence. Joint claims commissions often fail to reach an agreement, and tend to produce compromise settlements. When disputes cannot be resolved under such commissions, the parties may choose to use a mixed arbitral tribunal. A joint claims commission may sometimes be a quasi-permanent body, such as the International Joint Commission established by Canada and the United States in 1911 through the treaty of 1909 with the United Kingdom relating to boundary waters and other questions concerning the boundary between the United States and Canada.

See also: Chamizal arb.; Espousal; Int'l. claims; Mixed arbitral tribunal; Mixed claims comm'n.

Sources: M. HUDSON, *supra* Convention on the Pacific Settlement of Int'l. Disputes; *Treaty relating to boundary waters and questions arising along the boundary between the United States and Canada*, signed at Washington January 11, 1909, entered into force May 5, 1910. [36 Stat. 2448, T.S. 548, III Redmond 2607 as cited in 1969 TREATIES IN FORCE 226 (U.S. Dept. of State)].

JUDGMENT

The decision of a court on a proceeding brought before it.

A judgment may be enforced by legal procedures that vary from state to state. A judgment enables the prevailing party to satisfy his claim under the coercive procedures provided by law for that purpose. An arbitration award under modern arbitration statutes may be made enforceable when the successful party makes a motion to confirm the award in the court having jurisdiction. Judgment may then be entered on it.

See also: Confirming the award; Entry-of-judgment clause; Judgment-roll.

Sources: BLACK's LAW DICTIONARY (3d ed. 1933).

JUDGMENT-ROLL (IN ARBITRATION)

The documents which must be filed in a court in order to make the award a judgment so as to ensure its enforcement.

A judgment-roll may consist of the original or a copy of the contract containing the arbitration agreement, and each written extension of time within which the award is to be made, and each paper submitted to the court in connection with the arbitration, as well as each order of the court concerned with confirming the award.

See also: Confirming the award; Entry-of-judgment clause; Judgment.

Sources: ASS'N. OF THE BAR OF THE CITY OF N.Y., *supra* Award by confession.

JUDICIAL NOTICE

The recognition by a court or an arbitrator of the existence or the truth of anything in a case as being self-evident or common knowledge.

Judicial notice is a process whereby judges and arbitrators simply recognize statutory laws of other jurisdictions, the official acts of governmental agencies, the common practices in collective bargaining, the customary practices in modern industry, and all other such matters which are so generally known that trying to prove them would be a waste of time.

See also: Independent investigation by arbitrator.

Sources: M. BEATTY, LABOR-MANAGEMENT ARB. MANUAL 66 (1960); M. DOMKE, *supra* Adhesion contract at 246.

JUDICIAL REVIEW (IN ARBITRATION)

A review of the award by a court at the request of one of the parties to determine whether or not the award can be enforced.

A judicial review cannot concern itself with the sufficiency of evidence or the merits of the award, nor can the award be vacated because of alleged errors either of law or fact. Most arbitration statutes are explicit on these points. The two questions specifically left in labor arbitration by the Trilogy decisions for the court to determine are whether there exists an agreement to arbitrate, and whether the arbitrator remained within his authority in making his award. In the United States Supreme Court decision on *Enterprise Wheel & Car Corp.*, Justice Douglas declared: "The refusal of courts to review the merits of an arbitration award is the proper approach to arbitration under collective bargaining agreements. The federal policy of settling labor disputes by arbitration would be undermined if courts had the final say on the merits of the awards. . . . (The arbitrator's) award is legitimate only so long as it draws its essence from the collective bargaining agreement. When the arbitrator's words manifest an infidelity to this obligation, courts have no choice but to refuse enforcement of the award."

See also: Arbitrator's authority; Enforcement of award (Labor); Modifying the award; Prima Paint Corp. . . . ; Rehearing; Trilogy; Vacating an award.

Sources: United Steelworkers v. Enterprise Wheel & Car Corp., 363 U.S. 593 (1960); Ass'n. of the Bar of the City of N.Y., *supra* Award by confession at 24; Aaron, *Judicial Intervention in Labor Arb.*, 20 Stan. L. Rev. 41-56 (1967).

JURISDICTION

The legal power or right to exercise authority.

The jurisdiction of the arbitrator is defined and limited by the agreement of the parties in their contract. It may also be determined by certain statutes. A frequent cause for litigation has been the question whether or not the issue in a dispute lies within the authority or jurisdiction of the arbitrator.

See also: Arbitrability; Arbitrator's authority; Competence de la competence; Procedural arbitrability; Substantive arbitrability.

JURISDICTIONAL DISPUTES

A dispute between two unions about their right to represent workers, or between two unions and an employer over their right to certain work assignments.

There are two distinct types of jurisdictional disputes. The first, when two unions differ as to which will represent a specific employee group. These are often known as representational disputes. The AFL and the CIO set up machinery for resolving such disputes in their No-Raiding Agreement of 1954, and the subsequent AFL-CIO Internal Disputes Plan. The second type of jurisdictional dispute is one over the assignment of specific work to one of two contending unions. Such disputes are referred to as work assignment disputes. Jurisdictional disputes may be resolved by the National Labor Relations Board under the National Labor Relations Act § 8(b)(4)(D) and § 10(k) proceedings. Attempts may also be made to settle the disputes privately by means of such inter-union panels as the AFL-CIO Internal Disputes Plan, or by arbitrators under a collective bargaining agreement between the employer and one of the unions.

See also: AFL-CIO Internal Disputes Plan; Carey v. Westinghouse; Concurrent jurisdiction; Nat'l. Joint Board for the Settlement of Jurisdictional Disputes in the Building and Construction Industry; Nat'l. Labor Relations Board; No-Raiding Agreement (AFL and CIO); Representational disputes; § 10(k) proc.; Trilateral disputes; Work assignment disputes.

Sources: Cole, *supra* AFL-CIO Internal Disputes Plan at 454-460; Collister, *Standards for Assignment of Work in Jurisdictional Work Disputes*, 33 U. Mo. Kan. City L. Rev. 43 (1965); Stowe, *The Organizational Disputes Agreement, Industrial Union Department, AFL-CIO*, 10 Lab. L. J. 460-467 (1959).

JUSTICIABLE

Liable to trial in a court of justice.

Under some statutes, notably the United States Arbitration Act, a controversy is subject to arbitration over the objection of a party to an agreement to arbitrate, only if the dispute is justiciable, that is, when it becomes a proper subject for court action. The requirement of justiciability has been dropped from the New York Arbitration Act by the Civil Practice Law and Rules, which became effective in 1963. An international dispute will not be considered justiciable unless the parties have first tried to resolve it. Nor will such an international disagreement be considered a bona fide legal international dispute, if no attempt has been made to exhaust all domestic remedies. The parties may agree to waive the exhaustion of local remedies either by their own agreement or through adherence to an international convention, such as the Convention on the Settlement of Investment Disputes between States and Nationals of Other States.

Sources: Ass'n. of the Bar of the City of N. Y., *supra* Award by confession at 10; M. Domke, *supra* Appeal boards of adm. agencies at 63.

KANSAS COURT OF INDUSTRIAL RELATIONS

A compulsory arbitration tribunal established by the State of Kansas in 1920 after coal strikes in 1919 caused fuel shortages.

The Kansas Court of Industrial Relations was abolished in 1925.

See also: Compulsory arbitration.

Sources: 1-5 Kansas Court of Industrial Relations Ann. Rep. (1921-25); H. Roberts, Roberts' Dictionary of Industrial Relations (1966).

LA

Labor Arbitration Reports, published by the Bureau of National Affairs, Inc., 1231 25th Street, N.W., Washington, D.C. 20037.

The correct citation is the year, the abbreviation LA, and the page number, such as 1968 LA 592.

LABOR ARBITRATION

See: Labor arbitration (Voluntary).

LABOR ARBITRATION AWARDS

Arbitration awards published by Commerce Clearing House, Inc., 4025 West Peterson Avenue, Chicago, Illinois 60646.

Full texts of labor arbitration awards and opinions are given, to be cited as 68-1 ARB ¶ 8254, where 68-1 means the year and volume if more than one volume is published for that particular year. The paragraph cited in the volume is denoted by ¶ 8254. A topical index digest, table of awards, and arbitrators' biographies are also given.

See also: American Labor Arb. Awards (P-H); Labor Arb. Reports (BNA); Summary of Labor Arb. Awards (AAA); War Labor Reports (BNA).

LABOR ARBITRATION REPORTS

The successor to War Labor Reports published by the Bureau of National Affairs, Inc., Washington, D.C.

The *Labor Arbitration Reports* are in 51 volumes to date, not including the current volume. These volumes are to be cited as 48 LA 300 where 48 is the volume number, LA denotes Labor Arbitration, and 300 is the page number. These are the published labor arbitration awards, including the opinions which are given in full. Cases are classified and codified in a separate *Cumulative Digest and Index* by name of parties, arbitrators, and subject. These cumulative digest and index volumes are published at ten-year intervals, with a current paperback index published after five years.

See also: American Labor Arb. Awards (P-H); Labor Arb. Awards (CCH); Summary of Labor Arb. Awards (AAA); War Labor Reports (BNA).

LABOR ARBITRATION (VOLUNTARY)

The referral of a dispute by the parties through a voluntary arbitration clause in their collective bargaining agreement to an impartial third person for a final and binding resolution.

The dramatic evolution of labor arbitration has been the natural consequence of the urgent need of the concerned parties to resolve disputes arising out of the collective bargaining agreement. As the contending parties increasingly fought in the early years of the 20th century for what they strongly felt were their rights, they were forced to turn to labor arbitration as the one effective means of attaining these rights and settling disputes concerning them. Today labor arbitration is fast becoming integrated with federal and state courts, and with the National Labor Relations Board. This integration has been consolidated by thousands of decisions rendered by hundreds of arbitrators in disputes resolved solely through the parties' voluntary agreement to arbitrate, and without their seeking any prior or subsequent judicial intervention.*

See also: Arbitrator; Arsenal of weapons; Award; Cases. U.S. Supreme Court (Labor); Compulsory arb.; Concurrent jurisdiction; Discovery of documents; Enforcement of Award (Labor); Federal Mediation and Conciliation Service; Grievance arb.; Impartial chairman; Individual rights; Interest arb.; Jurisdictional disputes; Labor court; Loose-leaf services; Management rights; Mediation; Procedural arbitrability; Procedure (Arb.); Public employee; Railroad Industry; § 301 disputes; Substantive arbitrability; Trilogy (1960).

Sources: *Jones, *The Name of the Game Is Decision*, 46 TEXAS L. REV. 865-897 (1968); Murphy, *Current Trends in Labor Arb.*, in 11 N.Y. UNIVERSITY, PROC. OF THE ANNUAL CONF. ON LABOR 236-238 (1958); Shulman, *supra* Arbitrator.

LABOR COURT

A labor arbitration court of government origin and control for the purpose of resolving labor-management disputes.

Labor courts are common in many countries of the world. They may be bipartite or tripartite in organization. A typical example is the Danish Permanent Court of Arbitration, which is a 6 member Court, with 16 substitute members representing employers and employees, and a neutral president, 3 vice presidents, and a secretary. The president is to be elected each year by a majority vote of the union-management members of the Court. If the election does not occur by December 1st of each year, the president is elected from members of the Danish Supreme Court and other courts by their presidents. The Danish Labour Court, formerly known as the Permanent Court of Arbitration, deals with disputes rising out of an alleged breach of a collective bargaining contract, and more generally with rights disputes which cannot be settled through collective bargaining. Such a labor court has been successfully resisted in the United States as an erosion of our system of collective bargaining, but is still being supported vigorously by some members of the United States Congress.

See also: Compulsory arb.; Compulsory arb. Australia; Compulsory arb. Public employees; Conseil de prud'hommes; Labor arb. (Voluntary); Nat'l. Railroad Adjustment Board; Tripartite board.

Sources: Denmark Labor Court Act, No. 536 of October 4, 1919 as amended; K. Braun, Labor Disputes and Their Settlement (1955); T. Johnston, Collective Bargaining in Sweden (1962); Fleming, *The Labor Court Idea*, 65 Mich. L. Rev. 1551-1568 (1967).

LABOR DISPUTE

A conflict of claims or rights which may include a dispute between parties to a collective bargaining agreement over the terms or the interpretation of the terms of their contract.

The Norris-LaGuardia Act of March 23, 1932, at § 13(c), defines a labor dispute as follows: "The term 'labor dispute' includes any controversy concerning terms or conditions of employment, or concerning the association or representation of persons in negotiating, fixing, maintaining, changing, or seeking to arrange terms or conditions of employment, regardless of whether or not the disputants stand in the proximate relation of employer and employee."

See also: Norris-LaGuardia Act.

Sources: Norris-LaGuardia Act, 47 Stat. 70, 29 U.S.C.A. § 101 et seq. (1932).

LABOR MANAGEMENT RELATIONS ACT, 1947

See: Taft-Hartley Act.

LABOR-MANAGEMENT REPORTING AND DISCLOSURE ACT

See: Landrum-Griffin Act.

LACHES

The undue or unreasonable delay in asserting a right which might prevent the enforcement of that right or result in its loss.

Arbitrators may consider laches when searching for a remedy or determining a dispute. An arbitrator might rule that if a party has "slept on its claimed rights" for too long a time, it might therefore have lost all its claims to those rights. An example of such a ruling occurred in a case where a grievance was brought three and a half years after the company established a half-hour unpaid lunch period.* The company was upheld on the basis of laches. In another case, an arbitrator held that the doctrine of laches barred the discharge of an employee who had falsified his employment application six years previously. The arbitrator ordered the employee reinstated without back pay, because he felt that the employee should not be penalized so drastically six years later, since it had been the company which had been negligent in not checking the original employment application.**

See also: Statute of limitations; Time limits; Waiver of arb.

Sources: 5 AM. JUR., *supra* Death of the arbitrator at 558-559; AAA, SUMMARY OF LABOR ARB. AWARDS *50-16, **86-8.

LAKE ONTARIO CLAIMS TRIBUNAL (September 27, 1968)
(United States and Canada)

A tribunal established to arbitrate the claims of United States citizens against Canada in the Gut Dam controversy.

The United States consented in 1902 to the building by Canada of the Gut Dam on the St. Lawrence River, providing Canada agreed to compensate United States property owners for whatever damages might be caused by the construction and maintenance of the Dam. The Dam was built, but was subsequently dismantled in 1953. United States property owners filed several damage suits in 1952 against the Dominion of Canada for damages caused by high water levels in Lake Ontario and the St. Lawrence River. After the claimants themselves had failed to reach an agreement to arbitrate with Canada, they asked for State Department assistance in May 1954. Negotiations between the United States State Department and the Canadian Government were unsuccessful. By means of the Lake Ontario Claims Act of 1962, the United States Congress authorized the Foreign Claims Settlement Commission to determine the validity and amount of the claims. The Act became inoperative in 1965 when the United States and Canada agreed to arbitration through a three-member international arbitral tribunal. Under this agreement, each of the two governments was to appoint a national member, and the third member who would preside as Chairman was to be designated jointly by the two governments. The United States and Canada agreed to accept the decision of the Tribunal as final and binding. The Tribunal received 230 claims on behalf of United States citizens in the total amount of $653,386.02. The two governments entered into a compromise agreement on September 27, 1968, through which Canada agreed to pay the United States $350,000 in full satisfaction of the claims.

See also: Espousal; Foreign Claims Settlement Comm'n. of the U.S.; Int'l. claims; Mixed arbitral tribunal; Mixed claims comm'n.; Trail Smelter Arb.

Sources: *Canada-U.S. Lake Ontario (Gut Dam) Arb. Agreement*, 4 INT'L. LEGAL MATERIALS 468-472 (1965); *Canada-United States Settlement of Gut Dam Claims*, 8 *id.* 118 (1969); *The Foreign Claims Settlement Commission and the Lake Ontario Claims Program*, 4 *id.* 473-476 (1965); Lillich, *Gut Dam*, 59 AM. J. INT'L. L. 892-898 (1965); Re, *Int'l. Claims Adjudication: The U.S.-Canadian Agreement*, 17 BUFFALO L. REV. 125-134 (1967).

LANDRUM-GRIFFIN ACT OF 1959
(Labor-Management Reporting and Disclosure Act, 73 Stat. 519)

A federal act passed in 1959 which further amended the National Labor Relations Act, and added detailed, separate restrictions and regulations of internal union affairs.

The Landrum-Griffin Act also provided for the reporting and disclosure of certain financial transactions and administrative practices of both labor organizations and employers. The Act provided for election procedures, and for the prevention of abuses in the administration of trusteeships by labor organizations.

Sources: A. Cox & D. Bok, Cases and Materials on Labor Law 136-137 (6th ed. 1965); C. Gregory, Labor and the Law 572-578 (1961).

LANGUAGE OF THE ARBITRATION

The parties may designate the official language of the arbitration in their agreement to arbitrate or in their *compromis,* or the language of the arbitration may be determined by the arbitrator or by the rules of an agency or institution administering the arbitration.

Rule 20 of the Regulations and Rules of the International Centre for Settlement of Investment Disputes provides that the Tribunal meeting in preliminary procedural consultation shall determine the language or languages to be used in the proceedings. The rules of some administrative agencies have specific provisions for the translation of documents.

See also: Compromis.

Sources: U.N. ECE Hndbook, U.N. Doc. TRADE/WP.1/15/Rev. 1 (1958) at 52; U.N. ILC, *supra* Annulment . . . at 166; ICSID, supra Appeal boards of adm. agencies at 92.

LATIN AMERICA

See: Calvo Clause; Draft Convention on Int'l. Com'l. Arb.; Draft Convention to Improve the Climate for Investment in Latin America . . .; Draft Uniform Law on Inter-American Com'l. Arb.; Inter-American Com'l. Arb. Comm'n.; Montevideo Treaty; Organization of American States; Pact of Bogotá; Second Conf. on Inter-American Com'l. Arb.; Treaty of Guadalupe Hidalgo (1848).

LAW MERCHANT (LEX MERCATORIA)

A body of rules derived from custom and usage which governed the international transactions of merchants who traveled throughout the civilized world during the Middle Ages.

The *lex mercatoria* was applied as part of the common law by the merchants in their special tribunals. This body of trade rules, developed by the international business community rather than by lawyers, was almost as universal in medieval times as the law of the Church. International merchants sat in the *piepoudre* courts. Later this cosmopolitan and universal law merchant was incorporated into the national laws of the various countries. The law merchant is the equivalent of what is today the constant and continuing effort on the part of governmental and non-governmental organizations to develop uniform laws on arbitration and international trade law.

See also: Customary law; European Convention Providing a Uniform Law on Arb.; Piepoudre court; Draft Uniform Law on Inter-American Com'l. Arb.; U.N. Comm'n. on Int'l. Trade Law.

Sources: Schmitthoff, *The Unification of the Law of Int'l. Trade*, 1968 J. Bus. L. 105-119.

LAWYERS' ARBITRATION LETTER (1960-   )

A quarterly memorandum published by the American Arbitration Association on problems of law arising out of the enforcement of arbitration clauses and awards, and containing pertinent case citation and discussion.

The Lawyers' Letters were collected and bound in 1968 with an Appendix of Supplemental Cases. This volume may be ordered from the AAA. Supplemental issues will be published in the future.

See also: American Arbitration Association.

LEAGUE OF NATIONS

An association of States created in accordance with a Covenant of the Peace Conference at Paris, adopted on April 28, 1919, with the high purpose of reducing the likelihood of war, of establishing a system of collective security and cooperation, and encouraging the adoption of the principle of arbitration.

The Covenant of the Peace Conference provided for judicial and arbitral settlement of international disputes as one way of securing the principal objective of the organization, which was the prevention of war and the maintenance of world peace. The League of Nations was officially dissolved on April 18, 1946.

See also: European Convention on the Execution of Foreign Arbitral Awards; Protocol on Arb. Clauses.

Sources: WEBSTER'S INT'L. DICTIONARY (2d ed.).

LEGALISMS

Formal procedures and observances used to make an arbitration more closely resemble a case at law.

The use of such legalisms is often time-consuming, consisting of expensive disagreements over arbitrability between the parties, or between the parties and the arbitrator. Other legalisms may take the form of arguing over technical rules as to the admissibility of evidence, or the application of precedent. Also wasteful may be too great a reliance on transcripts, or the use of over-lengthy briefs, or a dependence on discovery and other pretrial procedures common in civil litigation.

See also: Discovery of documents; Stare decisis.

Sources: R. FLEMING, THE LABOR ARB. PROCESS 57 (1965); *Creeping Legalism in Labor Arb.*, 13 ARB. J. (n.s.) 129-132, 161 (1958).

LENA GOLDFIELDS ARBITRATION (September 3, 1930)
(*Lena Goldfields, Ltd.* v. *Soviet Union*)

An arbitration of a dispute arising from an exploring, mining, and transportation concession agreement granted in 1925 by the Soviet Union to a British company, Lena Goldfields, Ltd.

When the Soviet Union began to expropriate the company's mines and equipment in a series of nationalization measures, Lena Goldfields, Ltd. invoked the arbitration agreement. The arbitration tribunal held that the Soviet Union had unjustly enriched itself by this expropriation without adequately compensating the British company. Although the Soviet Government had appointed its own arbitrator, and joint selection of a super-arbitrator had been made, as well as the date set for the hearing, the U.S.S.R. later refused to attend the hearing on the grounds that the court lacked jurisdiction. The arbitration agreement had provided for a default award, "on condition that such decision is unanimous." The chairman and the Lena-appointed arbitrator met, and an award of £8,500,000 plus 12% interest was made on September 3, 1930. This award was repudiated by the Soviet Union. The British Government finally obtained a settlement in 1934 by linking the *Lena Goldfields Case* with trade agreement discussions. Although the proper law of the contract was Soviet law, the case was judged on the general principles of law recognized by civilized nations, and specifically on the doctrine of unjust enrichment.

See also: Applicable law. Int'l. pub. arb.; Concession contract; Default; Economic development agreements; Enforcement of award (Int'l. pub. arb.); General principles of law recognized by civilized nations; Int'l. claims; Int'l. law.

Sources: Text of the Award in the Lena Goldfields, Ltd. Arb., Sept. 3, 1930, in Nussbaum, *The Arb. between Lena Goldfields, Ltd. and the Soviet Government*, 36 CORNELL L. Q. 42-53 (1950); E. NANTWI, *supra* Annulment . . . ; Ssekandi, *Contracts between a State and a Foreign Private Company*, 2 E. AFRICAN L. J. 281-298 (1966).

LEX MERCATORIA

See: Law merchant.

LIABILITY OF ARBITRATOR

An arbitrator is immune from civil or legal action for any award he may render.

Without such immunity, the losing party could expose the arbitrator to all the hazards of a lawsuit.

See also: Arbitrator; Testimony of arbitrator.

Sources: 10 LAWYERS' LETTERS (1962), supra Adjournment of hearings at 1; 29 id. (1967) at 3.

LIE DETECTOR (POLYGRAPH)

An electronic device which records the changes in blood pressure, pulse, respiration, and perspiration of a person under questioning in order to determine whether or not he is telling the truth.

Arbitrators, like courts, usually exclude polygraph evidence in proceedings before them. Labor unions contend on principle that refusal to take a lie detector test is not in itself a just cause for discharge.

See also: Rules of evidence.

Sources: Burkey, Privacy, Property and the Polygraph, 18 LAB. L. J. 79-89 (1967).

LINCOLN MILLS

[Textile Workers Union of America v. Lincoln Mills of Alabama, 353 U.S. 448 (1957)]

A major U.S. Supreme Court decision ruling that specific performance of promises to arbitrate grievances is enforceable under federal law.

The Textile Workers-Lincoln Mills contract prohibited strikes and lockouts during its term, and required that grievances be handled under a specific procedure. The grievances in this particular dispute were processed through the required steps. When the union demanded arbitration, the company refused, and the union brought suit in the district court to compel arbitration. The Supreme Court first concerned itself with the question of whether § 301 of the Labor Management Relations Act might be considered a source of substantive law. "Plainly," the Court ruled, "the agreement to arbitrate grievance disputes is the *quid pro quo* for an agreement not to strike. Viewed in this light, the legislation does more than confer jurisdiction in the federal courts over labor organizations. It expresses a federal policy that federal courts should enforce these agreements on behalf of or against labor organizations and that industrial peace can be best obtained only in that way." The Court concluded that § 301 authorized federal courts to fashion a body of federal law for the enforcement of collective bargaining agreements in industries affecting interstate commerce, and that an essential element of this federal law was the enforcement of agreements to arbitrate. Following this decision, the three Trilogy cases of 1960 further confirmed the strength of arbitration in cases similiar to *Lincoln Mills*.

See also: Common law arb.; Enforcement of arb. agreements (Common law); Enforcement of arb. agreements (Federal statutes); Enforcement of award (Labor); Individual rights; Labor arb. (Voluntary); No-strike clause; § 301 disputes; Substantive arbitrability; Taft-Hartley Act; Trilogy.

Sources: Textile Workers v. Lincoln Mills of Alabama, 353 U.S. 448 (1957); Aaron, *On First Looking into the Lincoln Mills Decision*, in 12 PROC. OF THE NAT'L. ACADEMY OF ARBITRATORS 1-13 (1959); Bickel, *Legislative Purpose and the Judicial Process*, 71 HARV. L. REV. 1-39 (1957); Bunn, *Lincoln Mills and the Jurisdiction to Enforce Collective Bargaining Agreements*, 43 VA. L. REV. 1247-1259 (1957).

LIVINGSTON V. JOHN WILEY & SONS

See: Procedural arbitrability; Wiley & Sons v. Livingston.

LOCALE OF ARBITRATION

The place where the arbitration is held.

Where the contract provides for a possible place of arbitration, such a provision will be honored by the arbitrators. Proper selection of the place of arbitration is important because of the convenience of witnesses and the location of material, books, and other evidence under dispute. It has often been held that the parties in selecting a place of arbitration have also implied an agreement on the applicability of the law of that place. Reference in their agreement to the rules of an administrative agency determines that the rules of that agency shall apply as to locale when the parties have not designated in their agreement where the arbitration will be held. The International Chamber of Commerce in Article 18 of its rules provides that: "The proceedings before the arbitrator shall take place in the country determined by the Court of Arbitration, unless the parties shall have agreed in advance upon the place of arbitration."

See also: Applicable procedural law; Applicable substantive law; Arb. agreement; Procedure; Situs of arb.; Venue of arb.; U.N. ECE. Rules of Arb.; Wal Wal Arb.

Sources: AAA COM'L. ARB. RULES, *supra* Adm. appointment at § 10; M. BERNSTEIN, *supra* Appeal at ch. 15; M. DOMKE, *supra* Appeal boards of adm. agencies; 6 LAWYERS' LETTERS (1961), *supra* Adjournment of hearings at 3.

LOCAL REMEDIES RULE

See: Exhaustion of local remedies.

LONDON COURT OF ARBITRATION
(69 Cannon Street, London, E.C. 4, United Kingdom)

Established in 1892 under the auspices of the London Chamber of Commerce to provide facilities for domestic and international commercial arbitration.

The Court is administered by 24 members, 12 appointed by the Corporation of London, and 12 by the London Chamber of Commerce. The Rules of the Court are revised periodically as the arbitration law in England changes. From 1892 to 1902, the Court was known as the London Chamber of Arbitration. Its facilities are open to any person or organization of any country. The London Court is well known throughout the world for the skill and high quality of its arbitrators.

See also: Access to the arbitral tribunal; Chamber of commerce; Institutional arb.; Int'l. com'l. arb.

Sources: LONDON COURT OF ARB., [DESCRIPTIVE PAMPHLET] (1963); Hoare, *The London Court of Arb.*, 33 ARB. J. OF THE INST. OF ARBITRATORS 121-124 (1967); Macassey, *The London Court of Arb.*, 3 ARB. J. 351 (1939).

LONDON COURT OF ARBITRATION. ARBITRATION CLAUSE

The clause reads as follows: "The construction, validity and performance of this contract shall be governed by the law of England and all disputes which may arise under, out of, or in connection with, or in relation to this contract shall be submitted to the arbitration of the London Court of Arbitration under and in accordance with its Rules at the date hereof. The parties hereto agree that service of any notices in the course of such arbitration at their addresses as given in this contract shall be valid and sufficient."

See also: Future disputes clause; Service by mail; Standard arb. clause.

Sources: London Court of Arb., *supra* Adm. expenses.

LOOSE-LEAF SERVICES (LABOR ARBITRATION AWARDS)

See: American Labor Arb. Awards (P-H); Labor Arb. Awards (CCH); Labor Arb. Reports (BNA); Summary of Labor Arb. Awards (AAA); War Labor Reports (BNA).

LUMP SUM SETTLEMENT

A method of settling international claims through negotiation between governments of a single or lump sum to be paid without consideration for individual claims or recourse to international adjudication.

After such a lump sum settlement, the amount is divided among the various qualified claimants by the receiving government. A lump sum settlement is one which is negotiated rather than arbitrated. It is a quicker means of settling international claims, as the claimant is usually not required to exhaust his remedies in the foreign country before seeking the intervention of his own government. It is an inferior method of diplomatic protection from the standpoint of the individual, since he is given no opportunity to claim in direct suit the actual amount of compensation due him from the liable government. The success of the lump sum settlement procedure depends almost exclusively on the adequacy of the sum obtained from the foreign government.

See also: Espousal; Foreign Claims Settlement Comm'n. of the U.S.; Int'l. claims; Mixed arbitral tribunals.

Sources: 8 M. WHITEMAN, *supra* Calvo Clause at 1118ff; Re, *The Presettlement Adjudication of Int'l. Claims,* in INT'L. ARB. LIBER AMICORUM FOR MARTIN DOMKE 214ff. (P. Sanders ed. 1967).

MADDOX

See: Republic Steel v. Maddox.

MAJOR DISPUTES

See: National Mediation Board.

MANAGEMENT RIGHTS

Those rights which management retains in its contracts with a union.

Management rights can be divided into two categories: all decisions relating to the operation of the business, and those concerned with the supervision of employees. Rights concerning supervision are variously expressed in union contracts as the right to hire, promote, discharge, or discipline for cause. The collective bargaining agreement provides its own machinery in its grievance and arbitration procedures for testing and remedying violations of rights for both management and employees. Many arbitrations involve management rights which are not clearly expressed in the agreement, or which are based on past practice, or on some ambiguity in the contract. In its *Fibreboard* decision, the United States Supreme Court held that contracting out work is not, in itself, a management right, and in some instances must be subject to collective bargaining.

See also: Collective bargaining agreement; Exclusionary clause; Fibreboard Paper Products Corp. v. NLRB; Past practice; Residual rights; Subcontracting.

Sources: L. KELLER, THE MANAGEMENT FUNCTION 20-34 (1963); M. STONE, MANAGERIAL FREEDOM AND JOB SECURITY (1964); General Motors Corp.—UAW Collective Bargaining Agreement, effective Jan. 1, 1968; Goldberg, *Management's Reserved Rights,* in 9 PROC. OF THE NAT'L. ACADEMY OF ARBITRATORS 118-129 (1956).

MECHANIC'S LIEN

The security interest of a worker or contractor in a building or its land as a protection against loss of pay for work performed or materials used in the construction of that building.

The mechanic's lien ensures that the worker or contractor be paid first. Under New York State law, a filing of a notice for lien does not constitute a waiver of the right to arbitrate.

Sources: M. DOMKE, *supra* Adhesion contract at 268-269.

MEDIATION

An advisory intervention by a third party in dispute negotiations with the purpose of helping the parties concerned find a solution.

The parties may be a union and a company, or they may be two disputing nations. The success of this organized friendly aid depends on the skill of the mediator. In the early years as Impartial Chairman in the hosiery industry, George Taylor defined mediation as the development of "the consent to lose," on the part of one or the other of the disputing parties.* There are many types of government mediation available on the local, state, and national levels. The mediator may be invited to participate in crisis or non-crisis conditions. He may meet with the parties separately, carrying messages from one to the other, or he may arrange joint conferences. He may be able to persuade the parties to agree on arbitrating at least some of the issues in dispute. Since his is largely a persuasive and clarifying role, the mediator may offer suggestions, but rarely acts to force either party to accept a solution. In international law, mediation refers to a third-party procedure which is both informal and confidential.

See also: Arsenal of weapons; Atomic Energy Labor-Management Relations Panel; Conciliation; Emergency boards; Executive Order 10988; Fact-finding; Federal Mediation and Conciliation Service; Good offices; Grievance mediation; Impartial chairman system; Impasse; Labor arb. (Voluntary); Missile Sites Labor Commission; Nat'l. Defense Mediation Board; Office of Collective Bargaining; Preventive mediation; State boards of mediation; Taylor Law; Tennessee Valley Authority employee-management relations.

Sources: D. COLE, THE QUEST FOR INDUSTRIAL PEACE 160-161 (1963); *Killingsworth & Wallen, *supra* Board of arb. at 59-79; Stevens, *Mediation and the Role of the Neutral*, in FRONTIERS OF COLLECTIVE BARGAINING (J. Dunlop & N. Chamberlain eds. 1967).

MERGING SENIORITY LISTS

The combining of seniority lists for the protection of the seniority of employees when plants within a company, or departments within that company move or consolidate, or when a corporation is sold or merged with another.

Problems of seniority are becoming increasingly complex with the rapid advancement of technology. Companies and unions are developing principles for the clarification of seniority, such as the length-of-service method, the follow-the-work method where workers may be given the opportunity to move with the plant with full protection for their seniority rights, and the surviving-group principle where the employees of the purchasing company have preference over the employees of the acquired company. Many such seniority cases are referred to arbitration.

See also: Seniority.

Sources: Feinberg, *Do Contract Rights Vest?*, in 16 PROC. OF THE NAT'L. ACADEMY OF ARBITRATORS 192-237 (1963); Kennedy, *id.* at 1-44; Weber, *The Interplant Transfer of Displaced Employees*, in ADJUSTING TO TECHNOLOGICAL CHANGE 95-143 (G. Somers et al., ed. 1963).

MERITS OF A CASE

The intrinsic rights and wrongs in a dispute as determined by the substantial facts of the case itself.

In its Trilogy decisions, the United States Supreme Court ruled that judges are not to get into the merits of the case when they are determining arbitrability or enforcement. These decisions signified that the judges were not to substitute their judgment for that of the arbitrator.

See also: American Manufacturing Co.; Enterprise Wheel & Car Corp.; Motion to compel arb.; Trilogy.

Sources: United Steelworkers v. Warrior & Gulf Nav. Co., 363 U.S. 574 (1960).

MINOR DISPUTES

See: National Railroad Adjustment Board.

MISCONDUCT OF ARBITRATOR

Any conduct on the part of the arbitrator which might endanger a valid award.

Either party may challenge an arbitrator and ask that he be removed before he has made his award on the grounds of partiality or failure to conduct the hearings properly. Or a party may move to have the award vacated. The Uniform Arbitration Act at § 12 lists the grounds for vacating the award as follows: "(1) The award was procured by corruption, fraud or other undue means; (2) There was evident partiality by an arbitrator appointed as a neutral or corruption in any of the arbitrators or misconduct prejudicing the rights of any party; (3) The arbitrators exceeded their powers; (4) The arbitrators refused to postpone the hearing upon sufficient cause being shown therefor or refused to hear evidence material to the controversy or otherwise so conducted the hearing, contrary to the provisions of § 5, as to prejudice substantially the rights of a party; . . ."

See also: Adjournment of hearings; Annulment . . . ; Arbitrator; Bias; Challenge of arbitrator; Duty to disclose; Grounds of nullity; Independent investigation by arbitrator; Rehearing; Removal of arbitrator; Rules of evidence; Uniform Arb. Act; Vacating an award.

Sources: Uniform Arb. Act; M. DOMKE, *supra* Adhesion contract at 204-210, 231-251.

MISSILE SITES LABOR COMMISSION
(May 26, 1961—October 11, 1967)

A nine member, tripartite board composed of an equal number of labor, management, and public representatives appointed by the President of the United States to resolve present or future disputes at missile and space sites.

The Missile Sites Labor Commission was created by a Presidential Executive Order of President John F. Kennedy on May 26, 1961. The Secretary of Labor was Chairman, and the Director of the Federal Mediation and Conciliation Service was Vice Chairman of the Missile Sites Labor Commission. Procedures for settling disputes at the local level were set up through twenty-four local tripartite committees, including representatives from the Federal Mediation and Conciliation Service. Settlement of disputes was by mediation, though efforts could also be made to obtain agreement for arbitration. Like the Atomic Energy Labor-Management Panel, the Missile Sites Labor Commission was established to handle labor relations in government owned but privately operated plants. The Missile Sites Labor Commission was terminated on October 11, 1967, and its function transferred to the Federal Mediation and Conciliation Service.

See also: Atomic Energy Labor-Management Relations Panel; Federal Mediation and Conciliation Service; Mediation; Public employee; Tennessee Valley Authority employee-management relations; Tripartite board.

Sources: U.S. GPO, MISSILE SITES LABOR COMMISSION 1961 THRU 1967 (1969); J. Kuczma, *The Missile Sites Labor Story*, August 13, 1963 (address before the American Bar Association).

MIXED ARBITRAL TRIBUNAL

A special international tribunal to arbitrate mutual or unilateral claims.

Mixed arbitral tribunals may be resorted to after wars or insurrections, or in peacetime when established procedures for handling claims break down. These tribunals are usually composed of three members, one from each of the disputing States, and a president appointed jointly by the disputants, or by some designated public figure or institution. The parties in their agreement to arbitrate may make it clear that arbitration is to take place prior to the exhaustion of all other remedies. Examples of such tribunals were those set up by the Peace Treaties in 1919 and 1920. Conciliation Commissions to handle similar claims were established after World War II.*

See also: Espousal; Exhaustion of local remedies; Int'l. claims; Int'l. pub. arb.; Joint claims comm'n.; Lake Ontario Claims Tribunal; Lump sum settlement; Mixed claims comm'n.; Tribunal; Tripartite board.

Sources: *14 U.N.R.I.A.A. 3-523; K. CARLSTON, *supra* Annulment . . .; J. SIMPSON & H. Fox, *supra* Appointment of arbitrators; M. WHITEMAN, *supra* Calvo Clause at 779.

MIXED CLAIMS COMMISSION

The most common type of international arbitral tribunal.

The members of a mixed claims commission are selected by the States involved in a dispute. An odd member is selected jointly by these members, or by an authority appointed by them. The power of decision may be by majority vote, or if no such agreement is reached, the final decision rests with the odd member acting as umpire. Nations usually do not require that local remedies be exhausted first before the parties resort to arbitration. The question of the local remedy rule may be posed by one of the governments in its arguments before the tribunal. The Government of the United Kingdom used such an argument in 1956 in the *Ambatielos Case* (*Greece* v. *United Kingdom*). The Commission held that Mr. Ambatielos had not availed himself of all local remedies available to him, as required by the Treaty of 1886 which the parties had mutually agreed in their *compromis* was partially to govern the case, and his claim therefore was not allowed.

See also: Alabama Arb.; Espousal; Exhaustion of local remedies; Int'l. claims; Int'l. pub. arb.; Joint claims comm'n.; Lake Ontario Claims Tribunal; Mixed arbitral tribunal; Tripartite board.

Sources: The Ambatielos Claim, 12 U.N.R.I.A.A. 87-153 (1956); K. CARLSTON, *supra* Annulment . . .; M. HUDSON, *supra* Convention on the Pacific Settlement of Int'l. Disputes; J. RALSTON, THE LAW AND PROCEDURE OF INT'L. TRIBUNALS (1926); D. SANDIFER, EVIDENCE BEFORE INT'L. TRIBUNALS (1939); J. SIMPSON & H. Fox, *supra* Appointment of arbitrators.

MODEL RULES ON ARBITRAL PROCEDURE

A comprehensive set of procedural rules for international public arbitration prepared by the International Law Commission under the direction of Professor Georges Scelle.

The Model Rules on Arbitral Procedure were originally planned as an international convention to be approved initially by the General Assembly, and thereafter opened to signature and ratification by the member States. This convention was later drafted as Model Rules and submitted to the General Assembly with the recommendation that the Rules would not become binding on any United Nations Member State unless they were accepted by that State in an arbitration treaty or *compromis*. The *Commentary on the Draft Convention* pointed out that "The chief significance of the draft lies in the several means which it provides for ensuring that the obligation to carry out the agreement to arbitrate shall not be frustrated at any point by a subsequent failure by one of the parties to fulfill that obligation." The Model Rules incorporate the International Court of Justice as a supervisory authority.

See also: Annulment . . . ; Consent of the parties; Evasion of arb.; Exces de pouvoir; Grounds of nullity; Int'l. Law Comm'n.; Int'l. pub. arb.; Party autonomy; Procedure.

Sources: Model Rules, *supra* Appointment of arbitrators; U.N. ILC, *supra* Annulment . . . at 8.

MODERN ARBITRATION STATUTE

A modern arbitration statute provides that any agreement to submit future disputes to arbitration cannot be revoked and is specifically enforceable, that a party to a dispute may compel a reluctant party to arbitrate by means of a court order, and that any court action initiated in violation of an arbitration agreement may be stayed until arbitration has taken place in the agreed manner.

Most modern arbitration statutes grant the court the authority to appoint arbitrators on the application of a party, to fill vacancies when the parties fail to make such appointments, or when the arbitrators withdraw or are unable to serve. The court is not free to review the facts and findings in the award of an arbitrator. Modern statutes are generally useful in providing quicker procedures for confirming awards.

See also: Enforcement of arb. agreements (State statutes); Future disputes clause; Irrevocability of the arb. agreement; Modifying the award; Motion to compel arb.; Notice of intention to arbitrate; Stay of arb.; Stay of suit; Statutory arb.; Subpoena.

Sources: M. DOMKE, *supra* Adhesion contract at 20; 28 LAWYERS' LETTERS (1966), *supra* Adjournment of hearings at 6.

MODIFYING THE AWARD

The correction of errors in an award by a court or an arbitrator.

According to most statutes, an award may be corrected if there is a miscalculation of figures, or a mistake in the description of any person, thing or property referred to in the award. Under the New York State law, an application to modify the award must be made to the court in writing within 90 days after delivery of the award. The court may under some statutes have the power to order a rehearing by the arbitrators. Or it may order them to modify and correct the award. Or the court may itself modify the award. Or where the award is not mutual or final, the court may resubmit the matter to the arbitrators. The award must cover all issues under dispute as described in the submission in order to be final. Recent modern statutes, such as those of New York State and Illinois, provide that within a specified time after delivery of the award, a party may request the arbitrator to modify or correct the award. The New York State Civil Practice Law and Rules states that such an application must be in writing, and must be made within twenty days after the award has been delivered. The arbitrator in correcting errors such as a miscalculation of figures, is not to reexamine the merits of his decision.

See also: Appeal; Award; Challenge of award; Functus officio; Modern arbitration statute; Rehearing; Statutory arb.; Supplemental award.

Sources: Ill. Rev. Stat., ch. 10, § 109; N. Y. CPLR § 7509; M. DOMKE, supra Adhesion contract at 316-317; 34 LAWYERS' LETTERS (1968), *supra* Adjournment of hearings at 1-3.

MONTEVIDEO CONFERENCE (1933)

The Seventh International Conference of American States was held in 1933 at Montevideo, Uruguay, where a report was made by the Pan American Union recommending the establishment of an Inter-American commercial arbitration system.

The Montevideo Conference adopted Resolution XLI on December 23, authorizing what was eventually to become the Inter-American Commercial Arbitration Commission. The Conference also recommended the adoption by the American Republics of a set of legislative standards to make more uniform the various national arbitration laws.

See also: Draft Uniform Law on Inter-American Com'l. Arb.; Inter-American Com'l. Arb. Comm'n.

Sources: INTER-AMERICAN COMMERCIAL ARBITRATION COMMISSION, *supra* Inter-American Com'l. Arb. Comm'n. at Annex A; C. Norberg, Inter-American Com'l. Arb., a Report Submitted to the Inter-American Council of Commerce and Production, 1966 (prepared under a grant of the AAA); Pan American Union, Com'l. Arb. in the American Republics, Dec. 3, 1933 (documents for use of delegates to the Seventh Int'l. Conf. of American States, Montevideo, Uruguay, No. 2); Domke, *supra* Inter-American Com'l. Arb. Comm'n.; Watson, *supra* Inter-American Com'l. Arb. Comm'n. at 211-219.

MONTEVIDEO TREATY (March 19, 1940)
(Treaty of International Procedural Law)

A treaty signed by Argentina, Columbia, Bolivia, Brazil, Paraguay, Peru, and Uruguay at Montevideo, Uruguay, on March 19, 1940, at the Second South American Congress of International Private Law.

Title III, Articles 5 through 9 of the Montevideo Treaty declared that judgments and arbitral awards rendered in civil and commercial matters in any one of the Contracting States shall be enforceable in any of the other States, providing that certain procedural matters have been met. These requirements are that the award was rendered by a competent tribunal in the international sphere, that it had finality or the authority of res judicata in the state where it was rendered, and that it was not in conflict with public order in the country where it was to be enforced. Another essential requirement is that the losing party must have been legally summoned, and either represented at the arbitration, or declared in default in conformity with the law of the country where the arbitration was conducted.

See also: Default; Enforcement of foreign arbitral awards; Res judicata.

Sources: *Treaty of Int'l. Procedural Law*, 37 Am. J. Int'l. L. Supp. 116-122 (1943).

MOONLIGHTING

The practice of working after hours at another job.

In cases involving discharge for dual employment unions frequently maintain that the practice of moonlighting must first have been prohibited in the contract to make it a just cause for discharge. Some arbitrators draw the distinction between performing outside labor and engaging in business in competition with one's employer. Other arbitrators consider deterioration of work or frequent absence as important in determining the degree of discipline which would be fair to apply in cases of moonlighting.

Sources: Foster, *Disloyalty to the Employer*, 20 Arb. J. (n.s.) 157-167 (1965).

MOTION PICTURE INDUSTRY ARBITRATION SYSTEM

An arbitration system which came into existence under a consent decree as the result of a settlement of the anti-trust suit brought by the United States Government in 1938 against five major motion picture distributors.

The arbitrations in the motion picture industry were to be administered according to the rules of the American Arbitration Association, which was appointed the administrator of the entire arbitration system. The AAA was authorized to establish a Tribunal in 30 designated cities where arbitration proceedings were to be held, with an Appeal Board to be located in New York City. The arbitrators were to be impartial and have no connection of any kind with the motion picture industry. An exhibitor was not compelled to arbitrate but could bring suit in a court under the anti-trust laws. The exhibitors were entitled to arbitration in disputes concerning those subjects of distribution which had been declared discriminatory in the original case. The system ceased to operate after the United States Supreme Court decision of May 3, 1948, which held that the Government had never consented to a permanent system of arbitration under the consent decree no matter how efficient that system had proved itself to be.

See also: American Arb. Association; Consent decree.

Sources: U. S. v. Paramount Pictures et al., 334 U.S. 131, 176 (1948); AAA, ANN. REP. (1941); NAT'L. THEATRES CORP., HANDBOOK ANALYZING CERTAIN PROVISIONS OF THE CONSENT DECREE (1941).

MOTION TO COMPEL ARBITRATION

A form of legal notice used by the aggrieved party to petition a court to compel the other party to arbitrate.

A motion to compel arbitration is allowed under most arbitration statutes. At the hearing before the court, the supporting affidavits and documents of both parties should provide evidence that there is an agreement to arbitrate. Both the statement that a dispute exists under that agreement, and the opposing party's refusal to comply, should also be presented. Under the New York State statute, the court may determine only whether a valid agreement to arbitrate was made or complied with, or if one of the parties refused to arbitrate, or whether the claim is barred by certain statutory requirements, such as time limitations. The court cannot consider the merits of the controversy. This is generally the pattern of other modern statutes, including the United States Arbitration Act. In most labor cases, § 301 of the Taft-Hartley Act would be the applicable law. Any disposition of the case by the court would be controlled by the Trilogy.

See also: Enforcement of arb. agreements (Federal statutes); Enforcement of arb. agreements (State statutes); Merits of a case; Modern arb. statute; § 301 disputes; Statutory arb.; Trilogy; U. S. Arb. Act.

Sources: Labor Management Relations Act, 29 U.S.C.A. §§ 141-197; N.Y. CPLR § 7503; Ass'N. OF THE BAR OF THE CITY OF N. Y., *supra* Award by confession at 13.

MULTIPLE GRIEVANCES

The accumulation of many grievances by union and management which may be consolidated and heard in a single hearing by the same arbitrator.

Any such consolidation of multiple grievances depends on particular contract restrictions.

See also: Consolidation; Distressed grievance procedure; Joinder.

MUNICIPAL LAW

The law of an individual state or nation.

See also: Applicable procedural law; Int'l. com'l. arb.

NATIONAL ACADEMY OF ARBITRATORS

An organization founded in Chicago on September 14, 1947, to foster high standards of knowledge and skill on a professional level among those engaged in the arbitration of industrial disputes.

The National Academy of Arbitrators is not an agency for the selection or appointment of arbitrators. It meets annually in national convention and more often in regional meetings. Lectures on various aspects of arbitration delivered at its meetings are reprinted annually and published by the Bureau of National Affairs under the general title, *Proceedings of the Annual Meeting of the National Academy of Arbitrators*. The Academy maintains standing committees of Ethics and Grievance, Law and Legislation, and Membership. *The Code of Ethics and Procedural Standards*, prepared jointly by the Academy and the American Arbitration Association, and approved for arbitrations by the Federal Mediation and Conciliation Service, is subject to continuing study and interpretation by the Ethics Committee of the Academy. The National Academy had approximately 350 members as of January 1968.

See also: Code of Ethics and Procedural Standards for Labor-Management Arb.

Sources: Nat'l. Academy of Arbitrators, Membership Directory 1968-69 at 2-3.

NATIONAL CIVIC FEDERATION

A federation organized in 1900 which was influential in the early 20th century in efforts to promote industrial peace.

The National Civic Federation sponsored a National Conference on Industrial Conciliation held in New York in 1900, where the advantages of conciliation and arbitration were reviewed, and a Committee on Conciliation and Arbitration was set up to appeal to the American people for the creation of joint boards of conciliation, and the adoption of annual or semi-annual joint agreements. Such influential men as Mark Hanna, Samuel Gompers, Grover Cleveland, Charles W. Eliot, August Belmont, and Charles M. Schwab were among its members. The National Civic Federation was an outgrowth of the Civic Federation of Chicago, which sponsored the first Congress on Industrial Conciliation and Arbitration in Chicago in 1894. *The National Civic Federation Review* was sponsored by the National Civic Federation, and published at irregular intervals from 1903 to 1920.

See also: Congress on Industrial Conciliation and Arbitration.

Sources: E. WITTE, *supra* Arbitration Act of 1888 at 17-21.

NATIONAL DEFENSE MEDIATION BOARD

A tripartite board established before the United States was formally at war by Executive Order No. 8716 of President Franklin D. Roosevelt on March 19, 1941, to adjust labor disputes threatening to interfere with the defense effort.

The National Defense Mediation Board was created to cope with the number of strikes which increased from 147 to 316 in the period from December 1940 to March 1941. Three dispute settlement procedures were provided in the Executive Order. The first of these was mediation. If mediation failed, voluntary arbitration was to be recommended. If both mediation and voluntary arbitration proved ineffective, fact-finding recommendations for a settlement were to be made public. Disputes were to reach the Board only through certification by the Secretary of Labor. The Board was originally composed of eleven members designated by the President, three public members, four management, and four labor. Alternates from all three groups were eventually added, increasing the membership to 41. The Board was formally terminated by Executive Order No. 9017 of January 12, 1942, which at the same time created the National War Labor Board.

See also: Fact-finding; Labor arb. (Voluntary); Mediation; Nat'l. War Labor Board; No-strike, No-lockout Agreement of 1941; Tripartite board.

Sources: U. S. BUREAU OF LABOR STATISTICS BULL. No. 714, REPORT ON THE WORK OF THE NAT'L. DEFENSE MEDIATION BOARD, March 19, 1941–January 12, 1942 (1942).

NATIONALITY OF ARBITRATOR

The neutral arbitrator or umpire in international public and international private cases is usually of a nationality different from that of the parties.

The parties may designate the nationality of the arbitrator in their arbitration agreement or *compromis*. Under the International Chamber of Commerce Rules, sole arbitrators and third arbitrators must be nationals of countries other than those of the parties. The Commercial Arbitration Rules of the American Arbitration Association at § 15 state: "If one of the parties is a national or resident of a country other than the United States, the sole Arbitrator or the neutral Arbitrator shall, upon the request of either party, be appointed from among the nationals of a country other than that of any of the parties."

See also: Arbitrator.

Sources: AAA COM'L. ARB. RULES, *supra* Adm. appointment at § 15; ICC, *supra* Answering statement art. 7 (3).

NATIONAL JOINT BOARD FOR THE SETTLEMENT OF JURISDICTIONAL DISPUTES. BUILDING AND CONSTRUCTION INDUSTRY (1949-1969)

A panel set up by the building trade unions and employer groups in the construction industry to hear and decide work assignment disputes.

The original Joint Board was created in 1948, and was known as the Board of Trustees. The later National Joint Board for the Settlement of Jurisdictional Disputes was established in October 1949. The Procedural Rules and Regulations were reviewed and frequently amended. Article X of the Constitution of the Building and Construction Trades Department, AFL-CIO, provided that all jurisdictional disputes between or "among affiliated National and International Unions and their affiliated Local Unions and employers shall" be settled by means of the Plan for Settling Jurisdicitonal Disputes Nationally and Locally. The Board consisted of an impartial chairman, two regular and two alternate members each from both employers and employees. There was also an Appeals Board empowered to review and decide appeals from decisions of the Joint Board, consisting of an Impartial Umpire, and two regular and two alternate members each from employees and employers. The National Joint Board ceased operations September 30, 1969.

See also: Jurisdictional disputes; § 10(k) proceedings; Work assignment disputes.

Sources: BUILDING & CONSTRUCTION DEPT., AFL-CIO, PLAN FOR SETTLING JURISDICTIONAL DISPUTES NATIONALLY AND LOCALLY (April 1, 1965); NAT'L. JOINT BOARD FOR SETTLEMENT OF JURISDICTIONAL DISPUTES, PROCEDURAL RULES AND REGULATIONS . . . AND APPEALS BOARD PROCEDURES (July 21, 1965); The Associated General Contractors of America, *News Release*, Oct. 1, 1969; Sherman, *The Nat'l. Joint Board For Settlement of Jurisdictional Disputes in the Building and Construction Industry*, 10 LAB. L. J. 463 (1959).

NATIONAL LABOR-MANAGEMENT PANEL

A panel established under § 205 of the Taft-Hartley Act of 1947 to assist the Director of the Federal Mediation and Conciliation Service.

The purpose of the National Labor-Management Panel is to advise how industrial controversies may be avoided, and how mediation and other voluntary adjustment procedures may be administered in disputes affecting the national welfare. The National Labor-Management Panel is composed of six representatives from labor and six from management appointed by the President of the United States. Each member holds office for a term of three years.

NATIONAL LABOR RELATIONS ACT (NLRA)

See: Wagner Act.

NATIONAL LABOR RELATIONS BOARD (NLRB)

An independent federal agency created by Congress in 1935 to administer the National Labor Relations Act of July 5, 1935.

Under the National Labor Relations Act as amended in 1947 by the Taft-Hartley Act, the NLRB has two primary functions: first, to determine through agency-conducted secret ballot elections which union is to be the exclusive representative of employees for the purpose of collective bargaining, and second, to prevent and remedy unfair labor practices by both labor organizations and employers. The National Labor Relations Board has jurisdiction over work assignment disputes in accordance with § 10(k) of the National Labor Relations Act. When conflict of concurrent jurisdictions occurs between the Board and an arbitrator, the Board through its Spielberg doctrine has determined which shall have precedence. Since 1947, the Board has been composed of five members and a general counsel appointed by the President of the United States with the consent of the Senate.

See also: Concurrent jurisdiction; Jurisdictional disputes; Representational disputes; § 10(k) proceedings; Spielberg doctrine; Unfair labor practice; Wagner Act; Work assignment disputes.

Sources: 32 NLRB ANN. REP. 2ff. (1967).

NATIONAL MEDIATION BOARD

A private agency of the federal government created by the Railway Labor Act of 1926, as amended June 21, 1934, to supersede the United States Board of Mediation, to govern labor relations in the railroad industry.

The Railway Labor Act was further amended on April 10, 1936, to extend the jurisdiction of the Board to airlines engaged in interstate commerce or under mail contract. The three members of the National Mediation Board are appointed by the President of the United States to serve for three years. The National Mediation Board has two major duties. The first is the mediation of disputes between the railroads, or airlines, and the unions representing their employees in making new or changing existing agreements, disputes sometimes described as Major Disputes. The second duty is the supervision and certification of secret ballot elections to select the unions to represent these employees. The Board also interprets the terms of agreements, appoints neutral referees when requested by the various divisions of the National Railroad Adjustment Board, and arbitrators when necessary in arbitrations held under the Act, and notifies the President when labor disputes threaten to deprive any section of the country of essential transportation services. The President may then, and at his own discretion, appoint an emergency board to investigate and report to him on such critical disputes.

See also: Conciliation; Emergency boards; Fact-finding; Gov't. intervention; Interest arb.; Mediation; Nat'l. Railroad Adjustment Board; Railway Labor Act; Representational disputes.

Sources: Railway Labor Act, 45 U.S.C. §§ 151-163, 181-188; 33 NAT'L. MEDIATION BOARD ANN. REP. (1968).

NATIONAL RAILROAD ADJUSTMENT BOARD

A board established under the 1934 amendments to the Railway Labor Act to hear and decide disputes in the railroad industry concerned with employee grievances, and the application and interpretation of the collective bargaining agreement.

Disputes caused by employee grievances are known in the railroad industry as Minor Disputes. Major Disputes which involve the making or changing of the contract are assigned for resolution to the National Mediation Board. The National Railroad Adjustment Board is composed of 36 members, 18 chosen and compensated by the carriers, and 18 by the railway labor organizations. The Adjustment Board is separated into four divisions, each bipartite division having jurisdiction over a distinct class or craft of employees. Any grievance which is not settled by bargaining or mediation, or any other established procedure outlined in the agreement, is automatically submitted to the National Railroad Adjustment Board. When the members of any of the four divisions are unable to agree upon an award, they select a neutral person to sit with the division as a member, who will then make a final and binding award. This neutral member is known as a referee. Where the division is unable to agree on the referee, the National Mediation Board itself makes the appointment, and the referee then renders the award. This latter procedure closely resembles compulsory arbitration.

See also: Adjustment board; Bipartite board; Compulsory arb.; Compulsory arb. Australia; Grievance arb.; Labor court; Nat'l. Mediation Board; PL boards of adjustment; Railway Labor Act; Referee; Tripartite Board.

Sources: Railway Labor Act, 45 U.S.C. §§ 151-163, 181-188; 33 NAT'L. MEDIATION BOARD ANN. REP. 41-42 (1968).

NATIONAL WAGE STABILIZATION BOARD
(January 1, 1946—February 24, 1947)

A board which replaced the National War Labor Board so that economic stabilization procedures could be maintained.

The National Wage Stabilization Board was to make stabilization continuously effective by exercising indirect controls over wage or salary increases. It ruled on applications for approval of voluntary increases which might be used as a basis for increasing prices or rent ceilings, or which might result in higher costs to the Government. The Board enforced alleged violations of the wage-stabilization program. Arbitrators were used for minor dispute settlements when necessary because of prior agreements negotiated under the National War Labor Board. The National Wage Stabilization Board was tripartite, as was the subsequent National Wage Stabilization Board of 1950-1952, which was established during the period of the Korean War.

See also: Nat'l. War Labor Board; Tripartite board.

Sources: U.S. NAT'L. WAGE STABILIZATION BOARD, DOCUMENTARY HISTORY OF THE BOARD (1947).

NATIONAL WAR LABOR BOARD

A twelve man panel composed equally of public, industry, and labor members created by Executive Order No. 9017 of President Franklin D. Roosevelt in January 1942, in accordance with the 1941 no-strike, no-lockout agreement, to function as a labor court in settling labor-management disputes during World War II.

The National War Labor Board recommended arbitration clauses to determine future disputes over the application and interpretation of the collective bargaining agreement. The influence of the Board led to a considerable increase in the use of permanent arbitrators. The Board disposed of 17,807 disputes involving approximately 12,300,000 employees. With very few exceptions, employers and unions voluntarily complied with these decisions. The National War Labor Board was terminated on December 31, 1945. The Board was a major influence in promoting the use of grievance procedures, and especially of arbitration, in the settlement of disputes. The National War Labor Board of 1942 included compulsory arbitration within its jurisdiction.

See also: Compulsory arb.; Compulsory arb. Australia; Nat'l. Defense Mediation Board; Nat'l. Wage Stabilization Board; Nat'l. War Labor Board of 1918; No-strike, No-lockout Agreement of 1941; War Labor Disputes Act. World War II.

Sources: Boudin, *The Authority of the Nat'l. War Labor Board over Labor Disputes*, 43 MICH. L. REV. 335 (1944); Freidin & Ulman, *Arb. and the Nat'l. War Labor Board*, 58 HARV. L. REV. 310-311 (1945); Letter of Lloyd K. Garrison to President Truman, 1 WAR LAB. REP. iii (1942); Letter of Lloyd K. Garrison to President Truman, 28 WAR LAB. REP. i (1946); WAR LABOR REPORTS (1942-1945) (BNA).

NATIONAL WAR LABOR BOARD OF 1918

A Board established in 1918 by an Executive Order of President Woodrow Wilson to settle labor-management disputes through mediation and conciliation in industries crucial for the effective conduct of the war.

The National War Labor Board resolved a total of 1,251 disputes in its 16 months of existence. Its decisions were influential in labor legislation of the 1930s in such practices as reinstatement with back pay of employees discharged for union activity, requirements that employers bargain with unions, employees' choice of bargaining agent through secret ballot elections, and the establishment of the basic eight-hour working day.

See also: Nat'l. War Labor Board.

Sources: 1 WAR LAB. REP. *ix*, x, xi (1942).

NETHERLANDS ARBITRATION INSTITUTE (N.A.I.)
(General Secretariat, Oppert 34 Rotterdam-1. The Netherlands)

A Dutch institution established in 1950, which was patterned after the American Arbitration Association.

The Netherlands Arbitration Institute was revised and enlarged in 1952, in order to promote more effective arbitral proceedings, and to offer facilities for arbitrations, especially for parties who cannot or will not refer their disputes to the arbitration institutes of the organized branches of trade and industry. The N.A.I. has inter-association agreements with the AAA, The Deutscher Ausschuss für Schiedsgerichtswesen at Bonn (W. Germany), and the Japan Commercial Arbitration Association at Tokyo.

See also: Institutional arb.; Inter-association com'l. arb. agreements.

Sources: Letter from A.S. Fransen van de Putte, *supra* Arbitrale Rechtspraak; Sanders, *supra* Arbitrale Rechtspraak at 40-41.

NEUTRAL ARBITRATOR

Usually the third or impartial arbitrator mutually selected by both parties to serve on the arbitration board after each party has already appointed a member of its own.

The neutral arbitrator is the chairman of the arbitral tribunal. He may also be appointed by the partisan arbitrators or by some impartial official, in accordance with the agreement of the parties. This latter manner of appointment is frequent in international public arbitration.

See also: Arbitrator; Impartial chairman; Impartial chairman (ad hoc); Oath of office; Partisan arbitrator; Permanent arbitrator; Presiding arbitrator; Public member; Third arbitrator; Tripartite board; Umpire; Unanimity of award.

NEWLANDS ACT [Pub. L. No. 6 (38 Stat. 103) (1913)]

A federal act which provided for mediation, conciliation, and arbitration for the settlement of disputes in the railroad industry.

The Newlands Act empowered President Woodrow Wilson to create the United States Board of Mediation and Conciliation by appointing a Commissioner of Mediation and Conciliation, and two other members.

An Assistant Commissioner was also appointed to act in the absence of the Commissioner. The Board was authorized to intervene in railroad disputes if in its judgment such action seemed desirable. Employees or employers might invoke the Board of Mediation and Conciliation in disputes over wages, hours of labor, or conditions of employment which interrupted or threatened to interrupt services. If mediation proved unsuccessful, the Board was authorized to persuade the parties to arbitrate their differences. Such arbitration procedures were entirely voluntary. The parties were to select their own arbitrators, each choosing two members, and these four members then selecting by a majority vote the two remaining arbitrators. The Newlands Act remained in effect until it was virtually superseded by the Transportation Act of 1920. The enactment of the Adamson Act in 1916, and government seizure of the railroads during the First World War, further decreased the importance and effectiveness of the Newlands Act.

See also: Adamson Act; Arb. Act of 1888; Erdman Act; Railroad Arb. Act; Railway Labor Act; Transportation Act of 1920.

Sources: Compilation, *supra* Erdman Act; Wisehart, *Transportation Strike Control Legislation*, 66 MICH. L. REV. 1697-1722 (1968).

NEW YORK CHAMBER OF COMMERCE

See: Chamber of Commerce of the State of New York.

NEW YORK CITY. OFFICE OF COLLECTIVE BARGAINING

See: Office of Collective Bargaining (OCB). New York City.

NEW YORK STATE CHAMBER OF COMMERCE

See: Chamber of Commerce of the State of New York.

NEW YORK STATE PUBLIC EMPLOYMENT RELATIONS BOARD (PERB)

A board established under § 205 of the Taylor Law to resolve disputes concerning union representation, and to establish panels of persons qualified to serve as mediators or fact-finders when negotiations reach an impasse, and to conduct such hearings, administering them according to the provisions of the Taylor Law.

The New York State Public Employment Relations Board is composed of three members appointed by the Governor, with the advice and consent of the Senate, from persons representing the public. The members of the Board are to hold no other public office. The office of Chairman is a full-time position. The Public Employment Relations Board is empowered to collect data and statistics relevant to public employee labor relations, to review local procedures, and to recommend necessary legislation. The Board has been active since just before September 1, 1967, the date on which the Taylor Law became effective. Under the 1969 amendments to the Taylor Law, PERB was given jurisdiction over the enforcement of the code of unfair labor practices, beginning on September 1, 1969.

See also: Compulsory arb. Pub. employees; Fact-finding; Public employee; Taylor Committee Report; Taylor Law.

Sources: N. Y. (State) PERB, Official Decisions, Opinions, and Related Matters (1968); N.Y. (State) Governor's Comm. on Public Employee Relations, *supra* Compulsory arb. Public employees at 43-49; N.Y. (State) Governor's Committee on Public Employee Relations, *Recommendations for Changes in New York State Law*, GERR G-1 (No. 283, 1969); *id., supra* Taylor Committee Report.

NINTH INTER-AMERICAN CONFERENCE

See: Pact of Bogotá.

NON LIQUET (IT IS NOT CLEAR)

A term which refers to the refusal by an arbitrator to render an award on the grounds that the law which has been invoked to apply to the case does not exist.

The doctrine of *non liquet* derives from a theory of law which is in the process of being abandoned. A large number of municipal codes, as well as the majority of writers on international law, now hold that in case of a "gap" in the law, it is the arbitrator's duty to supplement the law and render a decision. Article XI of the Model Rules on Arbitral Procedure states that the tribunal should not bring in a finding of *non liquet* based on the ground of silence or obscurity in the applicable law.

See also: Applicable law. Int'l. pub. arb.; Award; Model Rules on Arbitral Procedure.

Sources: Stone, Legal Controls of Int'l. Conflict (1954); Higgins, *Policy Consideration and the Int'l. Judicial Process*, 17 Int'l. & Comp. L. Q. 58 (1968).

NO-RAIDING AGREEMENT (AFL AND CIO)

An agreement drafted by a Joint Committee of the American Federation of Labor and the Congress of Industrial Organizations, and adopted by both organizations as a preliminary step toward merger of the two unions, in an effort to control the raids made by one union on the membership of the other.

The No-Raiding Agreement became effective as of June 9, 1954, and was binding only on the affiliates of each organization which signed it.

Raids conducted by affiliates of both federations were a principle cause of friction between the two organizations. The No-Raiding Agreement attempted to control the practice by setting up dispute settlement procedures at the local level, with appeals through the authorized representatives of both unions up to an Impartial Umpire whose decisions should be final and binding. The No-Raiding Agreement was incorporated in the Constitution at the merger of the two federations in 1955. Those affiliates of both federations which signed the Agreement were to continue the settlement of disputes under its provisions, including the final step of decision by an Impartial Umpire. Affiliates which had not previously signed the Agreement were to have access to similar dispute settlement procedures, with the exception that the Impartial Umpire would make recommendations for settlement instead of decisions or awards. The No-Raiding Agreement was concerned only with representational matters, the key thought being that all affiliates must respect the established bargaining relationships of other affiliates. David L. Cole was named Impartial Umpire, and has continued to serve as such under the AFL-CIO Internal Disputes Plan which succeeded the No-Raiding Agreement.

See also: AFL-CIO Internal Disputes Plan; American Federation of Labor and Congress of Industrial Organizations; Jurisdictional disputes.

Sources: AFL-CIO, DECISIONS AND RECOMMENDATIONS OF THE AFL-CIO IMPARTIAL UMPIRE 235-239 (1954-1958).

NORRIS-LA GUARDIA ACT (ANTI-INJUNCTION ACT)
(Act of March 23, 1932, 47 Stat. 70, 29 U.S.C.A. §§ 101 et seq.)

An act passed in 1932 which limited the circumstances under which federal courts could issue restraining orders or injunctions in cases growing out of labor disputes.

The Norris-LaGuardia Act removed the restraints on trade union activities which had developed under the anti-trust laws. Section 8 of the Act reads: "No restraining order or injunctive relief shall be granted to any complainant who has failed to comply with any obligation imposed by law . . . or who has failed to make every reasonable effort to settle such dispute either by negotiation or with the aid of any . . . governmental machinery of mediation or voluntary arbitration." The United States Supreme Court in its decision *Sinclair Refining Co. v. Atkinson*, on June 8, 1962, ruled that an employer should not be allowed the benefits of the injunction along with the right which Congress had given him in § 301 of the Taft-Hartley Act to sue for breach of a collective bargaining agreement.

See also: Injunction; Labor dispute; Sinclair Refining Co. v. Atkinson; Wagner Act.

Sources: Sinclair Refining Co. v. Atkinson, 370 U.S. 195 (1962); A. Cox & D. BOK, *supra* Landrum-Griffin Act at 96-111 (1965).

NORTHEASTERN BOUNDARY ARBITRATION (1831)

A dispute between the United States and Great Britain, involved principally with the northwest angle of the Nova Scotia-Maine boundary, which was submitted to arbitration under the Convention of September 29, 1827.

Upon ratification of this convention, the contracting parties were mutually to choose some friendly sovereign or nation as arbitrator, who was to try to arrive at a decision within two years. The King of the Netherlands was appointed arbitrator. The award rendered in 1831 was accepted by Great Britain, but the United States Senate resolved in June 1832, thirty-five to eight, that the award was not binding on the ground that the arbitrator had exceeded his authority. The arbitrator had been asked to choose between two boundary lines as claimed respectively by the parties, but instead decided to recommend a third line. The dispute was eventually settled by treaty in 1842.

See also: Boundary disputes; Enforcement of award (Int'l. pub. arb.); Exces de pouvoir.

Sources: 1 J. Moore, *supra* Alabama Arbitration at 65-161.

NO-STRIKE CLAUSE

A clause in a contract whereby a union agrees it will not strike during the life of the contract.

The United States Supreme Court held in the *Lincoln Mills* case of 1957 that an agreement to arbitrate grievances in a collective bargaining agreement is the *quid pro quo* for a union's promise not to strike. The presence of an arbitration provision has been held to imply a promise not to strike, when the contract itself is silent on that point.

See also: Atkinson v. Sinclair Refining Co.; Breach of contract; Drake Bakeries, Inc.; Injunctive relief; Lincoln Mills; Second trilogy; § 301 disputes; Sinclair Refining Co. v. Atkinson.

Sources: Aaron, *supra* Enterprise Wheel & Car Corporation at 360-380; Aaron, *supra* Injunctive relief at 93-116; Givens, *Injunctive Enforcement of Arbitration Awards Prohibiting Strikes*, 17 Lab. L. J. 293 (1966); Marshall, *Federal Enforcement of a No-Strike Clause by Injunctive Relief*, in Symposium On Labor Relations Law 578 (R. Slovenko ed. 1961).

NO-STRIKE, NO-LOCKOUT AGREEMENT OF 1941

An agreement between management and labor reached at a conference called by President Franklin D. Roosevelt on December 17, 1941, which outlawed strikes and lockouts during World War II.

Twelve employer representatives participated in the conference and twelve labor representatives, six each from the American Federation of Labor and the Congress of Industrial Organizations. The text of the report was not made public, but its substance was disclosed in a letter which the President sent to the conference representatives, summing up the following points of agreement: that there shall be no strikes or lock-outs, that all disputes shall be settled by peaceful means, and that the President shall set up a proper War Labor Board to handle these disputes. The President eventually issued Executive Order No. 9017 on January 12, 1942, creating the National War Labor Board.

See also: Nat'l. Defense Mediation Board; Nat'l. War Labor Board.

Sources: U. S. BUREAU OF LABOR STATISTICS, BULL. No. 714, REPORT ON THE WORK OF THE NAT'L. DEFENSE MEDIATION BOARD, March 19, 1941– January 12, 1942 at 40-41 (1942).

NOTICE OF HEARING

A formal notification of the time and place of a hearing which is sent to both parties in a dispute by an arbitrator or an administrative agency.

A notice of hearing is submitted after the notice of intention to arbitrate has been sent by one disputing party to the other. Notice of intention is also called the Demand for Arbitration. Arbitration laws specify the time allowed between such notice of hearing and the hearing itself. The New York State CPLR § 7506(b) provides: "The arbitrator shall appoint a time and place for the hearing and notify the parties in writing personally or by registered or certified mail not less than eight days before the hearing. . . ." Administrative rules under which the arbitration is being conducted may differ slightly in the length of time allowed between the notice of hearing and the hearing itself. Section 20 of the Commercial Arbitration Rules of the American Arbitration Association provides that the arbitrator shall fix the time and place for each hearing. The AAA will then mail to each party such a notice at least five days in advance, unless the parties have provided differently in their contract, or have waived such notice by mutual agreement. Some arbitration agreements provide for expedited hearings in case of an emergency. Such a provision can be effective only with a trade association or commodity exchange which has its own available panels, or with a permanent arbitrator or umpire, or with a speedy and certain method of selecting an *ad hoc* arbitrator.

See also: Demand for arb.; Hearing; Notice of intention to arbitrate; Participation in arb.; Rotating panels; Service by mail; Summary proceeding.

Sources: AAA COM'L. ARB. RULES, *supra* Administrative appointment at § 20; ASS'N. OF THE BAR OF THE CITY OF N. Y., *supra* Award by confession at 19.

NOTICE OF INTENTION TO ARBITRATE (DEMAND FOR ARBITRATION)

A document submitted by one disputing party to the other in order to initiate an arbitration.

Notice of intention to arbitrate is also known as a Demand for Arbitration. A notice of intention to arbitrate is usually filed with the administrative agency when an arbitration is to be held under the rules of that agency. Demand forms may be furnished by the agency. According to the New York State statute, a notice of intention should specify the agreement under which arbitration is being sought. It should also give the name and address of the party serving the notice, and include the ten-day notice of preclusion, a statement usually referred to as the Ten-Day Notice. The Ten-Day Notice provides that an application to stay arbitration must be made by the person served within ten days after receipt of the Demand or he "shall thereafter be precluded from objecting that a valid agreement was not made or has not been complied with. . . ." The Ten-Day Notice has no validity unless it includes the address of the party demanding arbitration. It is to be served "in the same manner as a summons or by registered or certified mail, return receipt requested." Under the Rules of the International Chamber of Commerce, the notice of intention to arbitrate is known as a request for arbitration.

See also: Claimant; Demand for arb.; Modern arb. statute; Notice of hearing; Service by mail; Stay of arb.; Submission agreement; Time limits.

Sources: N. Y. CPLR § 7503; AAA Com'L. Arb. Rules, *supra* Adm. appointment at § 7; AAA Voluntary Lab. Arb. Rules, *supra* Affidavit at § 7; M. Domke, *supra* Adhesion contract at 139-142; ICC, *supra* Answering statement at art. 8; London Court of Arb., *supra* Adm. expenses at art. 31, 32.

NUMBER OF ARBITRATORS

The number of arbitrators selected to serve may vary from one to as many as seven or more, the number usually being odd, so as to ensure a majority when a vote to determine an award is finally taken.

The final decision as to the number of arbitrators rests with the parties and their agreement to arbitrate. Tripartite boards were formerly most common, and remain so in international tribunals. The single arbitrator has become more or less standard in commercial and labor arbitration. Some statutes, such as the California law, provide that where the number of arbitrators is not specified in the agreement, one arbitrator shall serve. Multi-arbitrator boards can be helpful where more than one kind of expert knowledge is required as in commercial arbitration, or where party-appointed arbitrators in labor arbitration may usefully act as consultants to the neutral arbitrator.

See also: Appointment of arbitrators; Tripartite board.

Sources: 9 Calif. Code of Civ. Proced. § 1282(a); U.N. ECE, *supra* Access to the arbitral tribunal.

OATH OF OFFICE

Some arbitration statutes provide that the arbitrator shall be sworn "to hear and decide the controversy faithfully and fairly by an officer authorized to administer an oath."

When no oath is required or is waived by the parties, the arbitrator should nevertheless observe the standards which such an oath may impose or imply. Under the rules of most agencies, when the oath is not mandatory by law, parties may waive this oath by written consent, or by participating in the proceedings without objecting to the failure of the arbitrator to be sworn. The oath of office is usually taken by the arbitrator and administered by a duly authorized person just before the hearing is to be opened. Administrative agencies vary in their procedures in administering the oath of office. In international arbitral agencies, key administrative personnel may also be required to take an oath of office.

See also: Arbitrator; Hearing; Procedure.

Sources: N.Y. CPLR § 7506(a); AAA COM'L. ARB. RULES, *supra* Adm. appointment at § 26; CODE OF ETHICS, *supra* Code of Ethics and Procedural Standards for Labor-Management Arb.; M. DOMKE, *supra* Appeal boards of adm. agencies; M. DOMKE, *supra* Adhesion contract at 233.

OBLIGATORY COMPROMIS (INTERNATIONAL PUBLIC ARBITRATION)

A document to take the place of the *compromis* or submission agreement when the parties cannot agree on one or more issues or clauses of the original agreement to arbitrate.

An obligatory *compromis* may permit the parties to request a third Power to appoint a person, or persons, to draw up the *compromis*. If this procedure fails, the arbitral tribunal, if one with jurisdiction is available, shall itself draw up the *compromis*. In Articles 53 and 54 of the Convention on the Pacific Settlement of International Disputes (1899-1907), provision is made for the *compromis* to be settled by a commission consisting of five members.

See also: Compromis.

Sources: Convention on the Pacific Settlement of Int'l. Disputes (The Hague, July 28, 1899, revised Oct. 18, 1907).

OCB

See: Office of Collective Bargaining (OCB). New York City.

OECD

See: Organisation for Economic Co-operation and Development.

OFFICE OF COLLECTIVE BARGAINING (OCB) (NEW YORK CITY)

An impartial tripartite agency established by the Mayor's Executive Order No. 52 of September 29, 1967, and the New York City Collective Bargaining Law of September 1, 1967, to administer labor relations between the city and its employees.

The Office of Collective Bargaining acts independently. Its director is the Chairman of the Board of Collective Bargaining, which consists of seven appointed members, of which two are city members appointed by the Mayor, and two labor members appointed by the Municipal Labor Committee. The Chairman and the two other impartial members are appointed by the unanimous vote of the city and labor members. The New York City Collective Bargaining Law at § 1173-8.f provides that written collective bargaining agreements with municipal employee organizations shall contain provisions for grievance procedures and impartial binding arbitration. The Law also provides for the use of mediation. The Office of Collective Bargaining maintains a register of arbitrators. OCB through its Board of Certification determines union representation through secret ballot elections. When contract negotiations between a public employer and a certified employee organization reach an impasse, impasse panels with power to mediate and review facts are appointed by the director of the Board of Collective Bargaining. OCB procedures do not cover all public employees of New York City. Unlike the Taylor Law, impasse procedures under the OCB are in practice more flexible in relation to a fixed budget submission date. The Taylor Committee in Recommendations for Changes in New York State's Public Employee Bargaining Law on January 30, 1969, advocated that the jurisdiction of OCB be expanded to cover all public employees and employer organizations which are fiscally dependent on New York City, and that a final impasse step be developed to serve as a substitute for the strike. The amended Taylor Law (1969) in providing a code of unfair labor practices assigned jurisdiction over its enforcement to the New York Public Employment Relations Board, OCB retaining jurisdiction until March 1, 1970.

See also: Compulsory arb. Public employees; Fact-finding; Grievance procedure; Impasse; Labor arb. (Voluntary); Mediation; Public employee; Tripartite board; Tripartite Panel to Improve Municipal Collective Bargaining Procedures in N.Y.C.

Sources: N. Y. City Collective Bargaining Law, Admin. code, ch. 54, Local law 53–1967; N. Y. City Exec. Order No. 52, in N. Y. (City) OCB, COLLECTIVE BARGAINING LAW (1967); N. Y. (City), Agreement between Representatives of Municipal Employee Organizations and the City of New York on Improved Collective Bargaining Procedures, March 31, 1966; N. Y. (City) OCB. *Statement to the Select Joint*

Legislative Comm. on Pub. Employee Relations, Feb. 27, 1969;
N. Y. (State) Governor's Comm. on Public Employee Relations,
supra Compulsory arbitration. Public employees.

OPEN-END GRIEVANCE PROCEDURE

A grievance procedure which has as its final step the right to strike rather
than to arbitrate.

The steps in the open-end grievance procedure are similar to those
where arbitration is the end result. Sometimes a final step calls for the
use of a federal or state mediator before a strike can be called. Open-end
agreements are not often employed. Over 94% of all contracts provide
for final and binding arbitration.

See also: Grievance procedure.

Sources: U.S. BLS, *supra* Ad hoc arbitrator at 5; Repas, *Grievance Procedures
without Arb.*, 20 IND. & LAB. REL. REV. 380-390 (1967).

OPENING STATEMENT

A brief statement made at the opening of a hearing by the parties concerned which acquaints the arbitrator with the nature of the dispute and
with the evidence they intend to present.

Though its use is often optional with the parties, the arbitrator may
sometimes specifically request that each party make an opening statement. It is usual for the claimant, that is the complaining party, to be
heard first. The arbitrator may vary this order at his own discretion.

See also: Procedure.

Sources: AAA MANUAL, *supra* Award at 12; M. DOMKE, *supra* Adhesion contract at 234; F. ELKOURI & E. ELKOURI, *supra* American Arb. Association.

OPINION

Usually a written document in which the arbitrator or arbitrators set
forth the reasons by which they arrived at their award.

An opinion almost invariably precedes the award in labor arbitration.
As the award itself states, the opinion is not considered to be part of the
award. The practice of giving an opinion is not common in commercial
arbitration in the United States, or in the countries of the British Commonwealth. In France and the Netherlands reasons usually accompany
the award. In international arbitration cases, any use of the word opinion
refers to the advisory opinions which judges of the Permanent Court of
International Justice, and subsequently the International Court of Justice,
may deliver under certain circumstances. Reasons for the award are
usually required in international public arbitration.

See also: Award; Enterprise Wheel & Car Corporation.

Sources: M. DOMKE, *supra* Appeal boards of adm. agencies at 91-92; 11 LAWYERS' LETTERS (1962), *supra* Adjournment of hearings at 2-3.

ORAL ARBITRATION AGREEMENT

An agreement by word of mouth as opposed to one which is written.

Most arbitration statutes require a written arbitration agreement. At common law, an oral agreement to arbitrate is sufficient to ensure an enforceable award.

See also: Common law arb.; Enforcement of arb. agreement (Common law).

Sources: N.Y. CPLR § 7501.

ORGANISATION FOR ECONOMIC CO-OPERATION AND DEVELOPMENT (OECD) (Chateau de la Muette, 2 rue André-Pascal, Paris 16, France)

An inter-governmental organization, successor to the Organisation for European Economic Co-operation which had been established in 1948 to institute joint European recovery programs and distribute Marshall Plan aid.

The OECD came into existence September 30, 1961, primarily to promote economic growth and to contribute to the economic development of the developing countries. There are 22 member nations in Europe, North America, and Japan. A Draft Convention on the Protection of Foreign Property was commended by a Resolution adopted by the OECD Council on October 12, 1967. Provisions for arbitration are included in Article 7 (Disputes), and in an Annex Relating to the Statute of the Arbitral Tribunal.

See also: Convention on the Settlement of Investment Disputes between States and Nationals of Other States; Council of Europe; OECD Draft Convention on the Protection of Foreign Property.

Sources: O.E.C.D. Draft Convention on the Protection of Foreign Property, Oct. 12, 1967, (O.E.C.D. Publication No. 23081, Nov. 1967); Consultative Assembly of the Council of Europe, *supra* Council of Europe at 133-150.

ORGANISATION FOR ECONOMIC CO-OPERATION AND DEVELOPMENT (OECD). DRAFT CONVENTION ON THE PROTECTION OF FOREIGN PROPERTY

A draft convention prepared by the OECD, and commended by its Council in a Resolution of October 12, 1967, as a means of protecting foreign private property in order to encourage the flow of capital for economic activity and development.

The Draft Convention on the Protection of Foreign Property declares that States shall pledge themselves to that general principle of international law which binds a State to respect and protect the property of nationals of other States within its boundaries. Article 7 of the Convention provides for the settlement of investment disputes by arbitration. If jurisdiction has been accepted by the host government, individuals and corporations may have access to an arbitral tribunal. According to the provisions in the Annex Relating to the Statute of the Arbitral Tribunal, the tribunal shall consist of three members. One arbitrator shall be appointed by each of the parties, and the third shall be appointed by the agreement of the parties. The draft convention was submitted to the Council of Europe for an opinion, which appeared as Opinion No. 39 (1963). The Opinion comments on the arbitral procedures in some detail, and also states as follows: "The fact that the draft Convention provides for an arbitral procedure is to be welcomed; indeed, the effective international protection of foreign property hinges in the last resort on the neutral arbitration of disputes, and there are those who believe that an adequate system of arbitration would in itself suffice to improve the investment climate."

See also: Abs-Shawcross Draft Convention on Investments Abroad; Convention on the Settlement of Investment Disputes between States and Nationals of Other States; Draft Convention to Improve the Climate for Investment in Latin America by Facilitating the Settlement of Disputes; Organisation for Economic Co-operation and Development.

Sources: Consultative Assembly of the Council of Europe, *supra* Council of Europe at 138; O.E.C.D. Draft Convention on the Protection of Foreign Property, Oct. 12, 1967, (O.E.C.D. Publication No. 23081, Nov. 1967); Haight, *O.E.C.D. Resolution on the Protection of Foreign Property*, 2 INT'L. LAWYER 326-353 (1968).

ORGANIZATION OF AMERICAN STATES (OAS)
(Pan American Union, Washington, D.C. 20006)

An organization of twenty-three American republics formed to strengthen the peace and security of the continent, to ensure the pacific settlement of disputes among member States, and to promote inter-governmental cooperation.

The OAS owed its inception to the First International Conference of American States which met at Washington, D.C., in 1889-1890. On April 14, 1890, the International Union of American Republics was established. Its secretariat or central office at that time was known as the Commercial Bureau, which was renamed the Pan American Union in 1910. The Organization of American States currently operates under the Charter of Bogotá of 1948. The Council of the Organization has three dependent bodies: the Inter-American Economic and Social Council, the Inter-American Council of Jurists, and the Inter-American Cultural Council.

See also: Pact of Bogotá; Draft Uniform Law on Inter-American Com'l. Arb.

Sources: ᴀ. Thomas & A. Thomas, The Organization of American States
(1963); U.S. Office of the Federal Register, *supra* Bureau of
Labor Statistics at 615-617.

OVERMAN

See: Umpire.

PACTA SUNT SERVANDA (CONTRACTS ARE TO BE KEPT)

A concept in international law that contracts and treaties are binding on
the parties and must be performed in good faith.

Pacta sunt servanda is generally acknowledged to be one among
those established principles of law recognized by civilized nations.
Arbitrators invoke these principles in cases where the law of the place
is either ambiguous or inapplicable. Ordinarily the *pacta* rule is only one
of many principles and policies which could play a part in determining
the final award.

See also: Binding character of award; General principles of law recognized by
civilized nations.

Sources: Garcia, (*Fourth*) *Report on International Responsibility*, 11 (II)
Y. B. Int'l. Law Comm'n. 24, U.N. Doc. A/CN.4/119 (1959);
S. Siksek, *supra* Concession contract.

PACT OF BOGOTA (April 30, 1948)
(The American Treaty of Pacific Settlement)

A pact which codified all previous Inter-American agreements concerned
with the peaceful settlement of international disputes.

The Pact of Bogotá included all types of peace-keeping machinery,
such as, good offices, mediation, investigation, conciliation, and judicial
settlement, as well as arbitration. When efforts at conciliation fail, legal
disputes are to be submitted to the International Court of Justice. If
the Court declares itself to be without jurisdiction, and the dispute is not
within the domestic jurisdiction of the State, and it is not a claim of a
national of one State against another, the parties are free to refer the
dispute to arbitration. Article 50 of the Treaty contains the following
provision: "If one of the High Contracting Parties should fail to carry
out the obligations imposed upon it by a decision of the International
Court of Justice or by an arbitral award, the other party or parties concerned shall, before resorting to the Security Council of the United
Nations, propose a Meeting of Consultation of Ministers of Foreign
Affairs (of the OAS) to agree upon appropriate measures of ensur(ing)
the fulfillment of the judicial or arbitral award." It was at the Bogotá
Conference of 1948 that the Inter-American System was reorganized to
become the Organization of American States.

See also: Enforcement of award (Int'l. pub. arb.).

Sources: Pact of Bogotá, 30 U.N.T.S. (1949) at 55ff; E. NANTWI, *supra* Annulment . . . at 171; Kunz, *The Pact of Bogotá*, 3 ARB. J. (n.s.) 147-155 (1948); Sohn, *Report on Int'l. Arb.*, in AMERICAN LAW ASSOCIATION, REPORT OF THE 52ND CONFERENCE, HELSINKI 1966 (1967).

PAN AMERICAN UNION

See: Organization of American States.

PANCHAYAT (INDIAN–ARBITRATION)

An arbitral proceeding before five persons who act as the sole and final judges of the matter referred to them by the parties.

These territorial arbitration boards, or village *panchayats,* which may be composed of one or as many as eleven members, existed in Pre-British India. They are still of considerable importance in many social and caste problems in India at the present time. The moral influence of these *panchayats* has been so great that the offending party has rarely been known to distort his case or to lie.

Sources: S. SINGH, THE LAW OF ARBITRATION (1966).

PARAMOUNT PICTURES. UNITED STATES V.

See: Motion Picture Industry Arbitration System.

PAROL AWARD

An award which is spoken rather than one which is written.

Arbitration laws in the United States declare that an award is not enforceable unless it be in writing. At common law in this country, if the submission requires that the award be in writing, that requirement must be met. In Great Britain, a parol award is usually valid unless the submission agreement or governing rules have provided that it be in writing. The Rules of the London Court of Arbitration state as follows: "The arbitrator, arbitrators, or umpire shall deliver his or their award in writing to the Court and any party to the reference may have a copy thereof on payment of the fees and expenses set out in the fifth Schedule hereto."

See also: Award.

Sources: AAA MANUAL, *supra* Award at 21; BLACK's LAW DICTIONARY (4th ed. 1951); W. GILL, *supra* Compensation of arbitrator.

PAROL EVIDENCE RULE

Evidence given by witnesses in a court of law or in an arbitration as to the making of a contract.

Parol evidence usually applies to testimony concerned with discussions held at the time of the negotiation of the agreement, in order to explain the meaning of a provision of that agreement. This testimony may refer to the "bargaining" history of negotiations between union and company representatives. It may also have reference to a contract in dispute in commercial transactions. If the wording of the agreement seems ambiguous, the arbitrator usually admits the evidence and determines what weight should be given to it.

See also: Hearing; Procedure; Rules of evidence.

Sources: BLACK'S LAW DICTIONARY (3d ed. 1933); Chicago Area Tripartite Comm. of the Nat'l. Academy of Arbitrators, *Report*, in 19 PROC. OF THE NAT'L. ACADEMY OF ARBITRATORS 95, 123 (1966); Coulson, *Appropriate Procedures for Receiving Proof in Com'l. Arb.*, 71 DICKINSON L. REV. 63-73 (1966); New York Tripartite Comm. of the Nat'l. Academy of Arbitrators, *Workshop on the Comm. Report*, in 19 PROC. OF THE NAT'L. ACADEMY OF ARBITRATORS 318, 319 (1966).

PARTICIPATION IN ARBITRATION

The taking part in the actual proceedings of an arbitration.

Participation includes such aspects as the selection of the arbitrators, and the actual attendance at the hearing. If a party to an arbitration agreement consents to participate in the arbitration proceedings without objection, he is automatically bound by the award made by the arbitrator, and cannot later claim that an agreement to arbitrate did not exist. Under New York State Law, when a party is served with a demand for arbitration, and receives a notice of hearing, he may choose not to participate altogether, or he may challenge the existence of an agreement to arbitrate by a motion to stay arbitration in advance of the hearings. In a procedure unique to New York State, the party who has been served with a demand, must apply to stay the arbitration within ten days, or lose the right thereafter to assert that a valid agreement to arbitrate had not been made. The statute clearly protects the right of a party to claim that he never agreed to bind himself to arbitrate. If he neither participated in the arbitration nor was served with a demand, he may under the New York State statute challenge the existence of the arbitration agreement by a motion to stay arbitration before the hearing begins, or to have the award vacated after it is made. But if he fails to act and absents himself completely from the hearing, an *ex parte* arbitration can result in an enforceable award.

See also: Default; Ex parte arb.; Lena Goldfields Arb.; Notice of intention to arbitrate; Stay of arb.; Vacating an award.

Sources: N.Y. CPLR § 7503(b), § 7506(c) & § 7511(b) 2(ii); 7 LAWYERS' LETTERS (1961), *supra* Adjournment of hearings at 1-3.

PARTISAN ARBITRATOR

An arbitrator chosen by one of the parties.

A partisan arbitrator may or may not act in the interest of the party which appointed him, though it is common for him to act in such a partisan manner. He is also known as the party-appointed arbitrator. In international arbitration, the partisan arbitrator is called the national arbitrator, or the national member of the tribunal, in order to emphasize the mixed character of his role. While a degree of partiality toward the appointing nation is tolerated, the international arbitrator is otherwise subject to the same requirements which apply to the third or neutral arbitrator.

See also: Tripartite board; Unanimity of award.

PARTY-APPOINTED ARBITRATOR

See: Partisan arbitrator.

PARTY AUTONOMY

The principle that the parties to an arbitration agreement retain their mutual right to control the rules and procedures which will govern the arbitration.

Party autonomy is rarely absolute. It is often limited by various statutes, governing conventions, or the general principles of law recognized by civilized nations. Nonetheless, the phrase *as the parties shall agree* is common to rules of arbitration, to conventions, and uniform arbitration laws. Procedures such as the method of appointing the arbitrators, the applicable law, the place of arbitration, or the official language to be used may be established by the parties in the arbitration agreement or *compromis*. The success of party autonomy depends on just how clearly the arbitration agreement defines the nature of the dispute, and how completely it develops adequate and legal procedures for resolving it.

See also: Consent of the parties; European Convention on Int'l. Com'l. Arb.; Model Rules on Arbitral Procedure; Permanent Court of Arb. Rules of Arb. and Conciliation for Settlement of Int'l. Disputes between Two Parties of Which Only One Is a State; Wal Wal Arb.

Sources: Ionasco & Nestor, The Limits of Party Autonomy, in THE SOURCES OF THE LAW OF INT'L. TRADE 167-200 (C. Schmitthoff ed. 1964).

PAST PRACTICE

A course of action knowingly adopted and accepted by a union and a company over a significant period of time regardless of whether or not the contract explicitly permits such action.

An action such as this is not accepted in the sense of both parties having specifically agreed to it, but rather that it is regarded by the workers involved as the normal and proper response. Past practice becomes significant in arbitration whenever one of the parties submits evidence of past practice to support its grievance or claim. United States Supreme Court Justice Douglas in the *Warrior & Gulf* case stated: "The labor arbitrator's source of law is not confined to the express provisions of the contract, as the industrial common law—the practices of the industry and the shop—is equally a part of the collective bargaining agreement although not expressed in it."

See also: Management rights; Warrior & Gulf Nav. Co.

Sources: Fuller, *Collective Bargaining and the Arbitrators*, in 15 PROC. OF THE NAT'L. ACADEMY OF ARBITRATORS 22 (1962); Jones, *supra* Discovery of documents at 1272; Mittenthal, *Past Practice and the Administration of Collective Bargaining Agreements*, in 14 PROC. OF THE NAT'L. ACADEMY OF ARBITRATORS 31-68 (1961).

PENNSYLVANIA COMPULSORY ARBITRATION OF SMALL CLAIMS

A system of compulsory arbitration for claims of a limited sum which the State of Pennsylvania established in 1952 in an effort to relieve its congested court calendars.

Under the Pennsylvania Compulsory Arbitration Statute, the court of common pleas in each county was permitted to provide by rule of court for compulsory arbitration in cases involving no more than $1,000 in claimed damages. The statute was amended in 1957 to include claims up to $2,000, and to apply to the Municipal Court of Philadelphia, and more recently to the County Court of Allegheny County (Pittsburgh). Each claim is heard by a panel of arbitrators who are members of the bar in the judicial district. Rules of evidence may be waived. The award arrived at by majority vote has the effect of a final judgment. The right to trial by jury is provided on appeal, but the appealing party must pay the cost of the arbitration and the fee of the arbitrator within prescribed limits.

See also: Compulsory arb.; Rules of evidence.

Sources: Pennsylvania Compulsory Arb. Statute, 5 Penn. Stat. Ann §§ 21 et seq. (Purdon 1963); INSTITUTE OF JUDICIAL ADMINISTRATION, COMPULSORY ARB. AND COURT CONGESTION (1956); *id*. SUPPLEMENTARY REPORT (1959); PHILADELPHIA COUNTY COURT, STATISTICAL REPORT AND EXPLANATORY REMARKS PERTAINING TO COMPULSORY ARB. (1962-1968); Rosenberg & Schubin, *Trial by Lawyer* 74 HARV. L. REV. 455-456 (1961).

PERB

See: New York State Public Employment Relations Board (PERB).

PERIODICALS

See: Arbitrale Rechtspraak; Arb. Journal; Arb. Magazine; Arb. News; Arbitration. The Journal of the Institute of Arbitrators; Indian Council of Arb. ICA Arb. Quarterly; Quarterly of the Japan Com'l. Arb. Association; Rassegna dell'Arbitrato; Revue de l'Arbitrage; U.N. ECAFE News Bulletin (at U.N. Economic Comm'n. for Asia and the Far East).

PERMANENT ARBITRATOR

An arbitrator who is selected to serve under the terms of a collective bargaining agreement for the life of the contract or a specified period of time.

The appointment of a permanent arbitrator is usually for the duration of the contract, which may be for a period of one or more years. The specific functions and responsibilities of the office of the permanent arbitrator are determined by the contract.

See also: Impartial chairman; Umpire.

Sources: F. ELKOURI & E. ELKOURI, supra American Arb. Association at 56-81.

PERMANENT COURT OF ARBITRATION. THE HAGUE
(Palais de la Paix, The Hague, The Netherlands)

An international agency established on July 29, 1899, by the Hague Convention of 1899, to provide facilities for the arbitration of international disputes which have not been settled by diplomacy or negotiation.

The Permanent Court of Arbitration also made available commissions of inquiry and conciliation. The Court provides administrative facilities and a list of qualified arbitrators. Each member nation may designate four qualified persons for terms of six years to serve as members of the Court. Procedures are established by The Hague Convention on the Pacific Settlement of International Disputes of July 28, 1899, as revised October 18, 1907. The administrative facilities are supported by contributions from member governments. Since the Court was established, there have been 24 arbitration cases, 4 cases have been referred to Commissions of Inquiry, and 3 cases to Commissions of Conciliation. The Pious Fund Case between Mexico and the United States was the first case referred to the Court. Although the machinery of the Permanent Court of Arbitration was originally devised for the settlement of disputes between governments, rules were drafted in 1962 for the arbitration of disputes between parties when only one is a State, and the other a private individual or corporation.

See also: Access to the arbitral tribunal; Convention on the Pacific Settlement of Int'l. Disputes of 1899 and 1907; Int'l. comm'n. of inquiry; Int'l. pub. arb.; Permanent Court of Arb. Rules of Arb. and Conciliation for Settlement of Int'l. Disputes between Two Parties of Which Only One Is a State; Pious Fund Case.

Sources: PERMANENT COURT OF ARB., RAPPORT DU CONSEIL ADMINISTRATIF
DE LA COUR PERMANENTE D'ARBITRAGE . . . 1967 (1968); YEAR-
BOOK OF INT'L. ORGANIZATIONS, *supra* Central Office for Int'l. Railway
Transport at 960.

PERMANENT COURT OF ARBITRATION. RULES OF ARBITRATION AND CONCILIATION FOR SETTLEMENT OF INTERNATIONAL DISPUTES BETWEEN TWO PARTIES OF WHICH ONLY ONE IS A STATE (1962)

Model rules of procedure prepared by the International Bureau of the
Permanent Court of Arbitration to provide ways and means for the settlement of disputes between States and private individuals or corporations
of another nation.

Parties to such an international dispute are under no obligation to
use these specific rules which are merely offered as a model to be followed. The Rules are based on principles customary to the general
practice of arbitration. The International Bureau of the Permanent Court
of Arbitration will act as administrator if the parties so wish. That State
which is a party to the arbitration must adhere to the Permanent Court
of Arbitration. The model rules are available to all nations which are
members of the United Nations, since all U.N. members have been
invited to adhere without specific time limits to the Permanent Court of
Arbitration.

See also: Consent of the parties; Convention; Party autonomy; Permanent
Court of Arb.

Sources: PERMANENT COURT OF ARB., *supra* Convention on the Pacific Settlement of Int'l. Disputes.

PERMANENT COURT OF INTERNATIONAL JUSTICE. THE HAGUE

A Court established under the auspices of the Council of the League of
Nations according to Article 14 of the Covenant, and under the Statute
of the Court, which was annexed to a Protocol of Signature of December
16, 1920.

The Permanent Court of International Justice was one of the first
international courts. It functioned continuously from January 1922, when
it held its first session at The Hague, until it was succeeded in 1945 by
the International Court of Justice. Sixty-five international disputes were
brought before the Court, most of them European in origin, and related to European questions. The Permanent Court of International
Justice was not a court of arbitration. The President of the Court might
be designated in an arbitration agreement to appoint an arbitrator in
cases where parties failed to agree. Judges of the Permanent Court did
not officiate as arbitrators.

Sources: M. HUDSON, THE PERMANENT COURT OF INT'L. JUSTICE (1945); M.
HUDSON, supra Convention on the Pacific Settlement of Int'l. Disputes; C. JENKS, supra Calvo Clause.

PERSONAL SERVICE

The serving of legal documents directly into the hands of all parties concerned with an arbitration.

Though most arbitration statutes declare that notice of the time and
place of hearing must be served, personal service of the notice is not
generally required. Statutes usually require notice of a stay of arbitration
and other court orders to be served in the same manner as a summons
or by registered or certified mail, return receipt requested. The Uniform
Arbitration Act, § 16 states: "Except as otherwise provided, an application to the court under this act shall be by motion. . . . Unless the parties
have agreed otherwise, notice of an initial application for an order shall
be served in the manner provided by law for the service of a summons in
an action." Where the rules of impartial agencies permit the service of
documents by ordinary mail, the courts have generally held that reference
to such rules constitute them part of the contract and therefore the
service of documents by mail is sustained.

See also: Procedure; Service by mail.

Sources: Freedman, Service of Applications to Court during Arbitral Proceedings, 161 N.Y. L. J., March 31, 1969, at 1, 3.

PIEPOUDRE (DUSTY-FOOTED COURT)

An impromptu arbitration court of laymen set up at fairs and markets to
decide on the spot all disputes between buyers and sellers.

The origins of the piepoudre court reach back to Saxon times, and
did not die out until well into the 19th Century.

See also: Law merchant.

Sources: 23, 46, 49 GROSS, SELECT CASES COVERING THE LAW MERCHANT
(1908-1932).

PIOUS FUND CASE (October 14, 1902)
(United States and Mexico)

This was the first case referred to the Permanent Court of Arbitration.

The Pious Fund Case was submitted through a compromis contained
in a treaty signed at Washington, D. C., on May 22, 1902, by Mexico
and the United States. This was the second time the Pious Fund was
arbitrated, and the arbitrators had to decide if the previous award was
governed by the principle of res judicata. The Pious Fund dated back to
the time of the Spanish rule of the 17th and 18th centuries. It was donated
by private persons to the Jesuit Fathers for the propagation of the faith

in the Californias. President Santa Anna of Mexico converted the fund into cash in 1842 and deposited it in the national treasury where it earned 6% interest to be used to promote the purposes of the original fund. When Upper California was ceded to the United States, the Mexican Government refused to pay the Prelates of the Church in Upper California any share of this interest. In 1875, the fund was the subject of an arbitration between the Governments of Mexico and the United States on a claim by the United States on behalf of the Archbishop of San Francisco and the Bishop of Monterey. The umpire, Sir Edward Thornton of England, ordered the Mexican government to pay the claim. Mexico paid the award but refused to make any further payments of interest due. The Prelates appealed again, and the two governments brought the matter to arbitration for the second time in October 1902. The United States was then awarded the sum of $1,420,682.67. The Government of Mexico was also required to pay an annuity of $43,050.99 Mexican, in perpetuity. Payments were interrupted in 1914. As a final act in the lengthy dispute, a Department of State press release dated August 1, 1967, announced that the two governments had concluded an agreement settling the Pious Fund claim. The agreement provided for a lump sum of $719,546 to be paid by the Government of Mexico to the United States Government as a final settlement of the case.

See also: Compromis; Enforcement of award (Int'l. pub. arb.); Espousal; Int'l. claims; Lump Sum Settlement; Permanent Court of Arb.; Res judicata.

Sources: THE HAGUE COURT REPORTS, *supra* Ex aequo et bono at 1-7, 48; 2 J. MOORE, *supra* Alabama Arbitration at 1348-1352; 9 U.N.R.I.A.A. XV-14 (1902).

PL BOARDS OF ADJUSTMENT

Regional or special boards of individual railroads and their employees, called PL Boards, or Public Law Boards, created under the 1966 amendment of § 3, second, of the Railway Labor Act to provide procedures for resolving grievances or minor disputes.

Regional boards may be established by the parties in their contract. A representative of any craft or class of employees may petition in writing any individual carrier for the establishment of a special board of adjustment to resolve disputes which otherwise would be referable to the National Railroad Adjustment Board. A dispute which has been pending before the Adjustment Board for 12 months may be referred to a PL Board. Such a regional board shall consist of one person selected by the carrier and one designated by the union. When the parties cannot agree, the National Mediation Board may be asked to appoint a member. If the two members cannot agree on an award, they may select a neutral member to make a decision. If either party is dissatisfied with the decision of a Regional or PL Board, that party may elect on 90 days' notice to the other party to come under the jurisdiction of the National Railroad Adjustment Board.

See also: Bipartite boards; Nat'l. Railroad Adjustment Act; Railway Labor Act.

Sources: Railway Labor Act, 45 U.S.C. §§ 151-163, 181-188.

POLYGRAPH

See: Lie detector.

POST-HEARING BRIEFS

Written documents requested by an arbitrator, or submitted to him by attorneys representing the parties in a dispute, as a supplement to the original presentation of the case after hearings have already been held.

Post-hearing briefs may be submitted first by one party, with the other party having opportunity for reply, or they may be submitted simultaneously. Usually the hearings are not declared closed until the date set by the arbitrator for receipt of the briefs. Post-hearing briefs give the parties an opportunity to quote in full the relevant portions of court decisions which pertain to the case as a means of reinforcing their oral evidence.

See also: Brief; Closing argument; Hearing; Procedure.

Sources: M. DOMKE, *supra* Adhesion contract at 251.

PRECEDENT (LABOR ARBITRATION)

The concept rarely true in labor arbitration that prior arbitration awards are binding on later decisions, establishing them either as a guide with only persuasive force, or as a precedent which must be followed.

Precedents are not expected to bind the labor arbitrator in making his decision. Decisions which are made within an industry or within a single company may tend to have value as precedent for the parties in the same industry in their collective agreements. This is especially true in permanent umpire systems. Harry Shulman, who served as Umpire for the Ford Motor Company and the United Automobile Workers, spoke of precedent in such a system as follows: ". . . (I)n this system a form of precedent and stare decisis is inevitable and desirable. I am not referring to the use in one enterprise, say United States Steel, of awards made by another arbitrator in another enterprise, say General Motors . . . (b)ut . . . the successive decisions within the same enterprise. . . . When the parties submit to arbitration in the system of which I speak, they seek not merely resolution of the particular stalemate, but guidance for the future, at least for similar cases."

See also: Chrysler-UAW Impartial Chairman System; Collateral estoppel; Ford-UAW Impartial Umpire System; General Motors-UAW Impartial Umpire System; Stare decisis.

Sources: F. ELKOURI & E. ELKOURI, *supra* American Arb. Association, ch. 11; Shulman, *supra* Arbitrator at 1020.

PREEMPTION

The doctrine of exclusive jurisdiction of either a court or government agency such as the National Labor Relations Board.

The exclusivity of NLRB jurisdiction in cases involving an unfair labor practice was made clear by the United States Supreme Court in 1953, in *Garner* v. *Teamsters' Union*. Previous cases cited in *Garner* had invoked the doctrine of preemption. However, with the *Lincoln Mills* case and its sanction of a union's right to sue to compel arbitration, and the later *Lucas Flour* v. *Teamsters Local 174* case, the doctrine of preemption was held not to apply to arbitration. As a result, the jurisdiction of the NLRB became increasingly a matter of coexistence or concurrent jurisdiction, the Board sometimes exercising its authority, and at other times relinquishing jurisdiction entirely.

See also: Concurrent jurisdiction; Spielberg doctrine; Unfair labor practice.

Sources: Joseph Garner v. Teamsters Local 776, 346 U.S. 485 (1953); Local 174, Teamsters Union v. Lucas Flour Co., 369 U.S. 95 (1962); Jones, *supra* Indifferent gentlemen at 767; Ordman, *Arb. and the NLRB*, in 20 PROC. OF THE NAT'L. ACADEMY OF ARBITRATORS 49-50 (1967); Sovern, § *301 and the Primary Jurisdiction of the NLRB*, 76 HARV. L. REV. 529-577 (1963).

PREHEARING CONFERENCE

A meeting of the arbitrator with the parties prior to the actual hearing in order to sift the issues in the case, and to examine the claims of the parties, and their various defenses.

At such a prehearing conference, the arbitrator could establish procedural rules as to evidence. He could also become acquainted with the issues in the case, and as a consequence, the parties might benefit from such an exploration of their case in depth. The grievances of the parties might then be resolved prior to arbitration. The prehearing conference is similar to the pretrial conference for which definite rules and procedures have been established. Parties meet with the judge, or with another judge who will not hear the actual case, for the purpose of stipulating facts, clarifying the nature of the case, and exploring possibilities of settlement. Some parties are opposed to having the same arbitrator who is to hear the case itself conduct the prehearing conference. A possible solution for this might be a system whereby apprentice arbitrators would conduct such preliminary conferences.*

See also: Discovery of documents; Hearing; Procedure; Provisional remedies; Stipulation.

Sources: R. COULSON, HOW TO STAY OUT OF COURT 22-25 (1968);* R. FLEMING, *supra* Arbitrator at 62-64; Brundage, *Applicability of Pretrial Procedures to Arb.*, 20 PROC. OF THE NAT'L. ACADEMY OF ARBITRATORS 366-375 (1967).

PRENTICE-HALL, INC.

See: American Labor Arbitration Awards.

PRESIDENT'S ADVISORY COMMITTEE ON LABOR-MANAGEMENT POLICY (3136 Labor Building, Washington, D.C. 20210)

A committee established by Executive Order 10918 of President John F. Kennedy on February 16, 1961, to encourage the use of collective bargaining as a means toward industrial peace.

The President's Advisory Committee on Labor-Management Policy is composed of the Secretary of Labor, the Secretary of Commerce, and five public, seven labor, and seven management representatives. The Committee's duties are primarily to advise on ways and means of preventing industrial disputes, to recommend sound wage and price policies, to promote higher standards of living, increased productivity, and free and responsible collective bargaining procedures, which labor, management, or the public may follow.

Sources: U.S. OFFICE OF THE FEDERAL REGISTER, *supra* Bureau of Labor Statistics at 591.

PRESIDENT'S COMMISSION ON LABOR RELATIONS IN THE ATOMIC ENERGY INSTALLATIONS

A commission appointed in 1948 by President Harry S. Truman after a threat of a strike at the Oak Ridge atomic energy plant.

William H. Davis was appointed chairman of the Commission, Aaron Horvitz and Edwin E. Witte, members, and John Dunlop, consultant. The Commission concluded that unions and managements in atomic energy must "forego all resort to strikes, lockouts, or other interruptions of atomic operations." It also suggested that a Panel be established with the power to mediate and issue recommendations for dispute settlements. The President accepted the suggestions, and in April of 1949 created the Atomic Energy Labor Relations Panel, appointing the Commission members as members of the Panel. Labor relations in the atomic energy field are unique in that the operations are government owned, but privately operated.

See also: Atomic Energy Labor-Management Relations Panel.

Sources: U.S. ATOMIC ENERGY LABOR-MANAGEMENT RELATIONS PANEL, *supra*
Atomic Energy Labor-Management Relations Panel; Johnson, *supra*
Atomic Energy Labor-Management Relations Panel at 38-53; Straus,
supra Atomic Energy Labor-Management Relations Panel at 233-259.

PRESIDENT'S TASK FORCE ON EMPLOYEE-MANAGEMENT RELATIONS IN THE FEDERAL SERVICE

A board appointed by President John F. Kennedy in June 1961, to recommend ways to improve employee-management relations in the Federal
Service.

Arthur J. Goldberg was the chairman, John W. Macy, Jr., the vice-
chairman, and the four other members were David E. Bell, J. Edward
Day, Robert F. McNamara, and Theodore C. Sorensen. The major recommendations of the Task Force were that federal employees should
have the right to join bona fide employee organizations, and that these
organizations should have the right to recognition by government
agencies. These recommendations were later incorporated in the President's Executive Orders 10987, which established agency systems for
appeals from adverse actions, and 10988, which was concerned with
employee-management cooperation in the Federal Service.

See also: Executive Order 10988.

Sources: A MANUAL FOR EMPLOYEE-MANAGEMENT COOPERATION IN THE FED-
ERAL SERVICE iii, iv, 2, 12-28 (H. Roberts ed., 3d ed. 1967).

PRESIDING ARBITRATOR

The arbitrator chosen by the vote of an impartial arbitration board or tribunal to act as chairman of that board when there is more than one
arbitrator.

When there is a neutral or public arbitrator who is a member of a
tripartite board that neutral arbitrator presides. The presiding arbitrator
in international arbitration is often designated in the agreement, either
by name, or to be chosen by the authority so specified.

See also: Arbitrator; Impartial chairman; Impartial chairman (Ad hoc); Neutral arbitrator; Public member; Third arbitrator.

Sources: CODE OF ARB. (F. Kellor ed. 1931).

PREVENTIVE MEDIATION

Mediation designed to discuss potential problems and disputes before
they reach a crisis stage.

Such preventive mediation may be on a continuous basis where
neutrals meet with joint labor-management committees throughout the
term of the contract in a consultative or advisory capacity. This is somewhat similar to the role the impartial chairman played in the early part

of the century. Mediation may be employed in contract discussions before any direct negotiation takes place.

See also: Federal Mediation and Conciliation Service; Mediation.

Sources: Stevens, *supra* Mediation at 273.

PRIMA PAINT CORPORATION V. FLOOD & CONKLIN MFG. CO.
[*Prima Paint Corp.* v. *Flood & Conklin Mfg. Co.*, 388 U.S. (1967)]

A United States Supreme Court landmark decision which held that if a contract had a broad arbitration clause, any charge that the contract had been induced by fraud is a question to be determined by an arbitrator and not by a court.

In making its decision, the Supreme Court relied on § 4 of the United States Arbitration Act which provides that a party "aggrieved by . . . the . . . refusal . . . of another to arbitrate under a written agreement" to do so, may obtain an order compelling arbitration if the federal court would otherwise have had jurisdiction. The Court reasoned that if it is claimed that the arbitration clause itself had been induced by fraud, the court would then have the power to adjudicate the claim. Otherwise the claim should be determined by the arbitrator. In the *Prima Paint* case, the claim was that Flood and Conklin had not fraudulently induced Prima Paint to enter into the arbitration agreement, but into the contract itself. The Court also held that the arbitration clause was separable from the container contract. The *Prima Paint* decision gave a broad reading to the interstate commerce provision of the United States Arbitration Act, and as a result, probably increased and widened its eventual application.

See also: Container contract; Enforcement of arb. agreements (Federal statutes); Fraudulent inducement of the contract; Judicial review; Separability doctrine; U.S. Arb. Act.

Sources: *Arb. Clauses and Fraudulent Inducement*, 42 WASH. L. REV. 620-631 (1967); Coulson, *Prima Paint: An Arb. Milestone*, 22 ARB. J. (n.s.) 237-245 (1967); *Federal Arb. Act and Application of the "Separability Doctrine" in Federal Courts*, 1968 DUKE L. J. 588-614; 25 LAWYERS' LETTERS (1966), *supra* Adjournment of hearings; 27 *id*.

PRINCIPLES OF LAW COMMON TO THE PARTIES

When there is a law common to different nationalities in an international public arbitration, this law may be used as a means of settling and enforcing the dispute.

Article 46 of the International Oil Consortium Agreement with the Government of Iran in 1954 states: "In view of the diverse nationalities of the parties to this agreement, it shall be governed . . . in accordance with principles of law common to Iran and the several nations in which the other parties to this agreement are incorporated, and in the absence of such common principles, then by and in accordance with principles of law recognized by civilized nations in general, including such of those principles as may have been applied by international tribunals." The Consortium represented Nationals from the United States, England, France, and the Netherlands.

See also: Applicable law. Int'l. pub. arb.; General principles of law recognized by civilized nations.

Sources: H. CATTAN, *supra* Concession contract at 59; Farmanfarma, *The Oil Agreement between Iran and the Int'l. Oil Consortium*, 34 TEXAS L. REV. 259-289 (1955).

PRIVACY OF ARBITRATION

The parties to an arbitration often expect that no publicity shall be given to any facts in the case without their express consent.

Part I, section 8(a) of the Code of Ethics and Procedural Standards for Labor-Management Arbitration states: "An arbitrator should not, without the approval of the parties, disclose to third persons any evidence, argument or discussions pertaining to the arbitration." The arbitrator should not disclose terms of the award until after it has been delivered simultaneously to both parties. Any publication or disclosure should be made only with the consent of the parties. If the subject matter of the arbitration is of such public interest as to warrant publicity, the parties should advise the arbitrator accordingly on the record or in writing. Administrative agencies always respect this principle of privacy. No one but the parties is allowed to gain any knowledge of the records and files without their written consent. Some trade associations make some awards accessible to their members as precedents for future transactions in their particular trade.

See also: Code of Ethics and Procedural Standards for Labor-Management Arb.

Sources: CODE OF ETHICS, *supra* Code of Ethics and Procedural Standards for Labor-Management Arb.; M. DOMKE, *supra* Adhesion contract at 248.

PROCEDURAL ARBITRABILITY

Arbitrability which an arbitrator determines by making certain that all grievance procedures prior to the final step of arbitration have been complied with as outlined in the collective bargaining agreement.

Matters of procedural arbitrability are usually determined by the arbitrator, unless the parties in their agreement expressly state that such decisions are to be made by the courts. The arbitrator has jurisdiction over such matters as time limits for filing the necessary documents for arbitration as imposed by the contract, as well as over such matters as whether all previous steps of the grievance procedure have been met prior to arbitration. The United States Supreme Court in its *Wiley* decision considered the question of procedural arbitrability, Mr. Justice Harlan stating as follows: "Once it is determined, as we have, that the parties are obligated to submit the subject matter of a dispute to arbitration, 'procedural' questions which grow out of the dispute and bear on its final disposition should be left to the arbitrator. . . ." Judge Medina in the decision of the United States Court of Appeals in *Livingston* v. *John Wiley & Sons* on January 11, 1963, gave this opinion on procedural arbitrability: ". . . (I)t may well be that the arbitrator can make his most important contribution to industrial peace by a fair, impartial and well-informed decision of these very procedural matters. To hold matters of procedure to be beyond the competence of the arbitrator to decide, would, we think, rob the parties of the advantages they have bargained for, that is to say, the determination of the issues between them by an arbitrator and not by a court. A contrary decision would emasculate the arbitration provisions of the contract. . . ."

See also: Arbitrability; Grievance procedure; Grievance procedure—Level of steps; Jurisdiction; Labor arb. (Voluntary); Substantive arbitrability; Warrior & Gulf Nav. Co.; Wiley v. Livingston.

Sources: Livingston v. John Wiley & Sons, 313F 2d 52, cert granted, 373 U.S. 908 (1963); Cox, *supra* Collective bargaining agreement at 1482-1518; Dunau, *Procedural Arbitrability—A Question for Court or Arbitrator?* 14 LAB. L. J. 1010-1016 (1963); Fleming, *Problems of Procedural Regularity in Labor Arb.*, 1961 WASH. U. L. Q. 221.

PROCEDURE (ARBITRATION)

An established manner of conducting an arbitration.

An arbitration procedure may be spelled out in detail by the parties in their arbitration agreement, *compromis*, or treaty. Administrative agencies create their own rules of procedure subject to statutory control. The mere mention in an arbitration clause of the rules of a specific agency is one way of incorporating these rules as part of the arbitration agreement. These procedures are concerned with such essential matters as the appointment of arbitrators, the choice of place, the applicable law, and the conduct of hearings. The ratification by nations of certain international conventions entitles citizens of those nations to arbitration under the specific procedures as established by the rules of those conventions.

See also: Adjournment of hearings; Answering statement; Applicable procedural law; Appointment of arbitrator; Arbitrator's authority; Brief; Com'l. arb.; Consolidation; Convention on the Settlement of Investment Disputes between States and Nationals of Other States; Delegation of the arbitrator's authority; Delivery of the award; Discovery of documents; Execution of award; Hearing; Independent investigation by arbitrator; Int'l. com'l. arb.; Int'l. pub. arb.; Labor arb. (Voluntary); Locale; Model Rules on Arbitral Procedure; Nationality of arbitrator; Notice of hearing; Notice of intention to arbitrate; Number of arbitrators; Oath of office; Opening statement; Parol evidence rule; Participation; Personal service; Post-hearing briefs; Prehearing conf.; Provisional remedies; Reopening of hearings; Rules of evidence; Service by mail; Signature on award; Transcript of hearing;

U.N. ECE. Rules of Arb.; U.N. Handbook of Nat'l. and Int'l. Institutions Active in the Field of Int'l. Com'l. Arb.

Sources: European Convention on Int'l. Com'l. Arb., U.N. Doc. E/ECE/423 & E/ECE/TRADE/48 (done at Geneva on 21 April 1961); *Procedural Problems in the Conduct of Arb. Hearings,* in 17 PROC. OF THE NAT'L. ACADEMY OF ARBITRATORS 1-32 (1964).

PROTOCOL OF PEACE

An agreement which ended a strike in the New York City ladies' cloak and suit industry in 1910, and which provided for labor arbitration in the clothing industry.

The Protocol of Peace was the first of a number of agreements which set up joint adjustment boards with permanent impartial chairmen through agreements with the clothing employers and the International Ladies' Garment Workers Union. It ". . . differed from the usual trade agreement in four ways: it had no definite time limit; it was a 'permanent treaty of peace' institutionalizing an industrial government; it established the preferential union shop as distinct from the closed shop; and it provided for permanent bodies of conciliation and arbitration."* A committee on grievances of four members, two from each side, was to consider and settle minor grievances. Louis D. Brandeis was largely responsible for the Protocol of Peace. The long-term benefit of the Protocol was that it influenced the attitude of the workers who began to recognize arbitration as the one effective substitute for strikes as a means of settling disputes.

See also: Adjustment board; Grievance arb. (Rights arb.); Impartial chairman; Labor arb. (Voluntary).

Sources: E. WITTE, supra Arb. Act of 1888 at 23-24; *Gomberg, *Special Study Committee* in FRONTIERS OF COLLECTIVE BARGAINING 243-246 (J. Dunlop & N. Chamberlain eds. 1967).

PROTOCOL ON ARBITRATION CLAUSES (1923)
(Geneva Protocol on Arbitration Clauses)

A protocol established under the auspices of the League of Nations to enforce the arbitration agreement in international trade disputes between nationals of different countries.

The Protocol on Arbitration Clauses provides that Contracting States shall recognize the validity of arbitration agreements which cover existing disputes or future differences between parties who reside in different countries. Under the Protocol, the parties agree to submit to arbitration all or any differences that may arise in connection with commercial matters which are capable of being settled through arbitration, whether or not the arbitration is to take place in a country where none of the parties resides. Each Contracting State reserves the right to limit the obligation mentioned above to contracts which are considered to be commercial under its national law. The protocol also provides that the courts of the contracting parties, on the application of either one of the parties, shall refer any dispute to the decision of an arbitrator, if the dispute is covered by the Protocol and includes an arbitration agreement.

See also: Convention on the Execution of Foreign Arbitral Awards; Enforcement of foreign arbitral awards.

Sources: Protocol on Arb. Clauses, (1923); M. DOMKE, *supra* Adhesion contract at 369; INT'L. TRADE ARB. 283-284 (M. Domke ed. 1958); Hoare, *supra* Convention on the Execution of Foreign Arbitral Awards at 36-37; Comm. on Com'l. Arb., *supra* Convention on the Execution of Foreign Arbitral Awards.

PROVISIONAL REMEDIES

Preliminary judicial relief granted by a court in a civil action to secure a plaintiff against loss, injury, or the dispersion or waste of the matter in dispute while the action is still pending.

Courts have generally held that the parties' choice of arbitration bars any court action other than that required to compel an arbitral proceeding, and convert an award into a judgment. The arbitrator determines the various kinds of relief available in arbitration, though he rarely orders the equivalent of a provisional remedy. Special circumstances, such as the examination of a witness who is unable to appear for the hearing, may justify the granting of preliminary relief without disturbing the arbitration process. To protect the parties from having their right to arbitration considered waived, § 46 of the American Arbitration Association Commercial Arbitration Rules provides: "No judicial proceedings by a party relating to the subject matter of the arbitration shall be deemed a waiver of the party's right to arbitrate. . . ."

See also: Discovery of documents; Examination before trial; Injunction; Prehearing conference; Procedure; Waiver of arb.

Sources: M. DOMKE, *supra* Adhesion contract at 263-267; 14 LAWYERS' LETTERS (1963), *supra* Adjournment of hearings at 4-6.

PUBLIC EMPLOYEE

A person who is employed by a government, or any of its agencies, and paid from public funds to perform its duties and services.

The term public employee applies equally to municipal, county, state, or federal employees. Such government agencies as the Atomic Energy Commission, NASA, or TVA may have public employees working side by side with private employees. The public employees are hired by the government agency. The private employees are employees of private corporations under government contract.

See also: Atomic Energy Labor-Management Relations Panel; Executive Order
10988; Missile Sites Labor Commission; New York State Public Employment Relations Board; Office of Collective Bargaining; Taylor
Committee Report; Taylor Law; Tennessee Valley Authority employee-management relations.

PUBLIC EMPLOYMENT RELATIONS BOARD (PERB)

See: New York State Public Employment Relations Board (PERB).

PUBLIC MEMBER

The neutral member of an arbitration board in cases where the public
interest is affected.

The public member is the non-partisan arbitrator as distinguished
from the arbitrators chosen respectively by labor and management. Such
arbitration courts are normally composed of three members, but may
sometimes have as many as five, or even more.

See also: Neutral arbitrator; Presiding arbitrator; Railroad Arb. Act; Third
arbitrator; Tripartite board; Tripartite Panel to Improve Municipal
Collective Bargaining Procedures in New York City.

PUBLIC REVIEW BOARD (UNITED AUTOMOBILE WORKERS)

An appeal board established as a court of final resort by the United Auto
Workers in April 1957, at its 16th Constitutional Convention, which en-
sured its individual members an impartial, final and binding decision in
complaints they may have against the local or international union.

The Public Review Board is composed of seven members who are
distinguished community leaders appointed by the UAW President,
subject to the approval of the International Executive Board and ratification by the convention, their terms to run until the next convention. The
Board has been granted independent authority and responsibility to
investigate and hold hearings. It also has the obligation to deal with
alleged violations of any AFL-CIO ethical practices codes. Appeals to
the Public Review Board usually proceed first to the membership of the
local union, and if not satisfactorily resolved, are then referred within
thirty days to the International Executive Board, and as a last resort
within an additional thirty days, either to the UAW convention, or to
the Public Review Board. The Board is not a substitute for local union
grievance machinery, nor does it have jurisdiction over cases involving
official collective bargaining policies of the UAW. The Board's jurisdiction in grievance cases is limited to situations where fraud, discrimination,
or collusion with management have been charged. The decisions of the
Public Review Board have been published continuously since 1957 with
a cumulative *Digest and Index of the Decisions of the Public Review*

Board, International Union, UAW. The Digest is of published decisions only.

See also: Appeal systems; Duty of fair representation; Individual rights.

Sources: PUB. REVIEW BOARD OF THE UAW, ANN. REPORTS (1957-1967); J. STIEBER et al., DEMOCRACY AND PUB. REVIEW (1960).

QUARTERLY OF THE JAPAN COMMERCIAL ARBITRATION ASSOCIATION

An English language quarterly, sometimes double and sometimes single leaf, which began publication in Japan in 1958 to serve as an exchange for information between the Japan Commercial Arbitration Association and foreign arbitration organizations.

The Quarterly publishes articles by experts on arbitration, texts of treaties containing arbitration agreements, copies of bilateral treaties and multilateral conventions on arbitration, and information on foreign national associations and conferences.

Sources: 1 Q. JAPAN COM'L. ARB. ASS'N. 1 (No. 1, 1958).

RAILROAD ARBITRATION ACT (JOINT RESOLUTION)
[PL 88-108 (77 Stat. 132) (1963)]

A federal law which provided for the settlement of a four year dispute between five railroad brotherhoods and the major railroads in the United States.

The Railroad Arbitration Act was passed by Congress as a Joint Resolution on August 28, 1963, at a time when the country was faced with the threat of a national railway strike. This act, which applied to a single dispute, provided for compulsory arbitration of the current work-rules dispute between the carriers and the railroad brotherhoods. The dispute involved the so-called feather-bedding issue of extra firemen on diesel engines. The parties had some choice in the selection of arbitrators, as each named two members of the seven member board, these four members then naming three additional members if they could come to an agreement on them. If no agreement was reached President John F. Kennedy was to name the neutral members, as he actually did. This tripartite Board was to render by majority vote within ninety days after enactment of the law an award binding for two years as to the use of firemen on diesel freight and yard locomotives, and on the make-up of road and yard crews. The Act further provided that the parties immediately resume collective bargaining of all secondary issues. By the terms of the award a majority of the 40,000 firemen involved, those with ten or more years seniority, were to remain employed until they retired, or left of their own accord, or were dismissed for just cause.

See also: Adamson Act; Compulsory arb.; Emergency boards; Erdman Act;
Gov't. intervention; Newlands Act; Public member; Seizure of plant;
Tripartite board.

Sources: U.S. National Mediation Bd., Arb. Bd. No. 282, Award, Nov. 26,
1963; Morgan, *The Adequacy of Collective Bargaining in Resolving
the Problem of Job Security and Technological Change*, 16 LAB. L. J.
87-99 (1965); *The 1963 Railroad Arb. Act*, 86 Mo. LAB. REV. 1187-
1188 (1963); Siegel & Lawton, *Stalemate in 'Major' Disputes under
the Railway Labor Act*, 32 GEO. WASH. L. REV. 8-22 (1963).

RAILROAD INDUSTRY

See: Adamson Act; Arb. Act of 1888; Central Office for Int'l. Railway Transport; Congress of Industrial Conciliation and Arb.; Erdman ｜Act;
Nat'l. Mediation Board; Nat'l. Railroad Adjustment Board; Newlands
Act; Railroad Arb. Act; Railway Labor Act; Transportation ｜Act of
1920.

RAILWAY LABOR ACT
[44 Stat. 577 (1926), 45 U.S.C. §§ 151-163, 181-188 (1966)]

A federal statute enacted in 1926 to provide for the prompt resolution of
disputes between railroads and their employees, amended in 1934, and
further amended in 1936 extending coverage to airlines.

The Railway Labor Act applies to all railroads and their subsidiaries,
to express and sleeping car companies engaged in interstate commerce,
and to airlines involved in interstate and foreign commerce and the
transportation of mail. The National Mediation Board in Washington,
D. C., and the National Railroad Adjustment Board in Chicago, Illinois,
are the two agencies which administer the provisions of this act. The
National Railroad Adjustment Board has no jurisdiction over airline
disputes. The Railway Labor Act guarantees and provides for collective
bargaining rights, and prescribes methods for the settlement of various
types of disputes, including arbitration as a mean of settlement. Section 2
of the Act reads in part as follows: "The purposes of the Act are: . . . (4)
to provide for the prompt and orderly settlement of all disputes concerning rates of pay, rules, or working conditions; (5) . . . (and) . . . of
all disputes growing out of grievances or out of the interpretation or
application of agreements covering rates of pay, rules, or working conditions." On June 20, 1966, Congress amended § 3, second [P.L. 89-456
(1966) 80 Stat. 208] of the Railway Labor Act in order to create a
special board of adjustment to resolve disputes otherwise referable to
the National Railroad Adjustment Board. These special boards are known
as PL Boards (Public Law Boards).

See also: Adamson Act; Arb. Act of 1888; Emergency board; Erdman Act;
Nat'l. Mediation Board; Nat'l. Railroad Adjustment Board; Newlands
｜Act; PL Boards of Adjustment; Transportation Act of 1888.

Sources: U.S. Bureau of Labor Statistics, Bull. No. 262, Federal Labor Laws and Programs 58-59 (1964).

RASSEGNA DELL'ARBITRATO
(Via Q. Sella, 69, Rome, Italy)

A quarterly arbitration journal first published in 1961 by the Associazione Italiana per l'Arbitrato.

Each issue of *Rassegna dell'Arbitrato* contains a scholarly article on arbitration as well as case comments, law notes, and brief notices of seminars, conferences, and international conventions.

RATE CLAUSES

Provisions in air transport agreements by which contracting nations agree on uniform rates for users of their air service.

Since agreement on rates is so vital and important to the nations involved, arbitration of rates is often provided either in a specific clause applicable to rate disagreement only, or under a general arbitration clause applicable to the entire agreement.

See also: Air transport agreements; Convention on Int'l. Civil Aviation.

RECIPROCITY

Mutual concessions in trade or other commercial interests granted by one country in exchange for special advantages granted to it by another nation.

Such extended reciprocal concessions may become permanent and operate as customary international law. Mutual agreements may also become parts of treaties. Since 1950, commercial treaties of the United States have provided for the reciprocal enforcement of arbitration agreements and awards regardless of the place of arbitration or the nationality of the arbitrators. Bilateral treaties of this kind are usually referred to as Treaties of Friendship, Commerce and Navigation.

See also: U.S. Treaties of Friendship, Commerce and Navigation.

RECOGNITION CLAUSE

A clause in the collective bargaining contract which states that the employer will bargain only with a particular union as the exclusive bargaining agent of the employees who have selected this union to represent them, subject to and in accordance with the provisions of law.

A recognition clause is the most basic clause of any labor relations contract. It is virtually required by the National Labor Relations Act which states that a company must recognize any union that has been shown to represent a majority of the employees in an appropriate bargaining unit. Even before the United States Supreme Court decision in *Fibreboard,* arbitrators would occasionally use this clause to prohibit subcontracting, holding that the union's right to exclusive recognition would otherwise be circumvented.

See also: Collective bargaining agreement; Duty of fair representation; Fibreboard Paper Products Corp.; Subcontracting.

Sources: Fairweather, *Implied Restrictions on Work Movements,* 38 Notre Dame Lawyer 518 (1963); General Motors Corp., *supra* Management rights at § .01a.

REFEREE

A person to whom a dispute is referred by a board or a court so that he may hear and settle it.

Such a referral may be made with or without the consent of the parties. Whenever the National Railroad Adjustment Board is unable to resolve a dispute, the term referee is applied to the neutral member who is selected by the members of the Board to make a final decision. In § 3(1), the Railway Labor Act describes the designation of referee as follows: "Upon failure of any division to agree upon an award because of a deadlock or inability to secure a majority vote of the division members, as provided in ¶(n) of this section, then such division shall forthwith agree upon and select a neutral person, to be known as 'referee,' to sit with the division as a member thereof, and make an award. . . ."

See also: Nat'l. Railroad Adjustment Board.

Sources: Railway Labor Act, 45 U.S.C. §§ 151-163, 181-188.

REHEARING

The reconsideration of an award which may result in a new arbitration before the same or different arbitrators.

A rehearing may be ordered by a court as a result of a challenge to an award on a motion to confirm, modify, or vacate the award. Under some statutes, application for modifying the award may be made to the arbitral tribunal which originally issued the award. Statutory grounds for changing an award may vary. The New York Civil Practice Law and Rules, § 7511(c) gives the court the following grounds for modifying the award: ". . . a miscalculation of figures or a mistake in the description of any person, thing or property referred to in the award; or the arbitrators have awarded upon a matter not submitted to them and the award may be corrected without affecting the merits of the decision upon the issues submitted; or the award is imperfect in a matter of form, not affecting the merits of the controversy." Some statutes declare that the court may recommit the matter to the same arbitrators where the award is not mutual, final and definite. If the grounds for vacating the award are corruption, fraud, or other misconduct of the arbitrators, a rehearing will then be ordered, usually before new arbitrators. If an arbitrator has made an error in his computations, and all that is required is a mechanical correction, some statutes do not demand a rehearing by the arbitrator. The court itself then makes the correction and enforces the award.

See also: Functus officio; Judicial review in arb.; Misconduct of arbitrator; Modifying the award; Vacating an award; Waiver of arb.

Sources: 5 AM. JUR., *supra* Death of the arbitrator at § 143.

REINSTATEMENT

The return of a discharged employee to his former job through the decision of an arbitrator.

A discharged employee may be reinstated with or without back pay. The crucial issue in discharge cases is whether the grievant fell short of the parties' standard of proper conduct as established in the collective bargaining agreement, and whether discharge was a fair and reasonable penalty. An arbitrator may reinstate an employee with full pay for the time lost, or with a portion of the pay, or with no pay at all. The extent of back pay awarded varies with the arbitrator's reasons for reinstatement.

See also: Back pay awards; Enterprise Wheel & Car Corp.

Sources: Ross, *supra* Distressed grievance procedures at 30-32 (1957).

REINSTATEMENT OF THE ARBITRATOR'S AUTHORITY

The jurisdiction of the arbitrator is reestablished when the award is vacated and recommitted by the court to the same or any other arbitrator.

The parties may have the right to reinstate the arbitrator's authority by written agreement. Under some modern statutes such as the New York State Civil Practice Law & Rules, the parties may request the arbitrator to remedy miscalculations of figures or certain errors of description of property or persons in the award.

See also: Arbitrator's authority; Modifying the award.

Sources: N.Y. CPLR § 7509; M. DOMKE, *supra* Adhesion contract at 215-217.

REMOVAL OF ARBITRATOR

The dismissal of an arbitrator for reasons of bias or misconduct before he renders his award.

Though most arbitration statutes contain ways and means for vacating an award, they do not often provide for the removal of an arbitrator before he has made his award. The court may occasionally remove an arbitrator. If it refuses to do so, the party may then choose to wait and try to have the award vacated. Under the rules of some administrative agencies, a party may challenge the arbitrator by presenting its claim to a special committee of the agency. If the challenge appears justified, the agency will vacate the office of arbitrator, and appoint another arbitrator before permitting the arbitration to proceed.

See also: Bias; Challenge of arbitrator; Disqualification of arbitrator; Duty to disclose; Misconduct of arbitrator; Vacating an award.

Sources: U.N. ECE, *supra* Access to the arbitral tribunal; M. DOMKE, *supra* Appeal boards of adm. agencies; LONDON COURT OF ARB., *supra* Adm. expenses at art. 12; 2 LAWYERS' LETTERS (1960), *supra* Adjournment of hearings.

REOPENING OF HEARINGS

Reconvening the hearings in an arbitration after they have been formally closed and before the award has been made.

An arbitrator may reopen a hearing on his own motion or at the request of a party. If reopening the hearings would delay the award beyond the time limit specified in the contract, the matter may not be reconvened unless the parties agree upon an extension of such a time limit. The arbitrator may wish to declare the hearings reopened if evidence appears insufficient, or if he wishes to have the parties clarify some of the facts. A party may also request a rehearing for the presentation of new evidence. Before deciding to reconvene the hearings, the arbitrator should offer the opposing party the opportunity to present his objections to such a reopening.

See also: Functus officio; Procedure; Time limits.

Sources: AAA COM'L. ARB. RULES, *supra* Adm. appointment at § 35; M. DOMKE, *supra* Adhesion contract at 251.

REPORTS

See: Citations of Labor Arbitration Awards.

REPRESENTATIONAL DISPUTES

A jurisdictional dispute involving a contest between two unions as to which one shall represent a specific group of employees.

Since the establishment in 1935 of the National Labor Relations Board under the National Labor Relations Act, a secret ballot representational election has been available for resolution of this type of jurisdictional dispute. Where one of the unions files a grievance leading to arbitration, the other may try to forestall a decision pending an NLRB ruling as to which union is the proper representative. Representational disputes are also resolved in such inter-union dispute settlement procedures as the AFL-CIO Internal Disputes Plan. Representational disputes in the railroads are handled by the National Mediation Board, as established by the Railway Labor Act (1926) as amended June 21, 1934.

See also: AFL-CIO Internal Disputes Plan; Carey v. Westinghouse; Jurisdictional disputes; Nat'l. Labor Relations Board; Nat'l. Mediation Board; No-Raiding Agreement (AFL & CIO); Work assignment disputes.

Sources: 32 Nat'l. Mediation Bd. Ann. Rep. 31-35 (1966); Collister, *supra* Jurisdictional disputes at 35-60; Dunlop, *Jurisdictional Disputes*, in 2 N. Y. University, Proc. of the Second Annual Conf. on Labor 478-479 (1949); Jones, *supra* Carey v. Westinghouse 328-329, 331.

REPUBLIC STEEL V. MADDOX
[*Republic Steel Corp.* v. *Maddox* 379 U.S. 650 (1965)]

A United States Supreme Court decision which held that where a grievance procedure has been made the exclusive method for resolving disputes, individual employees must try to obtain relief for any complaint by using the grievance procedure as established by the collective bargaining agreement, unless the union refuses to process the individual's claim, or the contract provides otherwise.

In the *Republic Steel* v. *Maddox* case, Maddox brought suit in a state court for severance pay amounting to $694.08, three years after his employment had been terminated when the company closed its plant. The agreement contained a three-step grievance procedure to be followed by arbitration, a procedure which Maddox had made no attempt to invoke. The Alabama courts permitted recovery. On appeal to the United States Supreme Court, the Alabama decision was reversed on the grounds that to "permit an individual employee to completely sidestep the available grievance procedures in favor of a law suit . . . would deprive employer and union of the ability to establish a uniform and exclusive method for orderly settlement of employee grievances. . . ."

See also: Grievance procedure; Individual rights; Vaca v. Sipes.

Sources: Republic Steel Corp. v. Maddox, 379 U.S. 650 (1965); Van Zile, *The Componental Structure of Labor-Management Contractual Relationships*, 43 U. Detroit L. J. 321-353 (1966).

REPUDIATION

The refusal of a losing party to comply with the award in an international arbitration.

See also: Annulment of the award . . . ; Compliance with the award; Enforcement of award (Int'l. pub. arb.); Grounds of nullity.

RESIDUAL RIGHTS

Those powers which an employer has held in the past and which have not been reduced or eliminated by court decisions or the collective bargaining agreement.

The residual rights doctrine gives management the benefit of the doubt concerning specific rights on which the contract is silent. When a court or an arbitrator does not find in the agreement anything to confirm the fact that the union is to perform a particular function, the court or the arbitrator may use the doctrine of residual rights as the legal basis for his decision.

See also: Collective bargaining agreement; Exclusionary clause; Management rights.

Sources: L. KELLER, *supra* Management rights at 41.

RES JUDICATA

A legal doctrine which holds that once a legal claim has come to a final conclusion it can never again be litigated.

The principle of res judicata is an attempt to prevent repetitious law suits. Once a case has gone to arbitration, and has been properly determined, its issues are res judicata, and can therefore never be raised again. Arbitration based on a valid contract has the same status as a law suit in the eyes of a court. A person challenging the enforcement of an award by an arbitrator cannot raise any issues already determined by the award.

See also: Binding character of award; Collateral estoppel; Pious Fund Case; Montevideo Treaty.

Sources: M. DOMKE, *supra* Adhesion contract at 295-297, 338; 14 LAWYERS' LETTERS (1963), *supra* Adjournment of hearings at 1.

RESPONDENT

The defendant, or party who receives a notice of intention to arbitrate from the claimant.

See also: Claimant; Counterclaim.

RESTAURANT INDUSTRY

See: Adjustment board.

RESTRICTIVE IMMUNITY

See: Tate Letter.

REVUE DE L'ARBITRAGE
(23 Rue d'Anjou, Paris VIII°, France)

A quarterly review published by the Comité Français de l'Arbitrage to cover all phases of arbitration law.

Each issue of the *Revue de l'Arbitrage* contains one or more articles on arbitration law, French and international case law, and reports of publications. In its recent issues, the *Revue* is publishing arbitral awards in order to further the knowledge of arbitral case law. Reports are also made in the *Revue* of the proceedings and resolutions of the various international congresses on arbitration, which have been fully reported in special issues of 1960 and 1966. The Editor of the *Revue de l'Arbitrage* is M. Jean Robert. Subscription is 30 fr a year through the Librairie Sirey, 22 rue Soufflot, Paris V. A complete file of issues since 1955 may be had through the Librairie Sirey.

See also: Comité Français de l'Arbitrage.

Sources: Memorandum by Jean Robert, *supra* Comité Français de 'lArbitrage.

RIGGED AWARD

See: Agreed award.

RIGHTS ARBITRATION

See: Grievance arbitration.

RIGHT TO COUNSEL

Each party to a dispute has a right to be represented by a lawyer.

The right of a party to enlist the aid of an attorney in an arbitration is included in the statutes of some states, including that of New York. This same right is extended and may not be waived at any future hearing. The New York State law also provides that such hearings remain valid even if the party has failed to exercise his right to counsel. Although the rules of some trade associations forbid representation by counsel in arbitration proceedings, a United Nations 1958 survey showed that most associations have rules or are governed by statutes providing for representation by a lawyer, a barrister or a solicitor.

Sources: N.Y. CPLR § 7506(d); Ass'n. of the Bar of the City of N.Y., *supra* Award by confession at 20; M. Domke, *supra* Adhesion contract at 233-234; 1 U.N. ECE, *supra* Access to the arbitral tribunal.

ROME INSTITUTE

See: International Institute for the Unification of Private Law.

ROTATING PANELS

A list of arbitrators in a collective bargaining agreement which is drawn up to function on a rotating basis for the life of the contract.

The number of names in a rotating panel varies from three to five with alternates to be used if necessary. These are variously called Contract Arbitrators or Rotating Panels. By such means, parties to a contract are able to expedite their arbitration case load, and take advantage at the same time of the benefits of a permanent arbitrator. If such rotating panels are set up by the American Arbitration Association, the arbitrations are held under the AAA rules.

See also: Ad hoc arbitrator; Appointment of arbitrators; Notice of hearing; Permanent arbitrator; Selection of arbitrators (AAA); Summary proceeding.

Sources: Hotel Employers Association of San Francisco, *supra* Adjustment board.

RULE-OF-COURT CLAUSE

A clause in a contract which states that any future dispute will be enforceable if the contract is filed with a court and made a rule of court, a provision which is also found in some older arbitration statutes.

Modern arbitration statutes frequently provide that the making of an arbitration agreement confers jurisdiction on the state courts to enforce the agreement and to enter judgment on the award. Some arbitration clauses, especially in the maritime industry still provide that the agreement be made a rule of court. Such clauses state that the agreement may be entered as a rule of court, and when thus entered, constitutes acceptance of the jurisdiction of the court in enforcing the award. This is especially important in charter parties to which foreign governments are parties, and which are therefore outside the jurisdiction of the court.

See also: Charter party; Enforcement of arb. agreements (State statutes); Entry-of-judgment clause; Standard arb. clause; Pennsylvania compulsory arb. of small claims.

Sources: Victory Transport, Inc. v. Comisaria General, 336 F 2d 354 (1964) cert den 381 U.S. 934 (1965); 5 AM. JUR., *supra* Death of the arbitrator at 637-638; M. DOMKE, *supra* Adhesion contract at 49-50.

RULE OF REASON

A means of challenging any management rule which threatens to deprive employees of their rights and privileges as guaranteed by the terms of the original contract.

Among those traditional rights which management has in controlling and directing the work of its employees is the right to set up specific rules of conduct, and the right to punish those employees who violate them. Management's authority in this respect may be limited by certain provisions of the collective bargaining agreement. If a contract does not contain a provision to protect employees against unjust discipline, then the contract as a whole is considered to provide such protection under the rule of reason.

See also: Individual rights; Management rights.

Sources: M. STONE, LABOR-MANAGEMENT CONTRACTS AT WORK 202 (1961);
*Arbiter Overrules New Jersey Township Dismissal of Probationary
Police Officer*, GOV'T. EMPLOYEE REL. REP. B-7 (No. 268, 1968).

RULES OF EVIDENCE

Limitations upon the admissibility of evidence as decided by the courts
or developed by statute.

Though rules of evidence as they apply to the courts do not control
in arbitration, they may have some influence upon the admissibility of
evidence in an arbitration. Purely formal procedures governing evidence
in arbitration are felt to be too restrictive in the flexible process of
a hearing which is adapted to the individual needs of the parties. The
arbitrator should be familiar with the rules of evidence, since his is the
ultimate decision on what to admit and what to reject as evidence.
Among those things he will have to determine for example are what is
hearsay and when it may be admitted, what is relevant, when to accept
a copy instead of the original document, and when to admit parol
evidence.

See also: Affidavit; Deposition; Lie detector; Parol evidence rule; Procedure.

Sources: 19 NAT'L. ACADEMY OF ARBITRATORS, *supra* Parol evidence rule.

SANCTIONS

Certain specified penalties which may be imposed on individuals or organizations or nations for failure to comply with the law.

Sanctions are used in the public sector of labor relations for the
primary purpose of preventing strikes. The New York State Taylor Law
may impose fines, as well as forfeiture of the union's right to automatic
dues check-off by management for a period not to exceed 18 months.
If there is a violation of any injunction, the union is subject to punishment up to a maximum fine of $10,000 a day or one week's dues which-
ever is less, for each day of contempt under the New York State Judiciary
Law § 751(2). Under § 751(1) of the same law, a public employee
charged with contempt is punishable by fine or imprisonment. The
amended Taylor Law of 1969 imposed even more severe sanctions.
Sanctions on the federal level are available to the President of the United
States when he invokes the seizure of a plant. The President may order
the army to occupy the struck plant in order to police and protect the
property. Striking employees may be discharged, and executives may be
temporarily replaced. Other kinds of sanctions may be made available
through court or legislative action, including anti-strike injunctions, proposed recommendations by the President, or by means of new or *ad hoc*
legislation.

See also: Arsenal of weapons; Compulsory arb.; Convention on Int'l. Civil Aviation; Enforcement of award (Int'l. pub. arb.); Gov't. intervention; Seizure of plant; Taylor Law.

Sources: McHugh, *New York's Experiment in Public Employee Relations*, 32 ALBANY L. REV. 58-95 (1967).

SCHOEFFEN

A term describing persons chosen from the German community of the 13th and 14th centuries who were considered worthy of trust and qualified to make decisions concerning the law, thus functioning very much like modern arbitrators.

The Schoeffen were permanent officers of good repute and influence, who were required to be selected from the landowning class. These early arbitrators sat in groups, sometimes 7 in number, and sometimes as many as 12 or 15. Later the Schoeffen evolved into a secret and almost inquisitorial society, delivering decisions and penalties which marked these private judges as full of pride, believing as they did that they represented the highest court in the world, becoming such a delusive law unto themselves that they soon withered and exhausted their usefulness.

See also: Arbitrator.

Sources: J. DAWSON, *supra* Indifferent gentlemen at 101; Jones, *supra* Indifferent gentlemen at 703.

SCOPE OF THE ARBITRATION AGREEMENT

The number and extent of issues, as specifically outlined in the arbitration agreement, which can be referred to arbitration in case of a dispute.

A narrow clause in an arbitration agreement may include only that which would relate to the validity, interpretation or performance of the agreement itself. What is termed a broad clause is so drafted as to include "any controversy or claim arising out of or relating to this contract, or the breach thereof. . . ." The standard arbitration clauses of the American Arbitration Association, the International Chamber of Commerce, and the London Court of Arbitration are designed to cover all disputes which might occur under the contract. Under such a broad clause, most courts allow the arbitrator to determine such questions as the fraudulent inducement of the contract.

See also: Arbitrability; Arb. agreement; Fraudulent inducement of the contract; Standard arb. clause.

Sources: M.DOMKE, *supra* Adhesion contract at 59-64, 99-104.

SECOND CONFERENCE ON INTER-AMERICAN COMMERCIAL ARBITRATION (Mexico City) (November 7-9, 1968)

A conference organized by the Chamber of Commerce of the City of

Mexico and the Mexican Bar Association in cooperation with the Inter-American Commercial Arbitration Commission and held at Mexico City on November 7-9, 1968.

The Second Conference on Inter-American Commercial Arbitration was attended by delegates from a variety of non-governmental bodies from 16 countries of the Western Hemisphere. The conference adopted a new arbitration clause to be recommended to the legal and business community for possible insertion in their contracts. The clause amplifies the former clause used by the Inter-American Commercial Arbitration Commission, providing for the appointment of arbitrators by the IACAC if the parties have made no such designation themselves, for the naming of the locale by the IACAC when the parties have not done so, for a time limit for making the award, and for compliance with the award. Article 4 of the Clause provides that the "parties hereby waive the right to any appeal or other remedies contesting the award; with the exception of annulment proceedings based on the . . . arbitrators having exceeded their authority or other reasons that may be considered admissible."

See also: Inter-American Com'l. Arb. Comm'n.

Sources: IACAC, RULES OF PROCEDURE 2 (1969); SEGUNDA CONFERENCIA INTERAMERICANA DE ARBITRAJE COMERCIAL, MEMORIA 73 (1968); Norberg, *supra* Bustamante Code at 25-41 (1969).

SECOND TRILOGY (1962)

Three decisions of the United States Supreme Court delivered simultaneously in 1962, which were concerned with the breach of the no-strike clause, and the further availability of arbitration to resolve such disputes.

See also: Atkinson v. Sinclair Refining Co.; Drake Bakeries, Inc.; No-strike clause; Sinclair Refining Co. v. Atkinson.

SECTION 10(K) PROCEEDING (WAGNER ACT)

A method of resolving work assignment disputes by the National Labor Relations Board.

The National Labor Relations Act at § 8(b)(4)(D) makes it an unfair labor practice for a union to strike or use restraint or coercion in order to force an employer to assign work to one particular group of employees rather than to another. After a strike or a threat of a strike or restraint and coercion, the Act gives the Board the authority to resolve this type of jurisdictional dispute under § 10(k). Section 10(k) also encourages voluntary settlement of such disputes, including the use of arbitration. This is particularly true since the United States Supreme Court decision of 1964 in *Carey* v. *Westinghouse*. Work assignment disputes in the construction industry formerly were assigned to the National Joint Board for Settlement of Jurisdictional Disputes in the Building and

Construction Industry. Work assignment disputes also come within the jurisdiction of the AFL-CIO Internal Disputes Plan.

See also: AFL-CIO Internal Disputes Plan; Carey v. Westinghouse; Jurisdictional disputes; Nat'l. Joint Board for the Settlement of Jurisdictional Disputes in the Building and Construction Industry; Nat'l. Labor Relations Board; Taft-Hartley Act.

Sources: Carey v. Westinghouse Electric Corp., 375 U.S. 261 (1964); Nat'l. Labor Relations Act, 29 U.S.C.A. § 141 et seq.; BUILDING & CONSTRUCTION TRADES DEPT., AFL-CIO, *supra* Nat'l. Joint Board for the Settlement of Jurisdictional Disputes.

SECTION 301 DISPUTES (TAFT-HARTLEY)

Section 301 reads as follows: "Suits for violation of contracts between an employer and a labor organization representing employees in an industry affecting commerce as defined in this Act, . . . may be brought in any district court of the United States having jurisdiction of the parties, without respect to the amount in controversy or without regard to the citizenship of the parties."

Suits may be brought under § 301 by either unions or employers or, in some instances, by one union against another union. Section 301 focuses either upon an alleged breach of the collective bargaining agreement by an employer or by a union, or upon a dispute between two unions. Awards as well as agreements to arbitrate may be enforced under § 301.

See also: American Manufacturing Co.; Atkinson v. Sinclair Refining Co.; Common law arb.; Drake Bakeries, Inc.; Enforcement of arb. agreements (Common law); Enforcement of arb. agreements (Federal statutes); Enforcement of award (Labor); Judicial review in arb.; Labor arb. (Voluntary); Lincoln Mills; Motion to compel arb.; No-strike clause; Sinclair Refining Co. v. Atkinson; Taft-Hartley Act; Vaca v. Sipes.

Sources: Labor Management Relations Act, 29 U.S.C.A. §§ 141-197; Gregory, *Arb. of Grievances under Collective Labor Agreements*, 1 GEORGIA L. REV. (1966); Jones, *Autobiography of a Decision*, 10 UCLA L. REV. 1020-1021 (1963).

SEIZURE OF PLANT

The taking over and temporary operation of a plant by the federal government during a strike or threat of a strike for the purpose of maintaining production in industries considered essential for the welfare of the nation.

There have been 71 such federal seizures since 1861, the beginning of the Civil War. Though most seizures have taken place during a time of war, they have also occurred in periods of peacetime rearmament or reconversion. Actual seizures have been ordered by Presidents Lincoln,

Wilson, Franklin D. Roosevelt, and Truman. The threat of seizure by President Theodore Roosevelt in 1902 may have been influential in persuading the anthracite mine owners to accept binding arbitration by the Presidential Anthracite Coal Strike Commission. There were three other occasions when two Presidents employed new legislation rather than seizure to avert threatened strikes in the railroad industry. These acts were the Newlands Act, with its voluntary arbitration procedure for railroad workers, approved by President Wilson on July 15, 1913; the Adamson Act, approved on September 5, 1916, by President Wilson, providing for a basic eight hour day with no reduction in pay for all train and engine workers; and a joint resolution of Congress, approved by President Kennedy on August 28, 1963, which prohibited a strike for six months over work rules, and provided for compulsory arbitration to resolve the issues in dispute.

See also: Adamson Act; Anthracite Coal Strike Comm'n.; Arsenal of weapons; Gov't. intervention; Newlands Act; Railroad Arb. Act; Sanctions; War Labor Disputes Act.

Sources: J. BLACKMAN, PRESIDENTIAL SEIZURE IN LABOR DISPUTES (1967).

SELECTION OF ARBITRATORS (AMERICAN ARBITRATION ASSOCIATION)

The submission of identical lists by the American Arbitration Association to both parties to a dispute for the selection of arbitrators when the AAA has been chosen to administer the arbitration under its own rules.

The parties, if they prefer, may provide in their agreement other means of selecting the arbitrators. Arbitrators on the Panels of the American Arbitration Association are classified as eligible to serve in labor, commercial, international, or accident claims disputes. The Voluntary Labor Arbitration Rules at § 12 describe this method of selecting arbitrators: "If the parties have not appointed an Arbitrator and have not provided any other method of appointment, the Arbitrator shall be appointed in the following manner: Immediately after the filing of the Demand or Submission, the AAA shall submit simultaneously to each party an identical list of names of persons chosen from the Labor Panel. Each party shall have seven days from the mailing date in which to cross off any names to which he objects, number the remaining names indicating the order of his preference, and return the list to the AAA. If a party does not return the list within the time specified, all persons named therein shall be deemed acceptable. From among the persons who have been approved on both lists, and in accordance with the designated order of mutual preference, the AAA shall invite the acceptance of an Arbitrator to serve. . . ." Biographical material on each arbitrator concerning his education and experience, and his *per diem* charges, is sent with the lists. Procedures are similar for the selection of commercial arbitrators.

In Accident Claims Tribunals, the AAA submits a list of three attorneys from which the parties are to select an arbitrator. When there is not a mutual choice, the Association then appoints the arbitrator.

See also: Adm. appointment; American Arb. Association; Appointment of arbitrators; Rotating panels; Selection of arbitrators (FMCS); Sole arbitrator.

Sources: AAA COM'L. ARB. RULES, *supra* Adm. appointment; M. DOMKE, *supra* Adhesion contract at 190-193.

SELECTION OF ARBITRATORS (FEDERAL MEDIATION AND CONCILIATION SERVICE)

The submission by the Federal Mediation and Conciliation Service of identical lists of suggested arbitrators to the disputing parties when they have been unable to agree on an arbitrator.

The Federal Mediation and Conciliation Service submits to the parties the names of seven arbitrators, unless the collective bargaining agreement provides for a different number. A short background statement is also furnished with the names, giving the qualifications, experience, and the *per diem* charge of each of the nominees. The parties have the choice of meeting together and alternately striking names from the list until the one chosen remains, or each party may advise the Service of its choice by numbering each name on the panel in order of preference.

See also: Appointment of arbitrators; Federal Mediation and Conciliation Service; Selection of arbitrators (AAA); Sole arbitrator.

Sources: U.S. FEDERAL MEDIATION AND CONCILIATION SERVICE, ARBITRATION POLICIES, FUNCTIONS AND PROCEDURES, ch. XII, pt. 1404 (1968).

SENIORITY

The length of service of an employee in his total employment or in some particular division or unit of the plant in which he works.

Competitive status seniority is the status of the employee in relation to other employees establishing certain preferences or rights as to layoff, to shift preference, as well as promotion. Benefit seniority refers only to the date of hiring of a particular employee, and affects such individual benefits as vacation, severance pay, and retirement benefits, and also partial protection from discharge because of length of service. Whatever seniority rights an employee has depend wholly on the contract. There are no enforceable seniority rights without a collective bargaining agreement. Seniority is often referred to as the "working man's most cherished possession."*

See also: Back pay awards; Grievance; Merging seniority lists; Sufficient ability clauses; Tests.

Sources: S. SLICHTER et al., *supra* Collective bargaining; CCH LAB. L. REP.
Union Contracts, Arbitration ¶ 58,581; Shulman, *supra* Arbitrator;
The Use of Tests in Promotions under Seniority Provisions, 21 VAND.
L. REV. (1967).

SEPARABILITY DOCTRINE

The principle that the arbitration clause is an agreement separate and
apart from the contract in which it appears.

The doctrine of separability has had varied acceptance. Federal law
in the United States recognizes the principle of separability and allows
the arbitrator to decide any issue so long as the arbitration clause is valid
and broad enough to cover the issue. In cases which include the issue of
fraudulent inducement of the contract, a dispute regarding the validity
of the main contract is to be determined by the arbitrator, while such
issues involving the arbitration clause must be determined by the court.

See also: Container contract; Fraudulent inducement of the contract; Irrevocability of the arb. agreement; Prima Paint Corp. . . . ; U. S. Arb.
Act; Scope of the arb. agreement.

Sources: Robert Lawrence Co. v. Devonshire Fabrics, Inc., 271 F. 2d 402
(2d Cir. 1959), cert. granted 362 U.S. 909, dismissed pursuant to
stipulation, 364 U.S. 801 (1960); M. DOMKE, *supra* Adhesion contract at 56-62; M. DOMKE, *supra* Appeal boards of adm. agencies
at 47; Bernstein, *supra* Container contract at 8-33 (1967); Collins,
supra Container contract at 736-756 (1966); 5 LAWYERS' LETTERS
(1961), *supra* Adjournment of hearings at 1-3; 25 *id*. (1966) at 4.

SERVICE BY MAIL

The rules of some administrative agencies state that any papers, notices,
or any process necessary or proper for the initiation or continuation of an
arbitration under their rules may be served upon each party by mail.

Service by mail is a way of acquiring jurisdiction over a party, especially when this party is not a resident in the state where the arbitration is to take place. The basis for the validity of this procedure lies in
the agreement of the parties to be bound by the rules of the agency.
Where service by registered or certified mail is required, the courts have
held that the mere refusal to accept registered mail will not be a ground
on which an award can be set aside. The courts also require an explana-
tion for the failure to accept such notices sent by registered mail.

See also: Personal service; Procedure; Notice of hearing; Notice of intention
to arbitrate.

Sources: AAA COM'L. ARB. RULES, *supra* Adm. appointment at § 39(b);
Aksen, *supra* Construction Industry Arb. Rules; Freedman, *supra* personal service; 3 LAWYERS' LETTERS (1960), *supra*, Adjournment of
hearings at 2.

SERVICES

See: Loose-leaf services.

SEVENTH INTERNATIONAL CONFERENCE OF AMERICAN STATES

See: Montevideo Conference (1933).

SIGNATURE ON AWARD

The affixing by an arbitrator of his name to an award.

Modern arbitration statutes vary in their requirements for the signing of the award by the arbitrators. The Uniform Arbitration Act, § 8(a) states that the award shall be in writing and signed by the arbitrators joining in making the award. The Rules and Regulations of the International Centre for Settlement of Investment Disputes require that the award be signed by those arbitrators who voted for the award. Similarly, the New York State statute requires that the award shall be signed and acknowledged by the arbitrator making it, within the time fixed by the agreement. The Commercial Arbitration Rules of the American Arbitration Association at § 41 declare that "(t)he award shall be in writing and shall be signed either by the sole Arbitrator or by at least a majority if there be more than one. . . ." As a safeguard to prove that the award is made in accordance with the agreement of the parties, it is usually advisable to have the dissenting arbitrator sign the award, and at the same time, note his dissent. Some state statutes require that the signing of the award be verified by witnesses or notarization.

See also: Delivery of award; Execution of award; Procedure.

Sources: N.Y. CPLR § 7507; Uniform Arb. Act § 8(a); M. DOMKE, *supra* Adhesion contract at 285; ICSID, *supra* Appeal boards of adm. agencies at rule 47(2).

SILK ASSOCIATION OF AMERICA

The association which was organized by 43 silk firms in New York City in 1872, and which later adopted arbitration as a means of settling disputes in the silk industry by appointing an Arbitration Committee in 1898.

The Arbitration Committee administered the arbitrations, established the rules, and compiled and published a *List of Official Arbitrators of the Silk Association of America, Inc.*, composed of members, as well as non-members selected from related trades. Arbitration is still used regularly in the industry. The Silk Association of America merged with the National Rayon Weavers Association to become the National Federation of Textiles, Inc. The successor association, the General Arbitration Council of the Textile Industry, was consolidated with the American Arbitration

Association in May of 1964. The arbitrator's fee in 1927 was $10 per hearing. At the present time, arbitrators serve without fee.

See also: Compensation of the arbitrator; General Arbitration Council of the Textile Industry. Arb. Rules.

Sources: AAA, YEARBOOK ON COM'L. ARB. IN THE U.S. at 772-783 (1927); A. Madigan, Memo [on the History of My Employment in the Arb. Field], Jan. 18, 1968.

SINCLAIR REFINING COMPANY V. ATKINSON
[*Sinclair Refining Co.* v. *Atkinson*, 370 U.S. 195 (1962)]

A United States Supreme Court decision which held that the federal courts are barred by § 4(a) of the Norris-LaGuardia Act from enjoining a strike even though the strike is in violation of a no-strike clause in the contract.

Under § 301 of the Taft-Hartley Act, the federal courts are given jurisdiction over suits between employers and unions for breach of collective bargaining agreements. Although violation of the no-strike clause is clearly a breach of the contract, the Supreme Court ruled that Congress did not intend the employer to enjoy the benefits of an injunction along with the right given him in § 301 to sue for breach of a collective bargaining agreement.

See also: Atkinson v. Sinclair Refining Co.; Breach of contract; Drake Bakeries, Inc.; Injunction; No-strike clause; Second trilogy; § 301 disputes.

Sources: Sinclair Refining Co. v. Atkinson, 370 U.S. 195 (1962); Smith & Jones, *Impact of the Emerging Federal Law, supra* Arbitrability at 831-912; Smith & Jones, *The Supreme Court, supra* Arbitrability at 751-808.

SITUS OF ARBITRATION

The place of arbitration.

See also: Locale of arb.; Venue of arb.

SMITH-CONNALLY ACT

See: War Labor Disputes Act. World War II.

SOLE ARBITRATOR

An arbitrator who is appointed to be solely responsible for making a final and binding award.

See also: Appointment of arbitrators; Arbitrator; Selection of arbitrators (AAA); Selection of arbitrators (FMCS).

Sources: CODE OF ARB., *supra* Presiding arbitrator (1931).

SOVEREIGN IMMUNITY

See: Tate Letter.

SPECIAL CASE (ENGLISH LAW)

The referral by an arbitrator to a court for a legal opinion on a point of law which has arisen during the course of the arbitration.

A special case may be stated in the form of a consultative case, or an interim award, or as an alternative final award. An arbitrator cannot refuse to state a special case on an arbitration in which a point of law arises, since to do so would constitute misconduct and be cause for vacating the award. The parties may request an arbitrator to state a special case. If the arbitrator refuses, either party may apply for a court order directing the arbitrator to do so, as provided in English law.

See also: Alternative final award; Applicable procedural law; Delegation of the arbitrator's authority; Doctrine of ouster; Interim award.

Sources: W. GILL, *supra* Compensation of arbitrator at 99-108; F. RUSSELL, *supra* Alternative final award; Schmitthoff, *supra* Doctrine of ouster at 293.

SPECIFIC PERFORMANCE

The decision by an arbitrator that one party to a dispute shall be required to perform the specific act he was bound to fulfill in the original contract.

An arbitrator can make an award on specific performance when he has been authorized to do so by the arbitration agreement, or when the parties have referred to the rules of an administrative agency which specifically authorize him to make use of such a remedy. The courts have clearly stated that such remedies are available in arbitration when the parties themselves have referred to rules providing for awards of specific performance. Such remedies are particularly important in personal service or construction contracts. The one specific performance which is always available to the disputing parties under modern arbitration statutes is the enforcement of the arbitration agreement itself.

See also: Injunction.

Sources: M. BERNSTEIN, *supra* Appeal at 597; M. DOMKE, *supra* Appeal boards of adm. agencies at 89-90; 4 LAWYERS' LETTERS (1960), *supra* Adjournment of hearings at 1-3.

SPIELBERG DOCTRINE (1955)

A landmark decision of the National Labor Relations Board, defining and establishing principles by which its own jurisdiction would be determined in any case where an arbitration award had already been made.

The Spielberg doctrine rules that the Board will honor an arbitration award under certain clearly declared conditions, even though it is plain that the jurisdiction of the Board over unfair labor practices is exclusive under § 10(a) of the National Labor Relations Act. In the *Spielberg Manufacturing Company* case, an unfair labor practice charge was filed with the National Labor Relations Board, following an arbitration award which had denied reinstatement after discharge to certain striking union members. Though the National Labor Relations Act had authorized the NLRB to accept jurisdiction, the Board declined on the grounds that "the proceedings appear to have been fair and regular, all parties had agreed to be bound by the award, and the decision of the arbitration panel is not clearly repugnant to the purposes and policies of the Act." The Board later added as part of the above requirements, that the arbitrator should consider the issue involved in the unfair labor practice in making his award.

See also: Concurrent jurisdiction; Nat'l. Labor Relations Board; Preemption; Unfair labor practice.

Sources: Spielberg Mfg. Co. v. NLRB, 112 NLRB 1080 (1955); Aaron, *supra* Judicial review in arb. at 54; Brown, *The Nat'l. Labor Policy, the NLRB, and Arb.*, in 21 Proc. of the Nat'l. Academy of Arbitrators at 83-93 (1968); Howlett, *The Arbitrator, the NLRB, and the Courts*, in 20 *id.* 67-110 (1967).

STANDARD ARBITRATION CLAUSE

An arbitration clause to be included in a contract as recommended by national and international administrative agencies such as the International Chamber of Commerce, the London Court of Arbitration, and the American Arbitration Association.

The Standard Arbitration Clause recommended by the American Arbitration Association reads as follows: "Any controversy or claim arising out of or relating to this contract, or the breach thereof, shall be settled by arbitration in accordance with the Rules of the American Arbitration Association, and judgment upon the award rendered by the Arbitrator(s) may be entered in any Court having jurisdiction thereof."

See also: Arb. agreement; Arb. clause; Construction Industry Arb. Rules; Entry-of-judgment clause; Future disputes clause; Institutional arb.; Int'l. Chamber of Commerce. Arb. clause; London Court of Arbitration. Arb. clause.

Sources: AAA Com'l. Arb. Rules, *supra* Adm. appointment at 2.

STARE DECISIS (TO STAND BY DECIDED MATTERS)

The doctrine of following rules or principles laid down in previous judicial decisions, accepting them as precedents which are obligatory and binding.

Under stare decisis, all courts exercising inferior jurisdiction are required to follow decisions of courts having superior jurisdiction. Arbitration awards are not considered to be judgments, and therefore cannot be viewed as precedents. Awards within organized arbitration systems may acquire persuasive value in guiding subsequent arbitrators. This is particularly true in certain trade associations where awards may become part of an internal system of case law for that particular trade. Since there is no hierarchy of courts in international public arbitration, stare decisis is not possible. International arbitration awards tend nevertheless to influence subsequent arbitrations. It is in this sense that Article 38(1)(d) of the Statute of the International Court of Justice recognizes "judicial decisions and the teachings of the most highly qualified publicists of the various nations, as subsidiary means for the determination of rules of law." This holds true, even though Article 59 of the same Statute cautions that: "The decision of the Court has no binding force except between the parties and in respect of that particular case."

See also: Precedent; Legalisms.

Sources: M. BEATTY, *supra* Judicial notice at 121; F. ELKOURI & E. ELKOURI, *supra* American Arb. Association at 251ff; Shulman, *supra* Arbitrator at 1020.

STATE BOARDS OF MEDIATION

A board vested by state law with authority to mediate labor disputes, and if mediation fails, to urge fact-finding and the use of voluntary arbitration as a means of settlement.

Such state boards are variously known as State Boards of Arbitration and Conciliation, or Boards of Mediation, or Industrial Commissions. Some states which have no such special boards authorize the Director of the Department of Labor to promote the use of voluntary mediation and conciliation in resolving labor disputes. The Taft-Hartley Act requires that state mediation agencies be notified of certain types of labor disputes, and in § 203 (b), in describing the duties of the Federal Mediation and Conciliation Service, states: "The Director and the Service are directed to avoid attempting to mediate disputes which would have only a minor effect on interstate commerce if State or other conciliation services are available to the parties. . . ." Some state mediation boards volunteer their services whenever they have knowledge of a labor dispute. Other boards wait until one or both parties specifically request such assistance.

See also: Appointing agency; Conciliation; Federal Mediation and Conciliation Service; Mediation.

Sources: 1 BD. OF MEDIATION & ARB. OF THE STATE OF N.Y., ANN. REP. (1888); N.J. STATE BOARD OF MEDIATION, MEDIATION AND THE DE-

VELOPMENT OF INDUSTRIAL RELATIONS IN NEW JERSEY (1966); U.S. BLS, BULL. No. 176, GUIDE TO STATE MEDIATION LAWS AND AGENCIES 531 (1958); Blumrosen, *Employee Rights, Collective Bargaining, and Our Future Labor Problem,* 15 LAB. L. J. (1964); Stark, *New Vistas in Mediation,* 6 LAB. L. J. 523-601 (1955).

STATUTE OF LIMITATIONS

A statute which determines the fixed statutory period after which an action cannot be taken to enforce any legal claim or right.

The courts sometimes apply a certain statute of limitations in arbitration cases or they leave to the discretion of the arbitrators whether such a statute should be applied. Courts usually uphold the self-imposed time limits which the parties provide in their arbitration agreements or collective bargaining agreements. These agreements may contain time limitations for performing various acts such as making a claim, or filing a grievance, or appealing the decision of an officer of the company in the grievance procedure. Both courts and arbitrators vary in their treatment of such provisions. Arbitration laws may specify a time limit within which an arbitration must begin. If this time limit is not met, arbitration under the statute is not available. The United States Supreme Court in *John Wiley & Sons v. Livingston* held that once the court determined that the parties are obligated to submit the subject of a dispute to arbitration, it would be for the arbitrator and not the court to make decisions on such procedural issues as compliance with time limitations provided in the contract.

See also: Laches; Notice of intention to arbitrate; Time limits; Vacating an award; Wiley v. Livingston.

Sources: BLACK'S LAW DICTIONARY (3d ed. 1933); 13 LAWYERS' LETTERS (1963), *supra* Adjournment of hearings at 3-5.

STATUTORY ARBITRATION

Arbitration for which rules and procedures are provided by a state or federal law for the conduct of arbitrations, and for the enforcement of arbitration agreements and awards.

The New York State Arbitration Law passed in 1920 was the first modern arbitration act in the United States. Most modern arbitration statutes apply to commercial arbitration. On the federal level, the U. S. Arbitration Act, the Labor Management Relations Act of 1947 (Taft-Hartley), the Railway Labor Act, and the Railroad Arbitration Act all provide for arbitration procedures.

See also: Appeal; Institutional arb.; Modern arb. statute; Modifying the award; Motion to compel arb.; § 301 disputes; Railroad . . . ; Vacating an award.

Sources: U.S. Arb. Act, 9 U.S.C. § 1-14; N.Y. CPLR §§ 7501-7514; M.BEATTY, *supra* Judicial notice at 19; M. DOMKE, *supra* Adhesion contract at 20; F. ELKOURI & E. ELKOURI, *supra* American Arb. Association at 21-22.

STAY OF ARBITRATION

The suspension by court order of all proceedings in an arbitration.

A stay of arbitration may occur when a party contests the existence of an agreement to arbitrate. Due process requires that the courts be open and available for the determination of such an issue. The New York State Arbitration Law at § 7503(b) states: ". . . a party who has not participated in the arbitration and who has not made or been served with an application to compel arbitration, may apply to stay arbitration on the ground that a valid agreement was not made or has not been complied with or that the claim sought to be arbitrated is barred by limitation under subdivision (b) of § 7502." The New York State statute requires that an application to stay arbitration must be made by a party who has been served with a notice of intention to arbitrate within ten days after receiving such a notice, and that "(n)otice of such application [to stay arbitration] shall be served in the same manner as a summons or by registered or certified mail, return receipt requested." Parties may provide in their agreement for other methods of service or for the rules of an impartial agency to apply which contain a service by mail clause. A court will also stay an arbitration until it determines whether certain issues lie within the scale of the arbitration agreement, and are therefore arbitrable.

See also: Arbitrability; Notice of intention to arbitrate; Participation in arbitration; Service by mail; Substantive arbitrability; Vacating an award.

Sources: N.Y. CPLR § 7503(b)(c); 5 AM. JUR., *supra* Death of arbitrator; Freedman, *supra* Personal service.

STAY OF SUIT

An attempt to violate an agreement to arbitrate may be stayed through court action until arbitration in the agreed manner has taken place.

Modern arbitration statutes include the provision that any court action instituted in violations of arbitral agreements may be stayed until arbitration takes place. If a party to a contract containing an arbitration clause brings a court action on a subject within the scope of the arbitration agreement, the other party may move to stay the action and request that the arbitration proceed as before.

See also: Enforcement of arb. agreements (Int'l. com'l. arb.); Enforcement of arb. agreements (State statutes); Evasion of arb.; Modern arb. statute; Waiver of arb. (Com'l.).

Sources: N.Y. CPLR § 7503.

STEEL INDUSTRY

See: Board of arbitration.

STEELWORKERS TRILOGY

See: Trilogy (1960).

STERLING IRON WORKS DISPUTE (January 1, 1771)

A wage dispute between the Sterling Iron Works and one of its employees which was the first industrial case administered by the Arbitration Committee of the New York State Chamber of Commerce.

The Sterling Iron Works constructed the famous iron chain which was stretched over the Hudson River at West Point to prevent British men-of-war from sailing up the river.

See also: Chamber of Commerce of the State of N.Y. Arb. Comm.

Sources: COMM. ON ιARB. OF THE CHAMBER OF COMMERCE OF THE STATE OF N.Y., ANN. REP. 2 (1943).

STIPULATION

Any verbal or written agreement between opposing attorneys in respect to the conduct of legal or arbitration proceedings.

See also: Board of arb.; Prehearing conference.

SUBCONTRACTING

An arrangement by an employer to have part or all of his product serviced or manufactured by an outside independent contractor.

The United States Supreme Court decision of *Fibreboard Paper Products* held that subcontracting may be a subject of collective bargaining.

See also: Collective bargaining agreements; Fibreboard Paper Products Corp. v. NLRB; Management rights; Recognition clause; Warrior & Gulf Nav. Co.

Sources: F. Young, *supra* Fibreboard Paper Products Corp. v. NLRB at 42; Smith, *Subcontracting and Union-Management Legal and Contractual Relations*, 17 W. RES. L. REV. 1272 (1966).

SUBMISSION AGREEMENT

A document used to initiate an arbitration of an existing dispute, stating the nature of the dispute, and affirming the parties intention to arbitrate and to abide by the award.

Parties not originally bound by an arbitration clause may use a submission agreement to refer their dispute to arbitration. The submission agreement establishes the extent and limit of the arbitrator's authority. It is through this agreement that he learns what issues are in question, and what relief is being sought. Submission agreements can only be used if both parties, having failed to settle their dispute by themselves, see the wisdom of seeking the assistance of an arbitrator. The more usual practice is to incorporate in the contract an arbitration clause which compels the use of arbitration in any future dispute occurring under the contract. Submission agreements must be in writing in New York State.

See also: Arb. agreement; Arbitrator's authority; Clause compromissoire; Common law arb.; Compromis; Consent of the parties; Enforcement of arb. agreements (Common law); Enforcement of arb. agreements (State statutes); Future disputes clause; Irrevocability of the arb. agreement; Notice of intention to arbitrate.

Sources: AAA LABOR ARB., *supra* American Arb. Association; AAA MANUAL, *supra* Award; CODE OF ARB., *supra* Presiding arbitrator at 27; Research Institute of America, *Com'l. Arb.: Pros and Cons*, Sept. 11, 1967.

SUBPOENA

A writ ordering the person designated in it to appear in court or at an arbitration hearing under a penalty for failure to do so.

A subpoena may also request that the person designated bring with him certain specified documents. Arbitration statutes of most states give the arbitrator the power to issue subpoenas. The U.S. Arbitration Act, § 7, provides that the arbitrator may issue subpoenas if the evidence sought is material to the proceedings. Under the New York State Civil Practice Law and Rules, § 7505, not only the arbitrator, but "any attorney of record in the arbitration proceeding" has the power to issue a subpoena.

See also: Modern arb. statute.

Sources: U.S. Arb. Act, 9 U.S.C. § 7 (1954); N.Y. CPLR § 7505; 16 LAWYERS' LETTERS (1963), *supra* Adjournment of hearings; O'Brien, *Should the NLRB Arbitrate Labor Contract Disputes?*, 6 WASHBURN L. J. (1966).

SUBPOENA DUCES TECUM

A subpoena compelling witnesses to appear in court or at an arbitration hearing together with any books or documents they may have which may illustrate or explain the subject matter of the trial or arbitration.

See also: Subpoena.

Sources: BLACK'S LAW DICTIONARY (3d ed. 1933).

SUBSTANTIVE ARBITRABILITY

A judicial resolution of arbitrability which determines whether or not an agreement to arbitrate exists, and if it does, whether the parties did or did not agree to arbitrate the particular dispute under review.

The two forums where the question of arbitrability can be raised are the courts and the arbitration hearing. The term arbitrability refers to two aspects of the same issue. The first one is whether the parties in their contract intended to arbitrate the matter under dispute. The second is whether all the procedural requirements in the labor agreement were complied with prior to arbitration. The courts must decide the first issue, and the arbitrators the second. The United States Supreme Court in its decision on *United Steelworkers of America* v. *Warrior and Gulf Navigation Co.* determined that substantive arbitrability is for the courts to decide, and defined such arbitrability as follows: "The Congress . . . has by § 301 of the Labor Management Relations Act, assigned the courts the duty of determining whether the reluctant party has breached his promise to arbitrate. For arbitration is a matter of contract and a party cannot be required to submit to arbitration any dispute which he has not agreed so to submit. . . ." The parties, however, may explicitly provide in their agreement that the arbitrator is to decide any dispute concerning the arbitrability of a particular claim. In this respect, Justice Brennan in concurring with the *Warrior* decision states: ". . . the parties may have provided that any dispute as to whether a particular claim is within the arbitration clause is itself for the arbitrator. Again the court . . . must send any dispute to the arbitrator, for the parties have agreed that the construction of the arbitration promise itself is for the arbitrator, and the reluctant party has breached his promise by refusing to submit the dispute to arbitration."

See also: American Manufacturing Co.; Arbitrability; Jurisdiction; Labor arb. (Voluntary); Procedural arbitrability; Stay of arb.; Warrior & Gulf Nav. Co.; Wiley v. Livingston.

Sources: John Wiley & Sons v. Livingston, 376 U.S. 543 (1964); McDermott, *supra* Arbitrability at 18-37.

SUFFICIENT ABILITY CLAUSE

A clause in a union contract which establishes ways and means for determining which of two employees shall be awarded a particular job.

Sufficient ability clauses are based on minimum acceptable qualifications for doing the work, provided the employee in question has seniority. The interpretation of the meaning of ability and seniority, and their interrelation, is a source of many disputes. If the parties cannot resolve them, the ultimate decision may be submitted to the arbitrator.

See also: Seniority; Tests.

Sources: *The Use of Tests, supra* Seniority.

SUI GENERIS

Unique as in a class by itself.

A term which may be applied to collective bargaining agreements in contrast with other types of contracts.

SUMMARY OF LABOR ARBITRATION AWARDS

A digest of labor arbitration awards published by the American Arbitration Association and appearing twelve times a year dated as of the fifteenth of each month.

The *Summary of Labor Arbitration Awards* was first published by the American Arbitration Association in April 1959. An index by arbitrator and subject covers the almost 2100 cases reported through July 1967. Subsequent cases are indexed on a quarterly and annual basis. The full text of each reported case is available at a nominal per page charge. Cases are cited as *108 AAA 18*, the 108 referring to the Report No. and the 18 referring to the case. The summaries from 1959 to 1967 have been published in a single volume. Supplemental volumes will appear annually.

See also: American Labor Arb. Awards (P-H); Labor Arb. Awards (CCH); Labor Arb. Reports (BNA); War Labor Reports (BNA).

SUMMARY PROCEEDING

A swift and simplified procedure for the hearing and resolution of a dispute.

Some contracts establish a permanent summary procedure with rotating panels of four or five arbitrators who may be summoned in turn for immediate hearings. Administrative agencies may often be called upon for speedy disposition of disputes as in theatre or labor disputes, when their rules so provide.

See also: Notice of hearing; Rotating panels.

SUPPLEMENTAL AWARD

An award in which the arbitrator corrects or supplements his original decision.

A supplemental award may be made only if the parties have agreed to give the arbitrators the authority to do so. If the supplemental award is a correction or modification or amendment of the earlier award, the final award should read: "In all other respects the Award dated . . . shall remain in full force and effect."

See also: Modifying the award.

Sources: M. DOMKE, *supra* Adhesion contract at 217, 295.

TAFT-HARTLEY ACT

(Labor Management Relations Act, Pub. L. No. 101, 80th Cong., 1st Sess.; 29 U.S.C.A. §§ 141-197)

An act passed in 1947 over President Harry S. Truman's veto which modified the National Labor Relations Act by restricting union activities.

The Taft-Hartley Law provided special machinery for handling national emergency disputes. It established a new agency to be known as the Federal Mediation and Conciliation Service. Title I of the Taft-Hartley Act became the new or amended National Labor Relations Act. Section 301 of Title III of the Taft-Hartley Act has had particular and specific importance for arbitration since the United States Supreme Court based its landmark decision of *Lincoln Mills* on this section, authorizing the enforcement of the arbitration agreement and of the subsequent award.

See also: Arbitrability; Emergency boards; Enforcement of arb. agreements (Federal statutes); Fact-finding; Federal Mediation and Conciliation Service; Gov't. intervention; Lincoln Mills; National Labor-Management Panel; § 301 disputes.

Sources: A. Cox & D. Bok, *supra* Landrum-Griffin Act at 129-135; C. Gregory, *supra* Landrum-Griffin Act at 341-442.

TATE LETTER

A letter of May 19, 1952, written by Jack B. Tate, Acting Legal Adviser to the State Department, in which the Department announced that it would recognize only public or purely governmental acts of foreign States in granting those States absolute immunity.

By means of this letter, the United States Government announced its adherence to the restrictive theory of sovereign immunity in suits against foreign governments. A number of European governments have long complied with these restrictive principles for certain activities. The Brussels Convention of 1926, for example, declared: "Sea going vessels owned or operated by States . . . are subject in respect of claims relating to the operation of such vessels . . . to the same rules of liability and to the same obligations as those applicable to private vessels, cargoes and equipment." As more arbitration clauses are being inserted in charter parties, and other maritime transactions to which foreign governments or their agencies are parties, more such cases are being determined by the courts. A federal court unequivocally upheld for the first time the restrictive theory of sovereign immunity in the *Victory Transport Case*, a dispute between an American corporation and a branch of the Spanish Ministry of Commerce. In this case, the United States Supreme Court on June 1, 1965, denied the petition for a writ of certiorari, refusing to grant permission to have the case reviewed. The Supreme Court thus supported the decision of the United States Court of Appeals for the Second Circuit of September 9, 1964, which had upheld the district court rule that the defense of sovereign immunity was not available because the transaction was "a commercial operation of the Spanish Government." The court of appeals affirmed the district court's order compelling arbitration in accordance with the agreement of the parties.

Sources: Petrol Shipping Corp. v. Kingdom of Greece, 360 F. 2d 103 (1966) cert den 385 U.S. 931 (1966); Victory Transport Inc., v. Comisaria General, 336 F. 2d 354 (1964) cert den 381 U.S. 934 (1965); Int'l. Convention for the Unification of Certain Rules Relating to the Immunity of State-Owned Vessels, April 10, 1926, 176 L.N.T.S. 199 (1937), as cited in 65 COLUM. L. REV. 1088-1089n (1965).

TAYLOR COMMITTEE REPORT (NEW YORK STATE)

A final report made on March 31, 1966, by Governor Nelson A. Rockefeller's Committee on Public Employee Relations.

Following the New York City transit strike in January 1966, Governor Rockefeller appointed a committee to review labor relations policies for public employees in New York State. George W. Taylor was appointed chairman. The other members were E. Wight Bakke, David L. Cole, John T. Dunlop, and Frederick H. Harbison. The published report of the Committee became the basis of the Taylor Law. The Taylor Law did not include all of the recommendations made by the Committee, summarized on pages 6 through 8 of the Report. These recommendations included repeal of the Condon-Wadlin Act, and the creation of a Public Employment Relations Board. A specific recommendation not included in the subsequent legislation had to do with a "show cause hearing" to be held before the appropriate state or local legislative body prior to final legislative action on the budget. Such a hearing would enable the parties to review and clarify their reasons for rejecting the recommendations of any fact-finding board before definite budget appropriations had been made. Though the Report rejected compulsory arbitration whenever there was an impasse, it did recommend that the parties establish mutually acceptable procedures to be followed in disputes. Among these was an advance commitment to submit a dispute voluntarily to arbitration on an *ad hoc* basis.

See also: Pub. Employment Relations Board; Taylor Law.

Sources: N.Y. (STATE) GOVERNOR'S COMM. ON PUB. EMPLOYEE RELATIONS, FINAL REPORT, March 31, 1966, (1966).

TAYLOR LAW (NEW YORK STATE)
(Public Employees' Fair Employment Act) (Ch. 392, L. 1967 and Article14, New York Civil Service Law, as amended by Ch. 24, L. 1969)

A law granting New York State public employees the right to join or refrain from joining labor organizations, and requiring state and local governments to negotiate with these employee organizations.

The Taylor Law was approved on April 21, 1967, and took effect September 1, 1967. Public employees are not granted the right to strike, but the act does establish a Public Employment Relations Board to assist in resolving disputes. The dispute settlement procedures include mediation, fact-finding, and a final resort to the legislative body of the government concerned. If either party rejects the report of the fact-finding board, the chief executive officer of the government involved shall submit the findings and recommendations of the fact-finding board with his own recommendations for settlement to the legislative body of the local government. The union also may submit its recommendations. A Taylor Law amendment was approved March 10, 1969, increasing the penalties on striking employees and adding a new provision describing unfair labor practices to be enforced by the Public Employment Relations Board.

See also: Condon-Wadlin Act; Fact-finding; Impasse; Mediation; N.Y. State Public Employment Relations Board; Public employee; Sanctions.

Sources: N.Y. State Public Employees' Fair Employment Act as amended by ch. 24, L. 1969; N.Y. (STATE) PERB, RULES OF PROCEDURE, A GUIDE TO THE TAYLOR LAW (1967); McHugh, *supra* Sanctions at 52-95.

TEN-DAY NOTICE

See: Notice of intention to arbitrate.

TENNESSEE VALLEY AUTHORITY EMPLOYEE-MANAGEMENT RELATIONS

Employee-management relations vested in the Tennessee Valley Authority which is a corporation created by an act of Congress on May 18, 1933, to conduct a unified program of the conservation and development of the natural resources in the Tennessee Valley region.

All functions of the Tennessee Valley Authority are contained in its three-member Board of Directors appointed by the President with the consent of the Senate. Both craft and clerical employees in the TVA have succeeded in securing favorable terms of employment in their negotiations with TVA management. If an impasse occurs in negotiations on contract terms, agreements provide for mediation which either side may request. If mediation fails, there is a provision for voluntary arbitration with certain wage rate restrictions, though such arbitration of contract terms may be invoked only if both parties consent to its use. As a final step in a three level grievance procedure, an appeal may be made by either party to an impartial third person whose decision is final and binding on both parties. An individual employee cannot request arbitration. The TVA experience in employee-management relations was unique in the federal service of the 1930's. The TVA has continued to favor collective bargaining.

See also: Labor arb. (Voluntary); Mediation; Missile Sites Labor Comm'n.; Pub. employee.

Sources: U.S. OFFICE OF THE FEDERAL REGISTER, *supra* Bureau of Labor Statistics; Thompson, *Collective Bargaining in the Pub. Service—the*

TVA Experience, 17 LAB. L. J. 89-98 (1966); Van Mol, *The TVA Experience,* in COLLECTIVE BARGAINING IN THE PUB. SERVICE 85 (K. Warner ed. 1967); Wagner, *TVA Looks at Three Decades of Collective Bargaining,* 22 IND. & LAB. REL. REV. 20-30 (1968).

TENTATIVE AWARD

A provisional award presented by the arbitrator to the parties for their consideration.

A tentative award is an effective means of testing principles and arguments not fully covered by the parties in the hearing. It also might impel the parties to explore certain implications of an award, to which they might be more sensitive than the arbitrator.

See also: Advisory opinion; Interim award.

Sources: M. BERNSTEIN, *supra* Appeal at 148; Garrett, *Some Potential Uses of the Opinion,* in 17 PROC. OF THE NAT'L. ACADEMY OF ARBITRATORS 114 (1964); Jones, *Arb. and the Dilemma of Possible Error,* 11 LAB. L. J. 1023 (1960).

TERRITORIAL DISPUTE

A controversy between States over the sovereignty of territory which each claims as its own.

See also: Boundary disputes.

TESTIMONY OF ARBITRATOR

An arbitrator cannot be compelled to give any testimony that would reveal his reasons for making an award.

Courts have uniformly held that an arbitrator may not be compelled to produce evidence that would impeach his award. All modern arbitration statutes recognize the need for specific grounds upon which an award may be set aside, such as the possible partiality or other misconduct of the arbitrators during the hearing. The courts have refused to compel an arbitrator to submit an affidavit explaining his award. "So long as no attempt is made to impeach an award by showing his own fraud or misconduct, an arbitrator's testimony is generally admissible to prove matters of fact in connection with the arbitration, in any case where other parol evidence can be received; and this is true, whether the purpose of the testimony is to sustain the award, or to show that it is a mere nullity. . . . Notwithstanding the rule against impeachment, it is usually held that testimony of arbitrators is admissible to show a mistake on their part."*

See also: Arbitrator; Enterprise Wheel & Car Corp.; Liability of arbitrator; Parol evidence; Vacating an award.

Sources: *6 C. J. S. ARBITRATION AND AWARD, § 131 as cited in M. BERNSTEIN, *supra* Appeal at 180; M. DOMKE, *supra* Adhesion contract at 227-230; 4 LAWYERS' LETTERS (1960), *supra* Adjournment of hearings.

TESTS

Written or oral means by which management measures the aptitude and ability of an employee to perform a particular job.

Tests are often used when hiring an employee, as well as in evaluating his qualifications for promotion. Arbitrators have generally held that tests used in determining ability for promotion must be related to the requirements of the job, and be reasonable and administered in good faith and without discrimination, and properly evaluated to ensure fairness.

See also: Seniority; Sufficient ability clause.

Sources: F. ELKOURI & E. ELKOURI, *supra* American Arbitration Association; *The Use of Tests*, *supra* Seniority.

TEXTILE ARBITRATION

See: General Arbitration Council of the Textile Industry; Int'l. Wool Textile Organisation; Silk Association of America.

THERAPY OF ARBITRATION

See: Carey v. Westinghouse.

THIRD ARBITRATOR

The neutral member of the arbitration board.

The third arbitrator as the neutral member is most frequent in tripartite boards where one of the arbitrators is elected by each of the parties and the third is chosen according to the agreement or the rules of the administrative agency. The parties may appoint the third arbitrator, or the two arbitrators selected by each of the parties may appoint him, or the administrative agency may designate the third arbitrator. He may also be appointed by a court, or any other outside official as the agreement may provide, such as the President of the International Court of Justice in international cases. In tripartite boards, a decision is usually reached by majority vote, unless the parties have provided that the third or neutral member of the board shall make the decision himself. The third arbitrator is variously known as the umpire, the referee, or the presiding or neutral arbitrator. In a three-man, impartial panel used in some commercial cases, the third arbitrator refers to no more than the third of three arbitrators.

See also: Arbitrator; Neutral arbitrator; Presiding arbitrator; Pub. member; Tripartite board; Umpire.

Sources: M. DOMKE, *supra* Adhesion contract at 197-201; 1 U.N. ECE, *supra* Access to the arbitral tribunal at 36-38.

TIME LIMITS

Specific limitations as to the time within which certain procedures must be performed in an arbitration.

Time limits are established by the parties in their contract, or by an administrative agency in its rules, or by a statute or treaty. Many contracts may set a time limit for submitting a demand for arbitration. This limit is enforced by the courts no matter how short the time limitation may be, although some statutes permit the arbitrator to determine whether a timely initiation of arbitration was made. Courts have generally ruled that a party loses all remedies and cannot later institute a court action after the time has expired for initiating an arbitration, unless there is a substantial reason for failure to initiate within the time limits. A party may forfeit by delay its right to appoint an arbitrator. The court may then make the appointment. Parties to an arbitration often fix the time within which an award must be rendered. An administrative agency may establish such a time limit in its rules, though there are usually no statutory limitations on the making of an award. A common feature of arbitration agreements in contemporary international loan contracts is that there are no time limits within which the award must be made.

See also: Appointment of arbitrators; Laches; Notice of intention to arbitrate; Procedural arbitrability; Reopening of hearings; Statute of limitations; Vacating an award.

Sources: N.Y. CPLR § 7502(b) & § 7503(c); G. DELAUME, *supra* Concession contract at 196; M. DOMKE, *supra* Adhesion contract at 146-148; 32 LAWYERS' LETTERS (1967), *supra* Adjournment of hearings at 1-3.

TORT

Any wrongful act, not involving a breach of contract, for which civil action can be taken.

Tort may be a direct invasion of some legal right, or the infraction of some public duty, or the violation of some private obligation which may damage the interests of an individual.

See also: Trail Smelter Arb.

Sources: BLACK'S LAW DICTIONARY (3d ed. 1933).

TRADE ASSOCIATION

A private nonprofit organization of businessmen or manufacturers in a particular trade or industry for the protection and advancement of their common interests.

Trade associations differ from chambers of commerce in this: membership is by industry rather than by locality. Many trade associations maintain their own arbitration facilities for the use of their members, or in some cases, for the general public. They may also maintain their own rules and panels of arbitrators. Procedures vary in formality and complexity. Some associations have only a few arbitrators who sit on all cases, or who may be assigned by the association to sit in rotation. In some associations, the arbitrators are appointed by an association official rather than by the parties, as in the London Shellac Trade Association where the Secretary of the Association appoints the arbitrators, with the parties allowed the right of challenge. Other associations provide that a council or arbitration committee should itself act as arbitrator. The Liverpool Provision Trade Association in its Rules, § IX (70)(a) has the following provision: "An Arbitration Committee shall consist of not less than three members of the Association appointed by the President, Vice-President and/or Secretaries. The Appeal Committee shall consist of the Board of Directors of the Association, seven of whom shall form a quorum."

See also: Adm. agency; Appointment of arbitrators; Institutional arb.; Inter-association com'l. arb. agreements; U.N. Handbook of Nat'l. and Int'l. Institutions Active in the Field of Int'l. Com'l. Arb.

Sources: U.N. ECE, supra Access to the arbitral tribunal; LIVERPOOL PROVISION TRADE ASSOCIATION, supra Appointment of arbitrators at 34; WEBSTER'S INTERNATIONAL DICTIONARY (3d ed. 1966); Subramanian, Arbitral Tribunals and Their Constitution, 3 INDIAN COUNCIL ARB. Q. 3-7 (1968).

TRAIL SMELTER ARBITRATION (April 16, 1938 and March 11, 1941)

An arbitration between the United States and Canada by special agreement under the Convention of Ottawa, April 15, 1935.

The Trail Smelter Arbitration arose out of a complaint by the Government of the United States that sulphur dioxide fumes from a smelter at Trail, British Columbia, were poisoning fisheries, lumber and fruit-growing trees, and crops and stock in the State of Washington. Article IV of the Convention of Ottawa instructed the Tribunal as follows: "The Tribunal shall apply the law and practice followed in dealing with cognate questions in the United States of America as well as international law and practice, and shall give consideration to the desire of the high contracting parties to reach a solution just to all parties concerned." Relevant decisions of the Supreme Court of the United States were considered, and scientific advisers were consulted. The Arbitrators then defined controls to be applied in operating the smelter, ruling out any which would unnecessarily hamper the operation and would not therefore constitute a "solution just to all parties concerned." The Trail Smelter Arbitration is generally considered a leading decision on the international law of tort, as well as one which clearly shows the role of equity in international arbitral judgments.

See also: Applicable law. Int'l. pub. arb.; Espousal; Equity; Int'l. claims; Lake Ontario Claims Tribunal; Tort.

Sources: Trail Smelter Case, 3 U.N.R.I.A.A. 1907 (1938 & 1941); C. Jenks, *supra* Calvo Clause at 408-410; Goldie, *Liability for Damage and the Progressive Development of Int'l. Law*, 14 Int'l. & Comp. L. Q. 1226 (1965).

TRANSCRIPT OF HEARING

A verbatim record of an arbitration hearing which is sometimes taped, but is more often in the form of a stenographic report.

Although the use of a reporter in arbitration is the exception rather than the rule, stenographic records can be very helpful in lengthy or complicated cases. A reporter may be used at the request of either party. If only one party asks for a transcript, that party is obliged to pay for it. Otherwise costs are shared by both parties.

See also: Hearing; Procedure.

Sources: F. Elkouri & E. Elkouri, *supra* American Arb. Association at 152-154.

TRANSPORTATION ACT OF 1920
(Esch-Cummins Act) [41 Stat. 456, 469 (1920)]

A federal act returning the railroads to private operation after World War I, and containing in its Title III provisions for settling disputes by the means of a Railroad Labor Board and voluntary Boards of Adjustment.

These voluntary Adjustment Boards could be created on local, regional, or national levels, and could intervene in cases involving grievances, rules, or working conditions. A Board could be invoked on its own motion, or at the Railroad Labor Board's request, or on application from one of the parties, or on the petition of 100 concerned workers. Such Boards could not act in wage disputes. If the Adjustment Board failed to resolve the dispute, it could then be referred to the Railroad Labor Board, which was a nine-member, tripartite board with three members each from employers, employees, and the public. This Board had exclusive jurisdiction over wage disputes, and disputes not settled by Adjustment Boards. Board decisions required the concurrence of at least five members, and in wage cases, one of these members was to be a public representative. The Board's effectiveness was hampered by an interpretation of the United States Supreme Court which held that the Board was intended to act as an arbitral agency whose decisions were enforceable only by public opinion. Both the carriers and the unions were dissatisfied with the Railroad Labor Board, and formed a joint committee in 1925 to assist in passing what was to become the Railway Labor Act of 1926.

See also: Adamson Act; Arb. Act of 1888; Erdman Act; Newlands Act; Railway Labor Act.

Sources: Esch-Cummins Act, in U.S. GPO, COMPILATION OF LAWS RELATING TO MEDIATION, CONCILIATION, AND ARB. 15-21 (1967); Lecht, *The Transportation Act of 1920*, in LEGISLATIVE REFERENCE SERVICE OF THE LIBRARY OF CONGRESS FOR THE SENATE COMM. ON LABOR & PUB. WELFARE, FEDERAL LEGISLATION TO END STRIKES 91-122 (1967); Wisehart, *supra* Newlands Act at 1697-1722.

TREATIES OF FRIENDSHIP, COMMERCE AND NAVIGATION

See: United States Treaties of Friendship, Commerce and Navigation.

TREATY

A pact or written agreement between sovereign States which establishes a legal relation between the cosigners.

Though a treaty or convention may be defined as a written instrument, States may incur legal obligations other than through such written agreements. Treaties usually refer to agreements between two nations and are bilateral in nature. Conventions usually refer to international agreements between more than two signatory nations. Customary usage allows the term multilateral treaty to be used instead of convention. International organizations, such as the United Nations or the International Bank for Reconstruction and Development, may of themselves have the authority to conclude international agreements with States.

See also: Collective bargaining; Compromis; Convention; Entry into force; Int'l. law.

Sources: U.N. ILC Draft Laws of Treaties, art. 2(1)(a).

TREATY OF GUADALUPE HIDALGO (February 2, 1848) (Treaty of Peace, Friendship, Limits, and Settlement)

A treaty between Mexico and the United States at the close of the Mexican War (1846-1848) which contained a permanent arbitration clause.

The Treaty of Guadalupe Hidalgo provides that in the event that future differences can not be settled by the two governments, "a resort shall not, on this account, be had to reprisals, aggression, or hostility of any kind, by the one republic against the other, until the government of that which deems itself aggrieved shall have maturely considered, in the spirit of peace and good neighborship, whether it would not be better that such difference should be settled by the arbitration of commissioners appointed on each side, or by that of a friendly nation. And should such course be proposed by either party, it shall be acceded to by the other, unless deemed by it altogether incompatible with the nature of the difference, or the circumstances of the case."

Sources: 9 THE STATUTES AT LARGE AND TREATIES OF THE UNITED STATES OF AMERICA 938-939, as cited in Fraser, supra Crucé, Eméric at 200; U.S. DEPT. OF STATE, TREATIES IN FORCE 145 (1968).

TREATY OF INTERNATIONAL PROCEDURAL LAW

See: Montevideo Treaty (March 19, 1940).

TRIBUNAL

A tribunal in arbitration is composed of one or more arbitrators with the authority to hear and decide disputes.

Tribunal may also be used as the site of a court or arbitration. It is also often referred to as an arbitration court.

See also: Mixed arbitral tribunal.

TRILATERAL ARBITRATION

See: Trilateral disputes.

TRILATERAL DISPUTES

Work assignment disputes in which three parties are involved, an employer and two unions.

Under the ordinary collective bargaining contract, when such a dispute is brought to arbitration, only two of these parties can be represented, the grieving union and the employer. The United States Supreme Court decision in Carey v. Westinghouse held that one union in a jurisdictional dispute can secure arbitration under its agreement with the employer, although the other union in the dispute will not be bound by such arbitration. In light of this decision, it has been suggested that such disputes might be settled with more certainty if an arbitrator would have the power to induce or compel the participation of the second union.

See also: Carey v. Westinghouse; Joinder; Jurisdictional disputes; Work assignment disputes.

Sources: Bernstein, supra Carey v. Westinghouse at 784; Jones, supra Indifferent gentlemen at 771-2.

TRILOGY (1960)

Three landmark decisions delivered simultaneously by the United States Supreme Court, dealing with the federal law of labor arbitration.

The Supreme Court Steelworkers Trilogy decisions ruled on arbitrability and on the enforcement of awards. On the issue of arbitrability it was held that the courts are limited to determining whether there is a collective bargaining agreement in existence, whether there is an arbitration clause, and whether there is an allegation that a provision of the agreement has been violated. If the arbitration clause is broad enough to include the alleged dispute, then arbitration must be ordered. On enforcement of awards the Court ruled, if the arbitrator stays within the submission and makes his award within his authority as established by the contract, then the award must be enforced. In either arbitrability or enforcement cases, the courts are not to examine the merits of the cases. They are not to substitute their judgment for that of the arbitrator, nor shall they refuse to require arbitration because they believe a claim is frivolous or baseless.

See also: American Manufacturing Co.; Arbitrability; Enforcement of award (Labor); Enterprise Wheel and Car Corp.; Judicial review in arb.; Labor arb. (Voluntary); Lincoln Mills; Merits of a case; Motion to compel arb.; Procedural arbitrability; Substantive arbitrability; Warrior and Gulf Nav. Co.

Sources: Davey, *supra* American Manufacturing Co. at 138-145; Meltzer, *supra* Arbitrability at 464-487; Smith & Jones, *supra* Arbitrability at 831-912.

TRILOGY (1962)

See: Second Trilogy (1962).

TRIPARTITE BOARD

An arbitration board usually composed of one or more members selected by each party, and a neutral member who is selected by both parties to act as chairman.

Tripartite boards may consist of more than one representative from each of the parties as well as from the public. In such cases, the agreement provides for the election of one of the neutral members as chairman. Tripartite boards may be permanent or temporary. The party-appointed members may act as advocates for their respective sides. The agreement that establishes the composition of the board may provide that a majority award shall be final and binding, or it may grant the neutral arbitrator the responsibility of making the final decision himself. Many parties feel that in a tripartite procedure, the neutral arbitrator is thus provided with background material necessary for making his decision, the party arbitrators acting somewhat in the role of advisors. The neutral arbitrator may meet with the party-appointed arbitrators in executive session to discuss ramifications of his decision before the award takes final form. Tripartite boards are used in commercial, international, and labor arbitration. Party-appointed arbitrators, usually referred to as national judges or national commissioners, participated in a majority of the international public arbitrations held during the last century and a half.

See also: Alabama Arb.; Impartial chairman; Impartial chairman (Ad hoc); Labor court; Missile Sites Labor Comm'n.; Mixed arbitral tribunal; Mixed claims comm'n.; Nat'l. Defense Mediation Board; Nat'l. Railroad Adjustment Board; Nat'l. Wage Stabilization Board; Neutral arbitrator; Number of arbitrators; Office of Collective Bargaining; Partisan arbitrator; Railroad Arbitration Act; Tripartite Panel to Improve Municipal Collective Bargaining in N.Y.C.; Unanimity of award.

Sources: Davey, *The Uses and Misuses of Tripartite Boards in Grievance Arb.*, in 21 PROC. OF THE NAT'L. ACADEMY OF ARBITRATORS 152-197 (1968); Herzog & Stone, *Voluntary Labour Arb. in the U.S.*, 82 INT'L. LAB. REV. 316 (1960); *The Use of Tripartite Boards in Labor, Com'l., and Int'l. Arb.*, 68 HARV. L. REV. 293 (1954).

TRIPARTITE PANEL TO IMPROVE MUNICIPAL COLLECTIVE BARGAINING PROCEDURES IN NEW YORK CITY

A fifteen member board consisting of four public members, two representatives of the city and nine from city employee organizations which recommended the establishment of an Office of Collective Bargaining.

Saul Wallen, Chairman, Philip A. Carey, Vern Countryman, and Peter Seitz were the public members. A Memorandum of Agreement was developed with the assistance of the Labor Management Institute of the American Arbitration Association. This memorandum of March 31, 1966, became the basis with some alterations for the New York City Collective Bargaining Law. The Agreement recommended the establishment of the Office of Collective Bargaining. Though it banned any strike for the life of the contract, it left to the New York State Legislature the ultimate decision on the right of public employees to strike.

See also: Office of Collective Bargaining; Public member; Tripartite board.

Sources: N.Y. (City) Agreement, *supra* Office of Collective Bargaining.

UAW PUBLIC REVIEW BOARD

See: Public Review Board (UAW).

UMPIRE

The neutral arbitrator who makes the final decision when the arbitrators appointed by the parties disagree on the merits of the dispute.

The use of an umpire in commercial cases is more common to European trade association arbitration. In Scots law, an umpire is sometimes referred to as an overman, or an arbitrator to settle disputes between arbitrators. As used in labor arbitration in this country, the umpire is a permanent arbitrator appointed jointly by labor and management, who is given limited jurisdiction under the terms of the contract, and who is solely responsible for his decision. The umpire is appointed by the parties to serve for a specified time and at a specified fee.

See also: Arbitrator; Ford-UAW Impartial Umpire System; General Motors-UAW Impartial Umpire System; Institutional arb.; Neutral arbitrator; Permanent arbitrator; Third arbitrator; Umpire system.

Sources: U.N. ECE, *supra* Access to the arbitral tribunal; M. DOMKE, *supra* Appeal boards of adm. agencies; WEBSTER'S INT'L. DICTIONARY (3d ed. 1966).

UMPIRE SYSTEM

A method of dispute settlement by means of a neutral arbitrator who is chosen by the parties concerned and whose authority is restricted to the interpretation and application of the existing collective bargaining agreement between the parties, and who arrives at his decision on the basis of evidence presented at a formal hearing.

The umpire serves for a specified length of time according to the will of the parties. His jurisdiction is limited by a detailed and specific collective bargaining agreement. The Umpire System was one of two distinct types of permanent arbitration to be developed in the United States, and was well-established by 1940. It originated in the anthracite coal industry with the award made in 1903 by the Anthracite Coal Strike Commission. This award provided for a Board of Conciliation with equal representation of management and labor, to which unresolved grievances were to be referred. Grievances not settled were to be referred to a neutral outsider to be known as the umpire. Unlike present practice, the umpire did not then meet with the board. Transcripts of hearings and other relevant documents were mailed to him. The umpire arrived at his decision, and then mailed it to the parties. His jurisdiction was limited to the interpretation and application of an existing agreement.

See also: Ad hoc arbitrator; Anthracite Board of Conciliation; Appeal systems; Appointment of arbitrators; Ford-UAW Impartial Umpire System; General Motors-UAW Impartial Umpire System; Grievance arb. (Rights arb.); Grievance procedure—Level of steps; Impartial chairman system; Labor arb. (Voluntary); Umpire.

Sources: ANTHRACITE BOARD OF CONCILIATION, AWARD OF THE ANTHRACITE COAL STRIKE COMMISSION 7-8 (July 1, 1953); Killingsworth & Wallen, *supra* Board of arb. at 59-62.

UNANIMITY OF AWARD

The unanimous decision of all the arbitrators in making an award.

The determination that the decision should be unanimous depends on the agreement between the parties. Most statutes and contracts permit a majority award. If there is no governing statute, and the parties have no express agreement, the common law rule requiring unanimity remains in effect. The impartial or third arbitrator of a tripartite board in labor arbitration frequently disregards the votes of the other arbitrators, and makes the final decision himself, if the agreement so permits.

See also: Award; Tripartite board.

Sources: 5 AM. JUR., *supra* Death of the arbitrator at 616; M. DOMKE, *supra* Adhesion contract at 282.

UNCITRAL

See: United Nations Commission on International Trade Law.

UNCONFIRMED AWARD

An award which has not as yet been made valid as a judgment in a court action so that it can be legally enforced.

When both parties consent to the award, and the losing party voluntarily complies with its terms, the award is rarely confirmed by the winning party. Voluntary compliance is the rule in nearly 90 per cent of arbitration cases. If the prevailing party feels that the losing party has no assets which can be attached, he may decide not to have the award confirmed. In some jurisdictions an unconfirmed award may be presented in attachment or other court cases as evidence of a debt which is still due. It may also have other legal significance, such as prohibiting a court suit of the same dispute.

See also: Award.

Sources: M. DOMKE, *supra* Appeal boards of adm. agencies at 94-96; M. DOMKE, *supra* Adhesion contract at 320-322.

UNFAIR LABOR PRACTICE

An act on the part of a union or an employer which interferes with the basic right of employees as set forth under § 7 of the National Labor Relations Act to join or refrain from joining labor unions and engaging in collective bargaining.

Sections 8(a)(b)(e) of this act make such conduct unlawful and empower the National Labor Relations Board to prevent or remedy it. State statutes may also declare certain acts as "unfair labor practices." Arbitrators have no jurisdiction over unfair labor practices except in those cases where such practices also violate collective bargaining agreements.

See also: Concurrent jurisdiction; Nat'l. Labor Relations Board; Preemption; Spielberg doctrine; Taylor Law.

Sources: A. COX & D. BOK, *supra* Landrum-Griffin Act at 162-165; Cushman, *Arb. and the Duty to Bargain*, 1967 WIS. L. REV. 615.

UNIDROIT

See: International Institute for the Unification of Private Law.

UNIFORM ARBITRATION ACT (UNITED STATES)

A uniform arbitration act covering voluntary agreements to arbitrate future, as well as existing disputes, drafted by a committee appointed by the National Conference of Commissioners on Uniform State Laws, and approved at Philadelphia, Pennsylvania, August 15-20, 1955 and amended at Dallas, Texas, August 24, 1956, and recommended for enactment in all states.

The Uniform Arbitration Act was also approved by the House of Delegates of the American Bar Association at its annual meeting on August 26, 1955, and the amendment was approved August 30, 1956. This act is not to be confused with a Uniform Arbitration Act which the Conference of Commissioners on Uniform Laws approved on August 25-31, 1925, and which was also approved by the American Bar Association in September 1925, and subsequently was adopted by a few states. The act of 1925 proved unsatisfactory and was withdrawn by the Conference. The various grounds which are specified in the Uniform Arbitration Act for confirming, vacating, or modifying an award are for the most part traditional ones embodied in similar modern arbitration statutes. A new provision, also included in some state statutes, permits arbitrators to correct minor errors in their award, or otherwise to clarify the award when necessary. Since 1956, at least fourteen states have passed statutes based more or less on the Uniform Arbitration Act.

See also: Adjournment of hearings; European Convention Providing a Uniform Law on Arb.; Draft Uniform Law on Inter-American Com'l. Arb.

Sources: Uniform Arb. Act; Nat'l. Conf. of Commissioners on Uniform State Laws, Proc. of the Comm. of the Whole, Uniform Arbitration Act, August 9-14, 1954; *Commissioners on Uniform State Laws*, in A.B.A. PROC. OF THE HOUSE OF DELEGATES 145-146 (1956); Pirsig, *The New Uniform Arb. Act*, 11 BUS. LAW. 44-51 (1956); *Uniform State Laws*, in A.B.A. PROC. OF THE HOUSE OF DELEGATES 172 (1955).

UNIFORM LAWS

See: Draft Uniform Law on Inter-American Commercial Arb.; European Convention Providing a Uniform Law on Arb. (Council of Europe); Int'l. Institute for the Unification of Private Law; UNCITRAL Uniform Arbitration Act (U.S.).

UNINSURED MOTORIST ARBITRATION

The arbitration of unresolved bodily injury claims resulting from automobile accidents between insured and uninsured motorists, provisions for which are contained in most uninsured motorist endorsements of insurance policies.

Arbitration is a method widely used to settle disputes between policy holders and their insurance carriers under this "Family Protection Endorsement" section of automobile liability policies. The standard form dealing with uninsured motorist insurance provides that, in the event of a disagreement, two things can be resolved by arbitration, one, whether the insured is legally entitled to recover damages from the owner or operator of an uninsured automobile, and two, the amount of damages due. The American Arbitration Association has been named an administrator of this type of arbitration under its Accident Claims Tribunal Rules in agreements with insurance companies since 1956.

See also: American Arb. Association; Selection of arbitrators (AAA).

Sources: AAA, Uninsured Motorists Arb. in the U.S., a Bibliography, April 1, 1969; Aksen, *Arb. of Automobile Accident Cases,* 1 CONN. L. REV. 70-92 (1968); Aksen, *Arb. of Uninsured Motorist Endorsement Claims,* 24 OHIO STATE L. J. 589-608 (1963); 9 LAWYERS' LETTERS (1962), *supra* Adjournment of hearings; 11 id. (1962); 33 *id.* (1968); 36 *id.* (1968).

UNITED AUTO WORKERS. PUBLIC REVIEW BOARD

See: Public Review Board.

UNITED NATIONS
(United Nations Plaza, New York, New York)

An organization of States which have accepted the obligations contained in the United Nations Charter drawn up and signed at the San Francisco Conference in 1945.

The United Nations Charter was drawn up by the representatives of 50 countries at the Conference on International Organization, San Francisco, April 25 to June 28, 1945. The Charter was signed on June 26, 1945. The United Nations has been particularly influential in the promotion of commercial arbitration through its Convention on the Recognition and Enforcement of Foreign Arbitral Awards, the European Convention on Commercial Arbitration, and the various regional arbitration systems developed in Europe and the Far East, and conferences and commissions created to further the use of arbitration in international trade disputes throughout the world. The International Law Commission formulated the Model Rules on Arbitration to be used in disputes in international public arbitration.

See also: Convention on the Recognition and Enforcement of Foreign Arbitral Awards; European Convention on Int'l. Com'l. Arb.; Int'l. Law Commission; Model Rules on Arbitral Procedure; U.N. Comm'n. on Int'l. Trade Law; U.N. Conf. on Int'l. Com'l. Arb.; U.N. ECAFE; U.N. ECE; U.N. Handbook of Nat'l. and Int'l. Institutions Active in the

Field of Int'l. Com'l. Arb.; U.N. Resolution of the U.N. Conference on Int'l. Com'l. Arb.

Sources: U.N. Comm'n. on Int'l. Trade Law, Int'l. Com'l. Arb., Report of the Secretary-General, U.N. Doc. A/CN.9/21 (1969); U.N., Directory (March 1969).

UNITED NATIONS COMMISSION ON INTERNATIONAL TRADE LAW (UNCITRAL)

A commission established by Resolution 2205(XXI) of the General Assembly on December 17, 1966, to harmonize all laws concerned with international trade.

The Resolution provided that the Commission on International Trade Law would consist of 29 member States. Representatives of these countries were to consider the interests of all peoples, and particularly those of the evolving countries, in the expansion of international trade. The General Assembly elected the member States on October 30, 1967, with due consideration to the adequate representation of the principal economic and legal systems of the world. Commercial arbitration was selected to be among those subjects which are to be studied. The Commission will undertake, with the assistance of experts, to prepare model and uniform laws and to promote wider acceptance of international trade terms and practices, including international commercial arbitration. The work is expected to extend over several years, coordinating all organizations concerned with the unification of the law of international trade. Each State appointed a representative from among its own experts in international trade. The Commission convened at its first meeting on January 29 through February 26, 1968.

See also: Int'l. com'l. arb.

Sources: Report of the Secretary-General, U.N. Doc. A/6396 at 58 and U.N. Doc. A/6396/corr. 2 at 2 (1966); U.N. Comm'n. on Int'l. Trade Law, Report on the Work of its First Session, Jan. 29-Feb. 26, 1968 23 U.N. GAOR Supp. 16, U.N. Doc. A/7216 (1968); Domke, *Progress in International Commercial Arbitration*, 1 NYU J. INT'L. L. & POLITICS 38-39 (1968).

UNITED NATIONS CONFERENCE ON INTERNATIONAL COMMERCIAL ARBITRATION (1958)

A conference held in New York City for the purpose of drafting a convention on the enforcement of foreign arbitral awards.

The United Nations Conference on International Commercial Arbitration was the result of a suggestion made in 1954 by the International Chamber of Commerce to the United Nations Economic and Social Council. On April 6, 1954, the Council established an *ad hoc* committee which prepared and submitted a draft convention. The Council decided to call a conference for the purpose of preparing a convention on the recognition and enforcement of foreign arbitral awards, and to consider other possible measures for increasing the effectiveness of international commercial arbitration. Forty-five nations were represented at the Conference. International non-governmental organizations were also represented.

See also: Convention on the Recognition and Enforcement of Foreign Arbitral Awards; Enforcement of foreign arbitral awards; Foreign arbitral awards; Int'l. non-governmental organization; U.N. Resolution of the U.N. Conf. on Int'l. Com'l. Arb.

Sources: Domke, *supra* Convention on the Recognition and Enforcement of Foreign Arbitral Awards.

UNITED NATIONS CONVENTION ON THE RECOGNITION AND ENFORCEMENT OF FOREIGN ARBITRAL AWARDS

See: Convention on the Recognition and Enforcement of Foreign Arbitral Awards.

UNITED NATIONS ECONOMIC COMMISSION FOR ASIA AND THE FAR EAST (ECAFE)
(Sala Santitham, Rajadamnern Avenue, Bangkok, Thailand)

A regional organization of the United Nations which promotes economic development and planning in Asian countries, and which has also been instrumental in furthering the use and development of arbitration.

The United Nations Economic Commission for Asia and the Far East is one of four regional commissions which report to the Economic and Social Council of the United Nations. ECAFE has established a Centre for Commercial Arbitration in Bangkok. The first issue of its *News Bulletin* was published by the ECAFE Centre in November 1964, and was largely devoted to articles and notes on arbitration. The Commission convened a Conference on Commercial Arbitration in Bangkok on January 5 to 8, 1966. Recommendations made at this Conference were approved by the Committee on Trade which met in Bangkok from January 24 to February 2, 1966. Preparations for the conference were made by a Working Party of Experts on Commercial Arbitration which had met in Bangkok on January 11 to 17, 1962. ECAFE Rules on Commercial Arbitration were prepared by the ECAFE Centre for Commercial Arbitration, and were printed in 1966.

See also: Applicable procedural law; Applicable substantive law; Int'l. com'l. arb.; U.N. ECE. Rules of Arb.; U.N. Resolution of the U.N. Conf. on Int'l. Com'l. Arb.

Sources: U.N. ECAFE RULES FOR INT'L. COM'L. ARB. (1966); U.N. ECAFE, Improvement of Existing Arb. Facilities and Techniques, TRADE/ARB. 7, 11 (1962); Domke, *supra* Applicable substantive law.

UNITED NATIONS ECONOMIC COMMISSION FOR EUROPE (ECE)
(Palais des Nations, 1211 Geneva 22, Switzerland)

A regional organization of the United Nations established to study the economic problems of Europe, and to further the use of arbitration.

The United Nations Economic Commission for Europe is one of the four regional commissions which report to the Economic and Social Council of the United Nations. ECE was instrumental in drafting the 1961 European Convention on International Commercial Arbitration. By October 1967, this convention had been ratified by 14 European countries. In addition to the European Convention, ECE has drafted a set of optional arbitration rules.

See also: Enforcement of arb. agreements (Int'l. com'l. arb.); European Convention on Int'l. Com'l. Arb.; U.N. ECE Rules of Arb.; U.N. Resolution of the U.N. Conf. on Int'l. Com'l. Arb.

Sources: *Development of Com'l. Arb. Facilities in the ECE Region*, TRADE/ CA/News 4 ECAFE Centre for Com'l. Arb. News Bull. 37-38 (1966); U.N. ECE, Arb. Rules, U.N. Doc. TRADE/Working Paper No. 23 (1965); Pointet, *The Geneva Convention on Int'l. Com'l. Arb.*, in 3 Int'l. Com'l. Arb. 263-321 (P. Sanders ed. 1965).

UNITED NATIONS ECONOMIC COMMISSION FOR EUROPE. RULES OF ARBITRATION

Modern arbitration rules developed through the United Nations Economic Commission for Europe for use in East-West European trade.

The drafting of these rules on arbitration, which was the result of some nine years work, coincided with the drafting of the European Convention on International Commercial Arbitration. The rules were completed in 1963. They are not compulsory in any way, but are simply a recommended form of procedure to be used in single cases only, and come into force in each instance as they are adopted by the parties. The rules are principally concerned with procedural matters based on modern arbitration practice, and may be modified at the discretion of the parties. These arbitration rules focus particularly on two problems which are the causes of frequent delays. The first is the selection of arbitrators, and the second, the designation of a place where the arbitration hearings may be held. Article 14 of the Rules of Arbitration states that the parties may select the place, and if they fail to do so, the selection is left to the arbitrators. When procedures are delayed by failure to appoint an arbitrator, the rules provide recourse to an "Appointing Authority." If the parties fail to agree in their contract on such an authority, but have agreed on the place of arbitration, then the Appointing Authority is the Chamber of Commerce of that particular place. If the parties have not agreed on the place, the initiating party may select an Appointing Authority from the Chamber of Commerce where the respondent resides, or from the Special Committee set up under the European Convention, or by the Court of Arbitration of the International Chamber of Commerce.

See also: Applicable procedural law; Appointment of arbitrators; Consent of the parties; European Convention on Int'l. Com'l. Arb.; Evasion of arb.; Locale; Party autonomy; Procedure; U.N. ECAFE; U.N. ECE.

Sources: U.N. ECE, *supra* United Nations Economic Commission for Europe; Benjamin, *New Arb. Rules for Use in Int'l. Trade*, in 3 INT'L. COM'L. ARB. 322-369 (P. Sanders ed. 1965); Cohn, *supra* European Convention on Int'l. Com'l. Arb.

UNITED NATIONS HANDBOOK OF NATIONAL AND INTERNATIONAL INSTITUTIONS ACTIVE IN THE FIELD OF INTERNATIONAL COMMERCIAL ARBITRATION (UNITED NATIONS) (TRADE/WP.1/15/Rev. 1, 3 December 1958)

A mimeographed five-volume study of arbitral institutions active in the field of international commercial arbitration.

The United Nations Handbook of National and International Institutions was prepared by the *Ad Hoc* Working Group on Arbitration of the Committee on the Development of Trade for the United Nations Economic Commission for Europe. The Handbook is a survey of arbitral procedures as practiced by 127 institutions in Europe and the United States, some of these making arbitration facilities available to the public, and others restricting them to certain specialized branches of trade. The Handbook was prepared for limited distribution, and does not reproduce rules or statutes, but merely summarizes and analyzes their main provisions. The institutions covered include arbitration courts of various chambers of commerce, national and international produce and commodity exchanges, and general arbitral institutions such as the International Chamber of Commerce and the American Arbitration Association.

See also: Appeal boards of adm. agencies; Institutional arb.; Int'l. com'l. arb.; Procedure; Trade association.

Sources: Benjamin, *supra* Appeal boards of adm. agencies at 350-397.

UNITED NATIONS RESOLUTION OF THE UNITED NATIONS CONFERENCE ON INTERNATIONAL COMMERCIAL ARBITRATION (June 10, 1958)

A resolution which was the secondary result of a conference, the major aim of which was the creation of the Convention on the Recognition and Enforcement of Foreign Arbitral Awards.

The United Nations Resolution of the United Nations Conference on International Commercial Arbitration contained proposals for increasing the effectiveness of arbitration in the settlement of private law disputes. It also encouraged the establishment of new facilities related to arbitration. The Resolution was submitted to the United Nations Economic and Social Council. It was subsequently implemented by the United Nations Economic Commission for Europe in its drafting of the European Convention on International Commercial Arbitration. The United Nations Commission for Asia and the Far East has also been instrumental in developing facilities for arbitration in the ECAFE Centre for Commercial Arbitration in Bangkok, Thailand.

See also: U.N. Conf. on Int'l. Com'l. Arb.; U.N. ECAFE; U.N. ECE.

Sources: U.S. Dept. of State, *supra* Convention on the Recognition and Enforcement of Foreign Arbitral Awards; DOMKE, *supra* Convention on the Recognition and Enforcement of Foreign Arbitral Awards.

UNITED STATES ARBITRATION ACT
(43 Stat. 883, as amended, 61 Stat. 669. 9 U.S.C. §§ 1-14)

The first federal modern arbitration statute in the United States.

As approved by President Calvin Coolidge on February 12, 1925, the United States Arbitration Act made written agreements valid and specifically enforceable for the arbitration of disputes arising out of maritime transactions, or contracts relating to commerce among States or Territories, or with foreign nations. The act was similar to the state arbitration laws of New York, New Jersey, Oregon, and Massachusetts. It provided for the enforcement of arbitration agreements and awards in federal courts. In order to invoke the Act in federal courts, some independent ground of federal court jurisdiction must exist. It is still an open question whether state courts must follow the United States Arbitration Act when the kind of contract is invoked which is enforceable under the Act.

See also: Container contract; Enforcement of arb. agreements (Federal statutes); Motion to compel arb.; Prima Paint Corp. . . . ; Separability doctrine.

Sources: Robert Lawrence Co. v. Devonshire Fabrics Inc. 271 F.2d 402 (2d Cir. 1959) cert. granted 362 U.S. 909, appeal dismissed per stipulation, 364 U.S. 801 (1960); SELECTED ARTICLES OF COM'L. ARB. (D. Bloomfield ed. 1927); M. DOMKE, *supra* Adhesion contract at 23-29; DOMKE, *supra* Institutional arb.

UNITED STATES ATOMIC ENERGY LABOR-MANAGEMENT RELATIONS PANEL

See: Atomic Energy Labor-Management Relations Panel.

UNITED STATES BOARD OF MEDIATION AND CONCILIATION

See: Newlands Act.

UNITED STATES BUREAU OF LABOR STATISTICS

See: Bureau of Labor Statistics.

UNITED STATES TREATIES OF FRIENDSHIP, COMMERCE AND NAVIGATION

Bilateral treaties between the United States and eighteen other nations providing among other things for the enforcement of arbitration agreements and awards in disputes between nationals and corporations of the respective countries.

The effectiveness of these treaties is not decisive. They provide specifically that enforcement cannot be denied for the reason that the award was rendered in another country or that the nationality of the arbitrator was not that of the party concerned.

See also: Enforcement of arb. agreements (Int'l. com'l. arb.); Enforcement of foreign arbitral awards; Reciprocity.

Sources: Treaty of Friendship, Commerce and Navigation between the U.S. and Japan, April 2, 1953, 4 U.S.T. 2063, T.I.A.S. 2863, 206 U.N.T.S. 143; M. DOMKE, supra Adhesion contract at 378-380.

UNITED STATES V. PARAMOUNT PICTURES

See: Motion Picture Industry Arbitration.

UNIVERSAL POSTAL UNION
(International Bureau, Schosshaldenstrasse 46, 3000 Berne, 15, Switzerland)

An international organization with headquarters in Berne, Switzerland, founded as the General Postal Union in 1874 to form a single postal territory for the reciprocal exchange of mail, and to encourage the development of international cooperation in the postal service of the member countries.

The Universal Postal Union is now a specialized agency of the United Nations with 138 States as members. A congress is held every five years, attended by government officials who examine and revise the Acts of the Union. The system of arbitration established by the Conventions of the Universal Postal Union is unique, providing for arbitrators to be chosen from the Union membership. The latest Convention was signed at Vienna July 10, 1964, and entered into force on January 1, 1966. Most countries, including the United States, have ratified the Convention. Chapter V, Article 126 of the General Regulations of the Universal Postal Union provides for arbitration, and specifies established procedures for the appointment of arbitrators.

See also: Central Office for Int'l. Railway Transport; Institutional arb.

Sources: Universal Postal Union, Constitution, Convention, and Related Documents, July 10, 1964, T.I.A.S. 5881; G. Codding, The Universal Postal Union (1964); M. Hudson, *supra* Convention on the Pacific Settlement of Int'l. Disputes; C. Jenks, *supra* Calvo Clause; Year-Book of Int'l. Organizations, *supra* Central Office for Int'l. Railway Transport at 18ff, 1042-1043.

VACATING AN AWARD

A court ruling to have an award set aside.

An award can be vacated on proof of partiality of an arbitrator appointed as a neutral, or when the arbitrators exceed their powers which the parties established in their agreement, or when they imperfectly execute the award. Other grounds for vacating an award are corruption, fraud, or other misconduct on the part of the arbitrator, or where the arbitration failed to follow the procedure established by the applicable statute. The right to object to such irregular procedure may be lost if the party shall have proceeded with the arbitration without making his objection known. An award also may be set aside under the New York State statute if the party neither participated in the arbitration nor was served with a demand, and can prove that there was no valid arbitration agreement or submission, or that this agreement was in violation of the statute of limitations. An award cannot be vacated "for mere errors of judgment, whether as to the law or as to the facts. If the (arbitrator) keeps within his jurisdiction and is not guilty of fraud, corruption or other misconduct affecting his award, it is unassailable, operates as a final and conclusive judgment, and . . . the parties must abide by it."* Under most modern arbitration statutes, a proceeding to vacate must be instituted within 30 to 90 days after the delivery of the award. The courts have also allowed any such motion to vacate to be made in opposition to a motion to confirm an award, even though the 90 day time limit may have expired. In New York State, such a motion to confirm may be made within one year after delivery of the award. When an award has been vacated under New York State law, a new arbitration is ordered by the court, to be heard before the same or before other arbitrators, depending upon the reasons for vacating the award.

See also: Adjournment of hearings; Appeal; Award; Bias; Challenge of award; Confirming the award; Disqualification of the arbitrator; Duty to disclose; Enforcement of award (Labor); Exces de pouvoir; Judicial review in arb.; Notice of intention to arbitrate; Participation in arb.; Rehearing; Removal of arbitrator; Statute of limitations; Statutory arb.; Stay of arb.; Testimony of arbitrator; Time limits; Waiver of the right to object to the arbitrator.

Sources: *Matter of Wilkins, 169 N.Y. 494, 62 N.E. 575 (1902), as cited in Ass'n. of the Bar of the City of N.Y., *supra* Award by confession at note 15; *id.* at 23-24; M. Domke, *supra* Adhesion contract at 303-311; 32 Lawyers' Letters (1967), *supra* Adjournment of hearings.

VACA V. SIPES
[*Vaca* v. *Sipes*, 386 U.S. 171 (1967)]

A United States Supreme Court decision which held that a union may refuse to process a worker's claim to arbitration, and that it subsequently cannot be sued unless the worker can prove that the union failed in its duty of fair representation.

The *Vaca* case involved an employee who had been discharged on grounds of poor health after his return from a medical leave of absence. The union refused to bring the grievance to arbitration when a medical examination proved unfavorable to the employee's case, suggesting instead that the grievant accept the company's offer of referral to a rehabilitation center. The employee refused and brought suit against the union, alleging that the union had breached its duty of fair representation. After a jury trial, a verdict was returned awarding the employee $7,000 compensatory, and $3,300 punitive damages, subsequently reduced to $3,000. The verdict was later set aside by the trial judge, and was eventually reversed by the Supreme Court of Missouri. The United States Supreme Court barred suit unless the employee could show that the union had acted in an arbitrary or discriminatory manner in refusing to bring his grievance to arbitration. The Court examined individual employee rights under § 301 of the Taft-Hartley Act, and held that the National Labor Relations Board did not have exclusive jurisdiction in such cases.

See also: Individual rights; Republic Steel v. Maddox; § 301 disputes.

Sources: Vaca v. Sipes, 386 U.S. 171 (1967); Comm. on Law and Legislation for 1967 of the Nat'l. Academy of Arbitrators, *Arb. and Federal Rights under Collective Agreements in 1967*, in 21 PROC. OF THE NAT'L. ACADEMY OF ARBITRATORS 201-206 (1968).

VENUE OF ARBITRATION

The place of arbitration.

See also: Locale of arb.; Situs of arb.

VOLUNTARY ARBITRATION

See: Arbitration (Voluntary).

VYNIOR'S CASE
[8 Co. 80a, 81b, 82a, 77 Eng. Rep. 595, 597, 599 (1609)]

The landmark case which allegedly reflected in its decision an early judicial hostility to the enforcement of arbitration agreements.

Lord C. J. Coke declared for the English Court in dictum that an arbitral agreement was revocable until it resulted in an award. Despite this apparently damaging opinion in the *Vynior's Case*, the court actually enforced the performance bond given by the defaulting party. Though the decision covers only recovery on the bond, the dictum seems to represent the common law of that time. The case resulted when Robert Vynior brought an action of debt against William Wilde, on a bond of £20. The bond contained the following arbitration agreement: "The condition of this obligation is such, that if the above bounden William Wilde do and shall from time to time, . . . keep the rule, . . . arbitrament, . . . and final determination of William Rugge, Esq., arbitrator indifferently named, . . . to, . . . adjudge, arbitrate, and finally determine, all matters, suits, . . . griefs, and contentions heretofore moved and stirred . . . touching or concerning the sum of two and twenty pence, heretofore taxed upon the said W. Wilde, for divers kind of parish business within the said parish of Themilthorpe; so as the said award be made and set down in writing, under the hand and seal of the said William Rugge at or before the feast of St. Michael the Archangel next ensuing after the date of these presents, that then this present obligation to be void and of no effect, or else the same to stand, abide, remain, and be in full force, power, strength, and virtue." In plain language, Robert Vynior held this bond and upon it sought and succeeded in holding Wilde, as the last sentence of the decision reads: "And afterwards judgement was given for the plaintiff." The Statute of Fines and Penalties later prohibited the enforcement of performance bonds beyond the amount of actually proved damages and thus the dictum in *Vynior's Case* became a precedent to prohibit the specific enforcement of the promise to arbitrate, since it can seldom be proved what the actual damage is in a breach of the promise to arbitrate.

See also: Common law arb.; Enforcement of arbitration agreements (Common law); Irrevocability of the arb. agreement.

Sources: Vynior's Case, as cited in J. COHEN, COM'L. ARB. AND THE LAW 87-88 (1918); Sayre, Development of Com'l. Arb. Law, 37 YALE L. J. 595-617 (1928).

WAGE STABILIZATION BOARD

See: National Wage Stabilization Board.

WAGNER ACT
(National Labor Relations Act, 49 Stat. 449 as amended by 61 Stat. 136 and 73 Stat. 519, 29 U.S.C. § 141 et seq.)

A federal act passed in 1935, which was designed to promote and protect the right of employees to organize.

Unlike the Norris-LaGuardia Act, the Wagner Act pledged government aid to employees in their efforts to organize. Section 7 of the Wagner Act specified what constitutes employee rights in this respect. The National Labor Relations Board was created to see that employers did not try to prevent employees from organizing. Title I of the Taft-Hartley

Act amended the National Labor Relations Act, and is commonly referred
to as the NLRA (1947).

See also: Concurrent jurisdiction; Nat'l. Labor Relations Board; Norris-La
Guardia Act.

Sources: A. Cox & D. Bok, *supra* Landrum-Griffin Act at 113-129; C. GREGORY,
supra Landrum-Griffin Act at 223-252.

WAIVER OF ARBITRATION (COMMERCIAL)

The voluntary relinquishment of the right to arbitrate.

A right to arbitrate may be waived by denying that there is anything
to arbitrate. It may also be waived by the failure to perform the preliminary steps leading to arbitration, or by being unjustifiably slow in doing
so, or by failing to protest the initiation of a court action by the other
party. When a party institutes a court action in violation of the arbitration
agreement, this action constitutes a waiver of the right to arbitrate. Such
a waiver is not often applied in labor arbitration.

See also: Laches; Mechanic's lien; Stay of suit.

Sources: 5 AM. JUR., *supra* Death of the arbitrator at 556-557; M. DOMKE,
supra Adhesion contract at 179-180.

WAIVER OF THE RIGHT TO OBJECT TO THE ARBITRATOR

The relinquishment of the right to object to an arbitrator once the arbitration begins.

If a party knows of facts concerning the arbitrator which would disqualify him and fails to act on these facts, that party may forfeit any
later opportunity to have the arbitrator removed or the award vacated.

See also: Duty to disclose; Vacating an award.

Sources: M.DOMKE, *supra* Adhesion contract at 211-214; 22 LAWYERS' LETTERS
(1965), *supra* Adjournment of hearings.

WAL WAL ARBITRATION (September 3, 1935)
(The Empire of Ethiopia and the Kingdom of Italy)

An arbitration between Italy and Ethiopia which tried to determine the
facts and fix the responsibility for the border incident of December 5 and
6, 1934, at Wal Wal, Ethiopia.

An Arbitration Commission was appointed under the Treaty of
Amity which had been signed by Ethiopia and Italy on August 2, 1928.
The arbitration is remarkable for two aspects unusual in international
public arbitration. The first was that the dispute was of a political nature
with national emotions involved, and therefore of a type rarely referred
to arbitration. The second aspect was that the Treaty of Amity was vague

in many important details, such as the determination of the place for the arbitration, the method of appointing arbitrators, as well as a clear definition of the central issue. The Commission ruled that no one could be considered responsible for the incident which involved troops of both countries in the remote desert outpost of Wal Wal. The Council of the League of Nations was instrumental in bringing the dispute to arbitration.

See also: Appointment of arbitrators; Int'l. pub. arb.; Locale of arb.

Sources: *Treaty between Ethiopia and Italy, Correspondence . . . Proceedings . . . and Decision of the Comm'n., Sept. 3, 1935*, in P. POTTER, THE WAL WAL ARB. (1938).

WAR LABOR BOARD

See: National War Labor Board.

WAR LABOR DISPUTES ACT. WORLD WAR II (June 25, 1943) (Smith-Connally Act) [Pub. L. No. 89 of the 78th Congress. (Chapter 144-1st session) (S. 796)]

A federal law enacted in 1943 to prevent strikes or any other cessation of the production of goods essential to the war effort.

The War Labor Disputes Act added to the powers of the then existing National War Labor Board. Under these wartime conditions, the powers granted by the Act made the Board virtually the compulsory arbitrator of labor disputes. If the United States Conciliation Service certified that a labor dispute existed which threatened the successful prosecution of the war, the Board might hear and resolve the dispute even though the parties failed to appear. The National War Labor Board was empowered to resolve the dispute by deciding the wages, hours, and other terms and conditions in controversy between the parties. The War Labor Disputes Act also provided for government seizure of plants under certain conditions.

See also: Compulsory arb.; Gov't. intervention; Nat'l. War Labor Board; Seizure of plant.

Sources: War Labor Disputes Act, in U.S. GPO, COMPILATION OF LAWS RELATING TO CONCILIATION, MEDIATION & ARB. 429-435 (1967).

WAR LABOR REPORTS (February 1942–December 1945)

Decisions of the National War Labor Board as published in 28 volumes by the Bureau of National Affairs, Washington, D.C.

The War Labor Reports include selected decisions by the regional boards and industry commissions of the National War Labor Board. Each decision is preceded by a statement of the rules laid down in the decision. The rules are classified and codified in an Index-Digest.

See also: Bureau of Nat'l. Affairs.

WARRIOR & GULF NAVIGATION COMPANY

[*United Steelworkers* v. *Warrior & Gulf Navigation Co.*, 363 U.S. 574 (1960)]

One of the three United States Supreme Court cases known as the 1960 Trilogy, in which the Court ruled on the question of arbitrability.

In the *Warrior and Gulf Navigation* case, the Supreme Court held that a grievance over the company's practice of subcontracting its maintenance work was arbitrable under the contract. This was true in spite of many unsuccessful attempts by the union to negotiate a specific limit on subcontracting, and also in spite of the presence of a clause in the contract excluding from arbitration those matters which were "strictly a function of management." The Supreme Court so held on the basis that doubts over arbitrability should be resolved in favor of arbitration, unless it may be said with "positive assurance" that the arbitration clause does not cover the dispute in question.

See also: American Manufacturing Co.; Arbitrability; Enterprise Wheel and Car Corp.; Grievance procedure; Procedural arbitrability; Subcontracting; Substantive arbitrability; Trilogy; Wiley v. Livingston.

Sources: United Steelworkers v. Warrior & Gulf Nav. Co., 363 U.S. 574 (1960); Aaron, *supra* Enterprise Wheel & Car Corp.; Davey, *supra* American Manufacturing Co.

WARSAW CONVENTION ON INTERNATIONAL AIR TRANSPORTATION (1929)

A code of private international law which provides, in particular, for limitation of carrier liability in airline accidents.

There are no arbitration agreements under this convention.

See also: Air transport agreements.

WILEY & SONS V. LIVINGSTON

[*John Wiley & Sons, Inc.,* v. *Livingston,* 376 U.S. 543 (1964)]

A United States Supreme Court decision which established the possibility of the survival of employee rights in a collective bargaining agreement after a business has been sold or merged with another.

In the *John Wiley & Sons* v. *Livingston* case, Interscience Publishers, Inc., a small publishing firm, merged with a larger, and all the employees were transferred to Wiley, the surviving corporation. The United States Supreme Court declared that Wiley, as the successor employer, was obligated to arbitrate the union's grievances in terms of the Interscience contract. In ruling on arbitrability, the Court made an important distinction as to when a court and when an arbitrator should determine matters of arbitrability. The Supreme Court held that a court should decide whether the arbitration provisions of the agreement survived the merger, and other matters of substantive arbitrability. Once it is determined by the court that the parties are obligated to submit the subject matter of a dispute to arbitration, the arbitrator must then determine questions of procedural arbitrability, such as whether there has been full compliance with the steps of the grievance procedure prior to arbitration.

See also: Arbitrability; Grievance procedure; Grievance procedure—Level of steps; Procedural arbitrability; Statute of limitations; Substantive arbitrability; Warrior & Gulf Nav. Co.

Sources: Livingston v. John Wiley & Sons, 313 F. 2d 52, cert. granted, 373 U.S. 908 (1963); Christensen, supra Arbitrability at 119-158; Comm. on Law & Legislation of the Nat'l. Academy of Arbitrators, Arb. and Rights under Collective Agreements, in 18 PROC. OF THE NAT'L. ACADEMY OF ARBITRATORS 219-223 (1965).

WITNESS

See: Expert witness.

WORK ASSIGNMENT DISPUTES

A dispute between an employer and two unions over the same work assignment.

Work assignment disputes have been the cause of costly jurisdictional strikes. In an attempt to solve the problem, the United States Congress enacted § 8(b)(4)(D) and § 10 (k) of the National Labor Relations Act in 1947, the first making such disputes unfair labor practices, and the second giving the National Labor Relations Board jurisdiction in solving them. The interpretation of § 10(k) proved difficult since its remedies could be implemented only by a strike or a threat of a strike. The United States Supreme Court in Carey v. Westinghouse, 1964, held that grievance arbitration between the employer and one of the unions could be used as an alternative remedy, thus avoiding the necessity for a strike before the NLRB could act. The NLRB subsequently did act in this case. From 1949 through September 1969, most work assignment disputes in the construction industry were settled by the National Joint Board for Settlement of Jurisdictional Disputes in the Building and Construction Industry. Work assignment disputes may also be resolved under the AFL-CIO Internal Disputes Plan.

See also: AFL-CIO Internal Disputes Plan; Carey v. Westinghouse; Concurrent jurisdiction; Joinder; Jurisdictional disputes; Labor arb. (Voluntary); Nat'l. Joint Board for the Settlement of Jurisdictional Disputes . . . ; Nat'l. Labor Relations Act; Representational disputes; § 10(k) proceedings; Trilateral disputes.

Sources: Carey v. Westinghouse Electric Corp., 375 U.S. 261 (1964); Nat'l. Labor Relations Act, 29 U.S.C.A. § 141 et seq; Jones, An Arbitral Answer to a Judicial Dilemma, 11 UCLA L. REV. 329 (1964).

WORKMEN'S COMPENSATION ARBITRATION PROCEEDINGS

Established procedures for arbitrating a dispute over a medical fee or bill in Workmen's Compensation Claims.

The Workmen's Compensation Arbitration Committee in New York consists of five physicians, two representing the Medical Society of the County in which the treatment was rendered, two designated by the Compensation Insurance Rating Board representing the carrier, and one selected by the chairman of the Workmen's Compensation Board, who acts as chairman of the Arbitration Committee.

Sources: N. CARTER, GUIDE TO WORKMEN'S COMPENSATION CLAIMS 183 (1965).

WORLD BANK (IBRD)

See: International Bank for Reconstruction and Development.

BIBLIOGRAPHIES

COMMERCIAL ARBITRATION
A SELECTED BIBLIOGRAPHY
Emphasizing Current Materials

BOOKS

American jurisprudence. 2d ed. Vol. 5. Rochester, N.Y., The Lawyers Co-operative Publishing Co., 1962. xx, 976 p. (Arbitration and award, p. 513-660).

Basu, Nrisinhadas. *The Arbitration act, 1940 (X of 1940).* Edited by Sudhir Kumar Bose. 5th ed. Calcutta, Eastern Law House, 1965. xliv, 879, cxxxvi p.

Baumbach, Adolf. *Schiedsgerichtsbarkeit; systematischer Kommentar zu den vorschriften der Zivilprozessordnung* . . . Begründet von Adolf Baumbach, fortgeführt von Karl Heinz Schwab. 2., neubearb. und erweiterte Aufl. München, Beck, 1960. xiv, 398 p.

Bernstein, Merton C. *Private dispute settlement.* New York, Free Press, 1968. xiv, 741 p.

Coulson, Robert. *How to stay out of court.* New York, Crown Publishers, 1968. 224 p. With an introduction by Arthur J. Goldberg.

Domke, Martin. *Commercial arbitration.* Englewood Cliffs, N.J., Prentice-Hall, 1965. xi, 116 p.

——————. *The law and practice of commercial arbitration.* Mundelein, Ill., Callaghan and Co., 1968. xiii, 469 p.

Gill, William H. *Evidence and procedure in arbitration.* With a foreword by the President of the Institute of Arbitrators. London, Sweet and Maxwell, 1965. vii, 200 p.

Lawyers' arbitration letters. Numbers 1 through 35, February 15, 1960-August 15, 1968. New York, American Arbitration Association, 1968. (variously paged).

Lazarus, Steven. *Resolving business disputes; the potential of commercial arbitration.* By Steven Lazarus et al. New York, American Management Association, 1965. 208 p.

Lebedev, C. N. *Mezhdunaroduyi torgovyi arbitrazh.* Moscow, 1965. 219 p.

Parker, Hubert, Lord Parker of Waddington. *The history and development of commercial arbitration;* and *Recent developments in the supervisory powers of the courts over inferior tribunals.* Jerusalem, Magnes Press, Hebrew University, 1959. 59 p. (Lionel Cohen lectures, sixth series—Jan. 1959).

Robert, Jean. *Arbitrage civil et commercial en droit interne et international privé. Suivi de formules pratiques.* 4th ed. Paris, Dalloz, 1967. 660 p.

Russell, Francis. *Russell on the law of arbitration.* 17th ed. by Anthony Walton. London, Stevens and Sons, Ltd., 1963. li, 477 p.

Sanjiva Row's the Arbitration act (act X of 1940), as amended up to date. 3d ed., rev. and enl. by M. Krishnaswami, 4th ed. by K. K. Singh. Allahabad, Law Publishers, 1963. lii, 637 p.

Singh, Shambhu Dayal. *The law of arbitration (including an exhaustive and analytical commentary on the Arbitration act, 1940 for India and Pakistan).* By S. D. Singh and V. D. Singh. 5th (revised and enlarged) ed. Allahabad, Ram Narain Lal Beni Madho, 1966. li, (20) 615 p.

PERIODICAL ARTICLES, ESSAYS, ETC.

Aeschlimann, Christopher John. "The arbitrability of patent controversies." *Journal of Patent Office Society.* 44:655-663. 1962.

Aksen, Gerald. "Arbitration of government subcontracting disputes." *Arbitration Journal.* (n.s.)20:34-40. 1965.

—————. "*Prima Paint* v. *Flood and Conklin*—what does it mean?" *St. John's Law Review.* 43:1-24. 1968.

—————. "Resolving construction contract disputes through arbitration." *Arbitration Journal.* (n.s.)23:141-161. 1968.

"Arbitration and protection of the child. A conversation on implications of . . . Sheets v. Sheets." Helen M. Buttenwieser, Henry H. Foster, Jr., Lawrence S. Kubie, Norman Moloshok, and Samuel A. Reinach. *Arbitration Journal.* (n.s.)21:215-222. 1966.

"Arbitration clauses and fraudulent inducement. Recent developments." *Washington Law Review.* 42:621-631. 1967.

Bernstein, Merton C. "The impact of the uniform commercial code upon arbitration: revolutionary overthrow or peaceful coexistence?" *NYU Law Review.* 42:8-33. 1967. (Also in *Arbitration Journal.* (n.s.)22:65-92. 1967).

Collins, Daniel G. "Arbitration and the uniform commercial code." *NYU Law Review.* 41:736-756. 1966. (Also in *Arbitration Journal.* (n.s.)21:193-214. 1966).

"Commercial arbitration." Part I. *Law and Contemporary Problems.* 17:471-629. 1952.

"Commercial arbitration." Part II. *Law and Contemporary Problems.* 17:630-710. 1952.

Coulson, Robert. "Appropriate procedures for receiving proof in commercial arbitration." *Dickinson Law Review.* 71:63-73. 1966.

—————. "Prima Paint: an arbitration milestone." *Arbitration Journal.* (n.s.) 22:237-245. 1967.

Domke, Martin. "Arbitration." In, New York University School of Law, *Annual survey of American law.* Dobbs Ferry, N.Y., Oceana Publications, 1952-1968.

—————. "Commercial arbitration in Mexico." *International Arbitration Journal.* 1:162-164. 1945.

—————. "Commercial arbitration in the United States." In, Union Internationale des Avocats, *Arbitrage international commercial.* Edited by Pieter Sanders. Paris, Dalloz et Sirey, 1956. Vol. 1, p. 196-215.

—————. "Education methods for commercial arbitration." Draft suggestions by Dr. Martin Domke for consideration of activities of the ECAFE Centre for Commercial Arbitration, to be presented at the Paris Preparatory Meeting of Experts on Commercial Arbitration on March 30, 1964. 5 p. Mimeographed.

"Erie, Bernhardt, and Section 2 of the United States arbitration act: a farrago of rights, remedies and a right to a remedy." *Yale Law Journal.* 69:847-867. 1960.

Falls, Raymond L., Jr. "Arbitration under the new civil practice law and rules in New York." *Arbitration Journal.* (n.s.)17:197-218. 1962.

"Federal arbitration act and application of the separability doctrine in federal courts." *Duke Law Journal.* 1968:588-614.

Feldman, Eddy S. "Arbitration law in California: private tribunals for private government." *Southern California Law Review.* 30:375-500. 1957.

——————. "Arbitration modernized—the new California arbitration act." *Southern California Law Review.* 34:413-444. 1961.

Goldberg, Arthur J. "A Supreme Court Justice looks at arbitration." *Arbitration Journal.* (n.s.)20:13-19. 1965.

Hoare, Frederick. "The London Court of Arbitration." *Arbitration*: The Journal of the Institute of Arbitrators. 33:121-127. 1967.

Hornstein, George D. "Arbitration in incorporated partnerships." *Arbitration Journal.* (n.s.)18:229-234. 1963.

Kay, Mark W. "Default judgments confirming ex parte arbitration awards." *University of Miami Law Review.* 15:138-160. 1960.

Kessler, Robert A. "Arbitration of intra-corporate disputes under New York laws." *Arbitration Journal.* (n.s.)19:1-22, 85-97. 1964.

Kronstein, Heinrich. "Arbitration is power." *NYU Law Review.* 38:661-700. 1963.

——————. "Business arbitration—instrument of private government." *Yale Law Journal.* 54:36-69. 1944.

Lorenzen, Ernest G. "Commercial arbitration—enforcement of foreign awards." *Yale Law Journal.* 45:39-68. 1935.

Mentschikoff, Soia. "Commercial arbitration." *Columbia Law Review.* 61:846-869. 1961.

New York Patent Law Association. "Arbitration and trademark problems." A colloquy among members of the Association: Cameron K. Wehringer, chm., John M. Calimafde, Rudolf Callmann, Francis J. Sullivan, and Stewart L. Whitman. *Arbitration Journal.* (n.s.)21:164-179. 1966.

O'Neal, F. Hodge. "Developments in the regulation of the close corporation." *Cornell Law Quarterly.* 50:641-662. 1965.

Phillips, Philip G. "Arbitration and conflicts of laws: a study of benevolent compulsion." *Cornell Law Quarterly.* 19:197-236. 1934.

——————. "A lawyer's approach to commercial arbitration." *Yale Law Journal.* 44:31-52. 1934.

——————. "The paradox in arbitration law: compulsion as applied to a voluntary proceeding." *Harvard Law Review.* 46:1258-1280. 1933.

——————. "A practical method for the determination of business fact." *University of Pennsylvania Law Review.* 82: 1934. 22 p.

——————. "Rules of law or laissez-faire in commercial arbitration." *Harvard Law Review.* 47:590-627. 1934.

Pirsig, Maynard E. "Arbitrability and the Uniform Act." *Arbitration Journal.* (n.s.) 19:154. 1964.

Rosenberg, Maurice. "Trial by lawyer: compulsory arbitration of small claims in Pennsylvania." By Maurice Rosenberg and Myra Schubin. *Harvard Law Review.* 74:448-471. 1961.

Rudnick, Harry L. "Arbitration of disputes between franchisers and franchisees." *Illinois Bar Journal.* 55:54-63. 1966.

Schmitthoff, Clive M. "The supervisory jurisdiction of the English courts." In, *International arbitration liber amicorum for Martin Domke.* Edited by Pieter Sanders. The Hague, Martinus Nijhoff, 1967. p. 289-300.

Stone, Morris. "A paradox in the theory of commercial arbitration." *Arbitration Journal.* (n.s.)21:156-163. 1966.

Sturges, Wesley A. "Arbitration—what is it?" *NYU Law Review*. 35:1031-1047. 1960.

——————. "Common-law and statutory arbitration: problems arising from their coexistence." By Wesley A. Sturges and Richard E. Reckson. *Minnesota Law Review*. 46:819-867. 1962.

Suratgar, David. "Arbitration in the Iranian legal system." *Arbitration Journal*. (n.s.)20:143-156. 1965.

Witte, Robert D. "Dispute settlement under government subcontracts." *Arbitration Journal*. (n.s.)18:193-204. 1963.

Wolaver, Earl S. "The historical background of commercial arbitration." *University of Pennsylvania Law Review*. 83:132-146. 1934.

BIBLIOGRAPHIES

American Arbitration Association Bibliographies prepared by the Eastman Arbitration Library:
> A basic arbitration library for medium-sized corporate law libraries
> Commercial arbitration
> Community disputes settlement procedures
> Limited partnerships and arbitration
> Patent arbitration
> Real estate arbitration and related fields
> Uninsured motorist arbitration in the United States

Association of the Bar of the City of New York. Library. "Selected list of materials of current interest on commercial arbitration." *Record*. 2:46-48. 1947.

——————. "Selected materials on commercial arbitration." *Record*. 17:145-156. 1962.

"Commercial arbitration in the United States; a bibliography." *Arbitration Journal*. (n.s.)17:227-234. 1962.

U. S. Library of Congress. Division of Bibliography. *List of references on commercial arbitration*. Washington, D.C., 1914. 9 p.

——————. *Supplementary list of references on commercial arbitration*. Aug. 7, 1922. Washington, D.C., 1922. 4 f. (Select list of references no. 662). Mimeographed.

DOCUMENTS

American Arbitration Association Commercial arbitration rules. . . . *As amended and in effect June 1, 1964*. New York. 11 p.

Association of the Bar of the City of New York. Committee on Arbitration. *An outline of procedure under the New York arbitration law*. New York, July 1, 1965. 31 p.

Institute of Judicial Administration. *Compulsory arbitration and court congestion; the Pennsylvania compulsory arbitration statute*. New York, 1956. 65 p. (Delay and congestion—suggested remedies series no. 11). Mimeographed.

Philadelphia. County Court. Compulsory Arbitration Division. *Statistical report and explanatory remarks pertaining to compulsory arbitration*. Philadelphia, Dec. 31, 1962-1968.

Research Institute of America. *Staff recommendations. Commercial arbitration: pros and cons*. New York, Sept. 11, 1967. 14 p. (File no. 33).

U. S. Congress. Senate. Committee on the Judiciary. Subcommittee on Antitrust and Monopoly (90.1). *Franchise legislation. Hearings before the subcommittee . . . pursuant to S. Res. 26 on S. 2507 . . . and S. 2321. Oct. 10, 11, 13, 16, 17, and 31, and Nov. 1, 1967.* Washington, D.C., Gov't. Printing Off., 1968. v, 553 p. Contains statement by Gerald Aksen, Counsel, American Arbitration Association, p. 91-98.

GENERAL ARBITRATION STATUTES IN THE UNITED STATES

United States Arbitration Act. 9 U.S.C. §§ 1-14; 61 Stat. 669, as amended by § 19 of Public Law 779, of September 3, 1954, 68 Stat. 1233.

Alabama. Code of Alabama (Recompiled 1960). Title 7, Ch. 19, §§ 829-844.

Alaska. Uniform Arbitration Act. Ch. 43, §§ 09, 43.010–09, 43.180. Effective date August 6, 1968.

Arizona. Arizona Revised Statutes. Ch. 9, §§ 12-1501–12-1516. 1962.

Arkansas. House Bill No. 463, enacted May 15, 1968.

California. Code of Civil Procedure. Part 3, Title 9, §§ 1280-1294.2 (Supp. 1961).

Colorado. Rules of Civil Procedure for the Courts of Record in Colorado, Colorado Revised Statutes. Vol. 1, Ch. 16, Rule 109(a) through (g). 1963.

Connecticut. General Statutes Annotated, Revision of 1958. Title 52, Ch. 909, §§ 52-408–52-424.

Delaware. Delaware Code Annotated. Title 10, Ch. 57, §§ 5701-5706. 1953.

District of Columbia. District of Columbia Code (1951 Edition). Vol. 2, note p. 907.

Florida. Florida Statutes Annotated. Ch. 682, §§ 682.01–682.22. 1967.

Georgia. Code of Georgia Annotated. Title 7, Ch. 7, §§ 7-101–7-111, 7-201–7-224.

Hawaii. Revised Laws of Hawaii 1955. Ch. 188, §§ 188-1–188-15.

Idaho. Idaho Code Annotated. Title 7, Ch. 9, §§ 7-901–7-910. 1948.

Illinois. Illinois Revised Statutes, 1961. Ch. 10 §§ 101-123. 1962 Cum. Ann. Pocket Part p. 192.

Indiana. House Enrolled Act No. 1266, Enacted May 1, 1969.

Iowa. Iowa Code Annotated. Ch. 679, §§ 679-1–679-18.

Kansas. General Statutes of Kansas (Annotated) 1963. Ch. 5, §§ 5-201–5-213.

Kentucky. Kentucky Revised Statutes 1960. Ch. 417, §§ 417.010–417.040.

Louisiana. Louisiana Revised Statutes (West, 1951). Title 9, Ch. 1, §§ 4201-4217.

Maine. Revised Statutes of the State of Maine, 1964. Title 14, Ch. 706, §§ 5927-5949 (Supp. 1968).

Maryland. Annotated Code of the Public General Laws of Maryland. Art. 7, §§ 1-23, as Revised by Acts 1965, Ch. 231, § 2.

Massachusetts. Annotated Laws of Massachusetts. Ch. 251, §§ 1-19 (Supp. 1966).

Michigan. Michigan Statutes Annotated. Title 27, Ch. 47, §§ 27.2483–27.2505, as Amended by Public Act No. 27 of 1963. Michigan Supreme Court Rules, Rule 769. 1963.

Minnesota. Minnesota Statutes Annotated. Vol. 37, Ch. 572, §§ 572.08–572.30, Laws 1957, c. 633, § 1, as Amended Laws 1963, c. 656, § 1 (Supp. 1965).

Mississippi. Mississippi Code 1942 Annotated (Recompiled 1956). Title 3, Ch. 1, §§ 279-297.

Missouri. Annotated Missouri Statutes (Vernon, 1952). Title 28, Ch. 435, §§ 435.010–435.280.

Montana. Revised Codes of Montana 1947 Annotated. §§ 93-201-1–93-201-10.

Nebraska. Revised Statutes of Nebraska 1943 (Reissue 1964). §§ 25-2103–25-2120.

Nevada. Assembly Bill No. 644, Enacted May 6, 1969.

New Hampshire. New Hampshire Revised Statutes Annotated 1955. Ch. 542, §§ 542:1–542:10.

New Jersey. New Jersey Statutes. Title 2A, Ch. 24, §§ 2A:24-1–2A:24-11.

New Mexico. New Mexico Statutes 1953 Annotated. §§ 22-3-1–22-3-8.

New York. Civil Practice Law and Rules. Art. 75, effective September 1, 1963, §§ 7501–7514 amended by N.Y. Laws 1962, Ch. 308.

North Carolina. General Statutes of North Carolina. Art. 45, §§ 1-544–1-567.

North Dakota. North Dakota Revised Code. Ch. 32-29, §§ 32-29-01–32-29-21.

Ohio. Ohio Revised Code Annotated (Page 1964). Ch. 2711, §§ 2711.01– 2711.16, as Amended on June 13, 1967 (Supp. 1968).

Oregon. Oregon Revised Statutes (1955 Replacement Parts). Ch. 33, §§ 33.210– 33.340.

Pennsylvania. Purdon's Pennsylvania Statutes Annotated. Title 5, Ch. 1-4, §§ 1-181.

Puerto Rico. Laws of Puerto Rico, Annotated. Ch. 259, §§ 3201-3229.

Rhode Island. General Laws of Rhode Island 1956. Title 10, Ch. 3, §§ 10-3-1– 10-3-20.

South Carolina. Code of Laws of South Carolina 1952. Title 10, Ch. 22, §§ 10-1901–10-1905.

Tennessee. Tennessee Code Annotated. Title 23, Ch. 5, §§ 23-501–23-519. 1955.

Texas. Revised Civil Statutes of the State of Texas (Vernon's Ann.) Title 10, Art. 224–238-6, as Revised and Amended by Acts 1965, 59 Leg. p. 1593, Ch. 689, § 1 (Supp. 1968).

Utah. Utah Code Annotated 1953. Title 78, Ch. 31, §§ 78-31-1–78-31-22.

Virginia. Code of Virginia 1950. Title 8, Ch. 22, §§ 8-503–8-507, as Amended by Acts 1968, Ch. 244 (Supp. 1968).

Washington. Revised Code of Washington. Title 7, Ch. 7.04, §§ 7.04-010– 7.04-220.

West Virginia. The West Virginia Code of 1961. Ch. 55, Art. 10, §§ 5499-5506.

Wisconsin. Wisconsin Statutes (West's Ann.). Title 27, Ch. 298, §§ 298-01– 298.18.

Wyoming. Wyoming Statutes, Title 1, Ch. 37, §§ 1-1048.1–1048.21 (Supp. 1965).

SYMPOSIA

Institute of Arbitrators. London. "Edinburgh symposium on arbitration, May 18, 1966." *Arbitration: the Journal of the Institute of Arbitrators.* (n.s.) 32:67-85. 1966.

"Symposium: arbitration and the courts. Scope of the U.S. aribtration act in commercial arbitration: problems in federalism." *Northwestern University Law Review.* 58:468-494. 1963.

"A symposium on arbitration." Chicago Bar Association, Seminar on arbitration, Nov. 5, 1964. *Chicago Bar Record.* 46:56-77. 1964.

"Symposium on arbitration." *Vanderbilt Law Review.* 10:657-829. 1957.

"Symposium on commercial arbitration." *Ohio State Law Journal.* 24:589-649. 1963.

"A symposium on industrial, commercial, and international arbitration." *NYU Law Quarterly Review.* 17:495-624. 1940.

Texas University. School of Law. *Proceedings of the conference held at the University of Texas School of Law. Commercial law of Mexico and the United States.* Austin, 1966. v, 220 p.

INTERNATIONAL COMMERCIAL ARBITRATION
A SELECTED BIBLIOGRAPHY
1958 - 1968

BOOKS

Becker, Elmar. *Die Rechsprechung der Sowjetischen Aussenhandelsschiedskommission.* Köln, Carl Heymanns Verlag KG, 1964. x, 185 p. (Fiwschriftenreihe Forschungsinstitut für Wirtschaftsverfassung und Wettbewerb E. V. Köln, Heft 17).

Bertheau, Theodor Richard. *Das New Yorker Abkommen vom 10. Juni 1958 über die Anerkennung und Vollstreckung ausländischer Schiedssprüche.* Zürich, Verlag Schulthess and Co., AG., 1965. xi, 136 p. (Zürcher Beitrage zur Rechtswissenschaft. Herausgegeben von Mitgliedern der Rechts- und staats- wissenschaftlichen Fakultät der Universität Zürich, Neue Folge, Heft 251).

Briseño Sierra, Humberto. *El arbitraje en el derecho privado; situación internacional.* México, D.F., Imprenta Universitaria, 1963. 429 p.

Committee for Economic Development Research and Policy Committee. *East-West trades; a common policy for the West.* A statement on national policy . . . Prepared in association with CEPES, the European Committee for Economic and Social Progress and Keizai Doyukai, Japan Committee for Economic Development. New York, May 1965. 69 p.

Domke, Martin, ed. *International trade arbitration; a road to worldwide cooperation.* New York, American Arbitration Association, 1958. ii, 311 p.

Fouchard, Philippe. *L'arbitrage commercial international.* Preface by B. Goldman. Paris, Librairie Dalloz, 1965. x, 611 p. (Bibliothèque de droit international privé, publieé sous la direction de Henri Batiffol et Ph. Francescakis, vol. II).

Francisco Brice, Angel. *Reconocimiento y ejecucion de sentencias arbitrales; convención adoptada por las Naciones Unidas en 1958.* Caracas, Comision Interamericana de Arbitraje Comercial, Seccion Venezolana, 1963. 47 p.

Haight, G. W. *Convention on the recognition and enforcement of foreign arbitral awards; summary analysis of record of United Nations conference, May/June 1958.* New York, October 1, 1958. iii, 108 p.

International arbitration liber amicorum for Martin Domke. Edited by Pieter Sanders. The Hague, Martinus Nijhoff, 1967. viii, 357 p. + bibliography of selected writings by Martin Domke.

International Association of Lawyers. *Arbitrage international commercial. International commercial arbitration.* Rapporteur général, Pieter Sanders. Paris, Dalloz et Sirey, 1956- . Vols. 2 and 3 have imprint. The Hague, M. Nijhoff. (Vol. 2, 1960; Vol. 3, 1965).

International Chamber of Commerce. *Commercial arbitration and the law throughout the world; summary of the rules concerning arbitration agreements, procedure, arbitral awards, enforcement of awards, means of recourse.* Basel, Verlag für Recht und Gesellschaft Ag., 1949. Lettered pages by countries. (Documents of the I.C.C. no. 11). Supplements 1-1951, 2-1958, 3-1964.

Rao, K. Krishna. *International commercial arbitration.* New Delhi, The Indian Society of International Law. 1964. vii, 398 p.

Robert, Jean. *Arbitrage civil et commercial en droit interne et international privé. Suivi de formules pratiques.* 4th ed. Paris, Dalloz, 1967. 660 p.

Rubellin-Devichi, Jacqueline. *L'arbitrage; nature juridique, droit interne et droit international privé.* Preface by J. Vincent. Paris, Librairie Générale de Droit et de Jurisprudence, 1965. 412 p. (Bibliothèque de droit privé, t. 63).

Schmitthoff, Clive M., ed. *The sources of the law of international trade, with special reference to East-West trade.* New York, Frederick A. Praeger, 1964. xxvi, 292 p.

PERIODICAL ARTICLES, ESSAYS, ETC.

Ambión, Bienvenido C. "Commercial arbitration facilities and procedures." *Philippine Law Journal.* 39:514-522. 1964.

——————. "Is Philippine legislative action necessary on twelve ECAFE-listed problems of commercial arbitration?" By Bienvenido C. Ambión, Elizabeth R. Tan, Filemon R. Balbastro, Jr. *Philippine Law Journal.* 38: 648-735. 1963.

Arets, Jean. "Réflexions sur la nature juridique de l'arbitrage." In, *Annales de la Faculté de droit de Liège, septième année,* 1962. p. 173-201.

Baxi, Upendra. "Allepey turmeric fingers and arbitral awards; spices in the conflict of laws." *Journal of the Indian Law Institute.* 10:149-170. 1968.

Benjamin, Peter I. "The developing nations and certain legislative obstacles in the field of international commercial arbitration." In, *International arbitration liber amicorum for Martin Domke.* Edited by Pieter Sanders. The Hague, Martinus Nijhoff, 1967. p. 1-11.

——————. "The European convention on international commercial arbitration." *British Yearbook of International Law.* 37:478-495. 1962.

——————. "Inter-institutional agreements designed to extend existing facilities for international commercial arbitration." *International and Comparative Law Quarterly.* 8:289-298. 1959.

Bongco, Gamaliel G. "The enforcement of foreign arbitration agreements and awards in the Philippines." *ECAFE Centre for Commercial Arbitration News Bulletin.* Trade/CA/News 5:1-15. 1966.

Bredin, Jean-Denis. "The paralysis of foreign arbitral awards through the abuse of remedies." *Journal du Droit International.* 89:639-665. 1962.

Boka, Ernest. "The sources of the law of international trade in the developing countries of Africa." In, *The sources of the law of international trade.* Edited by Clive M. Schmitthoff. New York, Frederick A. Praeger, 1964. p. 227-254.

Burstein, Herbert. "Arbitration of international commercial disputes." *Boston College Industrial and Commercial Law Review.* 6:569-577. 1965.

Carabiber, Charles. "Conditions of development of international commercial arbitration." In, *International trade arbitration: a road to world-wide cooperation.* Edited by Martin Domke. New York, American Arbitration Association, 1958. p. 149-163.

——————. "L'évolution de la jurisprudence en matière d'exécution des jugements étrangers et des sentences arbitrales étrangères et internationales." In, *Essays in honor of George S. Maridakis.* Athens, 1964. Vol. 3, p. 3-18.

——————. "Les tribunaux internationaux et les intérêts privés." In, *Etudes de droit contemporain; contributions françaises aux 111e et IVe congrès internationaux de droit comparé.* Paris, Sirey, 1959. p. 305-323. (Travaux et recherches de l'Institut de droit comparé de l'Université de Paris.)

Carlston, Kenneth S. "Psychological and sociological aspects of the judicial and arbitration process." In, *International arbitration liber amicorum for Martin Domke*. Edited by Pieter Sanders. Hague, Martinus Nijhoff, 1967. p. 44-45.

Cohn, E. J. "The rules of arbitration of the International Chamber of Commerce." *International and Comparative Law Quarterly*. 14:132-171. 1965.

——————. "The rules of arbitration of the United Nations Economic Commission for Europe." *International and Comparative Law Quarterly*. 16:946-981. 1967.

Czizmas, Michael. "Die Aussenhandelsarbitrage in Ungarn." *Osteuropa Recht*. 13:261-290. 1967.

David, René. "L'avenir de l'arbitrage." In, *International arbitration liber amicorum for Martin Domke*. Edited by Pieter Sanders. Hague, Martinus Nijhoff, 1967. p. 56-64.

Delaume, Georges R. "Arbitration." In, Delaume, Georges R., *American-French private international law*. 2d ed. Dobbs Ferry, N.Y., Oceana, 1961. p. 175-181.

Deleuze, Jean-Marie. "La rédaction des clauses compromissoires dans les contrats commerciaux internationaux." In, *Annales de la Faculté de droit de Liège*, neuvième année, 1964. p. 83-102.

Doi, Teruo. "International commercial arbitration in Japan." In, *International arbitration liber amicorum for Martin Domke*. Edited by Pieter Sanders. Hague, Martinus Nijhoff, 1967. p. 65-77.

Domke, Martin. "American arbitral awards: enforcement in foreign countries." *University of Illinois Law Forum*. 1965:399-410.

——————. "Arbitral awards without written opinions: comparative aspects of international commercial arbitration." In, *20th century comparative and conflicts law; legal essays in honor of Hessel E. Yntema*. Leyden, A. W. Sythoff, 1961. p. 249-261.

——————. "Arbitration of state-trading relations." *Law and Contemporary Problems*. 24:317-328. 1959.

——————. "Enforcement of foreign arbitral awards in the United States." *Arbitration Journal*. (n.s.)13:91-97. 1958.

——————. "Enforcement of foreign awards and judgments on awards." In, *The law and practice of commercial arbitration*. Chicago, Callaghan, 1968. p. 361-380.

——————. "International arbitration of commercial disputes." In, Institute on Private Investments Abroad, *Proceedings 1960*. Albany, N.Y., Matthew Bender and Co., 1960. p. 131-184.

——————. "International aspects of commercial arbitration in the Americas." In, Academia Interamericana de Derecho Comparado e Internacional, *Cursos Monográficos*. Havana, 1960. Vol. 8, p. 481-504.

——————. "International commercial arbitration in the International Cooperation Year." *Arbitration Journal*. (n.s.)20:226-233. 1965.

——————. "International commercial arbitration: its present status and future prospects." In, *World peace through law. The Washington World Conference*. St. Paul, Minn., West Publishing Co., 1965. p. 293-299.

——————. "Possible measures for increasing the effectiveness of international commercial arbitration." In, *International commercial arbitration*. Edited by Pieter Sanders. Hague, Martinus Nijhoff, 1960. Vol. 2, p. 328-347.

——————. "Progress in international commercial arbitration." *NYU Journal of International Law and Politics*. 1:37-43. 1968.

——————————. "The settlement of trade disputes in regional markets." In, *Legal problems of international trade and investment.* New Haven, Conn., Yale Law School, 1962. p. 131-144.

——————————. "The United Nations Conference on International Commercial Arbitration." *American Journal of International Law.* 53:414-426. 1959.

Eisemann, Frédéric. "L'arbitrage de la Chambre de Commerce internationale." In, *Annales de la Faculté de droit de Liège,* neuvième année, 1964. p. 103-127.

——————————. "L'arbitre-partie." In, *International arbitration liber amicorum for Martin Domke.* Edited by Pieter Sanders. Hague, Martinus Nijhoff, 1967. p. 78-88.

——————————. "The Court of arbitration. ICC's stake in the law of international trade." *Journal of World Trade Law.* 2:19-25. 1968.

Farago, L. "Decisions of the Hungarian Chamber of Commerce in 'Comecon' arbitrations." *International and Comparative Law Quarterly.* 14:1124-1143. 1965.

"Foreign arbitral awards and foreign judgments based upon such awards." *International and Comparative Law Quarterly.* 13:1465-1468. 1964.

"Foreign Trade Arbitration Commission of the U.S.S.R. Chamber of Commerce." In, Indian Council of Arbitration, *Facilities for international commercial arbitration in foreign countries.* New Delhi, 1967. p. 14-15.

Fragistas, Ch. N. "Arbitrage étranger et arbitrage international en droit privé." *Revue Critique de Droit International Privé.* p. 1-20. No. 1, 1960.

——————————. "Etapes dans le règlement international de l'arbitrage privé." In, Institute of Comparative Law, *Collection of studies on foreign and comparative law.* Belgrade, 1966. p. 109-124.

François, J.P.A. "La liberté des parties de choisir les arbitres dans les conflits entre les Etats." In, *International arbitration liber amicorum for Martin Domke.* Edited by Pieter Sanders. Hague, Martinus Nijhoff, 1967. p. 89-94.

Gentinetta, Joerg. "Was ist 'Lex Fori' privater Internationaler Schiedsgerichte?" *Zeitschrift für Schweizerisches Recht.* (n.f.)84:139-176. 1965.

Glossner, Ottoarndt. "International commercial arbitration, some practical aspects." In, *International arbitration liber amicorum for Martin Domke.* Edited by Pieter Sanders. Hague, Martinus Nijhoff, 1967. p. 95-102.

Goldman, Berthold. "Les conflits de lois dans l'arbitrage international de droit privé." *Académie de Droit International. Recueil des Cours II.* 109:347-483. 1963.

Goldman, Marvin G. "Arbitration in inter-American trade relations. Regional market aspects." *Inter-American Law Review.* 7:67-94. 1965.

Gormley, W. Paul. "The future role of arbitration within the EEC: the right of an arbitrator to request a preliminary ruling pursuant to Article 177." *Saint Louis University Law Journal.* 12:550-563. 1968.

——————————. "The place of commercial arbitration in multi-national and international organizations." *Ohio State Law Journal.* 24:619-635. 1963.

Habschied, Walter J. "L'expertise-arbitrage; étude de droit comparé." In, *International arbitration liber amicorum for Martin Domke.* Edited by Pieter Sanders. Hague, Martinus Nijhoff, 1967. p. 103-119.

Hariani, K.P. "Enforcement of foreign arbitration agreements and awards in India." *Indian Journal of International Law.* 7:31-44. 1967.

Hazard, John N. "Flexibility of law in Soviet state arbitration." In, *International arbitration liber amicorum for Martin Domke.* Edited by Pieter Sanders. Hague, Martinus Nijhoff, 1967. p. 120-132.

Ionasco, Trajan. "The limits of party autonomy." In, *The sources of the law of international trade*. Edited by Clive M. Schmitthoff. New York, Frederick A. Praeger, 1964. p. 167-200.

Jenard, Paul. "Projet de Convention européenne portant loi uniforme en matiére d'arbitrage en droit belge." In, *Annales de la Faculté de droit de Liége*, neuvième année, 1964. p. 39-66.

Kitagawa, Tokusuke. "Contractual autonomy in international commercial arbitration, including a Japanese perspective." In, *International arbitration liber amicorum for Martin Domke*. Edited by Pieter Sanders. Hague, Martinus Nijhoff, 1967. p. 133-142.

Klein, Frédéric-Edouard. "L'arbitrage international de droit privé: réalités et perspectives." *Annuaire Suisse de Droit International*. 20:41-62. 1965.

——————. "La Convention européenne sur l'arbitrage commercial international." *Revue Critque de Droit International Privé*. 2:621-640. 1962.

——————. "Zum Begriff des internationalen Schiedsverfahrens." In, *Festgabe zum Schweizerischen Juristentag*. Basel, Verlag Helbing and Lichtenhahn, 1963. p. 145-161.

Kopelmanas, Lazare. "L'arbitrage dans les rapports commerciaux Est-Ouest." In, *Annuales de la Faculté de droit de Liège*, neuvième année, 1964. p. 129-140.

Lagergren, Gunnar. "The limits of party autonomy." In, *The sources of the law of international trade*. Edited by Clive M. Schmitthoff. New York, Frederick A. Praeger, 1964. p. 201-224.

Larkin, Edwin M. "The effect of communism on international trade arbitration in the Soviet Union." *George Washington Law Review*. 33:728-739. 1965.

Leff, Eugene J. "The Foreign Trade Arbitration Commission of the U.S.S.R. and the West." *Arbitration Journal*. (n.s.)24:1-34. 1969.

Mann, F. A. "Lex facit arbitrum." In, *International arbitration liber amicorum for Martin Domke*. Edited by Pieter Sanders. Hague, Martinus Nijhoff, 1967, p. 157-183.

Mezger, Ernst. "La distinction entre l'arbitre dispensé d'observer la règle de la loi et l'arbitre statuant sans appel." In, *International arbitration liber amicorum for Martin Domke*. Edited by Pieter Sanders. Hague, Martinus Nijhoff, 1967. p. 184-198.

——————. "Enforcement of American awards in France." *Arbitration Journal*. (n.s.)17:74-84. 1962.

——————. "Das europäeische Ubereinkommen über die Handelsschiedsgerichtsbarkeit." *Rabels Zeitschrift*. 29:231-301. 1965.

——————. "Vers la consécration aux Etats-Unis de l'autonomie de la clause compromissoire dans l'arbitrage international." *Revue Critique de Droit International Privé*. 57:27-45. 1968.

Minoli, Eugenio. "L'Italie et la Convention de New York pour la réconnaissance et l'exécution des sentences arbitrales étrangères." In, *International arbitration liber amicorum for Martin Domke*. Edited by Pieter Sanders. Hague, Martinus Nijhoff, 1967. p. 199-207.

——————. "New York Convention on the recognition and enforcement of foreign arbitral awards." *Unification of Law Year Book 1958*. p. 156-197.

Motulsky, Henry. "L'exécution des sentences arbitrales étrangères". In, *Annales de la Faculté de droit de Liège*, neuvième année, 1964. p. 141-173.

Nestor, Ion. "De quelques problèmes relatifs à la compétence de l'arbitrage commercial." In, *Rechtsfragen der Kooperation zwischen Unternehmen in Ost und West*. Herrenalb (Schwarzwald), 1967. p. 107-123. (Studien des Instituts für Ostrecht, München.)

——————————. "A theoretical survey of arbitral practice in foreign trade issues." *Sciences Juridiques* (Bucarest). 11:245-261. 1967.

Norberg, Charles R. "Inter-American commercial arbitration." *American Journal of International Law.* 61:1028-1030. 1967.

——————————. "Inter-American Commercial Arbitration." *Lawyer of the Americas.* 1:25-41. 1969.

——————————. "Revitalization of commercial arbitration in the Western Hemisphere." *International Lawyer.* 3:109-121. 1968.

Ouchi, Kazuomi. "Problems of competence of international commercial arbitral tribunals." *Philippine International Law Journal.* 3:16-132. 1964.

Parra Aranguren, Gonzalo. "La function de la reciprocidad en el sistema venezolano del exequatur." *Revista de la Facultad de Derecho.* p. 39-122. No. 31, 1965.

Pearson, Neil. "Arbitration and the businessman." In, *International arbitration liber amicorum for Martin Domke.* Edited by Pieter Sanders. Hague, Martinus Nijhoff, 1967. p. 208-213.

Rajski, Jerzy. "The law of international trade of some European socialist countries and East-West trade relations." *Washington University Law Quarterly.* 1967:125-138.

Ramzaitsev, Dimitrii Fedorovich. "The law applied by arbitration tribunals." In, *The sources of the law of international trade.* Edited by Clive M. Schmitthoff. New York, Frederick A. Praeger, 1964. p. 138-153.

Reghizzi, Gabriele Crespi. "Legal aspects of trade with China: the Italian experience." *Harvard International Law Journal.* 9:85-139. 1968.

Reisman, William M. "Book review: International commercial arbitration liber amicorum for Martin Domke. Pieter Sanders, ed." *Syracuse Law Review.* 20:166-180. 1968.

Rivkin, Donald H. "International litigation and arbitration." *Kansas City Law Review.* 34:60-77. 1966.

Robert, Jean. "De la place de la loi dans l'arbitrage." In, *International arbitration liber amicorum for Martin Domke.* Edited by Pieter Sanders. Hague, Martinus Nijhoff, 1967. 226-239.

——————————. "Droit interne et droit international privé." *Revue de l'Arbitrage.* p. 83-91. juillet-septembre, 1967.

——————————. "Exposé introductif et général sur l'arbitrage." In, *Annales de la Faculté de droit de Liège,* neuvième année, 1964. p. 29-37.

Roberts, B. K. "International regional trade courts—need and feasibility." *International Lawyer.* 3:75-91. 1968.

Sanders, Pieter. "ECAFE rules for international commercial arbitration." In, *International arbitration liber amicorum for Martin Domke.* Edited by Pieter Sanders. Hague, Martinus Nijhoff, 1967. p. 252-267.

——————————. "Recent developments in international commercial arbitration." In, *Festschrift for Professor Fragistas,* 1967. p. 625-634.

——————————. "Venue of arbitration in international commercial arbitration." In, Indian Council of Arbitration, *International Seminar on Commercial Arbitration, New Delhi, 18th and 19th March, 1968.* New Delhi, 1968. p. 169-174.

Schachter, Oscar. "Conciliation procedures in the United Nations conference on trade and development." In, *International arbitration liber amicorum for Martin Domke.* Edited by Pieter Sanders. Hague, Martinus Nijhoff, 1967. p. 268-274.

Schlochauer, Hans-Jurgen. "Die Entwicklung der internationalen Schiedsgerichtsbarkeit." *Archiv des Volkerrechts.* 10:1-41. 1962.

Schmitthoff, Clive M. "The supervisory jurisdiction of the English courts." In, *International arbitration liber amicorum for Martin Domke.* Edited by Pieter Sanders. Hague, Martinus Nijhoff, 1967. p. 289-300.

——————. "The unification of the law of international trade." *Journal of Business Law.* 1968:105-119.

Schwab, Karl Heinz. "The legal foundations and limitations of arbitration procedures in the United States and Germany." In, *International arbitration liber amicorum for Martin Domke.* Edited by Pieter Sanders. Hague, Martinus Nijhoff, 1967. p. 301-312.

Seidl-Hohenveldern, Ignaz. "Arbitration by organs of international organizations." In, *International arbitration liber amicorum for Martin Domke.* Edited by Pieter Sanders. Hague, Martinus Nijhoff, 1967. p. 322-329.

"Some legal instruments governing trade relations between countries of different social systems." *Review of Contemporary Law.* p. 7-114. No. 2, 1967.

Straus, Donald B. "Inter-American commercial arbitration. Report of two meetings during April of 1967 in Buenos Aires and San Jose and subsequent action by Executive Committee of American Arbitration Association." New York, May 12, 1967. 8 p.

——————. "Inter-American commercial arbitration: unicorn or beast of burden?" *Business Lawyer.* 1965:43-58.

——————. "Remarks at the Conference of Inter-American commercial arbitration, Buenos Aires, April 3-4, 1967." 4 p.

Subramanian, S. "Arbitral tribunals and their constitution." *Indian Council Arbitration Quarterly.* 3:3-7. 1968.

Suratgar, David. "Arbitration in the Iranian legal system." *Arbitration Journal.* (n.s.) 20:143-156. 1965.

Szászy, István. "International aspects of arbitration." In, *International civil procedure; a comparative study.* Leyden, A. A. Sijthoff, 1967. p. 558-643.

——————. "Nationality of arbitral awards." In, International Law Association. Hungarian Branch, *Questions of international law 1966.* Budapest, 1966. p. 144-164.

Szászy, Stephen. "Arbitration of foreign trade transactions in the popular democracies." *American Journal of Comparative Law.* 13:441-450. 1964.

Szurski, Tadeusz. "Commercial arbitration." In, *The prospects of international arbitration.* Edited by Mohammed Ahsen Chaudhri. Karachi, Pakistan Publishing House, 1966. p. 21-51.

Tallon, Dennis. "The law applied by arbitration tribunals." In, *The sources of the law of international trade.* Edited by Clive M. Schmitthoff. New York, Frederick A. Praeger, 1964. p. 201-224.

Uchakow, Alexander. "Die Aussenhandelsarbitrage in Polen." *Osteropa-Recht.* 11:1-26. 1965.

Vaughter, James G. "Choice of law for international contracts: an American critique." *Texas International Law Forum.* 2:227-252. 1966.

Walker, Herman. "Dispute settlement: the chicken war." *American Journal of International Law.* 58:671-685. 1964.

Wartberg, Walter P. von. "Commercial arbitration and anti-trust matters in the European Economic Community." *Arbitration Journal.* (n.s.)21:65-97. 1966.

Wilner, Gabriel M. "Determining the law governing performance in international commercial arbitration: a comparative study." *Rutgers Law Review.* 19:646-691. 1965.

Wortley, B. A. "Quelques développements modernes qui touchent les controverses entre les particuliers et les états et les entités étatiques." In, *International arbitration liber amicorum for Martin Domke*. Edited by Pieter Sanders. Hague, Martinus Nijhoff, 1967. p. 348-357.

Zourek, Jaroslov. "New rules of arbitration proceeedings in Czechoslovakia." *Bulletin of Czechoslovakian Law*. 21:233-276. 1963.

BIBLIOGRAPHIES

Association of the Bar of the City of New York. Library. "Selected materials on international unification of private law." *Record*. 23:290-301. 1968.

"Bibliografia sobre arbitraje comercial en las Americas." Compiled by Marvin G. Goldman for the Second Inter-American Conference of Commercial Arbitration, November 7-9, 1968. In, Segunda Conferencia Interamericana de Arbitraje Comercial, *Memoria*. Nov., 1968.

Buenos Aires. Bolsa de Comercio. Biblioteca. *Arbitraje comercial; bibliografia*. Buenos Aires, 1967. 7 p.

de Angelis, Dante Barrios. "Bibliografía; el juicio arbitral." In, de Angelis, Dante Barrios, *El juicio arbitral*. Montevideo, 1956. p. 427-433.

Domke, Martin. "Bibliography (of international commercial arbitration) 1948-1958." In, *International trade arbitration: a road to world-wide cooperation*. Edited by Martin Domke. New York, American Arbitration Association, 1958. p. 296-311.

Fouchard, Philippe. "Bibliographie (sur l'arbitrage commercial international)." In, Fouchard, Philippe, *L'arbitrage commercial international*. Paris, Librairie Dalloz, 1965. p. 561-571.

International Chamber of Commerce. "Bibliography (on international commercial arbitration)." In, United Nations. Economic and Social Council. Committee on Non-Governmental Organizations, *Enforcement of international arbitral awards; statement submitted by the International Chamber of Commerce*. New York, Feb. 25, 1954. p. 4-8. (U.N. Doc. E/C.2/373/Add.1).

January, William H., comp. *Bibliografia sobre arbitraje comercial en Latino America*. Recopilada por William H. January para la Asociacion Americana de Arbitraje en la Biblioteca de Congreso de EE. UU. Washington, D.C., 1967. 10 p.

Rivkin, Donald H. "Bibliography on international litigation and arbitration." In, *A lawyer's guide to international business transactions*. Edited by Walter S. Surrey and Crawford Shaw. Philadelphia, Joint Committee on Continuing Legal Education of the American Law Institute and the American Bar Association, 1963. p. 993-1010.

United Nations. Commission on International Trade Law (2d session, Geneva, March 3, 1969). *Bibliography on arbitration law*. Geneva, 1969. 54 p. (U.N. Doc. A/CN.9/24/Add. 1, March 10, 1969).

Yale University. School of Law. "(Bibliography on international commercial arbitration)." In, Yale University. School of Law, *International finance and investment*. Dobbs Ferry, N.Y., Oceana, 1964. p. 696-701.

CONFERENCES, CONGRESSES, SYMPOSIA, ETC.

Buenos Aires. Bolsa de Comercio. *Antecedentes de la Primera Conferencia Interamericana de Arbitraje Comercial realizada en Buenos Aires durante los dias 2, 3 y 4 de Abril de 1967*. Buenos Aires, 1967. Variously paged.

Conferencia Interamericana de Arbitraje Comercial (primera). *Despachos de las comisiones que fueron considerados por la conferencia.* Buenos Aires, Federacion Argentina de Colegios de Abogados, April, 1967. 18 p.

Indian Council of Arbitration. *International seminar on commercial arbitration, 18th and 19th March, 1968.* New Delhi, 1968. 374 p.

——————————. *Seminar on international commercial arbitration, 15th March, 1967.* New Delhi, 1967. Variously paged.

"International arbitration: a symposium, Jan. 20, 1966, British Institute of International and Comparative Law. The principles and practice of international arbitration." *International and Comparative Law Quarterly.* 15:718-748. 1966.

Second International Arbitration Congress, Rotterdam, 6-9 July, 1966. "Reports." *Common Market Law Review.* 4:365-371. 1966.

Segunda Conferencia Interamericana de Arbitraje Comercial. *Memoria de la Segunda conferencia . . . ciudad de Mexico, Noviembre de 1968.* Mexico, D.F., La Camara Nacional de Comercio de la Ciudad de Mexico and Barra Mexicana-Colegio de Abogados, 1968. 73 p.

"Symposium—counseling mid-continent clients who trade abroad." *University of Missouri at Kansas City Law Review.* 34:1-93. 1966.

"Symposium on problems and processes of international commercial arbitration." *International Law Bulletin.* 2:44-75. 1963.

"A symposium on state trading." *Vanderbilt Law Review.* 20:253-578. 1967.

United Nations. Economic Commission for Asia and the Far East. "ECAFE Conference on Commercial Arbitration (held from 5-8 January, 1966 at Bangkok, Thailand.)" *ECAFE Centre for Commercial Arbitration News Bulletin.* TRADE/CA/NEWS 4:20-36. 1966.

United Nations. Economic Commission for Asia and the Far East. Committee on Trade (9th Session, 24 January—2 February, 1966, Bangkok, Thailand). *Report of the Conference on Commercial Arbitration.* Bangkok, Jan. 19, 1966. 29 p. (U.N. Doc. E/CN.11/TRADE/L.92 Corr. 1).

U.S. Department of State. *Official report of the U.S. delegation to the UN Conference on International Commercial Arbitration, New York, May 20-June 10, 1958.* Prepared by Charles H. Sullivan. Washington, D.C., Dept. of State, 1958. i, 27 p. Reproduced from typescript.

DOCUMENTS: GOVERNMENTS; INTER-GOVERNMENTAL ORGANIZATIONS; NON-GOVERNMENTAL ORGANIZATIONS

American Arbitration Association. *Inter-American commercial arbitration.* A report submitted to the Inter-American Council of Commerce and Production. By Charles Robert Norberg. New York, 1966. 10(4) p.

American Bar Association. Section of International and Comparative Law. Committee on International Unification of Private Law. *Report.* Washington, D.C., July, 1959. Variously paged.

American Bar Association. Special Committee on International Unification of Private Law. *Report.* By Soia Mentschikoff and Nicholas De B. Katzenbach. Chicago, American Bar Foundation, July, 1961. 88 p.

Buenos Aires. Bolsa de Comercio. *Antecedentes sobre el regimen arbitraje comercial.* Buenos Aires, 1966? Variously paged.

Council of Europe. *Agreement relating to application of the European convention on international commercial arbitration.* Strasbourg, (n.d.) 8 p. (European treaty series no. 42).

——————————. *Explanatory report of the European convention providing a uniform law on arbitration.* Strasbourg, 1967. 52 p.

Council of Europe. Consultative Assembly. *Report on arbitration in respect of international relations of private law. (Rapporteur: M. Wahl). Draft recommendation presented by the Legal committee.* Strasbourg, December 18, 1957. 26 p. (Its Doc. 769).

Czechoslovakia. Chamber of Commerce. *The Arbitration Court of the Chamber of Commerce of Czechoslovakia.* Prague, 1962. 71 p.

Gt. Brit. Private International Law Committee. *Recognition and enforcement of foreign arbitral awards. The fifth report of the . . . Committee, Oct., 1961.* London, H.M. Stationery Off., 1961. 33 p. (Cmnd. 1515).

Indian Council of Arbitration. *Facilities for international commercial arbitration in India.* New Delhi, June, 1966. 57 p.

——————————. *Standard contract forms and model arbitration clauses for use in foreign trade contracts.* New Delhi, June, 1966. 24 p.

Inter-American Commercial Arbitration Commission. *Inter-American commercial arbitration; a report submitted by the Commission to the National chambers of commerce and industry, the Inter-American council of commerce and production, bar associations, and international institutions of the Western hemisphere.* New York, April 1, 1968. 23 p. + annexes.

International Chamber of Commerce. *Guide to ICC arbitration.* Paris, Feb., 1963. 40 p.

International Institute for the Unification of Private Law. *Draft of a uniform law on arbitration in respect of international relations of private law and explanatory report.* Rome, 1954. 68 p.

International Olive Oil Council. *Model of standard international contract for the sale of olive oil.* Madrid, 1966. 2 p. (Its Doc. E.107/Doc. No. 1, 19th July, 1966).

International Wool Textile Organization. *International wool textile arbitration agreement. Revised text adopted at the 34th International wool conference, London, 1965.* London, 1965. 1 l.

Japan Commercial Arbitration Commission. "Articles of the Association; revised June 14, 1963." *ECAFE Centre for Commercial Arbitration News Bulletin.* TRADE/CA/NEWS 6:7-16. 1967.

Japan Shipping Exchange, Inc. Documentary Committee. *Notes on the "Beizai" Charter party 1964.* Tokyo, 1964. 18 p.

Latin American Free Trade Association. "Protocol for the settlement of disputes. (Done at Asunción, Paraguay, Sept. 2, 1967.)" *International Legal Materials.* 7:747-756. 1968.

United Nations. Commission on International Trade Law. *Report of the Commission . . . on the work of its first session, 29 Jan.–26 Feb., 1968.* New York, 1968. iv, 46p. (General Assembly official records, 23rd sess., supp. no. 16 (A/7216)).

——————————. (2d session, Geneva, March 3, 1969). *International commercial arbitration; report of the Secretary-General.* New York, Feb. 26, 1969. 68,2,2 p. (U.N. Doc. A/CN.9/21).

United Nations. Economic Commission for Asia and the Far East. Centre for Commercial Arbitration. *International commercial arbitration by the Centre . . . . Report submitted to the Seminar on international commercial arbitration (New Delhi, 18-19 March, 1968).* Bangkok, 1968. 56 p. + footnotes.

United Nations. Economic Commission for Asia and the Far East. Centre for the Promotion of Commercial Arbitration. *News Bulletin.* Nov., 1964- . (Its Doc. TRADE/CA/News 1-). Mimeo.

United Nations. Economic Commission for Asia and the Far East. Committee on Trade. *Improvement of existing arbitration facilities and techniques. Report by the Office of legal affairs of the United Nations Secretariat (for) the Working party of experts on commercial arbitration, 11-17 January, 1962, Bangkok, Thailand.* Bangkok, 1962. 18,2,2,23 p. (U.N. Doc. Trade/Arb/ 7,8,9,11, Jan. 9-10, 1962).

United Nations. Economic Commission for Europe. Committee on the Developments of Trade. Ad Hoc Working Group on Arbitration (6th session). *Final version of the handbook of national and international institutions active in the field of international commercial arbitration.* Geneva. United Nations, Dec. 3, 1958. 621 p. (U.N. Doc. Trade/WP1/15/Rev.1 Vol. I-V).

RULES

International Chamber of Commerce. *Rules of conciliation and arbitration in force on 1st June 1955.* Paris, 1967. 20 p.

International Olive Oil Council. *Rules of procedure of the International Arbitration Board set up within the International Olive Oil Council. (Art. 3 of the rules for reconciliation and arbitration).* Madrid, 1966. 7 p. (Its Doc. E.22/ Doc. No. 9, 25th April, 1966).

United Nations. Economic Commission for Asia and the Far East. Centre for Commercial Arbitration. *ECAFE rules for international commercial arbitration and ECAFE standards for conciliation.* Bangkok, 1966. 6 p.

United Nations. Economic Commission for Europe. *Arbitration rules.* Geneva, Jan., 1966. 9 p. (U.N. publication. Sales number: 66. II. E/Mim. 4.)

Zurich. Chamber of Commerce. *Conciliation and arbitration rules.* Zurich, [1961]. 10 p.

TREATIES AND CONVENTIONS

Council of Europe. *European convention providing a uniform law on arbitration.* Strasbourg, Jan. 20, 1966. 22 p. (European treaty series no. 56).

United Nations Conference on International Commercial Arbitration (New York, 20 May–10 June, 1958). *Final act and convention on the recognition and enforcement of foreign arbitral awards.* New York, 1958. 12 p. (U.N. Doc. E/CONF.26/8/Rev. 1, E/CONF.26/9/Rev. 1).

United Nations. Economic Commission for Europe. *Final act and European convention on international commercial arbitration. Special meeting of plenipotentiaries for the purpose of negotiating and signing a European convention on international commercial arbitration.* Geneva, April 21, 1961. 3 p. (U.N. Doc. E/ECE 423 and E/ECE/Trade/48).

U. S. Congress. Senate. *Convention on the recognition and enforcement of foreign arbitral awards. Message from the President of the United States transmitting the convention . . . . adopted at New York on June 10, 1958.* Washington, D. C., Govt. Printing Off., 1968. 44 p. (Executive E, 90th Cong., 2d session).

INTERNATIONAL PUBLIC ARBITRATION
A SELECTED BIBLIOGRAPHY

Emphasizing Current Materials

BOOKS

Carabiber, Charles. *L'arbitrage international entre gouvernements et particuliers.* Paris, Recueil Sirey, 1950. 102 p.

Carlston, Kenneth S. *The process of international arbitration.* New York, Columbia University Press, 1946. xiv, 318 p.

Cattan, Henry. *The evolution of oil concession in the Middle East and North Africa.* Dobbs Ferry, N.Y., Oceana Publications, 1967. xiv, 173 p.

——————. *The law of oil concessions in the Middle East and North Africa.* Dobbs Ferry, N.Y., Oceana Publications, 1967. xiv, 200 p.

Chapal, Philippe. *L'arbitrabilité des différends internationaux.* Préface de M. J. Charpentier. Paris, A. Pedone, 1967. 294 p. (Publications de la Revue générale de droit international public. Nouvelle série no. 10).

Chaudhri, Mohammed Ahsen, ed. *The prospects of international arbitration.* Karachi, Pakistan Publishing House, 1966. 131 p.

David Davies Memorial Institute of International Studies. *Report of a study group on the peaceful settlement of international disputes.* London, 1966. ii, 289 p.

Delaume, Georges R. *Legal aspects of international lending and economic development financing.* Dobbs Ferry, N.Y., Oceana Publications, 1967. xxiii, 371 p.

Fatouros, A. A. *Government guarantees to foreign investors.* New York and London, Columbia University Press, 1962. xxvi, 411 p.

Franck, Thomas M. *The structure of impartiality; examining the riddle of one law in a fragmented world.* New York, Macmillan, 1968. 344 p.

Friedmann, Wolfgang. *The changing structure of international law.* New York, Columbia University Press, 1964. xvi, 410 p.

Hudson, Manley O. *International tribunals past and future.* Washington, D.C., Carnegie Endowment for International Peace and Brookings Institution, 1944. xii, 287 p.

Iklé, Fred Charles. *How nations negotiate.* New York, Harper and Row, 1964. xii, 274 p.

International arbitration liber amicorum for Martin Domke. Edited by Pieter Sanders. The Hague, Martinus Nijhoff, 1967. viii, 357 p. + bibliography of selected writings by Martin Domke.

Jenks, C. Wilfred. *The prospects of international adjudication.* London, Stevens and Sons Ltd., 1964. xl, 805 p.

Jessup, Philip C. *Transnational law.* New Haven, Conn., Yale University Press, 1959 (c. 1956). 113 p.

Johnston, Douglas M. *The international law of fisheries; a framework for policy-oriented inquiries.* New Haven, Yale University Press, 1965. xxiv, 554 p.

Lall, Arthur. *Modern international negotiation; principles and practice.* By Arthur Lall. New York, Columbia University Press, 1966, xii, 404 p.

Lillich, Richard B. *International claims: postwar British practice.* Syracuse, N.Y., Syracuse University Press, 1967. 192 p.

——————. *International claims: their adjudication by national commissions.* Foreword by Martin Domke. Syracuse, N.Y., Syracuse University Press, 1962. 140 p.

——————. *International claims: their preparation and presentation.* By Richard B. Lillich and Gordon A. Christenson. Syracuse, N.Y., Syracuse University Press, 1962. 173 p.

——————. *The protection of foreign investment; six procedural studies.* Syracuse, N.Y., Syracuse University Press, 1965. 222 p.

Nantwi, E. K. *The enforcement of international judicial decisions and arbitral awards in public international law.* Leyden, A. W. Sijhoff, 1966. xv, 209 p.

Nwogugu, E. I. *The legal problems of foreign investment in developing countries.* Dobbs Ferry, N.Y., Oceana Publications, 1965. xxv, 320 p.

Sandifer, Durward V. *Evidence before international tribunals.* Chicago, Foundation Press, 1939. xii, 443 p.

Schwarzenberger, Georg. *International law. Vol. I—International law as applied by international courts and tribunals.* 2d ed. London, Stevens and Sons, Ltd., 1949. liv, 681 p.

Siksek, Simon G. *The legal framework for oil concessions in the Arab world.* Beirut, The Middle East Research and Publishing Center, 1960. xii, 140 p. (Middle East oil monographs no. 2).

Simpson, J. L. *International arbitration law and practice.* By J. L. Simpson and Hazel Fox. New York, Frederick A. Praeger, 1959. xx, 330 p.

Sørensen, Max, ed. *Manual of public international law.* London, Macmillan, 1968. lxv, 930 p.

Whiteman, Marjorie M. *Digest of international law.* Vol. 3, Oct. 1964, iv, 1261 p.; Vol. 8, Sept. 1967, v, 1291 p., Washington, D.C., Gov't. Pr. Off. (Dept. of State publications 7737, 8290).

PERIODICAL ARTICLES, ESSAYS, ETC.

Batiffol, Henri. "Arbitration clauses concluded between French government-owned enterprises and foreign private parties." *Columbia Journal of Transnational Law.* 7:32-47. 1968.

Broches, A. "The Convention on the settlement of investment disputes between states and nationals of other states: applicable law and default procedure." In, *International arbitration liber amicorum for Martin Domke.* Edited by Pieter Sanders. The Hague, Martinus Nijhoff, 1967. p. 12-22.

——————. "The Convention on the settlement of investment disputes; some observations on jurisdiction." *Columbia Journal of Transnational Law.* 5:263-280. 1966.

——————. "Development of international law by the International Bank for Reconstruction and Development." In, American Society of International Law, *Proceedings at its 59th annual meeting, April 22-24, 1965, Washington, D.C.* Washington, D.C., 1965. p. 33-38.

Carabiber, Charles. "L'immunité de juridiction et d'exécution des Etats, collectivités et établissements publics au regard de l'obligation assumée par une clause compromissoire insérée dans les contrats internationaux de droit privé." In, *International arbitration liber amicorum for Martin Domke.* Edited by Pieter Sanders. The Hague, Martinus Nijhoff, 1967. p. 23-43.

Carlston, Kenneth S. "International arbitration procedure." *Arbitration Journal.* (n.s.) 9:83-88. 1954.

Chaudhri, Mohammed Ahsen. "International arbitration since 1945." In, *The prospects of international arbitration.* Edited by Mohammed Ahsen Chaudhri. Karachi, Pakistan Publishing House, 1966. p. 1-20.

Delaume, Georges R. "Convention on the settlement of investment disputes between states and nationals of other states." *International Lawyer.* 1:64-80. 1966.

——————. "La convention pour le règlement des différends relatifs aux investissements, entre états et ressortissants d'autres états." *Journal du Droit International.* 93:26-61. 1966.

——————. "Jurisdictional aspects of international loans." *Columbia Journal of Transnational Law.* 3:3-18. 1964.

Dobrovir, William A. "A gloss on the Tate Letter's restrictive theory of sovereign immunity." *Virginia Law Review.* 54:1-19. 1968.

Domke, Martin. "The arbitration of international investment controversies." In, International Investment Law Conference, *Proceedings.* Washington, D.C., 1958. p. 1-13.

——————. "International civil aviation sets new pattern." *International Arbitration Journal.* 1:20-29. 1945.

——————. "The Israeli-Soviet oil arbitration." *American Journal of International Law.* 53:787-806. 1959.

——————. "A report of the 1961 Paris arbitration conference." *Arbitration Journal.* (n.s.) 16:131-142. 1961.

——————. "La risoluzione delle controversie in materia d'investimenti internazionali." *Rivista del Diritto Commerciale.* 55:92-101. 1957.

Farley, Andrew N. "Commentary: the Convention on the settlement of investment disputes between states and nationals of other states." *Duquesne University Law Review.* 5:19-30. 1966.

Farmanfarma, Abolbashar. "The oil agreement between Iran and the International Oil Consortium: the law controlling." *Texas Law Review.* 34:259-287. 1955.

Fraser, Henry S. "A sketch of the history of international arbitration." *Cornell Law Quarterly.* 11:179-208. 1926.

Goldie, L. F. E. "International arbitration and settlements." (From an article by L. F. E. Goldie, "Liability for damage and the progressive development of international law.") *International and Comparative Law Quarterly.* 14: 1226-1233. 1965.

Griffin, William L. "International claims of nationals of both the claimant and respondent states—the case history of a myth." *International Lawyer.* 1:400-423. 1967.

Haight, G. W. "O.E.C.D. resolution on the protection of foreign property." *International Lawyer.* 2:326-353. 1968.

Hussanein, Mohammed Tewfik. "The Permanent court of arbitration." In, *The prospects of international arbitration.* Edited by Mohammed Ahsen Chaudhri. Karachi, Pakistan Publishing House, 1966. p. 52-73.

Ketcham, William T., Jr. "Arbitration between a state and a foreign private party." In, Southwestern Legal Foundation, International and Comparative Law Center, *Rights and duties of private investors abroad.* Albany, Matthew Bender and Co., 1965. p. 403-425.

Kunz, Josef L. "The Pact of Bogotá." *Arbitration Journal.* (n.s.) 3:147-155. 1948.

Larsen, Paul B. "Arbitration in bilateral air transport agreements." *Arkiv for Luftrett.* 2:145-164. 1964.

Lillich, Richard B. "The Gut Dam claims agreement with Canada." *American Journal of International Law.* 59:892-898. 1965.

——————. "International claims: their settlement by lump sum agreements." In, *International arbitration liber amicorum for Martin Domke.* Edited by Pieter Sanders. The Hague, Martinus Nijhoff, 1967. p. 143-156.

Moore, Michael M. "International arbitration between states and foreign investors —the World Bank Convention." *Stanford Law Review.* 18:1359-1380. 1966.

Rao, P. Chandrasekhara. "Indo-Pakistan agreement on the Rann of Kutch: form and content." *Indian Journal of International Law.* 5:176-185. 1965.

Re, Edward D. "International claims adjudication: the United States–Canadian agreement." *Buffalo Law Review.* 17:125-134. Fall 1967.

——————. "The presettlement adjudication of international claims." In, *International arbitration liber amicorum for Martin Domke.* Edited by Pieter Sanders. The Hague, Martinus Nijhoff, 1967. p. 214-225.

Reisman, William M. "The enforcement of international judgments." *American Journal of International Law.* 63:1-27. 1969.

——————. "Book review: International arbitration liber amicorum for Martin Domke. Edited by Pieter Sanders." *Syracuse Law Review.* 20:166-180. 1968.

Rivkin, Donald H. "International litigation and arbitration." *University of Missouri at Kansas City Law Review.* 34:60-77. 1966.

Schachter, Oscar. "The enforcement of international judicial and arbitral decisions." *American Journal of International Law.* 54:1-24. 1960.

Scheuner, Ulrich. "Decisions ex aequo et bono by international courts and arbitral tribunals." In, *International arbitration liber amicorum for Martin Domke.* Edited by Pieter Sanders. The Hague, Martinus Nijhoff, 1967. p. 275-288.

Schrader, George D. "The Communications satellite corporation: a new experiment in government and business." *Kentucky Law Journal.* 53:732-742. 1965.

Schwarzenberger, G. "The arbitration pattern and the protection of property abroad." In, *International arbitration liber amicorum for Martin Domke.* Edited by Pieter Sanders. The Hague, Martinus Nijhoff, 1967. p. 313-321.

Schwebel, Stephen M. "Arbtration and the exhaustion of local remedies." By Stephen M. Schwebel and J. Gillis Wetter. *American Journal of International Law.* 60:484-501. 1966.

Sirefman, Josef P. "The World bank plan for investment dispute arbitration." *Arbitration Journal.* (n.s.)20:168-178.1965.

Sohn, Louis B. "Arbitration of international disputes ex aequo et bono." In, *International arbitration liber amicorum for Martin Domke.* Edited by Pieter Sanders. The Hague, Martinus Nijhoff, 1967. p. 330-337.

——————. "Report on international arbitration; Committee on the Charter of the United Nations." In, International Law Association, *Report of the 52nd Conference, Helsinki 1966.* London, 1967. p. 323-356.

Ssekandi, Francis M. "Contracts between a state and a foreign private company; reflections on the effectiveness of the arbitration process." *East African Law Journal.* 2:281-298. 1966.

Sucharitkul, Sompong. "Good offices as a peaceful means of settling regional differences." In, *International arbitration liber amicorum for Martin Domke.* Edited by Pieter Sanders. Hague, Martinus Nijhoff, 1967. p. 338-347.

Summers, Lionel M. "International arbitration." In, *World peace through law; the Washington World Conference.* St. Paul, Minn., West Publishing Co., 1967. p. 299-310.

Washburn, John N. "Arbitration procedures for INTELSAT's legal disputes." *Arbitration Journal.* (n.s.)23:97-102. 1968.

——————————. "INTELSAT: resort to arbitration after November 21, 1966 under the supplementary agreement on arbitration." Washington, D.C., 1967. 14 p. Reproduced from typescript.

BIBLIOGRAPHIES

American Arbitration Association. Library. *Selected bibliography on enforcement in the United States of arbitral agreements to which foreign governments are a party. Petrol Shipping Corp. v. Kingdom of Greece, remanded with instructions 332 F. 2d 370 (1964); and Victory Transport, Inc. v. Comisaria General de Abastecimientos y Transportes, 336 F. 2d 354 (1964), cert. den. 381 U.S. 934 (1965).* New York, 1966? 2 p.

Carnegie Endowment for International Peace. Library. *Bibliography on international arbitration.* Washington, D.C., January 20, 1928. 14 p. (Reading list no. 21).

Green, L. C., comp. "Selected bibliography (on international law as applied by international courts and tribunals)." In, Schwarzenberger, Georg, *International law.* 2d ed. Vol. I. London, Stevens and Sons, Ltd., 1949. p. 631-667.

United Nations. Secretariat. *Bibliography on arbitral procedure.* New York, June 20, 1950. 43 p. (U.N. Doc. A/CN/.4/29).

U.S. Library of Congress. Division of Bibliography. *List of references on international arbitration.* Compiled under the direction of Appleton Prentiss Clark Griffin, chief bibliographer. Washington, D.C., Gov't. Printing Off., 1908. 151 p.

——————————. *List of references on international courts with special reference to the Permanent Court of International Justice. October 10, 1923.* Washington, D.C., 1923. 27 p. (Select list of references, no. 774). Mimeo.

"World Bank Convention on investment disputes: a bibliographical note." *Arbitration Journal.* (n.s.)21:180-181. 1966.

CASES: ARBITRATION AWARDS

"Aramco arbitration." *International Law Reports.* 27:117-233. 1963.

"Arbitration tribunal established pursuant to the arbitration agreement signed at Paris on Jan. 22, 1963, between the United States of America and France, decided at Geneva on Dec. 22, 1963. Decision of the arbitration tribunal . . . ." *International Legal Materials.* 3:668-720. 1964. Also in *American Journal of International Law.* 58:101. 1964.

"Canada-United States Lake Ontario (Gut Dam) claims arbitration agreement." *International Legal Materials.* 4:468-472. 1965.

"Canada-United States settlement of Lake Ontario (Gut Dam) claims-report of the U. S. agent on the settlement." *International Legal Materials* 8:118-143. 1969.

Carnegie Endowment for International Peace. Division of International Law. *The Hague court reports* . . . Edited with an introduction by James Brown Scott. New York, Oxford University Press, 1916. cxi, 664 p.

Gt. Brit. Foreign Office. *Award of Her Majesty Queen Elizabeth II for the arbitration of a controversy between the Argentine Republic and the Republic of Chile concerning certain parts of the boundary between their territories.* London, H. M. Stationery Off., 1966. 85 p. map.

"Italy-U.S. air transport arbitration: advisory opinion of tribunal. (Given at Geneva, July 17, 1965)." *International Legal Materials.* 4:974-987. 1965.

Moore, John Bassett ed. *History and digest of the international arbitrations to which the United States has been a party . . .* Washingon, D.C., Gov't. Printing Off., 1898. 6 vols.

————— ed. *International adjudications ancient and modern; history and documents . . . Modern series, vols. 1 and 2: Saint Croix River arbitration.* New York, Oxford University Press, 1929, 1930. cxiii, 513 p. xv, 503 p.

"Petroleum Development Ltd. v. Sheikh of Abu Dhabi, (Lord Asquith of Bishopstone, umpire) September 1951." *International Law Reports.* 1951:144-161.

Sapphire International Petroleum Ltd. *Arbitral award delivered in the dispute between Sapphire International Petroleums Limited (Toronto, Canada) and National Iranian Oil Company (Teheran, Iran), March 15, 1963.* Lausanne, Canton of Vaud, Switzerland. 75 p.

Schiedsgerichtshof und Gemischte Kommission für das Abkommen über deutsche Auslandsschulden. *Entscheidungen und Gutachten.* Koblenz, 1956. 43 p.

—————. *Entscheidungen und Gutachten.* Koblenz, 1964. 11 p.

—————. *Entscheidungen und Gutachten.* Koblenz, 1961/I. 24 p.

Schiedskommission für Güter, Rechte und Interessen in Deutschland. *Entscheidungen der Schiedskommission für Güter, Rechte und Interessen in Deutschland.* v. 1- .Koblenz, 1958- .

United Nations. *Reports of international arbitral awards. Recueil des sentences arbitrales.* New York, United Nations. v. 1- . (1948) - .

United States-France Air Transport Arbitration: decision of the tribunal . . . decided at Geneva on December 22, 1963. 123 p.

CASES: CASE COMMENTS, ARBITRATION AWARDS

"A comparison of choice-of-law methods for arbitration of contracts between a state and a foreign corporation." *Saint Louis University Law Journal.* 10:408-414. 1966.

Dennis, William Jefferson, *Tacna and Arica; an account of the Chile-Peru boundary dispute and of the arbitrations by the United States.* Hamden, Conn., Archon Books, 1967. xviii, 332 p.

Gomez Robledo, Antonio. *Mexico y el arbitraje internacional; el Fondo piadoso de las Californias, la Isla de la Pasion, el Chamizal.* Mexico, D. F., Editorial Porrua, S. A., 1965. 407 p.

"International air transport—treaty interpretation. Italy-United States air transport arbitration. Advisory opinion of tribunal July 17, 1965." *American Journal of International Law.* 60:413-418. 1966.

Lalive, Jean-Flavien. "Unilateral alteration or abrogation by either party to a contract between a state and a foreign national." In, Southwestern Legal Foundation, International and Comparative Law Center, *Rights and duties of private investors abroad.* Albany, Matthew Bender and Co., 1965. p. 265-279.

Larsen, Paul B. "The United States-Italy air transport arbitration: problems of treaty interpretation and enforcement." *American Journal of International Law.* 61:496-520. 1967.

Metzger, Stanley D. "Treaty interpretation and the United States-Italy air transport arbitration." *American Journal of International Law.* 61:1007-1011. 1967.

Nussbaum, Arthur. "The arbitration between the Lena Goldfields, Ltd. and the Soviet government." *Cornell Law Quarterly.* 36:31-53. 1950.

Potter, Pitman B. *The Wal Wal arbitration.* Washington. D.C., Carnegie Endowment for International Peace, 1938. vii, 182 p.

Stuyt, A. M. *Survey of international arbitrations, 1794-1938.* The Hague, Martinus Nijhoff, 1939. xi, 479 p.

Suratgar, David. "The Sapphire arbitration award, the procedural aspects: a report and a critique." *Columbia Journal of Transnational Law.* 3:152-209. 1965.

Verdross, Alfred. "Zwei schweizer Schiedssprüche über quasi-völkerrechtliche Verträge." *Swiss Yearbook of International Law.* 21:15-24. 1964.

DOCUMENTS: GOVERNMENTS

"India-Pakistan agreement on cease-fire in Rann of Kutch. Signed at New Delhi, June 30, 1965." *International Legal Materials.* 4:921-923. 1965.

U.S. Congress. Senate. Committee on Foreign Relations (88.1). *Convention . . . for solution of . . . the Chamizal. Hearings . . . on Executive N, Dec. 12 and 13, 1963.* Washington, D.C., Gov't. Printing Off., 1963. 134 p.

DOCUMENTS: INTER-GOVERNMENTAL BODIES

Council of Europe. Consultative Assembly. 7th session. *Draft European Convention for the peaceful settlement of disputes. Draft recommendation presented on behalf of the Committee on legal and administrative questions by M. Rolin.* Strasbourg, June 21, 1955. 39 p. (Doc. 356).

——————. "Opinion on O.E.C.D. draft convention on the protection of foreign property. Opinion No. 39 (1963)" *International Legal Materials.* 3:133-150. 1964.

——————. 7th session. *Recommendation 79 (1955) on the draft European Convention for the peaceful settlement of disputes.* Strasbourg, 1955. 13 p.

——————. 6th session. *Request by the Committee of Ministers for an opinion on the Draft European convention for the peaceful settlement of disputes.* Strasbourg, September 13, 1954. 13 p. (Doc. 271).

Hague. Bureau International de la Permanent Court of Arbitration. *Rapport du Conseil administratif de la Cour permanente d'arbitrage . . . sur les travaux de la Cour, sur le fonctionnement des services administratifs et sur les dépenses de l'exercice 1968.* La Haye, 1969.

International Centre for Settlement of Investment Disputes. *Convention on the settlement of investment disputes between states and nationals of other states; documents concerning the origin and the formulation of the convention.* Washington, D.C., 1968. V. II, part 1, Doc. 1-43, part 2, Doc. 44-146; iii, 1088 p.

——————. *Annual report,* 1967- . Washington, D.C., 1967.

——————. *Model clauses recording consent to the jurisdiction of the . . . Centre.* Washington, D.C., 1968. 24 p.

International Telecommunications Satellite Consortium. *Supplementary agreement on arbitration. Entered into force Nov. 21, 1966.* 9 p. Reproduced from typescript.

Organization of Arab Petroleum Exporting Countries. "Agreement. (Done at Beirut, Lebanon, January 9, 1968)." *International Legal Materials*. 7:759-769. 1968.

United Nations. *Charter of the United Nations together with the Statute of the International Court of Justice. Signed at the United Nations Conference on International Organization, San Francisco, Calif., June 26, 1945.* Washington, D.C., Gov't. Printing Off., 1947. 84 p. (Dept. of State publications 2353, conference series 74).

United Nations. Economic and Social Council. Committee on Non-Governmental Organizations. *Enforcement of international arbitral awards; statement submitted by the International chamber of commerce* . . . New York, Feb. 2, 1954. 15 p. (U.N. Doc. E/C.2/R.19).

United Nations. Economic Commission for Africa. *Investment laws and regulations in Africa.* New York, 1965. 79 p. (U.N. Doc. E/CN.14/INR/28/REV. 2).

United Nations. International Law Commission. "Arbitral procedure." In, *Yearbook of the International Law Commission 1957.* Vol. II, p. 1-15 (U.N. Doc. A/CN.4/SER. A/1957/ADD. 1).

——————. *1958.* Vol. 1, p. 5-84, 95-100, 217-233 (U.N. Doc. A/CN.4/SER. A/1958).

United Nations. Secretariat. *Arbitral procedure; commentary on draft on arbitral procedure* . . . New York, May 5, 1953. 126 p. (U.N. Doc. A/CN.4/L.40).

——————. *Commentary on the draft convention on arbitral procedure, adopted by the International Law Commission at its fifth session.* New York, 1955. viii, 260 p. (U.N. Doc. A/CN.4/92).

DOCUMENTS: NON-GOVERNMENTAL BODIES

International Law Association. American Branch.
Proceedings and Committee Reports
1961-1962. p. 63-66
1963-1964. p. 137-141
1965-1966. p. 30-34
1967-1968. p. 45-49.
International Law Association.
Report of the 50th Conference, Brussels, 1962. p. 253-259.
Report of the 51st Conference, Tokyo, 1964. p. 894-899.
Report of the 52d Conference, Helsinki, 1966. p. 804-809.
Report of the 53rd Conference, Buenos Aires, 1968 – p.

CONFERENCES, CONGRESSES, SYMPOSIA, ETC.

Congres International d'Arbitrage. Rotterdam, 6-9 juillet 1966. *Rapport no. III, l'arbitrage dans les relations entre personnes de droit public et personnes de droit privé.* By M. A. Flamme. Rotterdam, 1966. 24 p.

"North Pacific fisheries. Symposium." *Washington Law Review.* 43:1-307. 1967.

The White House Conference on International Cooperation. Washington, D.C., Nov. 28-Dec. 1, 1965. *Report of the Committee on Business and Industry.* Appendix: Proposals submitted by the American Arbitration Association. 37 p.

——————. *Report of the Committee of Development of International Law.* 15 p.

——————. *Report of the Committee on Peaceful Settlement of Disputes.* 28 p.

RULES

"Model rules on arbitral procedure." In, U.N. International Law Commission, *Report . . . covering the work of its tenth session, 28 April-4 July 1958*. New York, 1958. p. 5-8. (General Assembly. Official records: 13th session Supp #9 (A 3859).

Permanent Court of Arbitration. *Rules of arbitration and conciliation for settlement of international disputes between two parties of which only one is a state. Elaborated by the International Bureau in Feb. 1962*. The Hague, 1962. 14 p. Reproduced from typescript.

International Centre for Settlement of Investment Disputes. *ICSID regulations and rules, in effect on January 1, 1968*. Washington, D.C., 1968. 140 p.

TREATIES AND CONVENTIONS

British Railways Board. *International convention concerning the carriage of goods by rail (CIM) of 25th February, 1961 together with the additional uniform regulations. (Applicable as from 1st January, 1965)*. London, 1965. 69 p.

————. *International convention concerning the carriage of passengers and luggage by rail (CIV) of the 25th February, 1961, together with additional uniform regulations. (Applicable as from 1st January, 1965)*. London, 1965. 37 p.

"Communications satellite system arbitration agreement. Opened for signature at Washington, June 4, 1965. Supplementary agreement on arbitration." *International Legal Materials*. 4:735-744. 1965. (T.I.A.S. 5646).

Council of Europe. Consultative Assembly. *Recommendation 36 on the establishment of a European court of justice and of a European act for the peaceful settlement of disputes. Text of a motion adopted at the fourth ordinary session (second part)*. Strasbourg, September, 1952. 4 p.

France. Treaties, etc. 1965. "Algeria-France oil accord. Signed at Algiers, July 29, 1965." *International Legal Materials*. 4:809-913. 1965.

Gt. Brit. Treaties, etc. "Draft treaty between the United Kingdom of Great Britain and Northern Ireland and the Republic of Guatemala relating to the resolution of the dispute over British Honduras (Belize). Mediator's proposals for settlement of the Anglo-Guatemalan dispute . . . 26th April, 1968." In, *Gazette Extraordinary*, British Honduras, Belize City, 29th April 1968. No. 19, p. 213.

Habicht, Max. *Post-war treaties for the pacific settlement of international disputes; a compilation and analysis of treaties of investigation, conciliation, arbitration, and compulsory adjudication, concluded during the first decade following the world war*. Cambridge, Harvard University Press, 1931. xxiv, 1109 p.

Hague. International Peace Conference, 1899. *The Hague Conventions of 1899(I) and 1907(I) for the pacific settlement of international disputes*. Washington, D.C., Carnegie Endowment for International Peace, Division of International Law, 1915. iv, 48 p.

Inter-American Institute of International Legal Studies. *Draft convention to improve the climate for investment in Latin America by facilitating the settlement of disputes. With commentary. Second special meeting on legal and institutional aspects of foreign private investment*. Rio de Janeiro, November 1-5, 1965. 11 p.

International Bank for Reconstruction and Development. *Convention on the settlement of investment disputes between states and nationals of other states submitted to governments by the executive directors of the International Bank for Reconstruction and Development, March 18, 1965.* Washington, D.C., 1965. 81 p. In English, French, and Spanish.

International Civil Aviation Organization. *Convention on international civil aviation.* 3d ed. 1963. 43 p. (Doc. 7300/3).

Manning, William R. ed. *Arbitration treaties among the American nations to the close of the year 1910.* New York, Oxford University Press, 1924. xl, 472 p.

Organisation for Economic Co-operation and Development. "Draft convention on the protection of foreign property; text with notes and comments." *International Legal Materials.* 7:118-143. 1968.

Organisation for Economic Co-operation and Development. *Draft convention on the protection of foreign property and resolution of the Council of the OECD on the draft convention.* Paris, 1967. 60 p.

United Nations. *Systematic survey of treaties for the pacific settlement of international disputes, 1928-1948.* Lake Success, N.Y., 1949. ix, 1202 p.

United Nations. Secretariat. *A survey of treaty provisions for the pacific settlement of international disputes, 1949-1962.* New York, United Nations, 1966. v, 901 p.

U. S. Treaties, etc. 1945-1953 (Truman). *Agreement between the government of the United States of America and the government of the United Kingdom relating to air services between their respective territories. Signed at Bermuda February 11, 1946.* Washington, D.C., 1946. 17 p. (T.I.A.S. 1507).

U. S. Treaties, etc., 1963-1969 (Johnson). *Claims: establishment of international arbitral tribunal to dispose of United States claims relating to Gut Dam. Agreement between the United States . . . and Canada. Signed at Ottawa, March 25, 1965. Ratified by President September 3, 1965. Entered into force October 11, 1966.* Washington, D.C., Govt. Printing Off., 1966. 8 p. (T.I.A.S. 6114).

U. S. Treaties, etc. 1963-1969 (Johnson). *Communications satellite system. Agreement between the United States of America and other governments and special agreement concluded by certain governments and entities designated by governments, establishing interim arrangements for a global commercial communications satellite system and special agreement. Done at Washington, August 20, 1964; entered into force August 20, 1964;* Washington, D.C., 1964. 28 p. (T.I.A.S. 5646).

U. S. Treaties, etc. 1963-1969 (Johnson). *Universal Postal Union. Constitution, convention, and related documents, between the United States of America and other governments revising the Universal Postal Convention of Oct. 3, 1957. Signed at Vienna, July 10, 1964.* Washington, D.C., Gov't. Printing Off., 1966. 325 p. (T.I.A.S. 5881).

LABOR ARBITRATION
A SELECTED BIBLIOGRAPHY
1960 - 1969

BOOKS

Beatty, Marion. *Labor-management arbitration manual.* New York, E. E. Eppler, 1960. viii, 186 p.

Bernstein, Merton C. *Private dispute settlement.* New York, Free press, 1968. xiv, 741 p.

Blackman, John L., Jr., *Presidential seizure in labor .disputes.* Cambridge, Mass., Harvard University Press, 1967. xvi, 351 p.

Braun, Kurt. *Labor disputes and their settlement.* Baltimore, Johns Hopkins Press, 1955. xvi, 343 p.

Brissenden, Paul F. *The settlement of labor disputes on rights in Australia.* Los Angeles, Institute of Industrial Relations, University of California, 1966. ix, 131 p.

Cole, David L. *The quest for industrial peace.* New York, McGraw-Hill Co., 1963. xi, 164 p.

Cox, Archibald. *Cases and materials on labor law.* By Archibald Cox and Derek Curtis Bok. 6th ed. Brooklyn, Foundation Press, 1965. xxix, 1160 p.

Dunlop, John T. *Frontiers of collective bargaining.* By John T. Dunlop and Neil W. Chamberlain, Editors. New York, Harper & Row, 1967. ix, 318 p.

Eggert, Gerald G. *Railroad labor disputes; the beginnings of Federal strike policy.* Ann Arbor, Mich., University of Michigan Press, 1967. viii, 313 p.

Elkouri, Frank. *How arbitration works.* By Frank Elkouri and Edna Asper Elkouri. Rev. (i.e. 2d) ed. Washington, D.C., Bureau of National Affairs, 1960. xviii, 498 p.

Fleming, Robben Wright. *The labor arbitration process.* Urbana, Ill., University of Illinois Press, 1965. ii. 233 p.

Government employee relations report. Washington, D.C., Bureau of National Affairs. No. 1-   . 1963-   .

Gregory, Charles Oscar. *Labor and the law.* 2d rev. ed., with 1961 supplement. New York, Norton, 1961. 619 p.

Hays, Paul R. *Labor arbitration, a dissenting view.* New Haven, Conn., Yale University Press, 1966. vii, 125 p.

Johnston, T. L. *Collective bargaining in Sweden; a study of the labour market and its institutions.* Cambridge, Mass., Harvard University Press, 1962. 358 p.

Kagel, Sam. *Anatomy of a labor arbitration.* Washington, D.C., Bureau of National Affairs, 1961. x, 182 p.

Keller, Leonard A. *The management function: a positive approach to labor relations.* Washington, D.C., Bureau of National Affairs, 1963. xi, 289 p.

Lieberman, Myron. *Collective negotiations for teachers; an approach to school administration.* By Myron Lieberman and Michael H. Moskow. Chicago, Rand McNally and Co., 1966. xxii, 745 p.

McPherson, William H. *The French labor courts: judgment by peers.* By William H. McPherson and Frederic Meyers. Urbana, Ill., Institute of Labor and Industrial Relations, University of Illinois, 1966. viii, 104 p.

Moskow, Michael H. *Teachers and unions.* Philadelphia, University of Pennsylvania, Wharton School of Finance and Commerce, Industrial Research Unit, 1966. xiii, 288 p.

Northrup, Herbert R. *Compulsory arbitration and government intervention in labor disputes; an analysis of experience.* Washington, D.C., Labor Policy Association, 1966. ix, 449 p.

Roberts, Harold S., ed. *The challenge of industrial relations in the Pacific-Asian countries.* Edited by Harold S. Roberts and Paul F. Brissenden. Honolulu, East-West Center Press, 1965. viii, 259 p.

——————. *Compulsory arbitration: panacea or millstone?* Honolulu, Industrial Relations Center, University of Hawaii, Dec. 1965. xii, 162 p.

——————. *A manual for employee-management cooperation in the Federal service.* 3d ed. Honolulu, University of Hawaii, Industrial Relations Center, Aug. 1967. xiii, 275 p.

Shils, Edward B. *Teachers, administrators and collective bargaining.* By Edward B. Shils and C. Taylor Whittier. New York, Thomas Y. Crowell Co., 1968. xi, 580 p.

Slichter, Sumner H. *The impact of collective bargaining on management.* By Summer H. Slichter, James J. Healy and E. Robert Livernash. Washington, D.C., Brookings Institution, 1960. xv, 982 p.

Stieber, Jack. *Democracy and public review; an analysis of the UAW Public Review Board.* By Jack Stieber, Walter E. Oberer, and Michael Harrington. Santa Barbara, Calif., Center for the Study of Democratic Institutions, 1960. 64 p.

Stone, Morris. *Labor-management contracts at work; analysis of awards reported by the American Arbitration Association.* New York, Harper and Brothers, 1961. viii, 307 p.

——————. *Managerial freedom and job security.* New York, Harper and Row, 1964. viii, 262 p.

Straus, Robert Beckwith. *Transit negotiations in New York City; a case study and theory of collective bargaining in the public sector.* Honors thesis, Harvard College, 1967. iv, 138 p.

Summers, Clyde W. *Cases and materials on labor law.* By Clyde W. Summers and Harry H. Wellington. Mineola, New York, Foundation Press, Inc., 1968. xxxviii, 1229 p.

Tracy, Estelle R. *Arbitration cases in public employment.* New York, American Arbitration Association, 1969. xiv, 366 p.

Trotta, Maurice S. *Labor arbitration; principles, practices, issues.* New York, Simmons-Boardman Publishing Corp., 1961. x, 438 p.

Updegraff, Clarence M. Arbitration of labor disputes. 2d ed. Washington, D.C., Bureau of National Affairs, 1961. xv, 321 p.

Vosloo, Willem B. *Collective bargaining in the United States Federal civil service.* Chicago, Public Personnel Association, 1966. x, 226 p.

Warner, Kenneth O., ed. *Collective bargaining in the public service: theory and practice.* Chicago, Public Personnel Association, 1967. viii, 200 p.

Young, F. John L. *The contracting out of work: Canadian and U.S.A. industrial relations experience.* Kingston, Ontario, Industrial Relations Centre, Queen's University, 1964. ix, 150 p.

PERIODICAL ARTICLES, ESSAYS, ETC.

Aaron, Benjamin. "Arbitration in the Federal courts: aftermath of the trilogy."
  UCLA Law Review. 9:360-380. 1962.

——————. "Emergency dispute settlement." In, Southwestern Legal Foundation, *Labor Law Developments,* 1967. Albany, Matthew Bender and Co.,
  1967. p. 185-208.

——————. *An employee relations ordinance for Los Angeles County; report
  and recommendations of the consultants' committee.* Submitted by Benjamin
  Aaron, chm., Lloyd H. Bailer and Howard Block. Los Angeles, July 25,
  1968. 34 p.

——————. "Judicial intervention in labor arbitration." *Stanford Law Review.*
  20:41-56. 1967.

——————. "Reflections on the legal nature and enforceability of seniority
  rights." *Harvard Law Review.* 75:1532-1564. 1962.

——————. "Some procedural problems in arbitration. Symposium on arbitration." *Vanderbilt Law Review.* 10:733-748. 1957.

——————. "The strike and the injunction—problems of remand and removal." In, *Proceedings of New York University eighteenth annual conference on labor.* Washington, D.C., Bureau of National Affairs, 1966. p.
  93-116.

Anderson, Arvid. "Evolving patterns of labor relations in public employment." In,
  Southwestern Legal Foundation, *Labor law developments; proceedings of
  11th annual institute on labor law, Dallas, October 15-17, 1964.* Washington,
  D.C., Bureau of National Affairs, 1965. p. 209-224.

Bernstein, Merton C. "Jurisdictional dispute arbitration: the jostling professors."
  For the complainant, by Merton C. Bernstein. For the respondent, by Edgar
  A. Jones, Jr. *UCLA Law Review.* 14:347-353. 1966.

——————. "Nudging and shoving all parties to a jurisdictional dispute
  into arbitration: the dubious procedure of National Steel." *Harvard Law
  Review.* 78:784-797. 1965.

Blaine, Harry R. "Discipline and discharge in the United States postal service:
  adverse action and appeal." By Harry R. Blaine, Eugene C. Hagburg, and
  Frederick A. Zeller. *Industrial and Labor Relations Review.* 19:92-98. 1965.

Burkey, Lee M. "Privacy, property and the polygraph." *Labor Law Journal.* 18:79-
  89. 1967.

Christensen, Thomas G. S. "Arbitration, Section 301, and the National Labor
  Relations Act." *NYU Law Review.* 37:411-447. 1962.

——————. "The developing law of arbitrability." In, Southwestern Legal
  Foundation, *Labor law developments; proceedings of 11th annual institute
  on labor law, Dallas, October 15-17, 1964.* Washington, D.C., Bureau of
  National Affairs, 1965. p. 119-158.

——————. "Labor arbitration and judicial oversight. Symposium (book
  review)." *Stanford Law Review.* 19:671-697. 1967.

Cole, David. "Inter-relationship: the settlement of jurisdictional disputes." *Labor
  Law Journal.* 10:454-460. 1959.

Collister, Edward G., Jr. "Standards for assignment of work in jurisdictional work
  disputes." *University of Missouri at Kansas City Law Review.* 33:35-60.
  1965.

Cox, Archibald. "The legal nature of collective bargaining agreements." *Michigan Law Review.* 57:1-36. 1958.

——————. "Reflections upon labor arbitration." *Harvard Law Review.* 72:1482-1518. 1959.

——————. "Rights under a labor agreement." *Harvard Law Review.* 69: 601-657. 1956.

"Creeping legalism in labor arbitration: an editorial." *Arbitration Journal.* (n.s.) 13:129-132, 161. 1958.

Cushman, Bernard. "Arbitration and the duty to bargain." *Wisconsin Law Review.* 1967:612-640.

——————. "Voluntary arbitration of new contract terms—a forum in search of a dispute." *Labor Law Journal.* 16:765-777. 1965.

Davey, Harold W. "The Supreme Court and arbitration: the musings of an arbitrator." *Notre Dame Lawyer.* 36:138-145. 1961.

Dunau, Bernard. "Procedural arbitrability—a question for court or arbitrator?" *Labor Law Journal.* 14:1010-1016. 1963.

——————. "Subcontracting and unilateral employer action." In, *Proceedings of New York University eighteenth annual conference on labor.* Washington, D.C., Bureau of National Affairs 1966. p. 219-234.

Dunlop, John T. "Jurisdictional disputes." In, *Proceedings of New York University the second annual conference on labor.* Albany, Matthew Bender and Co., 1949. p. 477-504.

Epstein, Lee. "The agreed case: a problem in ethics." *Arbitration Journal.* (n.s.) 20:41-48. 1965.

Fairweather, Owen. "Implied restrictions on work movements—the pernicious crow of labor contract construction." *Notre Dame Lawyer.* 38:518-554. 1963.

Farmer, Guy. "Compulsory arbitration—a management lawyer's view." *Virginia Law Review.* 51:396-409. 1965.

Feinberg, I. Robert. "Interim relief and provisional remedies in arbitration." In, *Proceedings of New York University 17th annual conference on labor.* Washington, D.C., Bureau of National Affairs, 1964. p 49-63.

Feller, David E. "Compulsory arbitration—a union lawyer's view." *Virginia Law Review.* 51:410-422. 1965.

Fleming, Robben Wright. "Arbitrators and the remedy power." *Virginia Law Review.* 48:1199-1225. 1962.

——————. "The labor court idea." *Michigan Law Review.* 65:1551-1568. 1967.

——————. "Problems of procedural regularity in labor arbitration." *Washington University Law Quarterly.* 1961:221-249.

——————. "Some problems of due process and fair procedures in labor arbitration." *Stanford Law Review.* 13:235-251. 1961.

Foster, Howard G. "Disloyalty to the employer: a study of arbitration awards." *Arbitration Journal.* (n.s.) 20:157-167. 1965.

Givens, Richard A. "Injunctive enforcement of arbitration awards prohibiting strikes; *Ruppert* v. *Engelhofer* as Federal law." *Labor Law Journal.* 17:292-296. 1966.

Gomberg, William. "Special study committees." In, *Frontiers of collective bargaining.* Edited by John T. Dunlop and Neil W. Chamberlain. New York, Harper and Row, 1967. p. 235-251.

Gorske, Robert H. "Arbitration back-pay awards." *Labor Law Journal.* 10:18-27. 1959.

Gregory, Charles O. "Arbitration of grievances under collective labor agreements." *Georgia Law Review.* 1:20-37. 1966.

Gross, James A. "Value judgments in the decisions of labor arbitrators." *Industrial and Labor Relations Review.* 21:55-72. 1967.

Herzog, Paul M. "Voluntary labor arbitration in the United States." By Paul M. Herzog and Morris Stone. *International Labour Review.* 82:301-326. 1960.

Hull, W. J. "Aspects of labour relations in Asia." In, *Labor relations in the Asian countries: proceedings of the Second International Conference on Industrial Relations, Tokyo, Japan, 1967.* Tokyo, Japan Institute of Labour, 1967. p. 63-81.

Johnson, David B. "Dispute settlement in atomic energy plants." *Industrial and Labor Relations Review.* 13:38-53. 1959.

Jones, Edgar A., Jr. "The accretion of federal power in labor arbitration—the example of arbitral discovery." *University of Pennsylvania Law Review.* 116: 830-887. 1968.

——————. "An arbitral answer to a judicial dilemma: the Carey decision and trilateral arbitration of jurisdictional disputes." *UCLA Law Review.* 11:327-357. 1964.

——————. "Autobiography of a decision: the function of innovation in labor arbitration, and the National Steel orders of joinder and interpleader." *UCLA Law Review.* 10:987-1040. 1963.

——————. "Blind man's buff and the *now*-problems of Apocrypha, Inc. and Local 711; discovery procedures in collective bargaining disputes." *University of Pennsylvania Law Review.* 116:571-610. 1968.

——————. "Compulsion and the consensual in labor arbitration." *Virginia Law Review.* 51:369-395. 1965.

——————. "Evidentiary concepts in labor arbitration: some modern variations on ancient legal themes." *UCLA Law Review.* 13:1241-1297. 1966.

——————. "The labor board, the courts, and arbitration—a feasibility study of tribunal interaction in grievable refusals to disclose." *University of Pennsylvania Law Review.* 116:1185-1259. 1968.

——————. "The name of the game is decision—some reflections on arbitrability and authority in labor arbitration." *Texas Law Review.* 46:865-897. 1968.

——————. "On nudging and shoving the national steel arbitration into a dubious procedure." *Harvard Law Review.* 79:327-348. 1965.

——————. "Power and prudence in the arbitration of labor disputes: a venture in some hypotheses." *UCLA Law Review.* 11:675-791. 1964.

——————. "A sequel in the evolution of the trilateral arbitration of jurisdictional labor disputes—the Supreme Court's gift to embattled employers." *UCLA Law Review.* 15:877-895. April 1968.

Katz, Isadore. "Arbitration—favored child of preemption." In, *Proceedings of New York University 17th annual conference on labor.* Washington, D.C., Bureau of National Affairs, 1964. p. 27-47.

King, Bernard T. "The Taylor Act—experiment in public employer-employee relations." *Syracuse Law Review.* 20:1-20. 1968.

Krinsky, Edward B. "Public employment fact-finding in fourteen states." *Labor Law Journal.* 17:532-540. 1966.

Kroner, Jack L. "Minor disputes under the Railway Labor Act: a critical appraisal." *NYU Law Review.* 37:41. 1962.

Kuczma, Julius E. "The missile site labor story." Address before the American Bar Association, Chicago, Ill., Aug. 13, 1963. 24 p.

Kuhn, James W. "The grievance process." In, *Frontiers of collective bargaining.* Edited by John T. Dunlop and Neil W. Chamberlain. New York, Harper and Row, 1967. p. 252-270.

"Labor law—company must arbitrate jurisdictional dispute although only one union will participate. (United States)." *University of Illinois Law Forum.* 1964:482-487.

Laffer, Kingsley M. "The working of Australian compulsory arbitration." In, *The challenge of industrial relations in the Pacific-Asian countries.* Edited by Harold S. Roberts and Paul F. Brissenden. Honolulu, East-West Center Press, 1965. p. 59-80.

Levinson, David. "The locomotive firemen's dispute." *Labor Law Journal.* 17:671-690. 1966.

McCulloch, Frank W. "Arbitration and/or the NLRB." *Arbitration Journal.* (n.s.) 18:3-16. 1963.

McDermott, Thomas J. "Arbitrability: the courts versus the arbitrator." *Arbitration Journal.* (n.s.) 23:18-37. 1968.

——————. "Enforcing no-strike provisions via arbitration." *Labor Law Journal.* 18:579-587. 1967.

——————. "Use of fact-finding boards in labor disputes." *Labor Law Journal.* (n.s.)23:18-37. 1968.

McHugh, William F. "New York's experiment in public employee relations: the Public Employee's Fair Employment Act." *Albany Law Review.* 32:58-95. 1967.

Meltzer, Bernard. "The Supreme Court, arbitrability and collective bargaining." *University of Chicago Law Review.* 28:464-487. 1961.

Miller, Richard Ulric. "Arbitration of new contract wage disputes: some recent trends." *Industrial and Labor Relations Review.* 20:250-264. 1967.

Morgan, C. Baird, Jr. "The adequacy of collective bargaining in resolving the problem of job security and technological change." *Labor Law Journal.* 16:87-99. 1965.

O'Brien, John D. "Should the NLRB arbitrate labor contract disputes?" *Washburn Law Journal.* 6:39-53. 1966.

O'Donoghue, Martin F. "Jurisdictional disputes in the construction industry since CBS." *Georgetown Law Journal.* 52:314. 1964.

"Procedural arbitrability under § 301 of the LMRA." *Yale Law Journal.* 73:1459-1476. 1964.

"The railway work rules dispute—a precedent for compulsory arbitration." *DePaul Law Review.* 14:115-129. 1964.

Sherman, Louis. "National Joint Board for Settlement of Jurisdictional Disputes in the Building and Construction Industry." *Labor Law Journal.* 10:463-474. 1959.

Shulman, Harry. "Reason, contract, and law in labor relations." *Harvard Law Review.* 68:999-1024. 1955.

Smith, Russell A. "Impact of the emerging Federal law of grievance arbitration on judges, arbitrators and parties." By Russell A. Smith and Dallas L. Jones. *Virginia Law Review.* 52:831-912. 1966.

——————. "Subcontracting and union-management legal and contractual relations." *Western Reserve Law Review.* 17:1272-1301. 1966.

——————. "The Supreme Court and labor dispute arbitration: the emerging Federal law." By Russell A. Smith and Dallas L. Jones. *Michigan Law Review.* 63:751-808. 1965.

284 A DICTIONARY OF ARBITRATION

Sovern, Michael I. "§ 301 and the primary jurisdiction of the NLRB." *Harvard Law Review.* 76:529-577. 1963.

Stevens, Carl M. "Mediation and the role of the neutral." In, *Frontiers of collective bargaining.* Edited by John T. Dunlop and Neil W. Chamberlain. New York, Harper and Row, 1967. p. 271-290.

——————. "Reply to Mr. Contini. (Is compulsory arbitration compatible with bargaining?)" *Industrial Relations: A Journal of Economy and Society.* 6:114-116. 1966.

Stieber, Jack. "Grievance arbitration in the United States: an analysis of its functions and effects." In, Gt. Brit. Royal Commission on Trade Unions and Employers' Associations, *Research papers 8; three studies in collective bargaining.* London, H. M. Stationery Off., 1968. p. 1-30.

Stowe, David H. "The Organizational disputes agreement, Industrial Union Dept., AFL-CIO." *Labor Law Journal.* 10:460-462. 1959.

Straus, Donald B. "Labor arbitration and its critics." *Arbitration Journal.* (n.s.) 20:197-211. 1965.

——————. "Labor disputes in Atomic Energy Commission experience." In, *Proceedings of the New York University fourth annual conference on labor.* Albany, Matthew Bender and Co., 1951. p. 233-259.

Summers, Clyde W. "Labor arbitration: a private process with a public function." *Revista Juridica de la Universidad de Puerto Rico.* 34:477-496. 1965.

——————. "Labor law in the Supreme Court: 1964 term." *Yale Law Journal.* 75:59-88. 1965.

Thompson, Arthur A. "Collective bargaining in the public service—the TVA experience and its implications for other government agencies". *Labor Law Journal.* 17:89-98. 1966.

"The use of tripartite boards in labor, commercial, and international arbitration." *Harvard Law Review.* 68:293-339. 1954.

Van Zile, Philip T., II. "The componential structure of labor-management contractual relationships: *Republic Steel Corp.* v. *Maddox* and *Humphrey* v. *Moore.*" *University of Detroit Law Review.* 43:321-353. 1966.

Wagner, Aubrey J. "TVA looks at three decades of collective bargaining." *Industrial and Labor Relations Review.* 22:20-30. 1968.

Wisehart, Arthur M. "Transportation strike control legislation: a congressional challenge." *Michigan Law Review.* 66:1697-1722. 1968.

BIBLIOGRAPHIES

Brickett, Margaret F. "Labor history resources in the U.S. Department of Labor Library." *Labor History.* 2:236-240. 1961.

Canberra, Australia. National Library. *Select bibliography on industrial conciliation and arbitration, with special reference to Australia and New Zealand.* Compiled by Kenneth Binns with the assistance of H. L. White and L. C. Key. Canberra, 1929. 60 p.

Illinois University. Institute of Labor and Industrial Relations. *Labor history in the United States; a general bibliography.* Compiled by Gene S. Stroud and Gilbert E. Donahue. Urbana, Ill., 1961. 167 p.

Jensen, Vernon H., comp. *Bibliography of dispute settlement by third parties.* Compiled by Vernon H. Jensen and Harold G. Ross. Ithaca, N.Y., New York State School of Industrial and Labor Relations at Cornell University, 1955. xxvi, 253 p. Supplements no. 1 and 2 issued 1959 and 1960.

Neufeld, Maurice F., comp. *A representative bibliography of American labor history*. Ithaca, N.Y., New York State School of Industrial and Labor Relations at Cornell University, 1964. ix, 146 p.

U. S. Federal Mediation and Conciliation Service. *Labor-management relations: a bibliography*. Washington, D.C., Nov. 1951. 27 p.

U. S. Library of Congress. Division of Bibliography. *List of recent references on industrial arbitration. January 5, 1920*. Washington, D.C., 1920. 9 f. (Select list of references, no. 350).

——————. *List of recent references on industrial arbitration. (Supplementary to mimeographed list, January 5, 1920) November 2, 1922*. Washington, D.C., 1922. 9 f. (Select list of references, no. 697).

——————. *Select list of references on industrial arbitration*. Compiled under the direction of A.P.C. Griffin, chief of Division of Bibliography. Washington, D.C., Gov't. Printing Off., 1903. 15 p.

U. S. National Labor Relations Board. Library. *Bibliography (on the) Labor Management Relations Act, 1947, as amended by the Labor-Management Reporting and Disclosure Act, 1959*. Compiled by Sylvia H. Washington. Washington, D.C., 1966. 78 (22) p.

——————. *Supplement I 1967*. Washington, D.C., 1967. 39 (6) p.

Vosloo, Willem B., comp. "Bibliography on U.S. government employees)." In,

Vosloo, Willem B., comp. "Bibliography (on U.S. government employees)." In, *service*. Chicago, Public Personnel Association, 1966. p. 183-193.

Warner, Kenneth O., comp. "Annotated bibliography (on public employees)." Compiled by Kenneth O. Warner and Mary L. Hennessy. In, *Public management at the bargaining table*. Edited by Kenneth O. Warner and Mary L. Hennessy. Chicago, Public Personnel Association, 1967. p. 435-474.

CASES: PUBLISHED ARBITRATION AWARDS AND OPINIONS

American Arbitration Association. *Summary of labor arbitration awards, 1959-1967*. New York, American Arbitration Association, 1968. Unpaged.

Bureau of National Affairs. *Labor arbitraton reports; awards of arbitrators, reports of fact-finding boards, court decisions on labor arbitration*. v. 1-   1946- Washington, D.C.

Commerce Clearing House. *Labor arbitration awards*. v. 61-1-   1961- Chicago.

Prentice-Hall, Inc., *Prentice-Hall American labor arbitration awards*. Englewood Cliffs, N.J., 1946-

DOCUMENTS: GOVERNMENTAL BODIES

Australia. Court of Conciliation and Arbitration. *Commonwealth arbitration reports. A report of cases* . . . v. 1- . 1905/07-   . Sydney, Law Book Co. of Australasia Pty. Ltd.

Gt. Brit. Royal Commission on Trade Unions and Employers' Associations. *Research papers 8; three studies in collective bargaining*. London, H. M. Stationery Off., 1968. viii, 64 p.

New York (City). 1966 (Lindsay). *Agreement between representatives of municipal employee organizations and the City of New York on improved collective bargaining procedures*. Includes statement of public members of tripartite panel: Saul Wallen, chm., Philip A. Carey, Vern Countryman, Peter Seitz. New York, American Arbitration Association, Labor Management Institute, March 31, 1966. 23 p.

New York (City). Department of Labor. *Unresolved disputes in public employment.* New York, Dec. 1955. 29 p. (Serial L.R. 9)

New York (City). Laws, statutes, etc. "Executive order no. 52. 'The conduct of labor relations bewteen the City of New York and its employees.'" In, New York (City) Office of Collective Bargaining, *New York City collective bargaining law; Executive order no. 52 . . . ; consolidated rules of the Office of Collective Bargaining.* New York, City Record, 1967. p. 13-23.

——————. "New York City collective bargaining law. (Administrative code, chapter 54; local law 53-1967)." In, New York (City) Office of Collective Bargaining, *New York City collective bargaining law; Executive order no. 52 . . . ; consolidated rules of the Office of Collective Bargaining.* New York, City Record, 1967. p. 1-12.

New York (State). Governor's Committee on Public Employee Relations. *Final report, March 31, 1966.* George W. Taylor, chm., E. Wight Bakke, David L. Cole, John T. Dunlop, Frederick H. Harbison. Albany, 1966. 63 p.

——————. *Interim report, June 17, 1968.* Albany, 1968. 35 p.

——————. "Recommendations for changes in New York State law, Jan. 30, 1969." *Government Employee Relations Report.* p. G-1. No. 283, 1969.

New York (State). Public Employment Relations Board. *Guide for fact-finders.* By Harold R. Newman. Albany, Oct. 23, 1968. 3 p. Mimeo.

——————. *Official decisions, opinions, and related matters.* Albany, Secretary of State, State of New York, 1968. 10 parts.

——————. *Rules of procedure; a guide to the Taylor law.* Albany, 1967. 80 p.

U. S. Atomic Energy Labor-Management Relations Panel. *Report—fiscal years 1957 through 1964.* Washington, D.C., Gov't. Printing Off., 1964. 23 p.

U. S. Bureau of Labor Statistics. *Major collective bargaining agreements. Arbitration procedures.* Washington, D. C., Gov't. Printing Off., 1966. vi, 167 p. (Bull. no. 1425-6)

——————. *Major collective bargaining agreements. Grievance procedures.* Washington, D.C., Gov't. Printing Off., 1964. iv, 80 p. (Bull. no. 1425-1)

U. S. Civil Service Commission. Office of Labor-Management Relations. *Union recognition in the Federal government; listings by Federal departments and agencies of recognitions and agreements under Executive order 10988.* Washington, D.C., Nov. 1967. 364 p.

U. S. Congress. Senate. Committee on the Judiciary. Subcommittee on Improvements in Judicial Machinery (90.1). *U. S. labor court. Hearing before the Subcommittee . . . on S. 176 providing for the establishment of a United States court of labor-management relations.* Oct. 17, 1967. Washington, D.C., Gov't. Printing Off., 1968. iii, 156 p.

U. S. Department of Labor. *Collective bargaining in the basic steel industry; a study of the public interest and the role of government.* Washington, D.C., Gov't. Printing Off., 1961. ix, 317 p.

U. S. Federal Mediation and Conciliation Service. *Memorandum and regulations (regarding disclosure of information by Federal mediators in the course of their official mediation and conciliation duties).* Washington, D.C., (n.d.). 10 p.

U. S. Laws, statutes, etc. *Compilation of laws relating to mediation, conciliation, and arbitration between employers and employees . . .* Compiled by Gilman G. Udell. Washington, D.C., Gov't. Printing Off., 1967. xv, 1035 p.

U. S. Library of Congress. Legislative Reference Service. *Federal legislation to end strikes: a documentary history.* Committee print, 90th Congress, 1st session, prepared for the Subcommittee on Labor of the Committee on Labor and Public Welfare, U. S. Senate. Washington, D.C., Gov't. Printing Off., May 1967. 2 parts, 1354 p.

U. S. President. 1961-1963 (Kennedy). "Executive order 10988; Employee-management cooperation in the Federal service. Jan. 17, 1962."

U. S. President. 1969-   (Nixon). "Executive order 11491; Labor-management relations in the federal service. October 29, 1969, replacing Executive Order 10988." In, *Special Supplement, Government Employee Relations Report,* BNA, No. 320, October 27, 1969.

DOCUMENTS. NON-GOVERNMENTAL BODIES

American Arbitration Association. *Labor arbitration, procedures and techniques.* New York, July 1968. 23 p.

American Federation of Labor and Congress of Industrial Organizations. *The AFL-CIO internal disputes plan. Determinations and reports 1962-63—* Washington, D.C.

——————. *Decisions and recommendations of the AFL-CIO Impartial Umpire.* v. 1- . 1954-58-   Washington, D.C.

American Federation of Labor and Congress of Industrial Organizations. Building and Construction Trades Department. *Plan for settling jurisdictional disputes nationally and locally. April 1, 1965.* Washington, D.C., 1965. 146 p.

Council on Industrial Relations for the Electrical Contracting Industry. (*Facts concerning the Council*). 8th ed. Washington, D.C., Jan. 1964. 38 p.

United Automobile Workers. Public Review Board. *Annual report to the membership of the U.A.W. 1957/58-*   Detroit.

PROCEEDINGS: CONFERENCES, CONGRESSES, SYMPOSIA

International Labour Conference (51st session). "Recommendation 130 . . . concerning the examination of grievances within the undertaking with a view to their settlement." In, International Labour Conference (51st session, Geneva, 1967), *Record of Proceedings.* Geneva, International Labour Office, 1968. p. 852-857.

International Labour Conference (51st session). Committee on Grievances and Communications. "Fifth item on the agenda: examination of grievances and communications within the undertaking. Appendix VIII." In, International Labour Conference (51st session, Geneva, 1967), *Record of Proceedings.* Geneva, International Labour Office, 1968. p. 716-732.

International Labour Office. "Conventions, recommendations, resolutions and additional texts adopted by the International Labour Conference at its 51st session (Geneva, 1967)." In, International Labour Office, *Official Bulletin,* supplement I. Vol. 50, no. 3, July 1967. 67 p.

Levin, Edward, ed. and comp. *New York State public employment relations; an ILR conference (held Nov. 15 1967, New York City).* Ithaca, N.Y., New York State School of Industrial and Labor Relations at Cornell University, April 1968. viii, 22 p.

National Academy of Arbitrators. *Proceedings of the annual meeting.* 1st-7th- 1948-54- . Washington, D.C., Bureau of National Affairs.

1954 cum.   The profession of labor arbitration (cumulative selection of addresses at the first seven annual meetings, 1948 through 1954)

1955, 8th annual meeting	Arbitration today
1956, 9th annual meeting	Management rights and the arbitration process
1957, 10th annual meeting	Critical issues in labor arbitration
1958, 11th annual meeting	The arbitrator and the parties
1959, 12th annual meeting	Arbitration and the law
1960, 13th annual meeting	Challenges to arbitration
1961, 14th annual meeting	Arbitration and public policy
1962, 15th annual meeting	Collective bargaining and the arbitrator's role
1963, 16th annual meeting	Labor arbitration and industrial change
1964, 17th annual meeting	Labor abitration—perspectives and problems
1965, 18th annual meeting	Proceedings of the 18th annual meeting
1966, 19th annual meeting	Problems of proof in arbitration
1967, 20th annual meeting	The arbitrator, the NLRB, and the courts
1968, 21st annual meeting	Developments in American and foreign arbitration

For reasons of space, the individual essays have not been listed in this bibliography. Citations for individual essays are generally to date and number of the annual meeting.

New York University. *Proceedings of the annual conference on labor.* 1st- 1948-   . New York, Matthew Bender and Co.

Rights and obligations of parties under collective agreements. Seminar on collective bargaining: 1966. Proceedings of twin seminars sponsored by Niagara University, St. Bonaventure University, Federal Mediation and Conciliation Service, and Society for the Promotion, Unification and Redevelopment of Niagara, Inc. (SPUR) May 6-7, 1966. St. Bonaventure, N.Y., St. Bonaventure University Press, 1967. xiii, 97 p.

Seminar on collective bargaining, Jamestown Community College and State University of New York at Buffalo, 1967. Proceedings of two seminars sponsored by Federal Mediation and Conciliation Service and others. Edited by Thomas R. Colosi and others. Foreword by William E. Simkin. Jamestown, N.Y., Jamestown Community College Press, 1968. xiii, 112 p.

Slovenko, Ralph, ed. *Symposium on labor relations law.* Baton Rouge, La., Claitor's Bookstore, 1961. xi, 795 p.

Southwestern Legal Foundation. *Labor law developments; proceedings of the annual institute on labor law, Dallas,* 1954-   . Washington, D.C., Bureau of National Affairs, 1955-   .

"Symposium. Arbitration and the courts." *Northwestern University Law Review.* 58:466-582. 1963.

A symposium on collective negotiations in education. Albany, Council for Administrative Leadership, 1968. vii, 60 p.

RULES

American Arbitration Association. *Voluntary labor arbitration rules as amended and in effect Jan. 1, 1970.* New York. 1968. 7 p.

National Joint Board for Settlement of Jurisdictional Disputes. *Procedural rules and regulations as amended . . . appeals board procedures.* (n.p.), July 21, 1965. 30 p.

U. S. Federal Mediation and Conciliation Service. *Arbitration policies, functions, and procedures.* Ch. XII, part 1404—arbitration . . . adopted Oct. 21, 1968. Washington, D.C., 1968. 4 p.

AMERICAN ARBITRATION ASSOCIATION COMMERCIAL ARBITRATION RULES

IMPORTANT

As amended and in effect June 1, 1964

When you include in your Agreements an arbitration clause naming the AAA, you rely on AAA service, and you place upon the Association the responsibility of providing that service. You will enable AAA to carry out that responsibility with maximum speed and efficiency **if you will advise the Association immediately whenever such a clause is used,** and not wait until a dispute arises to inform it of its responsibility.

For the Arbitration of future disputes:—

The American Arbitration Association recommends the following arbitration clause for insertion in all commercial contracts:

STANDARD ARBITRATION CLAUSE

Any controversy or claim arising out of or relating to this contract, or the breach thereof, shall be settled by arbitration in accordance with the Rules of the American Arbitration Association, and judgment upon the award rendered by the Arbitrator(s) may be entered in any Court having jurisdiction thereof.

For the Submission of existing disputes:—

We, the undersigned parties, hereby agree to submit to arbitration under the Commercial Arbitration Rules of the American Arbitration Association the following controversy: (cite briefly). We further agree that the above controversy be submitted to (one) (three) Arbitrators selected from the panels of Arbitrators of the American Arbitration Association. We further agree that we will faithfully observe this agreement and the Rules and that we will abide by and perform any award rendered by the Arbitrator(s) and that a judgment of the Court having jurisdiction may be entered upon the award.

COMMERCIAL ARBITRATION RULES

Section 1. AGREEMENT OF PARTIES — The parties shall be deemed to have made these Rules a part of their arbitration agreement whenever they have provided for arbitration by the American Arbitration Association or under its Rules. These Rules and any amendment thereof shall apply in the form obtaining at the time the arbitration is initiated.

Section 2. NAME OF TRIBUNAL — Any Tribunal constituted by the parties for the settlement of their dispute under these Rules shall be called the Commercial Arbitration Tribunal.

Section 3. ADMINISTRATOR — When parties agree to arbitrate under these Rules, or when they provide for arbitration by the American Arbitration Association and an arbitration is initiated thereunder, they thereby constitute AAA the administrator of the arbitration. The authority and obligations of the administrator are prescribed in the agreement of the parties and in these Rules.

Section 4. DELEGATION OF DUTIES — The duties of the AAA under these Rules may be carried out through Tribunal Administrator, or such other officers or committees as the AAA may direct.

Section 5. NATIONAL PANEL OF ARBITRATORS — The AAA shall establish and maintain a National Panel of Arbitrators and shall appoint Arbitrators therefrom as hereinafter provided.

Section 6. OFFICE OF TRIBUNAL — The general office of a Tribunal is the headquarters of the AAA, which may, however, assign the administration of an arbitration to any of its Regional Offices.

Section 7. INITIATION UNDER AN ARBITRATION PROVISION IN A CONTRACT — Arbitration under an arbitration provision in a contract may be initiated in the following manner:

(a) The initiating party may give notice to the other party of his intention to arbitrate (Demand), which notice shall contain a statement setting forth the nature of the dispute, the amount involved, if any, the remedy sought, and

(b) By filing at any Regional office of the AAA two (2) copies of said notice, together with two (2) copies of the arbitration provisions of the contract, together with the appropriate administrative fee as provided in the Administrative Fee Schedule.

The AAA shall give notice of such filing to the other party. If he so desires, the party upon whom the demand for arbitration is made may file an answering statement in duplicate with the AAA within seven days after notice from the AAA, in which event he shall simultaneously send a copy of his answer to the other party. If a monetary claim is made in the answer the appropriate fee provided in the Fee Schedule shall be forwarded to the AAA with the answer. If no answer is filed within the stated time, it will be assumed that the claim is denied. Failure to file an answer shall not operate to delay the arbitration.

Section 8. CHANGE OF CLAIM — After filing of the claim, if either party desires to make any new or different claim, such claim shall be made in writing and filed with the AAA, and a copy thereof shall be mailed to the other party who shall have a period of seven days from the date of such mailing within which to file an answer with the AAA. However, after the Arbitrator is appointed no new or different claim may be submitted to him except with his consent.

Section 9. INITIATION UNDER A SUBMISSION — Parties to any existing dispute may commence an arbitration under these Rules by filing at any Regional Office two (2) copies of a written agreement to arbitrate under these Rules (Submission), signed by the parties. It shall contain a statement of the matter in dispute, the amount of money involved, if any, and the remedy sought, together with the appropriate administrative fee as provided in the Fee Schedule.

Section 10. FIXING OF LOCALE — The parties may mutually agree on the locale where the arbitration is to be held. If the locale is not designated within seven days from the date of filing the Demand or Submission the AAA shall have power to determine the locale. Its decision shall be final and binding. If any party requests that the hearing be held in a specific locale and the other party files no objection thereto within seven days after notice of the request, the locale shall be the one requested.

Section 11. QUALIFICATIONS OF ARBITRATOR — No person shall serve as an Arbitrator in any arbitration if he has any financial or personal interest in the result of the arbitration, unless the parties, in writing, waive such disqualification.

Section 12. APPOINTMENT FROM PANEL — If the parties have not appointed an Arbitrator and have not provided any other method of appointment, the Arbitrator shall be appointed in the following manner: Immediately after the filing of the Demand or Submission, the AAA shall submit simultaneously to each party to the dispute an identical list of names of persons chosen from the Panel. Each party to the dispute shall have seven days from the mailing date in which to cross off any names to which he objects, number the remaining names indicating the order of his preference, and return the list to the AAA. If a party does not return the list within the time specified, all persons named therein shall be deemed acceptable. From among the persons who have been approved on both lists, and in accordance with the designated order of mutual preference, the AAA shall invite the acceptance of an Arbitrator to serve. If the parties fail to agree upon any of the persons named, or if acceptable Arbitrators are unable to act, or if for any other reason the appointment cannot be made from the submitted lists, the AAA shall have the power to make the appointment from other members of the Panel without the submission of any additional lists.

Section 13. DIRECT APPOINTMENT BY PARTIES — If the agreement of the parties names an Arbitrator or specifies a method of appointing an Arbitrator, that designation or method shall be fol-

lowed. The notice of appointment, with name and address of such Arbitrator, shall be filed with the AAA by the appointing party. Upon the request of any such appointing party, the AAA shall submit a list of members from the Panel from which the party may, if he so desires, make the appointment.

If the agreement specifies a period of time within which an Arbitrator shall be appointed, and any party fails to make such appointment within that period, the AAA shall make the appointment.

If no period of time is specified in the agreement, the AAA shall notify the parties to make the appointment and if within seven days thereafter such Arbitrator has not been so appointed, the AAA shall make the appointment.

Section 14. APPOINTMENT OF NEUTRAL ARBITRATOR BY PARTY-APPOINTED ARBITRATORS — If the parties have appointed their Arbitrators or if either or both of them have been appointed as provided in Section 13, and have authorized such Arbitrators to appoint a neutral Arbitrator within a specified time and no appointment is made within such time or any agreed extension thereof, the AAA shall appoint a neutral Arbitrator who shall act as Chairman.

If no period of time is specified for appointment of the neutral Arbitrator and the parties do not make the appointment within seven days from the date of the appointment of the last party-appointed Arbitrator, the AAA shall appoint such neutral Arbitrator, who shall act as Chairman.

If the parties have agreed that their Arbitrators shall appoint the neutral Arbitrator from the Panel, the AAA shall furnish to the party-appointed Arbitrators, in the manner prescribed in Section 12, a list selected from the Panel, and the appointment of the neutral Arbitrator shall be made as prescribed in such Section.

Section 15. NATIONALITY OF ARBITRATOR IN INTERNATIONAL ARBITRATION — If one of the parties is a national or resident of a country other than the United States, the sole Arbitrator or the neutral Arbitrator shall, upon the request of either party, be appointed from among the nationals of a country other than that of any of the parties.

Section 16. NUMBER OF ARBITRATORS — If the arbitration agreement does not specify the number of Arbitrators, the dispute shall be heard and determined by one Arbitrator, unless the AAA, in its discretion, directs that a greater number of Arbitrators be appointed.

Section 17. NOTICE TO ARBITRATOR OF HIS APPOINTMENT — Notice of the appointment of the neutral Arbitrator, whether appointed by the parties or by the AAA, shall be mailed to the Arbitrator by the AAA, together with a copy of these Rules, and the signed acceptance of the Arbitrator shall be filed prior to the opening of the first hearing.

Section 18. DISCLOSURE BY ARBITRATOR OF DISQUALIFICATION — Prior to accepting his appointment, the prospective neutral Arbitrator shall disclose any circumstances likely to create a presumption of bias or which he believes might dis-

ualify him as an impartial Arbitrator. Upon receipt
f such information, the AAA shall immediately
isclose it to the parties who, if willing to proceed
nder the circumstances disclosed, shall so advise
he AAA in writing. If either party declines to
vaive the presumptive disqualification, the vacancy
hus created shall be filled in accordance with the
pplicable provisions of these Rules.

Section 19. VACANCIES — If any Arbitrator
hould resign, die, withdraw, refuse, be disqualified
r be unable to perform the duties of his office, the
AAA may, on proof satisfactory to it, declare the
ffice vacant. Vacancies shall be filled in accordance
vith the applicable provisions of these Rules and
he matter shall be reheard unless the parties shall
gree otherwise.

Section 20. TIME AND PLACE — The Arbitrator
hall fix the time and place for each hearing. The
AAA shall mail to each party notice thereof at
east five days in advance, unless the parties by
nutual agreement waive such notice or modify the
erms thereof.

Section 21. REPRESENTATION BY COUNSEL
— Any party may be represented by counsel. A
arty intending to be so represented shall notify the
ther party and the AAA of the name and address
f counsel at least three days prior to the date set
or the hearing at which counsel is first to appear.
Vhen an arbitration is initiated by counsel, or where
n attorney replies for the other party, such notice
s deemed to have been given.

Section 22. STENOGRAPHIC RECORD — The
AAA shall make the necessary arrangements for the
aking of a stenographic record whenever such record
s requested by a party. The requesting party or
arties shall pay the cost of such record as provided
n Section 49.

Section 23. INTERPRETER — The AAA shall
nake the necessary arrangements for the services
f an interpreter upon the request of one or more
f the parties, who shall assume the cost of such
ervice.

Section 24. ATTENDANCE AT HEARINGS —
'ersons having a direct interest in the arbitration
re entitled to attend hearings. The Arbitrator shall
therwise have the power to require the retirement
f any witness or witnesses during the testimony
f other witnesses. It shall be discretionary with the
rbitrator to determine the propriety of the at-
endance of any other persons.

Section 25. ADJOURNMENTS — The Arbitrator
nay take adjournments upon the request of a party
r upon his own initiative and shall take such ad-
ournment when all of the parties agree thereto.

Section 26. OATHS — Before proceeding with the
irst hearing or with the examination of the file,
ach Arbitrator may take an oath of office, and if
equired by law, shall do so. The Arbitrator may, in
is discretion, require witnesses to testify under
ath administered by any duly qualified person or,
f required by law or demanded by either party,
hall do so.

Section 27. MAJORITY DECISION — Whenever
there is more than one Arbitrator, all decisions of
the Arbitrators must be by at least a majority. The
award must also be made by at least a majority
unless the concurrence of all is expressly required
by the arbitration agreement or by law.

Section 28. ORDER OF PROCEEDINGS — A
hearing shall be opened by the filing of the oath
of the Arbitrator, where required, and by the recording of the place, time and date of the hearing, the
presence of the Arbitrator and parties, and counsel,
if any, and by the receipt by the Arbitrator of the
statement of the claim and answer, if any.

The Arbitrator may, at the beginning of the hearing, ask for statements clarifying the issues involved.

The complaining party shall then present his claim
and proofs and his witnesses who shall submit to
questions or other examination. The defending party
shall then present his defense and proofs and his
witnesses, who shall submit to questions or other
examination. The Arbitrator may in his discretion
vary this procedure but he shall afford full and
equal opportunity to all parties for the presentation
of any material or relevant proofs.

Exhibits, when offered by either party, may be
received in evidence by the Arbitrator.

The names and addresses of all witnesses and
exhibits in order received shall be made a part of
the record.

**Section 29. ARBITRATION IN THE ABSENCE
OF A PARTY** — Unless the law provides to the
contrary, the arbitration may proceed in the absence
of any party, who, after due notice, fails to be
present or fails to obtain an adjournment. An award
shall not be made solely on the default of a party.
The Arbitrator shall require the party who is present
to submit such evidence as he may require for the
making of an award.

Section 30. EVIDENCE — The parties may offer
such evidence as they desire and shall produce such
additional evidence as the Arbitrator may deem
necessary to an understanding and determination of
the dispute. When the Arbitrator is authorized by
law to subpoena witnesses or documents, he may do
so upon his own initiative or upon the request of any
party. The Arbitrator shall be the judge of the
relevancy and materiality of the evidence offered
and conformity to legal rules of evidence shall not
be necessary. All evidence shall be taken in the
presence of all of the Arbitrators and of all the
parties, except where any of the parties is absent
in default or has waived his right to be present.

**Section 31. EVIDENCE BY AFFIDAVIT AND
FILING OF DOCUMENTS** — The Arbitrator shall
receive and consider the evidence of witnesses by
affidavit, but shall give it only such weight as he
deems it entitled to after consideration of any objections made to its admission.

All documents not filed with the Arbitrator at
the hearing, but arranged for at the hearing or
subsequently by agreement of the parties, shall be
filed with the AAA for transmission to the Arbitrator. All parties shall be afforded opportunity to
examine such documents.

Section 32. INSPECTION OR INVESTIGATION — Whenever the Arbitrator deems it necessary to make an inspection or investigation in connection with the arbitration, he shall direct the AAA to advise the parties of his intention. The Arbitrator shall set the time and the AAA shall notify the parties thereof. Any party who so desires may be present at such inspection or investigation. In the event that one or both parties are not present at the inspection or investigation, the Arbitrator shall make a verbal or written report to the parties and afford them an opportunity to comment.

Section 33. CONSERVATION OF PROPERTY — The Arbitrator may issue such orders as may be deemed necessary to safeguard the property which is the subject matter of the arbitration without prejudice to the rights of the parties or to the final determination of the dispute.

Section 34. CLOSING OF HEARINGS — The Arbitrator shall specifically inquire of all parties whether they have any further proofs to offer or witnesses to be heard. Upon receiving negative replies, the Arbitrator shall declare the hearings closed and a minute thereof shall be recorded. If briefs are to be filed, the hearings shall be declared closed as of the final date set by the Arbitrator for the receipt of briefs. If documents are to be filed as provided for in Section 31 and the date set for their receipt is later than that set for the receipt of briefs, the later date shall be the date of closing the hearing. The time limit within which the Arbitrator is required to make his award shall commence to run, in the absence of other agreements by the parties, upon the closing of the hearings.

Section 35. REOPENING OF HEARINGS — The hearings may be reopened by the Arbitrator on his own motion, or upon application of a party at any time before the award is made. If the reopening of the hearing would prevent the making of the award within the specific time agreed upon by the parties in the contract out of which the controversy has arisen, the matter may not be reopened, unless the parties agree upon the extension of such time limit. When no specific date is fixed in the contract, the Arbitrator may reopen the hearings, and the Arbitrator shall have thirty days from the closing of the reopened hearings within which to make an award.

Section 36. WAIVER OF ORAL HEARING — The parties may provide, by written agreement, for the waiver of oral hearings. If the parties are unable to agree as to the procedure, the AAA shall specify a fair and equitable procedure.

Section 37. WAIVER OF RULES — Any party who proceeds with the arbitration after knowledge that any provision or requirement of these Rules has not been complied with and who fails to state his objection thereto in writing, shall be deemed to have waived his right to object.

Section 38. EXTENSIONS OF TIME — The parties may modify any period of time by mutual agreement. The AAA for good cause may extend any period of time established by these Rules, except the time for making the award. The AAA shall notify the parties of any such extension of time and its reason therefor.

Section 39. COMMUNICATION WITH ARBITRATOR AND SERVING OF NOTICES —

(a) There shall be no communication between the parties and a neutral Arbitrator other than at oral hearings. Any other oral or written communications from the parties to the Arbitrator shall be directed to the AAA for transmittal to the Arbitrator.

(b) Each party to an agreement which provides for arbitration under these Rules shall be deemed to have consented that any papers, notices or process necessary or proper for the initiation or continuation of an arbitration under these Rules and for any court action in connection therewith or for the entry of judgment on any award made thereunder may be served upon such party by mail addressed to such party of his attorney at his last known address or by personal service, within or without the state wherein the arbitration is to be held (whether such party be within or without the United States of America), provided that reasonable opportunity to be heard with regard thereto has been granted such party.

Section 40. TIME OF AWARD — The award shall be made promptly by the Arbitrator and, unless otherwise agreed by the parties, or specified by law, no later than thirty days from the date of closing the hearings, or if oral hearings have been waived, from the date of transmitting the final statements and proofs to the Arbitrator.

Section 41. FORM OF AWARD — The award shall be in writing and shall be signed either by the sole Arbitrator or by at least a majority if there be more than one. It shall be executed in the manner required by law.

Section 42. SCOPE OF AWARD — The Arbitrator may grant any remedy or relief which he deems just and equitable and within the scope of the agreement of the parties, including, but not limited to, specific performance of a contract. The Arbitrator, in his award, shall assess arbitration fees and expenses in favor of any party and, in the event any administrative fees or expenses are due the AAA, in favor of the AAA.

Section 43. AWARD UPON SETTLEMENT — If the parties settle their dispute during the course of the arbitration, the Arbitrator, upon their request, may set forth the terms of the agreed settlement in an award.

Section 44. DELIVERY OF AWARD TO PARTIES — Parties shall accept as legal delivery of the award the placing of the award or a true copy thereof in the mail by the AAA, addressed to such party at his last known address or to his attorney, or personal service of the award, or the filing of the award in any manner which may be prescribed by law.

Section 45. RELEASE OF DOCUMENTS FOR JUDICIAL PROCEEDINGS — The AAA shall, upon the written request of a party, furnish to such party, at his expense, certified facsimiles of any papers in the AAA's possession that may be required in judicial proceedings relating to the arbitration.

Section 46. APPLICATIONS TO COURT —

(a) No judicial proceedings by a party relating ɔ the subject matter of the arbitration shall be ǝemed a waiver of the party's right to arbitrate.

(b) The AAA is not a necessary party in judicial ɔroceedings relating to the arbitration.

Section 47. ADMINISTRATIVE FEES — As a ɔnprofit organization, the AAA shall prescribe an ἰministrative fee schedule and a refund schedule ɔ compensate it for the cost of providing adminis- ɾative services. The schedule in effect at the time ỻ filing or the time of refund shall be applicable.

The administrative fees shall be advanced by the ἰitiating party or parties, subject to final apportion- ᴉent by the Arbitrator in his award.

When a matter is withdrawn or settled, the re- ɪnd shall be made in accordance with the refund ɔhedule.

The AAA, in the event of extreme hardship on ᴉe part of any party, may defer or reduce the ἀministrative fee.

Section 48. FEE WHEN ORAL HEARINGS ARE VAIVED — Where all Oral Hearings are waived ᴉder Section 36 the Administrative Fee Schedule ᴉall apply.

Section 49. EXPENSES — The expenses of wit- ᴇsses for either side shall be paid by the party ɾoducing such witnesses.

The cost of the stenographic record, if any is ɪade, and all transcripts thereof, shall be prorated ɋually among all parties ordering copies unless ᴉey shall otherwise agree and shall be paid for by ᴉe responsible parties directly to the reporting ɟency.

All other expenses of the arbitration, including ᴇquired travelling and other expenses of the Ar- ᴵtrator and of AAA representatives, and the ex- ᴇnses of any witness or the cost of any proofs ɾoduced at the direct request of the Arbitrator, ᴉall be borne equally by the parties, unless they ɟree otherwise, or unless the Arbitrator in his ᴗward assesses such expenses or any part thereof ᴇgainst any specified party or parties.

Section 50. ARBITRATOR'S FEE — Members of ᴉe National Panel of Arbitrators serve without fee ᴉ commercial arbitrations. In prolonged or special ᴀses the parties may agree to the payment of a fee.

Any arrangements for the compensation of a ᴇutral Arbitrator shall be made through the AAA ᴇnd not directly by him with the parties.

Section 51. DEPOSITS — The AAA may require ᴉe parties to deposit in advance such sums of ᴉoney as it deems necessary to defray the expense ỻ the arbitration, including the Arbitrator's fee if ᴉny, and shall render an accounting to the parties ᴇnd return any unexpended balance.

Section 52. INTERPRETATION AND APPLICA- ȚION OF RULES — The Arbitrator shall interpret ᴇnd apply these Rules insofar as they relate to his ᴏwers and duties. When there is more than one ᴀrbitrator and a difference arises among them con- cerning the meaning or application of any such Rules, it shall be decided by a majority vote. If that is unobtainable, either an Arbitrator or a party may refer the question to the AAA for final decision. All other Rules shall be interpreted and applied by the AAA.

ADMINISTRATIVE FEE SCHEDULE

The administrative fee of the AAA is based upon the amount of each claim as disclosed when the claim is filed, and is due and payable at the time of filing.

Amount of Claim	Fee
Up to $10,000	3% (minimum $50)
$10,000 to $25,000	$300, plus 2% of excess over $10,000
$25,000 to $100,000	$600, plus 1% of excess over $25,000
$100,000 to $200,000	$1350, plus ½% of excess over $100,000

The fee for claims in excess of $200,000 should be discussed with the AAA in advance of filing.

When no amount can be stated at the time of filing, the administrative fee is $200, subject to adjustment in accordance with the above schedule if an amount is subsequently disclosed.

If there are more than two parties represented in the arbitration, an additional 10% of the initiating fee will be due for each additional represented party.

OTHER SERVICE CHARGES

$30.00 payable by a party causing an adjournment of any scheduled hearing;

$25.00 payable by each party for each hearing after the first hearing;

$5.00 per hour payable by each party for hearings on Saturdays, legal holidays, and after 6:00 P.M. weekdays.

REFUND SCHEDULE

If the AAA is notified that a case has been settled or withdrawn before a list of arbitrators has been sent out, all the fee in excess of $50.00 will be refunded.

If the AAA is notified that a case has been settled or withdrawn thereafter but before the due date for the return of the first list, two-thirds of the fee in excess of $50.00 will be refunded.

If the AAA is notified that a case is settled or withdrawn thereafter but at least 48 hours before the date and time set for the first hearing, one-half of the fee in excess of $50.00 will be refunded.

AMERICAN ARBITRATION ASSOCIATION VOLUNTARY LABOR ARBITRATION RULES

AMERICAN ARBITRATION ASSOCIATION VOLUNTARY LABOR ARBITRATION RULES

1. **Agreement of Parties**—The parties shall be deemed to have made these Rules a part of their arbitration agreement whenever, in a collective bargaining agreement or submission, they have provided for arbitration by the American Arbitration Association (hereinafter AAA) or under its Rules. These Rules shall apply in the form obtaining at the time the arbitration is initiated.

2. **Name of Tribunal**—Any Tribunal constituted by the parties under these Rules shall be called the Voluntary Labor Arbitration Tribunal.

3. **Administrator**—When parties agree to arbitrate under these Rules and an arbitration is instituted thereunder, they thereby authorize the AAA to administer the arbitration. The authority and obligations of the Administrator are as provided in the agreement of the parties and in these Rules.

4. **Delegation of Duties**—The duties of the AAA may be carried out through such representatives or committees as the AAA may direct.

5. **National Panel of Labor Arbitrators**—The AAA shall establish and maintain a National Panel of Labor Arbitrators and shall appoint arbitrators therefrom, as hereinafter provided.

6. **Office of Tribunal**—The general office of the Labor Arbitration Tribunal is the headquarters of the AAA, which may, however, assign the administration of an arbitration to any of its Regional Offices.

7. **Initiation Under an Arbitration Clause in a Collective Bargaining Agreement**—Arbitration under an arbitration clause in a collective bargaining agreement under these Rules may be initiated by either party in the following manner:

   (a) By giving written notice to the other party of intention to arbitrate (Demand), which notice shall contain a statement setting forth the nature of the dispute and the remedy sought, and

   (b) By filing at any Regional Office of the AAA three copies of said notice, together with a copy of the collective bargaining agreement, or such parts thereof as relate to the dispute, including the arbitration provisions. After the Arbitrator is appointed, no new or different claim may be submitted to him except with the consent of the Arbitrator and all other parties.

8. **Answer**—The party upon whom the demand for arbitration is made may file an answering statement with the AAA within seven days after notice from the AAA, in which event he shall simultaneously send a copy of his answer to the other party. If no answer is filed within the stated time, it will be assumed that the claim is denied. Failure to file an answer shall not operate to delay the arbitration.

9. **Initiation under a Submission**—Parties to any collective bargaining agreement may initiate an arbitration under these Rules by filing at any Regional Office of the AAA two copies of a written agreement to arbitrate under these Rules (Submission), signed by the parties

and setting forth the nature of the dispute and the remedy sought.

10. **Fixing of Locale**—The parties may mutually agree upon the locale where the arbitration is to be held. If the locale is not designated in the collective bargaining agreement or submission, and if there is a dispute as to the appropriate locale, the AAA shall have the power to determine the locale and its decision shall be binding.

11. **Qualifications of Arbitrator**—No person shall serve as a neutral Arbitrator in any arbitration in which he has any financial or personal interest in the result of the arbitration, unless the parties, in writing, waive such disqualification.

12. **Appointment from Panel**—If the parties have not appointed an Arbitrator and have not provided any other method of appointment, the Arbitrator shall be appointed in the following manner: Immediately after the filing of the Demand or Submission, the AAA shall submit simultaneously to each party an identical list of names of persons chosen from the Labor Panel. Each party shall have seven days from the mailing date in which to cross off any names to which he objects, number the remaining names indicating the order of his preference, and return the list to the AAA. If a party does not return the list within the time specified all persons named therein shall be deemed acceptable. From among the persons who have been approved on both lists, and in accordance with the designated order of mutual preference, the AAA shall invite the acceptance of an Arbitrator to serve. If the parties fail to agree upon any of the persons named or if those named decline or are unable to act, or if for any other reason the appointment cannot be made from the submitted lists, the Administrator shall have power to make the appointment from other members of the Panel without the submission of any additional lists.

13. **Direct Appointment by Parties**—If the agreement of the parties names an Arbitrator or specifies a method of appointing an Arbitrator, that designation or method shall be followed. The notice of appointment, with the name and address of such Arbitrator, shall be filed with the AAA by the appointing party.

   If the agreement specifies a period of time within which an Arbitrator shall be appointed, and any party fails to make such appointment within that period, the AAA may make the appointment.

   If no period of time is specified in the agreement, the AAA shall notify the parties to make the appointment and if within seven days thereafter such Arbitrator has not been so appointed, the AAA shall make the appointment.

14. **Appointment of Neutral Arbitrator by Party-Appointed Arbitrators**—If the parties have appointed their Arbitrators, or if either or both of them have been appointed as provided in Section 13, and have authorized such Arbitrators to appoint a neutral Arbitrator within a specified time and no appointment is made within such time or any agreed extension thereof, the AAA may appoint a neutral Arbitrator, who shall act as Chairman.

   If no period of time is specified for appointment of the neutral Arbitrator and the parties do not make the appointment within seven days from the date of the

ppointment of the last party-appointed Arbitrator,
he AAA shall appoint such neutral Arbitrator, who
hall act as Chairman.

If the parties have agreed that the Arbitrators shall
ppoint the neutral Arbitrator from the Panel, the AAA
hall furnish to the party-appointed Arbitrators, in the
nanner prescribed in Section 12, a list selected from the
'anel, and the appointment of the neutral Arbitrator
hall be made as prescribed in such Section.

5. **Number of Arbitrators**—If the arbitration agreement
'oes not specify the number of Arbitrators, the dispute
hall be heard and determined by one Arbitrator, unless
he parties otherwise agree.

'6. **Notice to Arbitrator of His Appointment**—Notice of
he appointment of the neutral Arbitrator shall be mail-
d to the Arbitrator by the AAA and the signed ac-
eptance of the Arbitrator shall be filed with the AAA
rior to the opening of the first hearing.

7. **Disclosure by Arbitrator of Disqualification**—Prior
o accepting his appointment, the prospective neutral
Arbitrator shall disclose any circumstances likely to
reate a presumption of bias or which he believes might
lisqualify him as an impartial Arbitrator. Upon receipt
f such information, the AAA shall immediately disclose
t to the parties. If either party declines to waive the
resumptive disqualification, the vacancy thus created
hall be filled in accordance with the applicable pro-
isions of these Rules.

l8. **Vacancies**—If any Arbitrator should resign, die,
vithdraw, refuse or be unable or disqualified to perform
he duties of his office, the AAA shall, on proof satis-
actory to it, declare the office vacant. Vacancies shall
e filled in the same manner as that governing the
naking of the original appointment, and the matter
hall be reheard by the new Arbitrator.

l9. **Time and Place of Hearing**—The Arbitrator shall fix
he time and place for each hearing. At least five days
orior thereto the AAA shall mail notice of the time and
olace of hearing to each party, unless the parties other-
vise agree.

20. **Representation by Counsel**—Any party may be represented at the hearing by counsel or by other authorized representative.

21. **Stenographic Record**—Whenever a stenographic
record is requested by one or more parties, the AAA
will arrange for a stenographer. The total cost of
the record shall be shared equally among parties or-
lering copies, unless they agree otherwise.

22. **Attendance at Hearings**—Persons having a direct
interest in the arbitration are entitled to attend hearings. The Arbitrator shall have the power to require the
retirement of any witness or witnesses during the
testimony of other witnesses. It shall be discretionary
with the Arbitrator to determine the propriety of the
attendance of any other persons.

23. **Adjournments**—The Arbitrator for good cause shown
may adjourn the hearing upon the request of a party
or upon his own initiative, and shall adjourn when all
the parties agree thereto.

24. **Oaths**—Before proceeding with the first hearing,
each Arbitrator may take an Oath of Office, and if
required by law, shall do so. The Arbitrator may, in his
discretion, require witnesses to testify under oath administered by any duly qualified person, and if required
by law or requested by either party, shall do so.

25. **Majority Decision**—Whenever there is more than one
Arbitrator, all decisions of the Arbitrators shall be by
majority vote. The award shall also be made by majority
vote unless the concurrence of all is expressly required.

26. **Order of Proceedings**—A hearing shall be opened by
the filing of the oath of the Arbitrator, where required,
and by the recording of the place, time and date of
hearing, the presence of the Arbitrator and parties, and
counsel if any, and the receipt by the Arbitrator of the
Demand and answer, if any, or the Submission.

Exhibits, when offered by either party, may be received in evidence by the Arbitrator. The names and
addresses of all witnesses and exhibits in order received
shall be made a part of the record.

The Arbitrator may, in his discretion, vary the normal
procedure under which the initiating party first presents
his claim, but in any case shall afford full and equal
opportunity to all parties for presentation of relevant
proofs.

27. **Arbitration in the Absence of a Party**—Unless the
law provides to the contrary, the arbitration may proceed in the absence of any party, who, after due notice,
fails to be present or fails to obtain an adjournment.
An award shall not be made solely on the default of a
party. The Arbitrator shall require the other party to
sbumit such evidence as he may require for the making
of an award.

28. **Evidence**—The parties may offer such evidence as
they desire and shall produce such additional evidence
as the Arbitrator may deem necessary to an understanding and determination of the dispute. When the
Arbitrator is authorized by law to subpoena witnesses
and documents, he may do so upon his own initiative
or upon the request of any party. The Arbitrator shall
be the judge of the relevancy and materiality of the
evidence offered and conformity to legal rules of evidence shall not be necessary. All evidence shall be taken
in the presence of all of the Arbitrators and all of the
parties except where any of the parties is absent in
default or has waived his right to be present.

29. **Evidence by Affidavit and Filing of Documents**—The
Arbitrator may receive and consider the evidence of
witnesses by affidavit, but shall give it only such weight
as he deems proper after consideration of any objections made to its admission.

All documents not filed with the Arbitrator at the
hearing but which are arranged at the hearing or subsequently by agreement of the parties to be submitted,
shall be filed with the AAA for transmission to the
Arbitrator. All parties shall be afforded opportunity
to examine such documents.

30. **Inspection**—Whenever the Arbitrator deems it necessary, he may make an inspection in connection with
the subject matter of the dispute after written notice
to the parties who may, if they so desire, be present at
such inspection.

31. Closing of Hearings—The Arbitrator shall inquire of all parties whether they have any further proofs to offer or witnesses to be heard. Upon receiving negative replies, the Arbitrator shall declare the hearings closed and a minute thereof shall be recorded. If briefs or other documents are to be filed, the hearings shall be declared closed as of the final date set by the Arbitrator for filing with the AAA. The time limit within which the Arbitrator is required to make his award shall commence to run, in the absence of other agreement by the parties, upon the closing of the hearings.

32. Reopening of Hearings—The hearings may be reopened by the Arbitrator on his own motion, or on the motion of either party, for good cause shown, at any time before the award is made, but if the reopening of the hearing would prevent the making of the award within the specific time agreed upon by the parties in the contract out of which the controversy has arisen, the matter may not be reopened, unless both parties agree upon the extension of such time limit. When no specific date is fixed in the contract, the Arbitrator may reopen the hearings, and the Arbitrator shall have 30 days from the closing of the reopened hearings within which to make an award.

33. Waiver of Rules—Any party who proceeds with the arbitration after knowledge that any provision or requirement of these Rules has not been complied with and who fails to state his objection thereto in writing, shall be deemed to have waived his right to object.

34. Waiver of Oral Hearing—The parties may provide, by written agreement, for the waiver of oral hearings. If the parties are unable to agree as to the procedure, the AAA shall specify a fair and equitable procedure.

35. Extensions of Time—The parties may modify any period of time by mutual agreement. The AAA for good cause may extend any period of time established by these Rules, except the time for making the award. The AAA shall notify the parties of any such extension of time and its reason therefor.

36. Serving of Notices—Each party to a Submission or other agreement which provides for arbitration under these Rules shall be deemed to have consented and shall consent that any papers, notices or process necessary or proper for the initiation or continuation of an arbitration under these Rules and for any court action in connection therewith or the entry of judgment on an award made thereunder, may be served upon such party (a) by mail addressed to such party or his attorney at his last known address, or (b) by personal service, within or without the state wherein the arbitration is to be held.

37. Time of Award—The award shall be rendered promptly by the Arbitrator and, unless otherwise agreed by the parties, or specified by the law, not later than thirty days from the date of closing the hearings, or if oral hearings have been waived, then from the date of transmitting the final statements and proofs to the Arbitrator.

38. Form of Award—The award shall be in writing and shall be signed either by the neutral Arbitrator or by a concurring majority if there be more than one Arbitrator. The parties shall advise the AAA whenever they do not require the Arbitrator to accompany the award with an opinion.

39. Award Upon Settlement—If the parties settle their dispute during the course of the arbitration, the Arbitrator, upon their request, may set forth the terms of the agreed settlement in an award.

40. Delivery of Award to Parties—Parties shall accept as legal delivery of the award the placing of the award or a true copy thereof in the mail by the AAA, addressed to such party at his last known address or to his attorney, or personal service of the award, or the filing of the award in any manner which may be prescribed by law.

41. Release of Documents for Judicial Proceedings—The AAA shall, upon the written request of a party, furnish to such party at his expense certified facsimiles of any papers in the AAA's possession that may be required in judicial proceedings relating to the arbitration.

42. Judicial Proceedings—The AAA is not a necessary party in judicial proceedings relating to the arbitration.

43. Administrative Fee—As a nonprofit organization the AAA shall prescribe an administrative fee schedule to compensate it for the cost of providing administrative services. The schedule in effect at the time of filing shall be applicable.

44. Expenses—The expenses of witnesses for either side shall be paid by the party producing such witnesses.

Expenses of the arbitration, other than the cost of the stenographic record, including required traveling and other expenses of the Arbitrator and of AAA representatives, and the expenses of any witnesses or the cost of any proofs produced at the direct request of the Arbitrator, shall be borne equally by the parties unless they agree otherwise, or unless the Arbitrator in his award assesses such expenses or any part thereof against any specified party or parties.

45. Communication with Arbitrator—There shall be no communication between the parties and a neutral Arbitrator other than at oral hearings. Any other oral or written communications from the parties to the Arbitrator shall be directed to the AAA for transmittal to the Arbitrator.

46. Interpretation and Application of Rules—The Arbitrator shall interpret and apply these Rules insofar as they relate to his powers and duties. When there is more than one Arbitrator and a difference arises among them concerning the meaning or application of any such Rules, it shall be decided by majority vote. If that is unobtainable, either Arbitrator or party may refer the question to the AAA for final decision. All other Rules shall be interpreted and applied by the AAA.

Federal Mediation and Conciliation Service:
Arbitration Policies, Functions, and Procedures

CHAPTER XII—Federal Mediation and Conciliation Service

PART 1404—ARBITRATION

On June 21, 1968, notice of proposed rule changes was published in the FEDERAL REGISTER (68 F.R. 7358). There were set out therein the proposed revisions of Chapter XII, Title 29, of the Code of Federal Regulations, relating to the Service's arbitration policies and procedures. Comments which were received concerning the proposed regulations have been considered. The amendatory regulations as set forth below are hereby adopted to be effective October 21, 1968, and shall as of that date supersede the present regulations which are set forth in 29 CFR Part 1404.

Sec.
1404.1   Arbitration.
1404.2   Composition of roster maintained by the Service.
1404.3   Security status.
1404.4   Procedures; how to request arbitration services.
1404.5   Arbitrability.
1404.6   Nominations of arbitrators.
1404.7   Appointment of arbitrators.
1404.8   Status of arbitrators after appointment.
1404.9   Prompt decision.
1404.10 Arbitrator's award and report.
1404.11 Fees of arbitrators.
1404.12 Conduct of hearings.

AUTHORITY: The provisions of this Part 1404 issued under sec. 202, 61 Stat. 153, as amended; 29 U.S.C. 172. Interpret or apply sec. 3, 80 Stat. 250, sec. 203, 61 Stat. 153; 5 U.S.C. 552, 29 U.S.C. 173.

§ 1404.1 Arbitration.

The labor policy of the U.S. Government is designed to foster and promote free collective bargaining. Voluntary arbitration is encouraged by public policy and is in fact almost universally utilized by the parties to resolve disputes involving the interpretation or application of collective bargaining agreements. Also, in appropriate cases, voluntary arbitration or factfinding are tools of free collective bargaining and may be desirable alternatives to economic strife in determining terms of a collective bargaining agreement. The parties assume broad responsibilities for the success of the private juridical system they have chosen. The Service will assist the parties in their selection of arbitrators.

§ 1404.2 Composition of roster maintained by the Service.

(a) It is the policy of the Service to maintain on its roster only those arbitrators who are qualifiied and acceptable, and who adhere to ethical standards.

(b) Applicants for inclusion on its roster must not only be well-grounded in the field of labor-management relations, but, also, usually possess experience in the labor arbitration field or its equivalent. After a careful screening and evaluation of the applicant's experience, the Service contacts representatives of both labor and management since arbitrators must be generally acceptable to those who utilize its arbitration facilities. The responses to such inquiries are carefully weighed before an otherwise qualified arbitrator is included on the Service's roster. Persons employed full time as representatives of management, labor, or the Federal Government are not included on the Service's roster.

(c) The arbitrators on the roster are expected to keep the Service informed of changes in address, occupation or availability, and of any business connections with or of concern to labor or management. The Service reserves the right to remove names from the active roster or to take other appropriate action where there is good reason to believe that an arbitrator is not adhering to these regulations and related policy.

§ 1404.3 Security status.

The arbitrators on the Service's roster are not employees of the Federal Government, and, because of this status, the Service does not investigate their security status. Moreover, when an arbitrator is selected by the parties, he is retained by them and, accordingly, they must assume complete responsibility for the arbitrator's security status.

§ 1404.4 Procedures; how to request arbitration services.

The Service prefers to act upon a joint request which should be addressed to the Director of the Federal Mediation and Conciliation Service, Washington, D.C. 20427. In the event that the request is made by only one party, the Service may act if the parties have agreed that either of them may seek a panel of arbitrators, either by specific ad hoc agreement or by specific language in the applicable collective bargaining agreement. A brief statement of the nature of the issues in dispute should accompany the request, to enable the Service to submit the names of arbitrators qualified for the issues involved. The request should also include a copy of the collective bargaining agreement or stipulation. In the event that the entire agreement is not available, a verbatim copy of the provisions relating to arbitration should accompany the request.

§ 1404.5 Arbitrabitity.

Where either party claims that a dispute is not subject to arbitration, the Service will not decide the merits of such claim. The submission of a panel should not be construed as anything more than compliance with a request.

§ 1404.6 Nominations of arbitrators.

(a) When the parties have been unable to agree on an arbitrator, the Service will submit to the parties the names of seven arbitrators unless the applicable collective bargaining agreement provides for a different number, or unless the parties themselves request a different number. Together with the submission of a panel of suggested arbitrators, the Service furnishes a short statement of the background, qualifications, experience and per diem fee of each of the nominees.

(b) In selecting names for inclusion on a panel, the Service considers many factors, but the desires of the parties are, of course, the foremost consideration. If at any time both the company and the union suggest that a name or names be omitted from a panel, such name or names will be omitted. If one party only (a company or a union) suggests that a name or names be omitted from a panel, such name or names will generally be omitted, subject to the following qualifications: (1) If the suggested omissions are excessive in number or otherwise appear to lack careful consideration, they will not be considered; (2) all such suggested omissions should be reviewed after the passage of a reasonable period of time. The Service will not place names on a panel at the request of one party unless the other party has knowledge of such request and has no objection thereto, or unless both parties join in such request. If the issue described in the request appears to require special technical experience or qualifications, arbitrators who possess such qualifications will, where possible, be included in the list submitted to the parties. Where the parties expressly request that the list be composed entirely of technicians, or that it be all-local or non-local, such request will be honored. if qualified arbitrators are available.

(c) Two possible methods of selection from a panel are—(1) at a joint meeting, alternately striking names from the submitted panel until one remains, and (2) each party separately advising the Service of its order of preference by numbering each name on the panel. In almost all cases, an arbitrator is chosen from one panel of names. However, if a request for another panel is made, the Service will comply with the request, providing that additional panels are permissible under the terms of the agreement or the parties so stipulate.

(d) Subsequent adjustment of disputes is not precluded by the submission of a panel or an appointment. A substantial number of issues are being settled by the parties themselves after the initial request for a panel and after selection of the arbitrator. Notice of such settlement should be sent promptly to the arbitrator and to the Service.

(e) The arbitrator is entitled to be compensated whenever he receives insufficient notice of settlement to enable him to rearrange his schedule of arbitration hearings or working hours. In other situations, when an arbitrator spends an unusually large amount of time in arranging or rearranging hearing dates, it may be appropriate for him to make an administrative charge to the parties in the event the case is settled before hearing.

§ 1404.7 Appointment of arbitrators.

(a) After the parties notify the Service of their selection, the arbitrator is appointed by the Director. If any party fails to notify the Service within 15 days after the the date of mailing the panel, all persons named therein may be deemed acceptable to such party. The Service will make a direct appointment of an arbitrator based upon a joint request, or upon a unilateral request when the applicable collective bargaining agreement so authorizes.

(b) The arbitrator, upon appointment notification, is requested to communicate with the parties immediately to arrange for preliminary matters such as date and place of hearing.

§ 1404.8 Status of arbitrators after appointment.

After appointment, the legal relationship of arbitrators is with the parties rather than the Service, though the Service does have a continuing interest in the proceedings. Industrial peace and good labor relations are enhanced by arbitrators who function justly, expeditiously and impartially so as to obtain and retain the respect, esteem and confidence of all participants in the arbitration proceedings. The conduct of the arbitration proceeding is under the arbitrator's jurisdiction and control, subject to such rules of procedure as the parties may jointly prescribe. He is to make his own decisions based on the record in the proceedings. The arbitrator may, unless prohibited by law, proceed in the absence of any party who, after due notice, fails to be present or to obtain a postponement. The award, however, must be supported by evidence.

§ 1404.9 Prompt decision.

(a) Early hearing and decision of industrial disputes is desirable in the interest of good labor relations. The parties should inform the Service whenever a decision is unduly delayed. The Service expects to be notified by the arbitrator if and when (1) he cannot schedule, hear and determine issues promptly, and (2) he is advised that a dispute has been settled by the parties prior to arbitration.

(b) The award shall be made not later than 30 days from the date of the closing of the hearing, or the receipt of a transcript and any post-hearing briefs, or if oral hearings have been waived, then from the date of receipt of the final statements and proof by the arbitrator, unless otherwise agreed upon by the parties or specified by law. However, a failure to make such an award within 30 days shall not invalidate an award.

§ 1404.10 Arbitrator's award and report.

(a) At the conclusion of the hearing and after the award has been submitted to the parties, each arbitrator is required to file a copy with the Service. The arbitrator is further required to submit a report showing

a breakdown of his fees and expense charges so that the Service may be in a position to check conformance with its fee policies. Cooperation in filing both award and report within 15 days after handing down the award is expected of all arbitrators.

(b) It is the policy of the Service not to release arbitration decisions for publication without the consent of both parties. Furthermore, the Service expects the arbitrators it has nominated or appointed not to give publicity to awards they may issue, except in a manner agreeable to both parties.

§ 1404.11 Fees of arbitrators.

(a) No administrative or filing fee is charged by the Service. The current policy of the Service permits each of its nominees or appointees to charge a per diem fee for his services, the amount of which is certified in advance by him to the Service. Each arbitrator's maximum per diem fee is set forth on his biographical sketch which is sent to the parties at such time as his name is submitted to them for consideration. The arbitrator shall not change his per diem fee without giving at least 90 days advance notice to the Service of his intention to do so.

(b) In those rare instances where arbitrators fix wages or other important terms of a new contract, the maximum fee noted above may be exceeded by the arbitrator after agreement by the parties. Conversely, an arbitrator may give due consideration to the financial condition of the parties and charge less than his usual fee in appropriate cases.

§ 1404.12 Conduct of hearings.

The Service does not prescribe detailed or specific rules of procedure for the conduct of an arbitration proceeding because it favors flexibility in labor relations. Questions such as hearing rooms, submission of prehearing or posthearing briefs, and recording of testimony, are left to the discretion of the individual arbitrator and to the parties. The Services does, however, expect its arbitrators and the parties to conform to applicable laws, and to be guided by ethical and procedural standards as codified by appropriate professional organizations and generally accepted by the industrial community and experienced arbitrators.

In cities where the Service maintains offices, the parties are welcome upon request to the Service to use its conference rooms when they are available.

THE NEW YORK ARBITRATION LAW, ARTICLE 75, CIVIL PRACTICE LAW AND RULES

THE NEW YORK ARBITRATION LAW
Article 75, Civil Practice Law and Rules

§ 7501. Effect of arbitration agreement

A written agreement to submit any controversy thereafter arising or any existing controversy to arbitration is enforceable without regard to the justiciable character of the controversy and confers jurisdiction on the courts of the state to enforce it and to enter judgment on an award. In determining any matter arising under this article, the court shall not consider whether the claim with respect to which arbitration is sought is tenable, or otherwise pass upon the merits of the dispute.

§ 7502. Applications to the court; venue; statutes of limitation

(a) *Applications to the court; venue.* A special proceeding shall be used to bring before a court the first application arising out of an arbitrable controversy which is not made by motion in a pending action. The proceeding shall be brought in the court and county specified in the agreement; or, if none be specified, in a court in the county in which one of the parties resides or is doing business, or, if there is no such county, in a court in any county; or in a court in the county in which the arbitration was held. All subsequent applications shall be made by motion in the pending action or the special proceeding.

(b) *Limitation of time.* If, at the time that a demand for arbitration was made or a notice of intention to arbitrate was served, the claim sought to be arbitrated would have been barred by limitation of time had it been asserted in a court of the state, a party may assert the limitation as a bar to the arbitration on an application to the court as provided in section 7503 of subdivision (b) of section 7511. The failure to assert such bar by such application shall not preclude its assertion before the arbitrators, who may, in their sole discretion, apply or not apply the bar. Except as provided in subdivision (b) of section 7511, such exercise of discretion by the arbitrators shall not be subject to review by a court on an application to confirm, vacate or modify the award.

§ 7503. Application to compel or stay arbitration; stay of action; notice of intention to arbitrate

(a) *Application to compel arbitration; stay of action.* A party aggrieved by the failure of another to arbitrate may apply for an order compelling arbitration. Where there is no substantial question whether a valid agree-ment was made or complied with, and the claim sought to be arbitrated is not barred by limitation under sub-division (b) of section 7502, the court shall direct th-parties to arbitrate. Where any such question is raise-it shall be tried forthwith in said court. If an issu-claimed to be arbitrable is involved in an action pendin-in a court having jurisdiction to hear a motion t-compel arbitration, the application shall be made b-motion in that action. If the application is granted-the order shall operate to stay a pending or subsequen-action, or so much of it as is referable to arbitratio-

(b) *Application to stay arbitration.* Subject to th-provisions of subdivision (c), a party who has no-participated in the arbitration and who has not made o-been served with an application to compel arbitratio-may apply to stay arbitration on the ground that -valid agreement was not made or has not been complie-with or that the claim sought to be arbitrated is barre-by limitation under subdivision (b) of section 7502.

(c) *Notice of intention to arbitrate.* A party ma-serve upon another party a notice of intention t-arbitrate, specifying the agreement pursuant to whic-arbitration is sought and the name and address of th-party serving the notice, or of an officer or agen-thereof if such party is an association or corporatio-and stating that unless the party served applies t-stay the arbitration within ten days after such servic-he shall thereafter be precluded from objecting tha-a valid agreement was not made or has not bee-complied with and from asserting in court the bar of -limitation of time. Such notice shall be served in th-same manner as a summons or by registered or certi-fied mail, return receipt requested. An application t-stay arbitration must be made by the party serve-within ten days after service upon him of the notic-or he shall be so precluded. Notice of such applicatio-shall be served in the same manner as a summons o-by registered or certified mail, return receipt requeste-

§ 7504. Court appointment of arbitrator

If the arbitration agreement does not provide for -method of appointment of an arbitrator, or if th-agreed method fails or for any reason is not followe-or if an arbitrator fails to act and his successor ha-not been appointed, the court, on application of -party, shall appoint an arbitrator.

§ 7505. Powers of arbitrator

An arbitrator and any attorney of record in th-arbitration proceeding has the power to issue subpoenas-An arbitrator has the power to administer oaths.

§ 7506. Hearing

(a) Oath of arbitrator. Before hearing any testimony, an arbitrator shall be sworn to hear and decide the controversy faithfully and fairly by an officer authorized to administer an oath.

(b) Time and place. The arbitrator shall appoint a time and place for the hearing and notify the parties in writing personally or by registered or certified mail not less than eight days before the hearing. The arbitrator may adjourn or postpone the hearing. The court, upon application of any party, may direct the arbitrator to proceed promptly with the hearing and determination of the controversy.

(c) Evidence. The parties are entitled to be heard, to present evidence and to cross-examine witnesses. Notwithstanding the failure of a party duly notified to appear, the arbitrator may hear and determine the controversy upon the evidence produced.

(d) Representation by attorney. A party has the right to be represented by an attorney and may claim such right at any time as to any part of the arbitration or hearings which have not taken place. This right may not be waived. If a party is represented by an attorney, papers to be served on the party shall be served upon his attorney.

(e) Determination by majority. The hearing shall be conducted by all the arbitrators, but a majority may determine any question and render an award.

(f) Waiver. Except as provided in subdivision (d), a requirement of this section may be waived by written consent of the parties and it is waived if the parties continue with the arbitration without objection.

§ 7507. Award; form; time; delivery

Except as provided in section 7508, the award shall be in writing, signed and acknowledged by the arbitrator making it within the time fixed by the agreement, or, if the time is not fixed, within such time as the court orders. The parties may in writing extend the time either before or after its expiration. A party waives the objection that an award was not made within the time required unless he notifies the arbitrator in writing of his objection prior to the delivery of the award to him. The arbitrator shall deliver a copy of the award to each party in the manner provided in the agreement, or, if no provision is so made, personally or by registered or certified mail, return receipt requested.

§ 7508. Award by confession

(a) When available. An award by confession may be made for money due or to become due at any time before an award is otherwise made. The award shall be based upon a statement, verified by each party, containing an authorization to make the award, the sum of the award or the method of ascertaining it, and the facts constituting the liability.

(b) Time of award. The award may be made at any time within three months after the statement is verified.

(c) Person or agency making award. The award may be made by an arbitrator or by the agency or person named by the parties to designate the arbitrator.

§ 7509. Modification of award by arbitrator

On written application of a party to the arbitrators within twenty days after delivery of the award to the applicant, the arbitrators may modify the award upon the grounds stated in subdivision (c) of section 7511. Written notice of the application shall be given to other parties to the arbitration. Written objection to modification must be served on the arbitrators and other parties to the arbitration within ten days of receipt of the notice. The arbitrators shall dispose of any application made under this section in writing, signed and acknowledged by them, within thirty days after either written objection to modification has been served on them or the time for serving said objection has expired, whichever is earlier. The parties may in writing extend the time for such disposition either before or after its expiration.

§ 7510. Confirmation of award

The court shall confirm an award upon application of a party made within one year after its delivery to him, unless the award is vacated or modified upon a ground specified in section 7511.

§ 7511. Vacating or modifying award

(a) When application made. An application to vacate or modify an award may be made by a party within ninety days after its delivery to him.

(b) Grounds for vacating.

1. The award shall be vacated on the application of a party who either participated in the arbitration or was served with a notice of intention to arbitrate if the court finds that the rights of that party were prejudiced by:

(i) corruption, fraud or misconduct in procuring the award; or

(ii) partiality of an arbitrator appointed as a neutral, except where the award was by confession; or

(iii) an arbitrator, or agency or person making the award exceeded his power or so imperfectly executed it that a final and definite award upon the subject matter submitted was not made; or

(iv) failure to follow the procedure of this article, unless the party applying to vacate the award continued with the arbitration with notice of the defect and without objection.

2. The award shall be vacated on the application of a party who neither participated in the arbitration nor was served with a notice of intention to arbitrate if the court finds that:

(i) the rights of that party were prejudiced by one of the grounds specified in paragraph one; or

(ii) a valid agreement to arbitrate was not made; or

(iii) the agreement to arbitrate had not been complied with; or

(iv) the arbitrated claim was barred by limitation under subdivision (b) of section 7502.

(c) Grounds for modifying. The court shall modify the award if:

1. there was a miscalculation of figures or a mistake in the description of any person, thing or property referred to in the award; or

2. the arbitrators have awarded upon a matter not submitted to them and the award may be corrected without affecting the merits of the decision upon the issues submitted; or

3. the award is imperfect in a matter of form, not affecting the merits of the controversy.

(d) Rehearing. Upon vacating an award, the court may order a rehearing and determination of all or any of the issues either before the same arbitrator or before a new arbitrator appointed in accordance with this article. Time in any provision limiting the time for a hearing or award shall be measured from the date of such order or rehearing, whichever is appropriate, or a time may be specified by the court.

(e) Confirmation. Upon the granting of a motion to modify, the court shall confirm the award as modified; upon the denial of a motion to vacate or modify, it shall confirm the award.

§ 7512. Death or incompetency of a party

Where a party dies after making a written agreement to submit a controversy to arbitration, the proceedings may be begun or continued upon the applica-

tion of, or upon the notice to, his executor or administrator or, where it relates to real property, his distributee or devisee who has succeeded to his interest in the real property. Where a committee of the property or of the person of a party to such an agreement is appointed, the proceedings may be continued upon the application of, or notice to, the committee. Upon the death or incompetency of a party, the court may extend the time within which an application to confirm, vacate or modify the award or to stay arbitration must be made. Where a party has died since an award was delivered, the proceedings thereupon are the same as where a party dies after a verdict.

§ 7513. Fees and expenses

Unless otherwise provided in the agreement to arbitrate, the arbitrators' expenses and fees, together with other expenses, not including attorney's fees, incurred in the conduct of the arbitration, shall be paid as provided in the award. The court, on application, may reduce or disallow any fee or expense it finds excessive or allocate it as justice requires.

§ 7514. Judgment on an award

(a) Entry. A judgment shall be entered upon the confirmation of an award.

(b) Judgment-roll. The judgment-roll consists of the original or a copy of the agreement and each written extension of time within which to make an award; the statement required by section seventy-five hundred eight where the award was by confession; the award; each paper submitted to the court and each order of the court upon an application under sections 7510 and 7511; and a copy of the judgment.

THE UNIFORM ARBITRATION ACT

Introduction

The text of the Uniform Arbitration Law (Adopted ~~by~~ the National Conference of the Commissioners on ~~U~~niform State Laws in 1955 and amended in 1956, ~~a~~nd approved by the House of Delegates of the Amer~~i~~can Bar Association on August 26, 1955 and August ~~1~~0, 1956) has been reprinted by the American Ar~~bi~~tration Association in convenient form for the as~~si~~stance of legislators, lawyers, and businessmen who ~~w~~ish to improve the arbitration legislation in their ~~o~~wn states.

Many agreements to arbitrate are specifically en~~fo~~rceable under the Federal Arbitration Act and ~~u~~nder modern arbitration laws similar in content to ~~th~~e Uniform Act. In twenty-two states, the general ~~a~~dvantages of such modern laws are that they make ~~p~~ossible the use of future dispute arbitration clauses ~~i~~n a wide variety of contracts. At the same time, they ~~in~~clude minimum standards of procedure and rules ~~fo~~r confirming awards in court and invalidating ~~a~~wards for procedural defects. They establish pro~~c~~edures by which court actions in violation of agree~~m~~ents to arbitrate may be stayed. The effect of ~~m~~odern arbitration statutes is to endow agreements ~~to~~ arbitrate with the same legal protections that other ~~le~~gitimate private agreements have. This makes it ~~p~~ossible for the lawyer to use arbitration as one of ~~th~~e effective tools in his profession.

A list of citations to modern arbitration statutes is ~~p~~rinted on Page 11. It should be noted that some ~~of~~ these laws vary from the Uniform Law.

The American Arbitration Association is able to ~~a~~ct as a source of information on proposed arbitra~~ti~~on legislation. Inquiries should be directed to any ~~o~~ne of the regional offices listed on the back of this ~~p~~amphlet, or to the General Counsel of the Associa~~ti~~on in New York.

ACT RELATING TO ARBITRATION AND TO MAKE UNIFORM THE LAW WITH REFERENCE THERETO

SECTION 1. (*Validity of Arbitration Agreement.*) A written agreement to submit any existing controversy to arbitration or a provision in a written contract to submit to arbitration any controversy thereafter arising between the parties is valid, enforceable and irrevocable, save upon such grounds as exist at law or in equity for the revocation of any contract. This act also applies to arbitration agreements between employers and employees or between their respective representatives (unless otherwise provided in the agreement.)

SECTION 2. (*Proceedings to Compel or Stay Arbitration.*)

(a) On application of a party showing an agreement described in Section 1, and the opposing party's refusal to arbitrate, the Court shall order the parties to proceed with arbitration, but if the opposing party denies the existence of the agreement to arbitrate, the Court shall proceed summarily to the determination of the issue so raised and shall order arbitration if found for the moving party, otherwise, the application shall be denied.

(b) On application, the court may stay an arbitration proceeding commenced or threatened on a showing that there is no agreement to arbitrate. Such an issue, when in substantial and bona fide dispute, shall be forthwith and summarily tried and the stay ordered if found for the moving party. If found for the opposing party, the court shall order the parties to proceed to arbitration.

(c) If an issue referable to arbitration under the alleged agreement is involved in an action or proceeding pending in a court having jurisdiction to hear applications under subdivision (a) of this Section, the application shall be made therein. Otherwise and subject to Section 18, the application may be made in any court of competent jurisdiction.

(d) Any action or proceeding involving an issue subject to arbitration shall be stayed if an order for arbitration or an application therefor has been made under this section or, if the issue is severable, the stay may be with respect thereto only. When the application is made in such action or proceeding, the order for arbitration shall include such stay.

(e) An order for arbitration shall not be refused on the ground that the claim in issue lacks merit or bona fides or because any fault or grounds for the claim sought to be arbitrated have not been shown.

SECTION 3. (*Appointment of Arbitrators by Court.*) If the arbitration agreement provides a method of appointment of arbitrators, this method shall be followed. In the absence thereof, or if the agreed method fails or for any reason cannot be followed, or when an arbitrator appointed fails or is unable to act and his successor has not been duly appointed, the court on application of a party shall appoint one or more arbitrators. An arbitrator so appointed has all the powers of one specifically named in the agreement.

SECTION 4. (*Majority Action by Arbitrators.*) The powers of the arbitrators may be exercised by a majority unless otherwise provided by the agreement or by this act.

SECTION 5. (*Hearing.*) Unless otherwise provided by the agreement:

(a) The arbitrators shall appoint a time and place for the hearing and cause notification to the parties to be served personally or by registered mail not less than five days before the hearing. Appearance at the hearing waives such notice. The arbitrators may adjourn the hearing from time to time as necessary and, on request of a party and for good cause, or upon their own motion may postpone the hearing to a time not later than the date fixed by the agreement

for making the award unless the parties consent to a later date. The arbitrators may hear and determine the controversy upon the evidence produced notwithstanding the failure of a party duly notified to appear. The court on application may direct the arbitrators to proceed promptly with the hearing and determination of the controversy.

(b) The parties are entitled to be heard, to present evidence material to the controversy and to cross-examine witnesses appearing at the hearing.

(c) The hearing shall be conducted by all the arbitrators but a majority may determine any question and render a final award. If, during the course of the hearing, an arbitrator for any reason ceases to act, the remaining arbitrator or arbitrators appointed to act as neutrals may continue with the hearing and determination of the controversy.

SECTION 6. (*Representation by Attorney.*) A party has the right to be represented by an attorney at any proceeding or hearing under this act. A waiver thereof prior to the proceeding or hearing is ineffective.

SECTION 7. (*Witnesses, Subpoenas, Depositions.*)

(a) The arbitrators may issue (cause to be issued) subpoenas for the attendance of witnesses and for the production of books, records, documents and other evidence, and shall have the power to administer oaths. Subpoenas so issued shall be served, and upon application to the Court by a party or the arbitrators, enforced, in the manner provided by law for the service and enforcement of subpoenas in a civil action.

(b) On application of a party and for use as evidence, the arbitrators may permit a deposition to be taken, in the manner and upon the terms designated by the arbitrators, of a witness who cannot be subpoenaed or is unable to attend the hearing.

(c) All provisions of law compelling a person under subpoena to testify are applicable.

(d) Fees for attendance as a witness shall be the same as for a witness in the ....Court.

SECTION 8. (*Award.*)

(a) The award shall be in writing and signed by the arbitrators joining in the award. The arbitrators shall deliver a copy to each party personally or by registered mail, or as provided in the agreement.

(b) An award shall be made within the time fixed therefor by the agreement or, if not so fixed, within such time as the court orders on application of a party. The parties may extend the time in writing either before or after the expiration thereof. A party waives the objection that an award was not made within the time required unless he notifies the arbitrators of his objection prior to the delivery of the award to him.

SECTION 9. (*Change of Award by Arbitrators.*) On application of a party or, if an application to the court is pending under Sections 11, 12 or 13, on submission to the arbitrators by the court under such conditions as the court may order, the arbitrators may modify or correct the award upon the grounds stated in paragraphs (1) and (3) of subdivision (a) of Section 13, or for the purpose of clarifying the award. The application shall be made within twenty days after delivery of the award to the applicant. Written notice thereof shall be given forthwith to the opposing party, stating he must serve his objections thereto, if any, within ten days from the notice. The award so modified or corrected is subject to the provisions of Sections 11, 12 and 13.

SECTION 10. (*Fees and Expenses of Arbitration.*) Unless otherwise provided in the agreement to arbitrate, the arbitrators' expenses and fees, together with other expenses, not including counsel fees, incurred in the conduct of the arbitration, shall be paid as provided in the award.

SECTION 11. (*Confirmation of an Award.*) Upon application of a party, the Court shall confirm an award, unless within the time limits hereinafter imposed grounds are urged for vacating or modifying or cor-

recting the award, in which case the court shall proceed as provided in Sections 12 and 13.

SECTION 12. (*Vacating an Award.*)

(a) Upon application of a party, the court shall vacate an award where:

(1) The award was procured by corruption, fraud or other undue means;

(2) There was evident partiality by an arbitrator appointed as a neutral or corruption in any of the arbitrators or misconduct prejudicing the rights of any party;

(3) The arbitrators exceeded their powers;

(4) The arbitrators refused to postpone the hearing upon sufficient cause being shown therefor or refused to hear evidence material to the controversy or otherwise so conducted the hearing, contrary to the provisions of Section 5, as to prejudice substantially the rights of a party; or

(5) There was no arbitration agreement and the issue was not adversely determined in proceedings under Section 2 and the party did not participate in the arbitration hearing without raising the objection;

But the fact that the relief was such that it could not or would not be granted by a court of law or equity is not ground for vacating or refusing to confirm the award.

(b) An application under this Section shall be made within ninety days after delivery of a copy of the award to the applicant, except that, if predicated upon corruption, fraud or other undue means, it shall be made within ninety days after such grounds are known or should have been known.

(c) In vacating the award on grounds other than stated in clause (5) of Subsection (a) the court may order a rehearing before new arbitrators chosen as provided in the agreement, or in the absence thereof, by the court in accordance with Section 3, or, if the award is vacated on grounds set forth in clauses (3), and (4) of Subsection (a) the court may order a rehearing before the arbitrators who made the award or their successors appointed in accordance with

Section 3. The time within which the agreement requires the award to be made is applicable to the rehearing and commences from the date of the order.

(d) If the application to vacate is denied and no motion to modify or correct the award is pending, the court shall confirm the award.

SECTION 13. (*Modification or Correction of Award.*)

(a) Upon application made within ninety days after delivery of a copy of the award to the applicant, the court shall modify or correct the award where:

(1) There was an evident miscalculation of figures or an evident mistake in the description of any person, thing or property referred to in the award;

(2) The arbitrators have awarded upon a matter not submitted to them and the award may be corrected without affecting the merits of the decision upon the issues submitted; or

(3) The award is imperfect in a matter of form, not affecting the merits of the controversy.

(b) If the application is granted, the court shall modify and correct the award so as to effect its intent and shall confirm the award as so modified and corrected. Otherwise, the court shall confirm the award as made.

(c) An application to modify or correct an award may be joined in the alternative with an application to vacate the award.

SECTION 14. (*Judgment or Decree on Award.*) Upon the granting of an order confirming, modifying or correcting an award, judgment or decree shall be entered in conformity therewith and be enforced as any other judgment or decree. Costs of the application and of the proceedings subsequent thereto, and disbursements may be awarded by the court.

* [SECTION 15. (*Judgment Roll, Docketing.*)

(a) On entry of judgment or decree, the clerk

---

* *Brackets and parenthesis enclose language which the Commissioners suggest may be used by those States desiring to do so.*

shall prepare the judgment roll consisting, to the extent filed, of the following:

(1) The agreement and each written extension of the time within which to make the award;

(2) The award;

(3) A copy of the order confirming, modifying or correcting the award; and

(4) A copy of the judgment or decree.

(b) The judgment or decree may be docketed as if rendered in an action.]

SECTION 16. (*Applications to Court.*) Except as otherwise provided, an application to the court under this act shall be by motion and shall be heard in the manner and upon the notice provided by law or rule of court for the making and hearing of motions. Unless the parties have agreed otherwise, notice of an initial application for an order shall be served in the manner provided by law for the service of a summons in an action.

SECTION 17. (*Court, Jurisdiction.*) The term "court" means any court of competent jurisdiction of this State. The making of an agreement described in Section 1 providing for arbitration in this State confers jurisdiction on the court to enforce the agreement under this Act and to enter judgment on an award thereunder.

SECTION 18. (*Venue.*) An initial application shall be made to the court of the (county) in which the agreement provides the arbitration hearing shall be held or, if the hearing has been held, in the county in which it was held. Otherwise the application shall be made in the (county) where the adverse party resides or has a place of business or, if he has no residence or place of business in this State, to the court of any (county). All subsequent applications shall be made to the court hearing the initial application unless the court otherwise directs.

SECTION 19. (*Appeals.*)

(a) An appeal may be taken from:

(1) An order denying an application to compel arbitration made under Section 2;

(2) An order granting an application to stay arbitration made under Section 2(b);

(3) An order confirming or denying confirmation of an award;

(4) An order modifying or correcting an award;

(5) An order vacating an award without directing a rehearing; or

(6) A judgment or decree entered pursuant to the provisions of this act.

(b) The appeal shall be taken in the manner and to the same extent as from orders or judgments in a civil action.

SECTION 20. (*Act Not Retroactive.*) This act applies only to agreements made subsequent to the taking effect of this act.

SECTION 21. (*Uniformity of Interpretation.*) This act shall be so construed as to effectuate its general purpose to make uniform the law of those states which enact it.

SECTION 22. (*Constitutionality.*) If any provision of this act or the application thereof to any person or circumstance is held invalid, the invalidity shall not affect other provisions or applications of the act which can be given without the invalid provision or application, and to this end the provisions of this act are severable.

SECTION 23. (*Short Title.*) This act may be cited as the Uniform Arbitration Act.

SECTION 24. (*Repeal.*) All acts or parts of acts which are inconsistent with the provisions of this act are hereby repealed.

SECTION 25. (*Time of Taking Effect.*) This act shall take effect ....

MODERN ARBITRATION STATUTES IN THE UNITED STATES

UNITED STATES ARBITRATION ACT. U. S. Code, Title 9, Sections 1-14; 61 Stat. 669, as amended by Sec. 19 of Public Law 779, of September 3, 1954, 68 Stat. 1233.

ARIZONA. Arizona Revised Statutes (1962), Chapter 9, Sections 12-1501 to 12-1516.

CALIFORNIA. Code of Civil Procedure, Part 3, Title 9, Sections 1280 to 1294 (Supp. 1961).

CONNECTICUT. General Statutes Annotated, Revision of 1958, Title 52, Chapter 902, Sections 52-401 to 52-424.

FLORIDA. Florida Statutes Annotated, Chapter 57, Sections 57.10 to 57.31.

HAWAII. Revised Laws of Hawaii 1955, Chapter 188, Sections 188-1 to 188-15.

ILLINOIS. Illinois Rev. Statutes, 1961, sect. 101, 1962 Cum. Ann. Pocket Part p. 192.

LOUISIANA. Louisiana Revised Statutes (West, 1951), Title 9, Chapter 1, Sections 4201 to 4217.

MARYLAND. Act 1965, ch. 231, Art. 7, eff. June 1, 1965.

MASSACHUSETTS. Annotated Laws of Massachusetts, Chapter 251, Sections 1 to 19 (Supp. 1961).

MICHIGAN. Michigan Statutes Annotated, Title 27, Chapter 47, Sections 27.2483 to 27.2505, as amended by Public Act No. 27 of 1963; Michigan Supreme Court Rules, Rule 769 (1963).

MINNESOTA. Minnesota Statutes Annotated, Vol. 37, Chapter 572, Sections 572.08 to 572-30 (Supp. 1961).

NEW HAMPSHIRE. New Hampshire Revised Statutes Annotated 1955, Chapter 542, Sections 542:1 to 542:10.

NEW JERSEY. New Jersey Statutes, Title 2A, Chapter 24, Sections 2A:24-1 to 2A:24-11.

NEW YORK. Civil Practice Law and Rules, Art. 75, effective September 1, 1963; sect. 7501 amended by N. Y. Laws 1962, Chap. 308.

OHIO. Ohio Revised Code Annotated (Page, 1954), Chapter 2711, Sections 2711.01 to 2711.15, as amended on June 30, 1955 (Laws of Ohio, vol. 126, p. 304); 1961 Supp. p. 46.

OREGON. Oregon Revised Statutes (1955 Replacement Parts), Chapter 33, Sections 33.210 to 33.340.

PENNSYLVANIA. Purdon's Pennsylvania Statutes Annotated, Title 5, Chapters 1 to 4, Sections 1 to 181.

RHODE ISLAND. General Laws of Rhode Island 1956, Title 10, Chapter 3, Sections 10-3-1 to 10-3-20.

TEXAS. Vernon's Ann. Civ. St. arts 224-238-6, eff. Jan. 1, 1966.

WASHINGTON. Revised Code of Washington, Title 7, Chapter 7.04, Sections 7.04-010 to 7.04-220.

WISCONSIN. Wisconsin Statutes (West's Ann.), Title 27, Chapter 298, Sections 298-01 to 298-18.

WYOMING. Wyoming Stat. 1963 Supp. Chapter 37.

THE UNITED STATES ARBITRATION ACT

THE UNITED STATES ARBITRATION ACT

Title 9, U.S. Code §§ 1-14, first enacted February 12, 1925 (43 Stat. 883), codified July 30, 1947 (61 Stat. 669), and amended September 3, 1954 (68 Stat. 1233).

ARBITRATION

§1. Maritime transactions and commerce defined; exceptions to operation of title.

§2. Validity, irrevocability, and enforcement of agreements to arbitrate.

§3. Stay of proceedings where issue therein referable to arbitration.

§4. Failure to arbitrate under agreement; petition to United States court having jurisdiction for order to compel arbitration; notice and service thereof; hearing and determination.

§5. Appointment of arbitrators or umpire.

§6. Application heard as motion.

§7. Witnesses before arbitrators; fees; compelling attendance.

§8. Proceedings begun by libel in admiralty and seizure of vessel or property.

§9. Award of arbitrators; confirmation; jurisdiction; procedure.

§10. Same; vacation; grounds; rehearing.

§11. Same; modification or correction; grounds; order.

§12. Notice of motions to vacate or modify; service; stay of proceedings.

§13. Papers filed with order on motions; judgment; docketing; force and effect; enforcement.

§14. Contracts not affected.

"Maritime Transactions" and "Commerce" Defined; Exceptions to Operation of Title

§ 1. "Maritime transactions," as herein defined, means charter parties, bills of lading of water carriers, agreements relating to wharfage, supplies furnished vessels or repairs of vessels, collisions, or any other matters in foreign commerce which, if the subject of controversy, would be embraced within admiralty jurisdiction; "commerce," as herein defined, means commerce among the several States or with foreign nations, or in any Territory of the United States or in the District of Columbia, or between any such Territory and another, or between any such Territory and any State or foreign nation, or between the District of Columbia and any State or Territory or foreign nation, but nothing herein contained shall apply to contracts of employment of seamen, railroad employees, or any other class of workers engaged in foreign or interstate commerce.

Validity, Irrevocability, and Enforcement of Agreements to Arbitrate

§ 2. A written provision in any maritime transaction or a contract evidencing a transaction involving commerce to settle by arbitration a controversy thereafter arising out of such contract or transaction, or the refusal to perform the whole or any part thereof, or an agreement in writing to submit to arbitration an existing controversy arising out of such a contract, transaction, or refusal, shall be valid, irrevocable, and enforceable, save upon such grounds as exist at law or in equity for the revocation of any contract.

Stay of Proceedings Where Issue Therein Referable to Arbitration

§ 3. If any suit or proceeding be brought in any of the courts of the United States upon any issue referable to arbitration under an agreement in writing for such arbitration, the court in which such suit is pending, upon being satis-

310

fied that the issue involved in such suit or proceeding is referable to arbitration under such an agreement, shall on application of one of the parties stay the trial of the action until such arbitration has been had in accordance with the terms of the agreement, providing the applicant for the stay is not in default in proceeding with such arbitration.

Failure to Arbitrate Under Agreement; Petition to United States Court Having Jurisdiction for Order to Compel Arbitration; Notice and Service Thereof; Hearing and Determination

§ 4. A party aggrieved by the alleged failure, neglect, or refusal of another to arbitrate under a written agreement for arbitration may petition any United States district court which, save for such agreement, would have jurisdiction under Title 28, in a civil action or in admiralty of the subject matter of a suit arising out of the controversy between the parties, for an order directing that such arbitration proceed in the manner provided for in such agreement. Five days' notice in writing of such application shall be served upon the party in default. Service thereof shall be made in the manner provided by the Federal Rules of Civil Procedure. The court shall hear the parties, and upon being satisfied that the making of the agreement for arbitration or the failure to comply therewith is not in issue, the court shall make an order directing the parties to proceed to arbitration in accordance with the terms of the agreement. The hearing and proceedings, under such agreement, shall be within the district in which the petition for an order directing such arbitration is filed. If the making of the arbitration agreement or the failure, neglect, or refusal to perform the same be in issue, the court shall proceed summarily to the trial thereof. If no jury trial be demanded by the party alleged to be in default, or if the matter in dispute is within admiralty jurisdiction, the court shall hear and determine such issue. Where

such an issue is raised, the party alleged to be in default may, except in cases of admiralty, on or before the return day of the notice of application, demand a jury trial of such issue, and upon such demand the court shall make an order referring the issue or issues to a jury in the manner provided by the Federal Rules of Civil Procedure, or may specially call a jury for that purpose. If the jury find that no agreement in writing for arbitration was made or that there is no default in proceeding thereunder, the proceeding shall be dismissed. If the jury find that an agreement for arbitration was made in writing and that there is a default in proceeding thereunder, the court shall make an order summarily directing the parties to proceed with the arbitration in accordance with the terms thereof.

Appointment of Arbitrators or Umpire

§ 5. If in the agreement provision be made for a method of naming or appointing an arbitrator or arbitrators or an umpire, such method shall be followed; but if no method be provided therein, or if a method be provided and any party thereto shall fail to avail himself of such method, or if for any other reason there shall be a lapse in the naming of an arbitrator or arbitrators or umpire, or in filling a vacancy, then upon the application of either party to the controversy the court shall designate and appoint an arbitrator or arbitrators or umpire, as the case may require, who shall act under the said agreement with the same force and effect as if he or they had been specifically named therein; and unless otherwise provided in the agreement the arbitration shall be by a single arbitrator.

Application Heard as Motion

§ 6. Any application to the court hereunder shall be made and heard in the manner provided by law for the making and hearing of motions, except as otherwise herein expressly provided.

Witnesses Before Arbitrators; Fees; Compelling Attendance

§ 7. The arbitrators selected either as prescribed in this title or otherwise, or a majority of them, may summon in writing any person to attend before them or any of them as a witness and in a proper case to bring with him or them any book, record, document, or paper which may be deemed material as evidence in the case. The fees for such attendance shall be the same as the fees of witnesses before masters of the United States courts. Said summons shall issue in the name of the arbitrator or arbitrators, or a majority of them, and shall be signed by the arbitrators, or a majority of them, and shall be directed to the said person and shall be served in the same manner as subpoenas to appear and testify before the court; if any person or persons so summoned to testify shall refuse or neglect to obey said summons, upon petition the United States court in and for the district in which such arbitrators, or a majority of them, are sitting may compel the attendance of such person or persons before said arbitrator or arbitrators, or punish said person or persons for contempt in the same manner provided on February 12, 1925, for securing the attendance of witnesses or their punishment for neglect or refusal to attend in the courts of the United States.

Proceedings Begun by Libel in Admiralty and Seizure of Vessel or Property

§ 8. If the basis of jurisdiction be a cause of action otherwise justiciable in admiralty, then, notwithstanding anything herein to the contrary the party claiming to be aggrieved may begin his proceeding hereunder by libel and seizure of the vessel or other property of the other party according to the usual course of admiralty proceedings, and the court shall then have jurisdiction to direct the parties to proceed with the arbitration and shall retain jurisdiction to enter its decree upon the award.

Award of Arbitrators; Confirmation; Jurisdiction; Procedure

§ 9. If the parties in their agreement have agreed that a judgment of the court shall be entered upon the award made pursuant to the arbitration, and shall specify the court, then at any time within one year after the award is made any party to the arbitration may apply to the court so specified for an order confirming the award, and thereupon the court must grant such an order unless the award is vacated, modified, or corrected as prescribed in sections 10 and 11 of this title. If no court is specified in the agreement of the parties, then such application may be made to the United States court in and for the district within which such award was made. Notice of the application shall be served upon the adverse party, and thereupon the court shall have jurisdiction of such party as though he had appeared generally in the proceeding. If the adverse party is a resident of the district within which the award was made, such service shall be made upon the adverse party or his attorney as prescribed by law for service of notice of motion in an action in the same court. If the adverse party shall be a nonresident, then the notice of the application shall be served by the marshal of any district within which the adverse party may be found in like manner as other process of the court.

Same; Vacation; Grounds; Rehearing

§ 10. In either of the following cases the United States court in and for the district wherein the award was made may make an order vacating the award upon the application of any party to the arbitration—

(a) Where the award was procured by corruption, fraud, or undue means.

(b) Where there was evident partiality or corruption in the arbitrators, or either of them.

(c) Where the arbitrators were guilty of misconduct in refusing to postpone the hearing, upon sufficient cause shown, or in refusing to hear evidence pertinent and material to the controversy; or of any other misbehavior by which the rights of any party have been prejudiced.

(d) Where the arbitrators exceeded their powers, or so imperfectly executed them that a mutual, final, and definite award upon the subject matter submitted was not made.

(e) Where an award is vacated and the time within which the agreement required the award to be made has not expired the court may, in its discretion, direct a rehearing by the arbitrators.

Same; Modification or Correction; Grounds; Order

§ 11. In either of the following cases the United States court in and for the district wherein the award was made may make an order modifying or correcting the award upon the application of any party to the arbitration—

(a) Where there was an evident material miscalculation of figures or an evident material mistake in the description of any person, thing, or property referred to in the award.

(b) Where the arbitrators have awarded upon a matter not submitted to them, unless it is a matter not affecting the merits of the decision upon the matter submitted.

(c) Where the award is imperfect in matter of form not affecting the merits of the controversy.

The order may modify and correct the award, so as to effect the intent thereof and promote justice between the parties.

Notice of Motions to Vacate or Modify; Service; Stay of Proceedings

§ 12. Notice of a motion to vacate, modify, or correct an award must be served upon the adverse party or his attorney within three months after the award is filed or delivered. If the adverse party is a resident of the district within which the award was made, such service shall be made upon the adverse party or his attorney as prescribed by law for service of notice of motion in an action in the same court. If the adverse party shall be a nonresident then the notice of the application shall be served by the marshal of any district within which the adverse party may be found in like manner as other process of the court. For the purposes of the motion any judge who might make an order to stay the proceedings in an action brought in the same court may make an order, to be served with the notice of motion, staying the proceedings of the adverse party to enforce the award.

Papers Filed with Order on Motions; Judgment; Docketing; Force and Effect; Enforcement

§ 13. The party moving for an order confirming, modifying, or correcting an award shall, at the time such order is filed with the clerk for the entry of judgment thereon, also file the following papers with the clerk:

(a) The agreement; the selection or appointment, if any, of an additional arbitrator or umpire; and each written extension of the time, if any, within which to make the award.

(b) The award.

(c) Each notice, affidavit, or other paper used upon an application to confirm, modify, or correct the award, and a copy of each order of the court upon such an application.

The judgment shall be docketed as if it was rendered in an action.

The judgment so entered shall have the same force and effect, in all respects, as, and be subject to all the provisions of law relating to, a judgment in an action; and it may be enforced as if it had been rendered in an action in the court in which it is entered.

Contracts Not Affected

§ 14. This title shall not apply to contracts made prior to January 1, 1926.

CONVENTION ON THE RECOGNITION AND ENFORCEMENT OF FOREIGN AWARDS (UNITED NATIONS) (NEW YORK CONVENTION)

CONVENTION ON THE RECOGNITION AND ENFORCEMENT OF FOREIGN ARBITRAL AWARDS
June 10, 1958

Article I

1. This Convention shall apply to the recognition and enforcement of arbitral awards made in the territory of a State other than the State where the recognition and enforcement of such awards are sought, and arising out of differences between persons, whether physical or legal. It shall also apply to arbitral awards not considered as domestic awards in the State where their recognition and enforcement are sought.

2. The term "arbitral awards" shall include not only awards made by arbitrators appointed for each case but also those made by permanent arbitral bodies to which the parties have submitted.

3. When signing, ratifying or acceding to this Convention, or notifying extension under article X hereof, any State may on the basis of reciprocity declare that it will apply the Convention to the recognition and enforcement of awards made only in the territory of another Contracting State. It may also declare that it will apply the Convention only to differences arising out of legal relationships whether contractual or not, which are considered as commercial under the national law of the State making such declaration.

Article II

1. Each Contracting State shall recognize an agreement in writing under which the parties undertake to submit to arbitration all or any differences which have arisen or which may arise between them in respect of a defined legal relationship, whether contractual or not, concerning a subject matter capable of settlement by arbitration.

2. The term "agreement in writing" shall include an arbitral clause in a contract or an arbitration agreement, signed by the parties or contained in an exchange of letters or telegrams.

3. The court of a Contracting State, when seized of an action in a matter in respect of which the parties have made an agreement within the meaning of this article, shall, at the request of one of the parties, refer the parties to arbitration, unless it finds that the said agreement is null and void, inoperative or incapable of being performed.

Article III

Each Contracting State shall recognize arbitral awards as binding and enforce them in accordance with the rules of procedure of the territory where the award is relied upon, under the conditions laid down in the following articles. There shall not be imposed substantially more onerous conditions or higher fees or charges on the recognition or enforcement of arbitral awards to which this Convention applies than are imposed on the recognition or enforcement of domestic arbitral awards.

Article IV

1. To obtain the recognition and enforcement mentioned in the preceding article, the party applying for recognition and enforcement shall, at the time of the application, supply:
   (a) the duly authenticated original award or a duly certified copy thereof;
   (b) the original agreement referred to in article II or a duly certified copy thereof.

2. If the said award or agreement is not made in an official language of the country in which the award is relied upon, the party applying for recognition and enforcement of the award shall produce a translation of these documents into such language. The translation shall be certified by an official or sworn translator or by a diplomatic or consular agent.

Article V

1. Recognition and enforcement of the award may be refused, at the request of the party against whom it is invoked, only if that party furnishes to the competent authority where the recognition and enforcement is sought, proof that:
   (a) the parties to the agreement referred to in article II were, under the law applicable to them, under some incapacity,

or the said agreement is not valid under the law to which the parties have subjected it or, failing any indication thereon, under the law of the country where the award was made; or

(b) the party against whom the award is invoked was not given proper notice of the appointment of the arbitrator or of the arbitration proceedings or was otherwise unable to present his case; or

(c) the award deals with a difference not contemplated by or not falling within the terms of the submission to arbitration, or it contains decisions on matters beyond the scope of the submission to arbitration, provided that, if the decisions on matters submitted to arbitration can be separated from those not so submitted, that part of the award which contains decisions on matters submitted to arbitration may be recognized and enforced; or

(d) the composition of the arbitral authority or the arbitral procedure was not in accordance with the agreement of the parties, or, failing such agreement, was not in accordance with the law of the country where the arbitration took place; or

(e) the award has not yet become binding on the parties, or has been set aside or suspended by a competent authority of the country in which, or under the law of which, that award was made.

2. Recognition and enforcement of an arbitral award may also be refused if the competent authority in the country where recognition and enforcement is sought finds that:

(a) the subject matter of the difference is not capable of settlement by arbitration under the law of that country; or

(b) the recognition or enforcement of the award would be contrary to the public policy of that country.

Article VI

If an application for the setting aside or suspension of the award has been made to a competent authority referred to in Article V paragraph (1) (e), the authority before which the award is sought to be relied upon may, if it considers it proper, adjourn the decision on the enforcement of the award and may also, on the application of the party claiming enforcement of the award, order the other party to give suitable security.

Article VII

1. The provisions of the present Convention shall not affect the validity of multilateral or bilateral agreements concerning the recognition and enforcement of arbitral awards entered into by the Contracting States nor deprive any interested party of any right he may have to avail himself of an arbitral award in the manner and to the extent allowed by the law or the treaties of the country where such award is sought to be relied upon.

2. The Geneva Protocol on Arbitration Clauses of 1923 and the Geneva Convention on the Execution of Foreign Arbitral Awards of 1927 shall cease to have effect between Contracting States on their becoming bound and to the extent that they become bound, by this Convention.

Article VIII

1. This Convention shall be open until 31 December 1958 for signature on behalf of any Member of the United Nations and also on behalf of any other State which is or hereafter becomes a member of any specialized agency of the United Nations, or which is or hereafter becomes a party to the Statute of the International Court of Justice, or any other State to which an invitation has been addressed by the General Assembly of the United Nations.

2. This Convention shall be ratified and the instrument of ratification shall be deposited with the Secretary-General of the United Nations.

Article IX

1. This Convention shall be open for accession to all States referred to in article VIII.

2. Accession shall be effected by the deposit of an instrument of accession with the Secretary-General of the United Nations.

Article X

1. Any State may, at the time of signature, ratification or accession, declare that this Convention shall extend to all or any of the territories for the international relations of which it is responsible. Such a declaration shall take effect when the Convention enters into force for the State concerned.

2. At any time thereafter any such extension shall be made by notification addressed to the Secretary-General of the United Nations and shall take effect as from the ninetieth day after the day of receipt by the Secretary-General of the United Nations of this notifica-

tion, or as from the date of entry into force of the Convention for the State concerned, whichever is the later.

3. With respect to those territories to which this Convention is not extended at the time of signature, ratification or accession, each State concerned shall consider the possibility of taking the necessary steps in order to extend the application of this Convention to such territories, subject, where necessary for constitutional reasons, to the consent of the Governments of such territories.

Article XI

1. In the case of a federal or non-unitary State, the following provisions shall apply:

(a) With respect to those articles of this Convention that come within the legislative jurisdiction of the federal authority, the obligations of the federal Government shall to this extent be the same as those of Contracting States which are not federal States;

(b) With respect to those articles of this Convention that come within the legislative jurisdiction of constituent states or provinces which are not, under the constitutional system of the federation, bound to take legislative action, the federal Government shall bring such articles with a favourable recommendation to the notice of the appropriate authorities of constituent states or provinces at the earliest possible moment;

(c) A federal State party to this Convention shall, at the request of any other Contracting State transmitted through the Secretary-General of the United Nations, supply a statement of the law and practice of the federation and its constituent units in regard to any particular provision of this Convention, showing the extent to which effect has been given to that provision by legislative or other action.

Article XII

1. This Convention shall come into force on the ninetieth day following the date of deposit of the third instrument of ratification or accession.

2. For each State ratifying or acceding to this Convention after the deposit of the third instrument of ratification or accession, this Convention shall enter into force on the ninetieth day after deposit by such State of its instrument of ratification or accession.

Article XIII

1. Any Contracting State may denounce this Convention by a written notification to the Secretary-General of the United Nations. Denunciation shall take effect one year after the date of receipt of the notification by the Secretary-General.

2. Any State which has made a declaration or notification under article X may, at any time thereafter, by notification to the Secretary-General of the United Nations, declare that this Convention shall cease to extend to the territory concerned one year after the date of the receipt of the notification by the Secretary-General.

3. This Convention shall continue to be applicable to arbitral awards in respect of which recognition or enforcement proceedings have been instituted before the denunciation takes effect.

Article XIV

A Contracting State shall not be entitled to avail itself of the present Convention against other Contracting States except to the extent that it is itself bound to apply the Convention.

Article XV

The Secretary-General of the United Nations shall notify the States contemplated in article VIII of the following:

(a) Signature and ratifications in accordance with article VIII;

(b) Accessions in accordance with article IX;

(c) Declarations and notifications under articles I, X and XI;

(d) The date upon which this Convention enters into force in accordance with article XII;

(e) Denunciations and notifications in accordance with article XIII.

Article XVI

1. This Convention, of which the Chinese, English, French, Russian and Spanish texts shall be equally authentic, shall be deposited in the archives of the United Nations.

2. The Secretary-General of the United Nations shall transmit a certified copy of this Convention to the States contemplated in article VIII.

CONVENTION ON THE SETTLEMENT OF INVESTMENT DISPUTES BETWEEN STATES AND NATIONALS OF OTHER STATES (IBRD) (MARCH 18, 1965). CHAPTERS IV-VII ARBITRATION

Submitted to Governments

by the Executive Directors of the

INTERNATIONAL BANK FOR RECONSTRUCTION AND DEVELOPMENT

March 18, 1965

ARBITRATION.   Chapters IV—VIII

CHAPTER IV

Arbitration

SECTION 1

Request for Arbitration

Article 36

(1) Any Contracting State or any national of a Contracting State wishing to institute arbitration proceedings shall address a request to that effect in writing to the Secretary-General who shall send a copy of the request to the other party.

(2) The request shall contain information concerning the issues in dispute, the identity of the parties and their consent to arbitration in accordance with the rules of procedure for the institution of conciliation and arbitration proceedings.

(3) The Secretary-General shall register the request unless he finds, on the basis of the information contained in the request, that the dispute is manifestly outside the jurisdiction of the Centre. He shall forthwith notify the parties of registration or refusal to register.

Section 2

Constitution of the Tribunal

Article 37

(1) The Arbitral Tribunal (hereinafter called the Tribunal) shall be constituted as soon as possible after registration of a request pursuant to Article 36.

(2) (a) The Tribunal shall consist of a sole arbitrator or any uneven number of arbitrators appointed as the parties shall agree.

(b) Where the parties do not agree upon the number of arbitrators and the method of their appointment, the Tribunal shall consist of three arbitrators, one arbitrator appointed by each party and the third, who shall be the president of the Tribunal, appointed by agreement of the parties.

Article 38

If the Tribunal shall not have been constituted within 90 days after notice of registration of the request has been dispatched by the Secretary-General in accordance with paragraph (3) of Article 36, or such other period as the parties may agree, the Chairman shall, at the request of either party and after consulting both parties as far as possible, appoint the arbitrator or arbitrators not yet appointed. Arbitrators appointed by the Chairman pursuant to this Article shall not be nationals of the Contracting State party to the dispute or of the Contracting State whose national is a party to the dispute.

Article 39

The majority of the arbitrators shall be nationals of States other than the Contracting State party to the dispute and the Contracting State whose national is a party to the dispute; provided, however, that the foregoing provisions of this Article shall not apply if the sole arbitrator or each individual member of the Tribunal has been appointed by agreement of the parties.

Article 40

(1) Arbitrators may be appointed from outside the Panel of Arbitrators, except in the case of appointments by the Chairman pursuant to Article 38.

(2) Arbitrators appointed from outside the Panel of Arbitrators shall possess the qualities stated in paragraph (1) of Article 14.

SECTION 3

Powers and Functions of the Tribunal

Article 41

(1) The Tribunal shall be the judge of its own competence.

(2) Any objection by a party to the dispute that that dispute is not within the jurisdiction of the Centre, or for other reasons is not within the competence of the Tribunal, shall be considered by the Tribunal which shall determine whether to deal with it as a preliminary question or to join it to the merits of the dispute.

Article 42

(1) The Tribunal shall decide a dispute in accordance with such rules of law as may be agreed by the parties. In the absence of such agreement, the Tribunal shall apply the law of the Contracting State party to the dispute (including its rules on the conflict of laws) and such rules of international law as may be applicable.

(2) The Tribunal may not bring in a finding of *non liquet* on the ground of silence or obscurity of the law.

(3) The provisions of paragraphs (1) and (2) shall not prejudice the power of the Tribunal to decide a dispute *ex aequo et bono* if the parties so agree.

Article 43

Except as the parties otherwise agree, the Tribunal may, if it deems it necessary at any stage of the proceedings,

- (a) call upon the parties to produce documents or other evidence, and
- (b) visit the scene connected with the dispute, and conduct such inquiries there as it may deem appropriate.

Article 44

Any arbitration proceeding shall be conducted in accordance with the provisions of this Section and, except as the parties otherwise agree, in accordance with the Arbitration Rules in effect on the date on which the parties consented to arbitration. If any question of procedure arises which is not covered by this Section or the Arbitration Rules or any rules agreed by the parties, the Tribunal shall decide the question.

Article 45

(1) Failure of a party to appear or to present his case shall not be deemed an admission of the other party's assertions.

(2) If a party fails to appear or to present his case at any stage of the proceedings the other party may request the Tribunal to deal with the questions submitted to it and to render an award. Before rendering an award, the Tribunal shall notify, and grant a period of grace to, the party failing to appear or to present its case, unless it is satisfied that that party does not intend to do so.

Article 46

Except as the parties otherwise agree, the Tribunal shall, if requested by a party, determine any incidental or additional claims or counter-claims arising directly out of the subject-matter of the dispute provided that they are within the scope of the consent of the parties and are otherwise within the jurisdiction of the Centre.

Article 47

Except as the parties otherwise agree, the Tribunal may, if it considers that the circumstances so require, recommend any provisional measures which should be taken to preserve the respective rights of either party.

SECTION 4

The Award

Article 48

(1) The Tribunal shall decide questions by a majority of the votes of all its members.

(2) The award of the Tribunal shall be in writing and shall be signed by the members of the Tribunal who voted for it.

(3) The award shall deal with every question submitted to the Tribunal, and shall state the reasons upon which it is based.

(4) Any member of the Tribunal may attach his individual opinion to the award, whether he dissents from the majority or not, or a statement of his dissent.

(5) The Centre shall not publish the award without the consent of the parties.

Article 49

(1) The Secretary-General shall promptly dispatch certified copies of the award to the parties. The award shall be deemed to have been rendered on the date on which the certified copies were dispatched.

(2) The Tribunal upon the request of a party made within 45 days after the date on which the award was rendered may after notice to the other party decide any question which it had omitted to decide in the award, and shall rectify any clerical, arithmetical or similar error in the

award. Its decision shall become part of the award and shall be notified to the parties in the same manner as the award. The periods of time provided for under paragraph (2) of Article 51 and paragraph (2) of Article 52 shall run from the date on which the decision was rendered.

SECTION 5

Interpretation, Revision and Annulment of the Award

Article 50

(1) If any dispute shall arise between the parties as to the meaning or scope of an award, either party may request interpretation of the award by an application in writing addressed to the Secretary-General.

(2) The request shall, if possible, be submitted to the Tribunal which rendered the award. If this shall not be possible, a new Tribunal shall be constituted in accordance with Section 2 of this Chapter. The Tribunal may, if it considers that the circumstances so require, stay enforcement of the award pending its decision.

Article 51

(1) Either party may request revision of the award by an application in writing addressed to the Secretary-General on the ground of discovery of some fact of such a nature as decisively to affect the award, provided that when the award was rendered that fact was unknown to the Tribunal and to the applicant and that the applicant's ignorance of that fact was not due to negligence.

(2) The application shall be made within 90 days after the discovery of such fact and in any event within three years after the date on which the award was rendered.

(3) The request shall, if possible, be submitted to the Tribunal which rendered the award. If this shall not be possible, a new Tribunal shall be constituted in accordance with Section 2 of this Chapter.

(4) The Tribunal may, if it considers that the circumstances so require, stay enforcement of the award pending its decision. If the applicant requests a stay of

enforcement of the award in his application, enforcement shall be stayed provisionally until the Tribunal rules on such request.

Article 52

(1) Either party may request annulment of the award by an application in writing addressed to the Secretary-General on one or more of the following grounds:

    (a) that the Tribunal was not properly constituted;

    (b) that the Tribunal has manifestly exceeded its powers;

    (c) that there was corruption on the part of a member of the Tribunal;

    (d) that there has been a serious departure from a fundamental rule of procedure; or

    (e) that the award has failed to state the reasons on which it is based.

(2) The application shall be made within 120 days after the date on which the award was rendered except that when annulment is requested on the ground of corruption such application shall be made within 120 days after discovery of the corruption and in any event within three years after the date on which the award was rendered.

(3) On receipt of the request the Chairman shall forthwith appoint from the Panel of Arbitrators an *ad hoc* Committee of three persons. None of the members of the Committee shall have been a member of the Tribunal which rendered the award, shall be of the same nationality as any such member, shall be a national of the State party to the dispute or of the State whose national is a party to the dispute, shall have been designated to the Panel of Arbitrators by either of those States, or shall have acted as a conciliator in the same dispute. The Committee shall have the authority to annul the award or any part thereof on any of the grounds set forth in paragraph (1).

(4) The provisions of Articles 41–45, 48, 49, 53 and 54, and of Chapters VI and VII shall apply *mutatis mutandis* to proceedings before the Committee.

(5) The Committee may, if it considers that the circumstances so require, stay enforcement of the award pending its decision. If the applicant requests a stay of enforcement of the award in his application, enforcement shall be stayed provisionally until the Committee rules on such request.

(6) If the award is annulled the dispute shall, at the request of either party, be submitted to a new Tribunal constituted in accordance with Section 2 of this Chapter.

Section 6

Recognition and Enforcement of the Award

Article 53

(1) The award shall be binding on the parties and shall not be subject to any appeal or to any other remedy except those provided for in this Convention. Each party shall abide by and comply with the terms of the award except to the extent that enforcement shall have been stayed pursuant to the relevant provisions of this Convention.

(2) For the purposes of this Section, "award" shall include any decision interpreting, revising or annulling such award pursuant to Articles 50, 51 or 52.

Article 54

(1) Each Contracting State shall recognize an award rendered pursuant to this Convention as binding and enforce the pecuniary obligations imposed by that award within its territories as if it were a final judgment of a court in that State. A Contracting State with a federal constitution may enforce such an award in or through its federal courts and may provide that such courts shall treat the award as if it were a final judgment of the courts of a constituent state.

(2) A party seeking recognition or enforcement in the territories of a Contracting State shall furnish to a competent court or other authority which such State shall have designated for this purpose a copy of the award certified by the Secretary-General. Each Contracting State shall notify

328 A DICTIONARY OF ARBITRATION

the Secretary-General of the designation of the competent
court or other authority for this purpose and of any subsequent change in such designation.

(3) Execution of the award shall be governed by the
laws concerning the execution of judgments in force in the
State in whose territories such execution is sought.

Article 55

Nothing in Article 54 shall be construed as derogat-
ing from the law in force in any Contracting State relating
to immunity of that State or of any foreign State from
execution.

CHAPTER V

Replacement and Disqualification of Conciliators and Arbitrators

Article 56

(1) After a Commission or a Tribunal has been constituted and proceedings have begun, its composition shall
remain unchanged; provided, however, that if a conciliator
or an arbitrator should die, become incapacitated, or resign,
the resulting vacancy shall be filled in accordance with the
provisions of Section 2 of Chapter III or Section 2 of
Chapter IV.

(2) A member of a Commission or Tribunal shall
continue to serve in that capacity notwithstanding that he
shall have ceased to be a member of the Panel.

(3) If a conciliator or arbitrator appointed by a
party shall have resigned without the consent of the Commission or Tribunal of which he was a member, the Chairman shall appoint a person from the appropriate Panel to
fill the resulting vacancy.

Article 57

A party may propose to a Commission or Tribunal
the disqualification of any of its members on account of any
fact indicating a manifest lack of the qualities required by
paragraph (1) of Article 14. A party to arbitration proceedings may, in addition, propose the disqualification of

an arbitrator on the ground that he was ineligible for appointment to the Tribunal under Section 2 of Chapter IV.

Article 58

The decision on any proposal to disqualify a conciliator or arbitrator shall be taken by the other members of the Commission or Tribunal as the case may be, provided that where those members are equally divided, or in the case of a proposal to disqualify a sole conciliator or arbitrator, or a majority of the conciliators or arbitrators, the Chairman shall take that decision. If it is decided that the proposal is well-founded the conciliator or arbitrator to whom the decision relates shall be replaced in accordance with the provisions of Section 2 of Chapter III or Section 2 of Chapter IV.

CHAPTER VI

Cost of Proceedings

Article 59

The charges payable by the parties for the use of the facilities of the Centre shall be determined by the Secretary-General in accordance with the regulations adopted by the Administrative Council.

Article 60

(1) Each Commission and each Tribunal shall determine the fees and expenses of its members within limits established from time to time by the Administrative Council and after consultation with the Secretary-General.

(2) Nothing in paragraph (1) of this Article shall preclude the parties from agreeing in advance with the Commission or Tribunal concerned upon the fees and expenses of its members.

Article 61

(1) In the case of conciliation proceedings the fees and expenses of members of the Commission as well as the

charges for the use of the facilities of the Centre, shall be borne equally by the parties. Each party shall bear any other expenses it incurs in connection with the proceedings.

(2) In the case of arbitration proceedings the Tribunal shall, except as the parties otherwise agree, assess the expenses incurred by the parties in connection with the proceedings, and shall decide how and by whom those expenses, the fees and expenses of the members of the Tribunal and the charges for the use of the facilities of the Centre shall be paid. Such decision shall form part of the award.

CHAPTER VII

Place of Proceedings

Article 62

Conciliation and arbitration proceedings shall be held at the seat of the Centre except as hereinafter provided.

Article 63

Conciliation and arbitration proceedings may be held, if the parties so agree,

(a) at the seat of the Permanent Court of Arbitration or of any other appropriate institution, whether private or public, with which the Centre may make arrangements for that purpose; or

(b) at any other place approved by the Commission or Tribunal after consultation with the Secretary-General.

CHAPTER VIII

Disputes between Contracting States

Article 64

Any dispute arising between Contracting States concerning the interpretation or application of this Convention which is not settled by negotiation shall be referred to the International Court of Justice by the application of any party to such dispute, unless the States concerned agree to another method of settlement.

MODEL RULES ON ARBITRAL PROCEDURE,
ADOPTED BY THE INTERNATIONAL LAW COMMISSION

REPORT OF THE
INTERNATIONAL LAW
COMMISSION

COVERING THE WORK OF ITS TENTH SESSION
28 APRIL — 4 JULY 1958

GENERAL ASSEMBLY

OFFICIAL RECORDS : THIRTEENTH SESSION

SUPPLEMENT No. 9 (A/3859)

New York, 1958

MODEL RULES ON ARBITRAL PROCEDURE

Preamble

The undertaking to arbitrate is based on the following fundamental rules:

1. Any undertaking to have recourse to arbitration in order to settle a dispute beween States constitutes a legal obligation which must be carried out in good faith.

2. Such an undertaking results from agreement between the parties and may relate to existing disputes or to disputes arising subsequently.

3. The undertakng must be embodied in a written instrument, whatever the form of the instrument may be.

4. The procedures suggested to States parties to a dispute by these model rules shall not be compulsory unless the States concerned have agreed, either in the *compromis* or in some other undertaking, to have recourse thereto.

5. The parties shall be equal in all proceedings before the rbitral tribunal.

THE EXISTENCE OF A DISPUTE AND THE SCOPE OF THE UNDERTAKING TO ARBITRATE

Article 1

1. If, before the constitution of the arbitral tribunal, the parties to an undertaking to arbitrate disagree as to the existence of a dispute, or as to whether the existing dispute is wholly or partly within the scope of the obligation to go to arbitration, such preliminary question shall, at the request of any of the parties and failing agreement between them upon the adoption of another procedure, be brought before the International Court of Justice for decision by means of its summary procedure.

2. The Court shall have the power to indicate, if it considers that circumstances so require, any provisional measures which ought to be taken to preserve the respective rights of either party.

3. If the arbitral tribunal has already been constituted, any dispute concerning arbitrability shall be referred to it.

THE compromis
Article 2

1. Unless there are earlier agreements which suffice for the purpose, for example in the undertaking to arbitrate itself, the parties having recourse to arbitration shall conclude a *compromis* which shall specify, as a minimum:

(*a*) The undertaking to arbitrate according to which the dispute is to be submitted to the arbitrators;

(*b*) The subject-matter of the dispute and, if possible, the points on which the parties are or are not agreed;

(*c*) The method of constituting the tribunal and the number of arbitrators.

2. In addition, the *compromis* shall include any other provisions deemed desirable by the parties, in particular:

(i) The rules of law and the principles to be applied by the tribunal, and the right, if any, conferred on it to decide *ex aequo et bono* as though it had legislative functions in the matter;

(ii) The power, if any, of the tribunal to make recommendations to the parties;

(iii) Such power as may be conferred on the tribunal to make its own rules of procedure;

(iv) The procedure to be followed by the tribunal; provided that, once constituted, the tribunal shall be free to override any provisions of the *compromis* which may prevent it from rendering its award;

(v) The number of members required for the constitution of a *quorum* for the conduct of the hearings;

(vi) The majority required for the award;

(vii) The time limit within which the award shall be rendered;

(viii) The right of the members of the tribunal to attach dissenting or individual opinions to the award, or any prohibition of such opinions;

(ix) The languages to be employed in the course of the proceedings;

(x) The manner in which the costs and disbursements shall be apportioned;

(xi) The services which the International Court of Justice may be asked to render.

This enumeration is not intended to be exhaustive.

CONSTITUTION OF THE TRIBUNAL

Article 3

1. Immediately after the request made by one of the States parties to the dispute for the submission of the dispute to arbitration, or after the decision on the arbitrability of the dispute, the parties to an undertaking to arbitrate shall take the necessary steps, either by means of the *compromis* or by special agreement, in order to arrive at the constitution of the arbitral tribunal.

2. If the tribunal is not constituted within three months from the date of the request made for the submission of the dispute to arbitration, or from the date of the decision on arbitrability, the President of the International Court of Justice shall, at the request of either party, appoint the arbitrators not yet designated. If the President is prevented from acting or is a national of one of the parties, the appointments shall be made by the Vice-President. If the Vice-President is prevented from acting or is a national of one of the parties,

the appointments shall be made by the oldest member of the Court who is not a national of either party.

3. The appointments referred to in paragraph 2 shall, after consultation with the parties, be made in accordance with the provisions of the *compromis* or of any other instrument consequent upon the undertaking to arbitrate. In the absence of such provisions, the composition of the tribunal shall, after consultation with the parties, be determined by the President of the International Court of Justice or by the judge acting in his place. It shall be understood that in this event the number of the arbitrators must be uneven and should preferably be five.

4. Where provision is made for the choice of a president of the tribunal by the other arbitrators, the tribunal shall be deemed to be constituted when the president is selected. If the president has not been chosen within two months of the appointment of the arbitrators, he shall be designated in accordance with the procedure prescribed in paragraph 2.

5. Subject to the special circumstances of the case, the arbitrators shall be chosen from among persons of recognized competence in international law.

Article 4

1. Once the tribunal has been constituted, its composition shall remain unchanged until the award has been rendered.

2. A party may, however, replace an arbitrator appointed by it, provided that the tribunal has not yet begun its proceedings. Once the proceedings have begun, an arbitrator appointed by a party may not be replaced except by mutual agreement between the parties.

3. Arbitrators appointed by mutual agreement between the parties, or by agreement between arbitrators already appointed, may not be changed after the proceedings have begun, save in exceptional circumstances. Arbitrators appointed in the manner provided for in article 3, paragraph 2, may not be changed even by agreement between the parties.

4. The proceedings are deemed to have begun when the president of the tribunal or the sole arbitrator has made the first procedural order.

Article 5

If, whether before or after the proceedings have begun, a vacancy should occur on account of the death, incapacity or resignation of an arbitrator, it shall be filled in accordance with the procedure prescribed for the original appointment.

Article 6

1. A party may propose the disqualification of one of the arbitrators on account of a fact arising subsequently to the constitution of the tribunal. It may only propose the disqualification of one of the arbitrators on account of a fact arising prior to the constitution of the tribunal if it can show that the appointment was made without knowledge of that fact or as a result of fraud. In either case, the decision shall be taken by the other members of the tribunal.

2. In the case of a sole arbitrator or of the president of the tribunal, the question of disqualificaton shall, in the absence of agreement between the parties, be decided by the International Court of Justice on the application of one of them.

3. Any resulting vacancy or vacancies shall be filled in accordance with the procedure prescribed for the original appointments.

Article 7

Where a vacancy has been filled after the proceedings have begun, the proceedings shall continue from the point they had reached at the time the vacancy occurred. The newly appointed arbitrator may, however, require that the oral proceedings shall be recommenced from the beginning, if these have already been started.

POWERS OF THE TRIBUNAL AND THE PROCESS OF ARBITRATION

Article 8

1. When the undertaking to arbitrate or any supplementary agreement contains provisions which seem sufficient for the purpose of a *compromis*, and the tribunal has been constituted, either party may submit the dispute to the tribunal by application. If the other party refuses to answer the application on the ground that the provisions above referred to are insufficient, the tribunal shall decide whether there is already sufficient agreement between the parties on the essential elements of a *compromis* as set forth in article 2. In the case of an affirmative decision, the tribunal shall prescribe the necessary measures for the institution or continuation of the proceedings. In the contrary case, the tribunal shall order the parties to complete or conclude the *compromis* within such time limits as it deems reasonable.

2. If the parties fail to agree or to complete the *compromis* within the time limit fixed in accordance with the preceeding paragraph, the tribunal, within three months after the parties report failure to agree—or after the decision, if any, on the arbitrability of the dispute—shall proceed to hear and decide the case on the application of either party.

Article 9

The arbitral tribunal, which is the judge of its own competence, has the power to interpret the *compromis* and the other instruments on which that competence is based.

Article 10

1. In the absence of any agreement between the parties concerning the law to be applied, the tribunal shall apply:

(*a*) International conventions, whether general or particular, establishing rules expressly recognized by the contesting States;

(*b*) International custom, as evidence of a general practice accepted as law;

(*c*) The general principles of law recognized by civilized nations;

(*d*) Judicial decisions and the teachings of the most highly qualified publicists of the various nations, as subsidiary means for the determination of rules of law.

2. If the agreement between the parties so provides, the tribunal may also decide *ex aequo et bono*.

Article 11

The tribunal may not bring in a finding of *non liquet* on the ground of the silence or obscurity of the law to be applied.

Article 12

1. In the absence of any agreement between the parties concerning the procedure of the tribunal, or if the rules laid down by them are insufficient, the tribunal shall be competent to formulate or complete the rules of procedure.

2. All decisions shall be taken by a majority vote of the members of the tribunal.

Article 13

If the languages to be employed are not specified in the *compromis*, this question shall be decided by the tribunal.

Article 14

1. The parties shall appoint agents before the tribunal to act as intermediaries between them and the tribunal.

2. They may retain counsel and advocates for the prosecution of their rights and interests before the tribunal.

3. The parties shall be entitled through their agents, counsel or advocates to submit in writing and orally to the tribunal any arguments they may deem expedient for the prosecution of their case. They shall have the right to raise objections and incidental points. The decisions of the tribunal on such matters shall be final.

4. The members of the tribunal shall have the right to put questions to agents, counsel or advocates, and to ask them for explanations. Neither the questions put nor the remarks made during the hearing are to be regarded as an expression of opinion by the tribunal or by its members.

Article 15

1. The arbitral procedure shall in general comprise two distinct phases: pleadings and hearing.

2. The pleadings shall consist in the communication by the respective agents to the members of the tribunal and to the opposite party of memorials, counter-memorials and, if necessary, of replies and rejoinders. Each party must attach all papers and documents cited by it in the case.

3. The time limits fixed by the *compromis* may be extended by mutual agreement between the parties, or by the tribunal when it deems such extension necessary to enable it to reach a just decision.

4. The hearing shall consist in the oral development of the parties' arguments before the tribunal.

5. A certified true copy of every document produced by either party shall be communicated to the other party.

Article 16

1. The hearing shall be conducted by the president. It shall be public only if the tribunal so decides with the consent of the parties.

2. Records of the hearing shall be kept and signed by the president, registrar or secretary; only those so signed shall be authentic.

Article 17

1. After the tribunal has closed the written pleadings, it shall have the right to reject any papers and documents not yet produced which either party may wish to submit to it without the consent of the other party. The tribunal shall, however, remain free to take into consideration any such papers and documents which the agents, advocates or counsel of one or other of the parties may bring to its notice, provided that they have been made known to the other party. The latter shall have the right to require a further extension of the written pleadings so as to be able to give a reply in writing.

2. The tribunal may also require the parties to produce all necessary documents and to provide all necessary explanations. It shall take note of any refusal to do so.

Article 18

1. The tribunal shall decide as to the admissibility of the evidence that may be adduced, and shall be the judge of its probative value. It shall have the power, at any stage of the proceedings, to call upon experts and to require the appearance of witnesses. It may also, if necessary, decide to visit the scene connected with the case before it.

2. The parties shall co-operate with the tribunal in dealing with the evidence and in the other measures contemplated by paragraph 1. The tribunal shall take note of the failure of any party to comply with the obligations of this paragraph.

Article 19

In the absence of any agreement to the contrary implied by the undertaking to arbitrate or contained in the *compromis*, the tribunal shall decide on any ancillary claims which it considers to be inseparable from the subject-matter of the dispute and necessary for its final settlement.

Article 20

The tribunal, or in case of urgency its president subject to confirmation by the tribunal, shall have the power to indicate, if it considers that circumstances so require, any provisional measures which ought to be taken to preserve the respective rights of either party.

Article 21

1. When, subject to the control of the tribunal, the agents, advocates and counsel have completed their presentation of the case, the proceedings shall be formally declared closed.

2. The tribunal shall, however, have the power, so long as the award has not been rendered, to re-open the proceedings after their closure, on the ground that new evidence is forthcoming of such a nature as to constitute a decisive factor, or if it considers, after careful consideration, that there is a need for clarification on certain points.

Article 22

1. Except where the claimant admits the soundness of the defendant's case, discontinuance of the proceedings by the claimant party shall not be accepted by the tribunal without the consent of the defendant.

2. If the case is discontinued by agreement between the parties, the tribunal shall take note of the fact.

Article 23

If the parties reach a settlement, it shall be taken note of by the tribunal. At the request of either party, the tribunal may, if it thinks fit, embody the settlement in an award.

Article 24

The award shall normally be rendered within the period fixed by the *compromis*, but the tribunal may decide to extend this period if it would otherwise be unable to render the award.

Article 25

1. Whenever one of the parties has not appeared before the tribunal, or has failed to present its case, the other party may call upon the tribunal to decide in favour of its case.

2. The arbitral tribunal may grant the defaulting party a period of grace before rendering the award.

3. On the expiry of this period of grace, the tribunal shall render an award after it has satisfied itself that it has jurisdiction. It may only decide in favour of the submissions of the party appearing, if satisfied that they are well-founded in fact and in law.

DELIBERATIONS OF THE TRIBUNAL

Article 26

The deliberations of the tribunal shall remain secret.

Article 27

1. All the arbitrators shall participate in the decisions.

2. Except in cases where the *compromis* provides for a quorum, or in cases where the absence of an arbitrator occurs without the permission of the president of the tribunal, the arbitrator who is absent shall be replaced by an arbitrator nominated by the President of the International Court of Justice. In the case of such replacement the provisions of article 7 shall apply.

THE AWARD

Article 28

1. The award shall be rendered by a majority vote of the members of the tribunal. It shall be drawn up in writing and shall bear the date on which it was rendered. It shall contain the names of the arbitrators and shall be signed by the president and by the members of the tribunal who have voted for it. The arbitrators may not abstain from voting.

2. Unless otherwise provided in the *compromis*, any member of the tribunal may attach his separate or dissenting opinion to the award.

3. The award shall be deemed to have been rendered when it has been read in open court, the agents of the parties being present or having been duly summoned to appear.

4. The award shall immediately be communicated to the parties.

Article 29

The award shall, in respect of every point on which it rules, state the reasons on which it is based.

Article 30

Once rendered, the award shall be binding upon the parties. It shall be carried out in good faith immediately, unless the tribunal has allowed a time limit for the carrying out of the award or of any part of it.

Article 31

During a period of one month after the award has been rendered and communicated to the parties, the tribunal may, either of its own accord or at the request of either party, rectify any clerical, typographical or arithmetical error in the award, or any obvious error of a similar nature.

Article 32

The arbitral award shall constitute a definitive settlement of the dispute.

INTERPRETATION OF THE AWARD

Article 33

1. Any dispute between the parties as to the meaning and scope of the award shall, at the request of either party and within three months of the rendering of the award, be referred to the tribunal which rendered the award.

2. If, for any reason, it is found impossible to submit the dispute to the tribunal which rendered the award, and if within the above-mentioned time limit the parties have not agreed upon another solution, the dispute may be referred to the International Court of Justice at the request of either party.

3. In the event of a request for interpretation, it shall be for the tribunal or for the International Court of Justice, as the case may be, to decide whether and to what extent execution of the award shall be stayed pending a decision on the request.

Article 34

Failing a request for interpretation, or after a decision on such a request has been made, all pleadings and documents in the case shall be deposited by the president of the tribunal with the International Bureau of the Permanent Court of Arbitration or with another depositary selected by agreement between the parties.

VALIDITY AND ANNULMENT OF THE AWARD

Article 35

The validity of an award may be challenged by either party on one or more of the following grounds:

(a) That the tribunal has exceeded its powers;

(b) That there was corruption on the part of a member of the tribunal;

(c) That there has been a failure to state ·the reasons for the award or a serious departure from a fundamental rule of procedure;

(d) That the undertaking to arbitrate or the *compromis* is a nullity.

Article 36

1. If, within three months of the date on which the validity of the award is contested, the parties have not agreed on another tribunal, the International Court of Justice shall be competent to declare the total or partial nullity of the award on the application of either party.

2. In the cases covered by article 35, sub-paragraphs (a) and (c), validity must be contested within six months of the rendering of the award, and in the cases covered by sub-paragraphs (b) and (d) within six months of the discovery of the corruption or of the facts giving rise to the claim of nullity, and in any case within ten years of the rendering of the award.

3. The Court may, at the request of the interested party, and if circumstances so require, grant a stay of execution pending the final decision on the application for annulment.

Article 37

If the award is declared invalid by the International Court of Justice, the dispute shall be submitted to a new tribunal constituted by agreement between the parties, or, failing such agreement, in the manner provided by article 3.

REVISION OF THE AWARD

Article 38

1. An application for the revision of the award may be made by either party on the ground of the discovery of some fact of such a nature as to constitute a decisive factor, pro-

vided that when the award was rendered that fact was unknown to the tribunal and to the party requesting revision and that such ignorance was not due to the negligence of the party requesting revision.

2. The application for revision must be made within six months of the discovery of the new fact, and in any case within ten years of the rendering of the award.

3. In the proceedings for revision, the tribunal shall, in the first instance, make a finding as to the existence of the alleged new fact and rule on the admissibility of the application.

4. If the tribunal finds the application admissible, it shall then decide on the merits of the dispute.

5. The application for revision shall, whenever possible, be made to the tribunal which rendered the award.

6. If, for any reason, it is not possible to make the application to the tribunal which rendered the award, it may, unless the parties otherwise agree, be made by either of them to the International Court of Justice.

7. The tribunal or the Court may, at the request of the interested party, and if circumstances so require, grant a stay of execution pending the final decision on the application for revision.